The Dark Kingdoms

Books by
ALAN SCHOLEFIELD

Novels
A View of Vultures
Great Elephant
The Eagles of Malice
Wild Dog Running
The Young Masters
The Hammer of God
Lion in the Evening

History
The Dark Kingdoms

The Dark Kingdoms

*The Impact of White Civilization on Three
Great African Monarchies*

Alan Scholefield

WILLIAM MORROW AND COMPANY, INC.
NEW YORK   1975

Passages from *Congo to Cape, Early Portuguese Explorers* by Eric Axelson are reprinted by permission of Faber and Faber Ltd. and Barnes and Noble Books, Harper & Row, New York.

Library of Congress Cataloging in Publication Data

Scholefield, Alan.
  The dark kingdoms.

  Bibliography: p.
  1. Congo (Kingdom)—History. 2. Dahomey—History.
  3. Lesotho—History. I. Title.
DT655.S43   960   75-12593
ISBN 0-688-02958-2

Printed in the United States of America.

1 2 3 4 5   79 78 77 76 75

For
Brian and Birgitta
Barrow

Contents

List of Illustrations

Introduction

AT ONE time Africa was a land of many kingdoms, stretching north to south, east to west. There were those that were little more than tribal chieftainships holding a few hundred people in feu, but others were great and flourishing, with long histories, and a pageantry that matched the pre-Renaissance courts of the West. Some of the powerful kingdoms lasted well into the nineteenth century when, having withstood for centuries the attacks of their neighbours, they were finally destroyed by the white invaders who changed the face of Africa.

Although each kingdom collapsed in its own particular way the struggle for survival was often long and bitter. Some kings, sensing they had come into contact with a technologically more powerful people, decided to co-operate; others, afraid of being swamped by inexplicable and alien customs, withdrew into the heartland of their countries and fought savage wars of attrition. It did not seem to matter which philosophy was adopted towards the arrival of the whites, the end was nearly always the same.

But there was a third category: the few kingdoms which survived the white colonial era either because of their remoteness or their poverty or their astuteness.

This is the story of three kingdoms. Two of them succumbed to white pressure and disappeared. One of them survives. Each is seen at a critical period in its history, when black met white head-on.

There is no better example of a country welcoming a white race as friend and ally than the Old Kingdom of Congo on the arrival of the Portuguese. Congo, or Kongo (not to be confused with the modern Congo) flourished in northern Angola in the sixteenth century. Under its most famous king, Affonso I, it went to extraordinary lengths to adopt Portuguese culture and religion, and this period might have been a watershed for a multi-racial Africa had Portugal's greed and militancy not wasted the kingdom internally.

Dahomey, by contrast, was a kingdom that tried as best it could to keep its own identity. Forced to trade in slaves for survival, its kings attempted to keep all contact with whites to the sea coast while they themselves held court fifty miles inland at the capital of Abomey. For more than 250 years a succession of kings allowed few travellers to penetrate the country. But it was only a matter of time before the Dahomean army, with its famous brigade of female warriors, was fighting white forces in a last, vain attempt to save the kingdom.

The surviving kingdom, now with a constitutional monarch, is Lesotho (Basutoland) which still miraculously exists, completely surrounded by South Africa. Its critical period spans the life-time of its founder, Moshesh, who not only withstood attacks by black armies, but also a war with Britain and two wars with the Boers.

Not the least of the factors on which the fate of the dark kingdoms depended was the *kind* of white people who arrived from Europe. What must the citizens of the Old Kingdom have made of a Christianity whose representatives preached on Sundays and slaved for the rest of the week? What can Dahomeans have felt about a Britain that sent Richard Burton, a man who made no effort to conceal his contempt for them, to put pressure on them to change the customs and traditions on which the kingdom was founded?

Moshesh was lucky. The first whites he dealt with made up a small group of French Protestant missionaries who arrived in South Africa with an intense desire to give, wanting nothing in return. Their arrival, a few years ahead of settlers hungry for land, gave him enough time to adjust to new philosophies and a different way of life. He was a man of great quality, a visionary as well as a cunning diplomat. His success lay in the fact that he, unlike the kings of Congo and Dahomey, quickly learnt to play the white game of statesmanship; not only learnt it, but was able to beat the whites themselves at it.

PART ONE

'Royal Brothers'

'Imagination reels at the thought of so much grandeur and so much abasement.'
— Armattoe: *The Golden Age of West African Civilization*

A Portuguese caravel

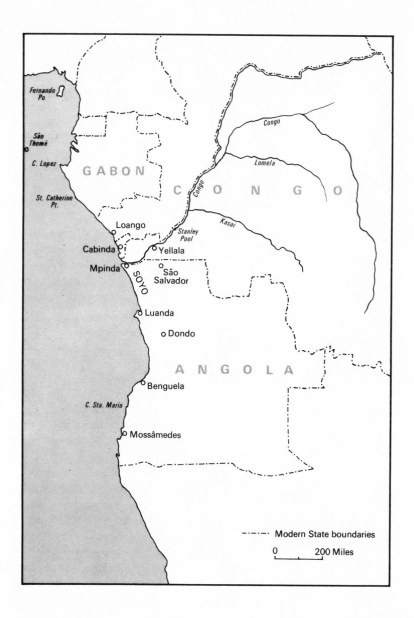

Fernando
Po

São
Thomé

C. Lopez

St. Catherine
Pt.

GABON

CONGO

Congo

Lomela

Congo

Kasai

Loango

Stanley
Pool

Cabinda

Yellala

Mpinda

SOYO

São
Salvador

Luanda

o Dondo

ANGOLA

Benguela

C. Sta. Maria

Mossâmedes

---·--- Modern State boundaries

0   200 Miles

1

WHEN THE Portuguese explorer, Diogo Cão, arrived at the mouth of the Congo River in the early 1480s, Africa south of the equator was as little known as anywhere on earth. Indeed it was not even certain the southern portion of the continent existed. Until a few years earlier the cartographers' world was still that of the *mappamundi*, maps produced in the Middle Ages, based on the Scriptures, often showing the world as a flat disc with Jerusalem at the centre, Paradise somewhere near the top, and the whole surrounded by the great Ocean. Cão had something better to work from. In 1475 a new map of the world was printed but even this, though a great advance over its predecessors and accurate for its day, was unable to speculate on the southern end of Africa.

Cão sailed from the Tagus in 1482 and picked his way carefully round the bulge of Africa into the Bight of Benin and down the west coast. The coastline had already been sketchily explored by earlier Portuguese captains as far south as the present state of Gabon, but once Cão was past Point St Catherine, almost half-way down the Gabon coastline, he was in unknown seas.

Today the big liners sailing between Southampton and the tip of Africa do the journey in less than a fortnight. At most times of the year the seas appear benign, even idyllic; a fresh breeze cools the tropical air, the colour of the water varies between translucent green and deep sky blue. But the farther south one travels, the more dangerous the coast becomes, with icy fogs, contrary winds, shoaling sandbanks and currents that set to the north.

In his recent book, *Congo to Cape*, Professor Eric Axelson of the University of Cape Town, who has made a special study of early Portuguese voyages off the coast of Africa, describes Cão's arrival at the mouth of the Congo the following year: 'From Cabinda to the mouth of the Congo Cão sailed beside a low coastline, luxuriant and green, from which the seabed

3

sloped very gradually, so that the off-shore waters remained extremely shallow; inland rose reddish hills that continued to the mouth of the Congo. At last Cão's ship rounded the point which he called the Cabo das Palmas covered to this day with palm trees and terminating in a rufous-coloured hillock which led later seamen to give it the more colourful name of Red Devil's Point (Ponta do Diablo Vermelho); situated at latitude 5° 44′N, this low cape marked the beginning of the estuary of the great river.'

The Zaïre or Congo is the third largest river in the world. It drains the centre of Africa and flows three thousand miles before it reaches the sea. More than a million cubic feet of its water enter the Atlantic every second. As the caravel entered the mouth it was dwarfed by the very immensity of the river with its towering tree-lined banks and its maze of islands, some more than ten miles long.

No one has described the river better than Joseph Conrad who went out to it in 1890 as captain of a small steamer. In *The Heart of Darkness* he wrote: 'Going up that river was like travelling back to the beginnings of the world, when vegetation rioted on the earth and the big trees were kings. An empty stream, a great silence, an impenetrable forest. The air was warm, thick, heavy, sluggish. There was no joy in the brilliance of sunshine. The long stretches of the waterway ran on, deserted, into the gloom of overshadowed distances. On silvery sandbanks hippos and alligators sunned themselves side by side. The broadening waters flowed through a mob of wooded islands; you lost your way on that river as you would in a desert...'

As Cão's ship moved slowly upstream the only sound that broke over the dense encroaching bush was the voice of the leadsman calling the marks. They could have had no idea of the importance of the moment. Diogo Cão, a very plain sailor, descendant of a bailiff at the Villa Real in Trasos Montes, was on the threshold of one of the greatest experiments in co-existence between black and white in African history. He was about to start a period that has drawn from scholars such words as 'glorious', 'refined', 'graceful', 'noble'.

Yet, apart from his visit and a mention in Camões' *Lusiads*, written in the middle of the sixteenth century and describing it as 'a river which no ancient knew', the Congo faded from man's interest. In 1816 part of it was explored by a Captain Tuckey of the Royal Navy, but even then nothing much was heard for another sixty years, until the great exploratory journeys of Livingstone and Stanley, when the river passed into modern history.

Cão anchored his ship a few miles upstream and almost at once his crew became aware of figures on the bank. They came down to the water's edge openly and allowed themselves to be taken aboard the caravel where they traded ivory for cloth.

These black people were descendants of tribes which had reached the Congo centuries before in the great migrations that populated Africa south of the Equator. They belonged to a race that had moved away from the cradles of early civilization and had become isolated from the main currents of history and culture. It was probable that they had never seen a white person before and doubtful, so complete was their isolation, that they had ever heard of such people. With Cão's arrival this isolation was to disappear for ever.

'Cão's interpreters attempted to converse with them,' wrote Professor Axelson, 'but could not understand the language, though they did gather that the river itself was called the Zaïre, that it ran through a mighty kingdom called Congo, and that the king of this realm lived a considerable way off in the interior.

'Gathering the impression of a well-ordered society Cão took the risk of asking the local tribesmen to guide to their king a small delegation of Portuguese. He proposed to await their return at an agreed time.'

While he waited he erected a *padrão*—a stone pillar he had brought with him from Lisbon—on which was inscribed: 'In the year 6681 of the creation of the World, and in that of 1482 since the birth of our Lord Jesus Christ, the most serene, most excellent and potent prince, King D. Joao (John) of Portugal, did order this land to be discovered and these *padrãos* to be set up by Dº Cão, an esquire of his household.'

Weeks passed with no sign of the men returning and Cão decided to continue his journey. He made his way a further seven hundred miles south to the present Cape Santa Maria in Angola where he planted his second *padrão* before returning to the mouth of the Congo. The men were not there. He seized four black visitors to the ship and sent a message ashore that they would be returned on his next voyage if his own men were brought safely back. He then sailed for Portugal.

That is how things might have ended, with friendship giving way to animosity, peace to violence. But it did not. Cão did return, not because he specifically wished to exchange the hostages, that was a side issue; he returned because his voyages were part of a pattern by Portuguese and Castilian sailors that were extending the boundaries of the known world. Europe was changing, it was moving out of the Middle Ages into the Renaissance and it had developed a thirst for knowledge.

The pressures to penetrate the unknown parts of the earth were so great that by 1521, less than forty years after Cão's voyage, Dias and Da Gama had opened the sea-route to the east, America had been discovered and the globe circumnavigated.

The particular reasons behind Cão's voyage of 1482–83 and those of Dias and Da Gama later owed much to a mixture of avarice and religious zeal. In sending out his caravels, King John was following the footsteps of his illustrious forebear, Prince Henry the Navigator. News had reached him of great wealth to be found in the interior of Africa and along the western coast; of gold, ivory and slaves. Then there was the question of the spice trade. During the Middle Ages spices had reached Europe from the east by land caravan. But since the fall of Constantinople to the Turks in 1453 the land-routes had become more difficult and more expensive. Cão was attempting to find a sea-route to the east which would give Portugal the spice trade.

There was another reason and it is like a thumbprint of the age: the search for Prester John. It was this, as much as gold and spices, that sent the Portuguese caravels round the tip of Africa. Looking back now on the desperate search for this fabulous monarch one discerns a flavour of Arthur and the Grail. Whether Prester John existed or not there seemed a need at the time to believe in him. Although Christianity was a thousand years old by the time he is first mentioned, the Crusades had ended in disaster and the Holy Places were in the hands of Islam. Christendom itself seemed to be weakening. Superstition was rife; the physical world was not understood and was therefore a dark and menacing place. People clung to their faith and were afraid. Then, in 1145, news of a Christian King living beyond Persia and Armenia, in the depths of the Orient, was brought to the Papal Palace. The legend grew. By 1165 a letter was circulating, purporting to come from this King, who modestly described himself as 'Presbyter Joannes by the power and virtue of God and of the Lord Jesus Christ, Lord of Lords'. It dealt at length with the wonders of his Empire. It was his desire, he said, to visit the Holy Sepulchre with a great army and destroy the enemies of the Cross. He said that seventy-two kings, reigning over as many kingdoms, were his tributaries. His empire extended over the three Indies, including that farther India where the body of St Thomas lay, as far as the world where the sun rose and all the way back again to the ruins of Babylon and the Tower of Babel.

In war, the letter continued, thirteen great crosses made of gold and jewels were carried in wagons before him as his standards and each was followed by ten thousand knights and one hundred thousand footmen. There were no poor in his dominions, no thief nor robber, no flatterer nor miser, no dissension, no lies and no vices. Before his palace was a great mirror erected on a many-storeyed pedestal and by looking at this he could discern everything that went on in his dominions. He was waited on by seven kings at a time, by sixty dukes and 365 counts; twelve archbishops sat at his right hand and twenty bishops at his left.

By the middle of the fifteenth century, this legendary figure had grown in stature; rumour had become fact. Thousands in Europe believed implicitly in his existence. None more so than King John of Portugal. He was a man of short temper, big, bulky and red-faced, who had dealt with an awkward magnate, the Duke of Viseu, by simply murdering him with his own hands. The King foresaw the strategic possibilities of a combined war on Islam, the armies of Christian Europe attacking from the front, those of Prester John from behind;

between them they would crush the enemy But first Prester John had to be found. By the time Cão was voyaging down Africa Prester John was thought to be the Emperor of Ethiopia and the search was drawing to a close.

2

CAO SET off from Lisbon for the second time towards the end of 1485 and the task was the same as before: to turn the southern continent and break into the eastern seas. But in other aspects the voyage was different from the first; this time he commanded a fleet of two or three ships, nor was he any longer a plain 'esquire'; he had been raised to cavalier in the royal household, had been granted a handsome annuity and had been ordered a coat-of-arms charged with replicas of the two *padrãos* he had planted. He had with him, as promised, the four hostages he had taken.

These men, too, were very different from the time they had come aboard his caravel in the River Congo to barter for cloth. They had arrived in Lisbon with Cão at the beginning of 1484 and had spent nearly two years there. Much had been made of them: they had met the king, who was greatly impressed; they had been clothed, converted to Christianity and taught to speak some Portuguese; they had been objects of not unkind curiosity and had been entertained by the nobility. Now they were to be restored to their homeland.

Professor Axelson has said that Cão was given a cordial welcome when the local inhabitants saw he had brought back their compatriots and that they had been well treated. 'According to the chronicler Barros (João Barros, who wrote in the sixteenth century), Cão sent one of the hostages to the King of Congo informing him of his arrival in the river, telling him that the caravels would continue their voyage southward along the coast, and asking that on his return the Portuguese messengers be waiting for him. On their safe delivery he promised to release the three Congolese hostages whom he had still not set free . . . He added that on his return to the river he would seek conversations with the King. Apparently the King replied so promptly that the Portuguese messengers arrived in the charge of one of his captains even before Cão had departed southward; Cão immediately released the remaining hostages and entrusted the Congolese captain with rich presents for his king.'

After journeying up the Congo River as far as the cataract at Yellala where he cut an inscription, he returned to visit the King of Congo at his capital.

Here is Professor Axelson again: 'The chronicler Rui de Pina suggests and Barros insists that Cão went in person to visit the King of Congo and it is likely that (he) followed the old trade route, which in fact was nothing more than a simple footpath, winding its way round boulders, termite mounds and trees, clambering up hillsides, plunging into valleys, seeking out fords to cross the intervening streams and tenuously linking village and village. A later Portuguese official in 1881, when conditions had changed very little from those Cão endured, noted that it took thirty-five and three-quarter hours of actual travel to cover the ninety or a hundred miles from the Congo to São Salvador, by which name the King's city came to be known in the sixteenth century with the arrival of a Jesuit mission. The journey could be covered in five days, but six or seven was more usual, owing to the ardours of the mode of travel.

'Cão's journey, with the armed men necessary to maintain his king's dignity and the native porters needed to carry provisions and gifts for the king and his courtiers must thus have taken the greater part of a week each way. The day's march would start with the light of dawn, and on the first day the stony path switchbacked up and down over a succession of steep and barren hills. In places it crossed great slabs of smooth rock where the booted Europeans had difficulty maintaining their balance, and in the airless valleys the over-clothed Portuguese roasted in the heat reflected from the rocky hillsides. In the late morning the caravan would halt at some village, usually located on a smooth-topped hill close to a source of water, and there, in return for a present of cloth or beads or brass the headman would place a hut at the disposal of the strangers to rest during the heat of the afternoon.

'By the second day the travellers passed into an area of

lush forest inhabited by flocks of brilliant red birds with black necks, and on the third day they entered a fertile and populated region which was fed by many streams beside which grew trees with bright scarlet flowers. The narrow path made its way through grass that was often as high as fifteen or twenty feet, and the close walls of vegetation hindered the porters who carried their burdens in bales covered with palm-frond matting. In the early morning the plants were heavy with dew and the travellers were quickly soaked to the skin, so that they envied the naked porters who were spared the discomfort of walking in wet clothes.

'On the fourth or fifth day the travellers crossed the fourth of the steep ridges that lay between them and their destination and descended into the valley of the Lunda, one of the tributaries of the Congo. Since Cão contrived to reach Yellala without mishap in the gorges of the Lower Congo, we can reasonably assume that he was not journeying in the season of the rains, when travel in the Lunda valley is extremely difficult because the rivers are swollen and floods spread over the low-lying ground which can be crossed only by rafts. In the season of low water, the marshes could be crossed by causeways made of tree trunks laid in the water and covered with intertwined branches, and it is likely that Cão and his party crossed the Lunda River, which even in the dry season is a hundred feet wide, by one of the curious suspension bridges, constructed of twisted branches and hung from two anchoring trees, which were a feature of the region: he would probably have been delayed for a long palaver with the local chief or headman who demanded toll at such crossings. Down in the valley the nights were made almost unbearable by the falsetto whining of blood-hungry mosquitoes, whose silent sisters carried the malaria-causing parasites.

'On the last day of the journey the path ascended a steep hillside where a precipice yawned on one side of the travellers; it crossed another wide valley, and then climbed to a ridge of high ground at the southern end of which lay the King's *mbanza*. This capital of the realm of Congo occupied a healthy site, well watered and admirably suited for agriculture, at an altitude of about two thousand feet, between the Luebi and Coco Rivers, looking out over grassland, with the forest in the

10

distance. It was a place that had long been inhabited and cultivated.

'One can imagine Cão and the King meeting in the shade of one of those giant baobab or fig trees which were favoured sites for palavers, with the drums bellowing in the background and soft strains played on horns made out of whole tusks of ivory.'

Cão then sailed south and planted a *padrão* on the coast of the Namib Desert to mark the limit of his voyage. Soon afterwards, for reasons that are not known, he died.

* * *

The next contact between Portugal and the Kingdom of Congo came in 1490. A fleet left Portugal in December and included missionaries, 'secular priests', Franciscan monks, armed soldiers, peasants, masons, carpenters and a few women. They sailed in three vessels which contained, as well as the tools which the artisans would use, church objects and ornaments. There were even building materials. It was a grim voyage. Plague had been raging in Lisbon when the fleet sailed and it had been brought aboard; several of the expedition leaders died.

At the end of March, 1491, the caravels reached the Congo coast in the province of Soyo and were welcomed by the provincial chief, who put on a great show of thudding drums and dancing warriors, and allowed himself to be baptized in the name of Dom Manuel on Easter Sunday.

The Portuguese caravan set off for the City of Congo a few days later. The paths had been cleared and widened and in some parts even swept as though for a royal progress. The more important of the Portuguese were carried on 'wooden horses', poles covered with saddles of oxhide which must have been excruciatingly uncomfortable. It took them twenty days.

At that time, according to an early chronicler, Mbanza Congo was not much more than a dusty bush town. Narrow paths ran in all directions through the tall grass. The huts of the important citizens were close to the King's enclosure, and were of unadorned straw except for the interiors where there were patterned mats. The only distinction between the homes of the nobility and those of the ordinary people was in the size and number of painted mats. And there was the traditional large tree, under which the chief sat to dispense justice. In the centre of the town was a large square on one side of which was the King's enclosure, the circumference of which was about one thousand metres. There were several gates, each guarded by warriors and trumpeters. Then came a second enclosure and a wall of branches which surrounded the palace. It was approached through a maze.

There is a description by the merchant and traveller Duarte Lopez, written towards the end of the sixteenth century after the Portuguese had been there for many years. It seems transformed, with sweet water, fine buildings and churches, a population of 100,000 and a Portuguese quarter occupying nearly a mile of housing. Olfert Dapper, a Flemish traveller who reached Mbanza Congo about one hundred years later, has even left us a sketch of the town. It is built on the top of high river bluffs and has several imposing buildings. A flag on the King's palace snaps in the breeze. Altogether the situation is lofty and airy and must have been a pleasant destination after the wet heat of the Congo valley, which, in years to come, was to kill off so many Portuguese missionaries and traders before they even reached the capital.

When the first great Portuguese mission entered the town in 1491 almost the entire population came out to meet them. Again there was much singing and dancing. The black nobility carried buffalo shields and ironwood swords, the proletariat bows and arrows. It was with this triumphant train that the Portuguese were led to the large huts which had been prepared for them. They were then taken to meet the King, the Mani Congo himself, Nzinga a Knuwu, who was seated on a chair inlaid with ivory and raised on a platform. The visitors came forward with their gifts of brocade, velvet fabrics, lengths of satin and silk, linen, magnificent garments, horse-tails mounted and chased with silver and various trinkets, as well as a cage of red pigeons.

It was an impressive show to a king who was simply dressed in a loin-cloth which had been given him by Cão, copper bracelets and a cap of palm-cloth. The badge of kingship, a zebra tail, hung from his left shoulder. He at once asked to be baptized.

It is difficult to imagine a more auspicious beginning. Here was a powerful monarch in the middle of Africa with no experience of Western ways wishing to embrace the God of his visitors—a God they were importing for this specific reason—almost the moment they arrived. The Portuguese might well have considered this a miracle had a more obvious reason not presented itself. When, a few weeks earlier, the provincial chief of Soyo had been baptized, the Portuguese had completed the celebrations by firing off their muskets in a show of power. Long before they reached Mbanza the Mani Congo had heard of the weapons; seeing them completed his conversion to Christianity. He was hastily baptized John I after the King of Portugal and his wife took the name Eleanor. Various black dignitaries who became known as 'counts', were also baptized, as was the King's son, the 'Duke' of Nsundi. He was given the name Affonso which, as one chronicler has it, 'he was to make glorious'. To round off these sacred ceremonies, building was started on the first church in Mbanza.

It was only then the Portuguese learnt the real reason for the quick conversion; the kingdom was on the point of civil war. Several tribes were rebelling against the central power and the Mani Congo was about to help his son Affonso put down the revolt. Naturally he wanted Portuguese aid. One must try to imagine the Portuguese at this moment: there were not many of them by comparison with their black hosts, they had come to this remote place to proselytize and begin a trading organization—and within a few weeks of their arrival, they were being asked to take part in a war which did not concern them in the least. But the request came from a brother in Christ and it was not possible to refuse. So, a black army marched out on to the central African field of battle under the banner of the Cross, accompanied by a number of white mercenaries carrying muskets. It is hardly surprising that they won the day and returned to the capital in triumph. In gratitude the Mani Congo settled the Portuguese in one section of the town not too far from his own palace and the two races lived in such amity that doors, it is said, were never closed and there was no need for guards. The co-existence had begun.

IT WOULD be hard to imagine two countries more dissimilar than Portugal and Congo at the close of the fifteenth century. Portugal was in the midst of the greatest surge of discovery the world had known and was poised at the start of a colonizing age. The list of her voyages and discoveries in the latter part of the fifteenth and early sixteenth centuries is like a drum-roll: the Cape of Good Hope doubled in 1488, proving that the Indian Ocean was accessible by sea; India reached by Da Gama in 1498; Greenland in 1500; Brazil in 1500; Madagascar in 1501; Mauritius in 1507 . . . and so on. By 1540 the Portuguese empire extended along the coasts of Brazil, East and West Africa, Malabar, Ceylon, Persia, Indo-China, the Malay archipelago, Goa and Malacca.

As the south-westernmost of the free peoples of Europe they were the natural inheritors of the tradition of exploration which had been carried on during the Middle Ages by the Arabs. They began where the Arabs left off by penetrating far into the Atlantic and it was Prince Henry the Navigator who channelled and organized their energy. The compass had been improved and the quadrant and the astrolabe, long used by astronomers, had been adapted for ships so that seamen could establish latitude. Prince Henry placed at the disposal of his captains the vast resources of the Order of Christ (the Portuguese section of the Knights Templar), the best information, the most up-to-date maps.

But as exploration overseas was bringing honour to Portugal the country itself was deteriorating. In mid-century civil war broke out with the Regent, Don Pedro, Duke of Coimbra, leading one faction and the Duke of Braganza the other. In 1449 Don Pedro was defeated and killed and the Duke of Braganza became the most powerful noble in the kingdom, said at one time to own one-third of the entire country. When King John II reached the throne in 1481 he noted acidly that the liberality of former kings had left the crown 'no estates except the high roads'. He crushed the feudal nobility and seized its lands. Ferdinand, Duke of Braganza, was beheaded for high treason in 1483 and a year later the king stabbed to death the Duke of Viseu, his own brother-in-law. For this and other acts he was given the title John the Perfect. He died in 1495 just after his fleet containing priests and presents had sailed for the Congo, and was succeeded by King Manuel I who is known as The Fortunate, because in his reign the sea-route to India was discovered and a Portuguese empire begun.

In contrast to this feverish and thrusting society, the old Kingdom of Congo had been cultivating its own back garden out of sight of the world. At one time it had occupied both banks of the Congo as far as Stanley Pool, but by the time the Portuguese arrived, the Kingdom had shrunk and the capital lay eighty miles south of the river. It was a palm-tree culture. Just as the plains Indians of North America adapted their lives to the buffalo, so did the Bakongo to the palm tree. There were several species of palms which gave the landscape a distinctive appearance and from these the Bakongo extracted oil, wine, vinegar and a kind of bread. The oil came from the pulp of the fruit and looked like greenish butter; they used it for cooking and rubbing into the skin. The bread was made from the kernel of the fruit which, according to Duarte Lopez, was rather like a hard almond. Wine was obtained by fermenting the sap and if allowed to go on fermenting it became vinegar. Lopez says that the wine was drunk fresh 'and is such a diuretic that in this country nobody suffers from gravel or stones in the bladder. It intoxicates when drunk in excess; it is very nourishing'. Apart from sustaining the body the palm tree also gave its fibres for the weaving of mats, baskets, storage containers, clothing, the woven roofs of huts, game traps and fishermen's snares.

The Bakongo knew how to work metals, including iron and copper, and they were fairly skilled potters. They had domesticated several animals—pigs, sheep, chickens and, in some districts, cattle—but unlike most Bantu tribes made no use of the milk.

Apart from the capital, the Bakongo lived in small villages in huts made from wattle frames and mat coverings and travellers would often come on to these villages without warning, for the huts were low and hidden by high elephant grass. Their agricultural implements were limited to the hoe and the

15

axe and they grew a little millet and sorghum. There were bananas and citrus fruits for the picking and an abundance of all kinds of game. Tribal law and custom regulated their daily lives and the witch-doctors had great power. They did not have a written language.

One has the impression of a timelessness which can still be found in Africa today away from the main roads. Enough work is done to exist, no more. As long as there is food and drink ambition is stilled, for the Bantu has never been an acquisitive person. The tenor of life was relaxed, slow, and without worry. Into this calm pond the Portuguese were to toss the doctrine of original sin and moral guilt.

They were particularly indignant at the sexual practices of the Bakongo. In Cavazzi's history of the Old Kingdom, published in 1687, their sins are described as those of 'sensuality or of lust with several women'. At the beginning of the seventeenth century Bishop Manuel Baptista observed angrily that few people 'regard the vices of the senses as sins'. Since many of the missionaries, including monks and friars, had themselves taken black mistresses, perhaps the good bishop was not only fulminating against the Bakongo who were, like many other African tribes, polygamous. Polygamy to the Portuguese meant promiscuity. One writer has managed to trace the sexual appetites of the Bakongo even further and blames the influence of spiced food.

This theme of sexual licence is a constant one in the early writings of missionaries and travellers in Africa and becomes even more widespread, once slavery had begun, as one more way of rationalizing the act of enslavement by disparaging the slave. In fact, Africa was no hot-bed of depravity; on the contrary, there was a rigid morality often amounting to a Victorian sternness. What misled many of the early travellers was the openness with which the African treats sexual matters, the understanding of the need for the sexual release of tension. Among the Zulus, for instance, copulation between unmarried couples was tolerated provided the girl was not deflowered and this led to a form of sexual contact which was safe, but which also gave satisfaction.

Bakongo children were separated from infancy, the boys, as they grew older, sleeping in a place reserved for men, the girls in a separate building reserved for females. Both were instructed by adults in self-control and, as one contemporary Congolese recalls, 'when and how to give in or refuse ... where the-normal-limits of horseplay lay'. The most overt sexual display came in their dances. The partners alternately stamped and rushed towards one another to simulate the sexual act. Once again, like many African dances, these were symbolic of the act of procreation, the natural growth of society. The Portuguese confused representation and fact, symbolic behaviour and licence. One missionary wrote: 'The pen of a devout person refuses to put such things on paper.'

Young people experimented with sex just as young people do everywhere, some experiments went too far, others were more successful. The laws were harsh for the libertine. Promiscuity among young people often resulted in the parties being sold into slavery. Sexual attempts on women returning from work or while bathing in the river carried the same punishment. Masturbation was not looked upon as a vice but homosexuals were severely dealt with. The defloration of a young girl meant reparation to the parents for it was considered that harm had been done to the family. Adultery was considered to transgress religious taboos as well as to cut at the fabric of society itself and for this crime the participants were often wrapped in dried banana leaves and turned into human torches. If their lives were spared they were sold as slaves. It is not surprising that a missionary described adultery as being 'very rare'. Incest was the most heinous of all sexual crimes and was said to cause drought, famine, sudden death, the sterility of women and of the earth.

Sexually mature young men were free to try their charms on the young girls, sometimes they were successful, sometimes not. Occasionally, they might make use of a slave woman owned by a wealthy noble but later on, once the whites had arrived in numbers, prostitution flourished, and then along with the religion, language and culture of the Portuguese, the Congo was to acquire their syphilis as well. The coming of the whites also produced a change in feminine modesty and soon the women were covering their breasts.

But neither the sexual attitudes of the Portuguese nor the changes they brought seemed to make any difference to the warmth with which the Bakongo welcomed them. Historians have been quick to see an affinity between the Bakongo's willingness to adopt Western ways and those of the Japanese 350 years later. But whereas the Japanese wanted the blueprints of a successful technology while keeping their own religions and customs, the people of the old Congo kingdom seemed to want to *be* Portuguese, at least at the beginning.

4

SOME TIME between 1506 and 1509, the Mani Congo, John I, died. He had, in many ways, been a disappointment to the Portuguese. Quite soon after he had been baptized it became clear that he had become a Christian for reasons of state and he returned to his fetishes and his harem. Traditional elements among the black nobility had never been happy about his baptism and spoke darkly of ancestors betrayed, of sorcery and vengeance. But what hastened John's apostasy was the uncompromising attitude of the Portuguese towards his marriages. They saw them as unchristian and tried to bring pressure on him to reject all his wives save one. What they did not realize was that the Mani Congo took on wives for precisely the same diplomatic reasons as European royalty: they represented power blocs. By many careful marriages the Mani Congo was able to make his position virtually unassailable. When the Portuguese remained intractably moral the Mani Congo reacted: he rejected their religion. About 1495 most of the missionaries and with them certain black nobles who had been converted were obliged to leave the City of Congo. They were led by the king's son who had been baptized Affonso and he settled them in the province of Nsundi well out of the Mani Congo's way. The anti-Christian faction was headed by Affonso's half-brother Prince Mpanza.

The accounts of what happened when the Mani Congo died are rich with romantic legend—and none the worse for that, for they fit snugly into traditional Christian mythology. The story goes that when the king died his wife, Eleanor, allowed no one near his quarters, nor did she release news of his death for three days. During that time she was able to send runners—the

Old Kingdom had developed a fast messenger relay system rather like that of the Incas—to Affonso who, with his small band of Christians, hurried through the bush and suddenly appeared in the city. The death of John I and the accession of Affonso I, as he became known, were announced simultaneously.

But Prince Mpanza now gathered a large army—the number has been given as nearly two hundred thousand—and marched on the capital. Here they were awaited by an army of ten thousand and possibly one hundred black Christians and Portuguese.

From the heights of the City of Congo, the defenders gazed down at the besieging force and many, realizing how badly outnumbered they were, prepared to give up the fight. Affonso told them to trust in God, but their faith must have been weak for they were on the point of deserting when they were checked by the chief of the province of Soyo, one of the earliest converts. This old man is quoted by Lopez as saying, 'Behold my age is now one hundred years and yet I take arms, being zealous for the religion I have adopted, and for the homage and honour I owe to my king, and do you, who are in the flower of your age, show timidity and so little fealty to your lawful sovereign? At least if you will not fight yourselves, animate your vassals, and do not discourage them, but let us await the first encounter with the enemy, and we shall have time after that in which to make plans for our safety.' Then Lopez goes on: 'With these comforting words he reassured the fallen spirits of these men and they turned back with him to seek the king, who was in the church praying and asking help from God.'

On the eve of battle, Affonso's men were greatly heartened by a sudden vision in the sky of five flaming swords. The following day a vision was seen by the enemy; this time of a lady in white, and a knight riding a white horse. When Affonso heard of the vision he sent a message to his half-brother identifying the Virgin Mary and St James, sent by God to defend the right. This was too much for the besieging army; they were routed and put to flight and Prince Mpanza was captured and executed.

Affonso's coronation took place in an open space before the

palace. A low wall separated him from the great crowd that had come to see the ceremony. It must have been a magnificent spectacle. All were dressed in their finest skins and palm cloth, their oiled black bodies shining, the breast-plates of the Portuguese soldiers glinting in the sunlight, the cowled monks in their brown or white habits, the Portuguese civilians in crimson doublets and green hose, and over everything the cobalt blue of the sky, the burning orange sun, the dust rising from thousands of unshod feet.

We have an account of the crowning in 1622 of Pedro II: the throne 'of crimson velvet, all fringed with silk and gold' stood on a magnificent rug. On each side of the throne stood young black nobles holding the royal insignia. One of them had charge of the large Congo flag sent as a gift from the King of Portugal, another held a coat of arms and a third the royal seal. Behind the throne stood a second group bearing the traditional crests of the royal family; these were designs of feathers stuck down on 'curtains of braided straw' hanging from poles six or seven feet high.

There were two other sanctified areas near the throne. One contained an altar stone and crucifix which was symbolic of the King's Christianity. The second was the great royal drum which symbolized his aggressiveness and embodied absolute power. Like all the kings of Congo themselves, who were never permitted contact with the ground and had to be carried everywhere, the drum stood on a piece of ornately woven cloth. It was trimmed with leopard skins and with gold and silver embroidery from which the teeth of rebels were strung. With its grisly relics it was the most dreaded symbol in all the Kingdom and was only displayed on three occasions: a royal death, a coronation, or when the nation went to war.

At a given moment, a melancholy fanfare was repeated twelve times and the coronation ceremony began. First there was a Christian ceremony, brief to the point of abruptness. The King placed his hands on the book of Holy Gospels and swore on the altar to perform faithfully the duties of a Christian king. He was blessed by a priest and that was that. The traditional ceremony, by contrast, was slow and majestic and comprised three parts: the presentation of the regalia, such objects as a small cap of palm leaves and a necklace of iron;

the ceremony of homage in which the important men came forward to kiss the King's hand and pay homage, and then his return to the palace followed by his court.

What sort of man was Affonso I? Here is a priest, Rui d' Aguiar, writing to the King of Portugal in 1516: 'May your Highness be informed that his (Affonso's) Christian life is such that he appears to me not as a man but as an angel sent by the Lord to this kingdom to convert it, especially when he speaks and when he preaches. For I assure your Highness that it is he who instructs us; better than we, he knows the Prophets and the Gospel of Our Lord Jesus Christ and all the lives of the saints and all things regarding our Mother the Holy Church, so much so that if your Highness could observe him himself, he would be filled with admiration.

'He expresses things so well and with such accuracy that it seems to me that the Holy Spirit speaks always through his mouth. I must say, Lord, that he does nothing but study and that many times he falls asleep over his books; he forgets when it is time to dine, when he is speaking of the things of God. So delighted is he with the reading of the Scripture that he is as if beside himself. When he gives audience or when he dispenses justice, his words are inspired by God and by the examples of the saints.

'He studies the Holy Gospel and when the priest finishes the Mass he asks him for benediction. When he has received it, he begins to preach to the people with great skill and great charity, imploring them to be converted and to give themselves to God; in such wise that his people are amazed and we others even more so, before the virtue and faith of this man. Every day he does this, every day he preaches as I have just said. Your Highness will be pleased to learn also that he is very assiduous in the exercise of justice, that he punishes with rigour those who worship idols and that he has them burned along with those idols.'

In other words, Affonso is a *nonpareil*: not only has he learned to speak and read Portuguese fluently, but he has absorbed the faith of his teachers to such a degree that he out-proselytizes the proselytizers. In his study of the Old Kingdom, M. Georges Balandier reminds us that the majority of the documentation is of missionary origin and dates for the most part from the period of militant Catholicism. So that what the Portuguese saw as good they magnified into magnificent; what they saw as bad into abomination.

One of Affonso's first acts on becoming king was to murder a close maternal relative. Some accounts have it that it was his own mother, others that it was her slave. This was a ritual killing. The victim was made to lie on a mat covering an open grave. The mat could not support the weight and the victim fell into the hole. He or she was then buried alive. One theory explains this in terms of symbolism; that the King had to demonstrate in a symbolic manner that he had renounced all family ties, that he had become solitary and was placed over everyone. This may be so but it seems hardly likely that his own mother would have kept her husband's death secret for three days while she sent for Affonso if she knew his first royal duty was to bury her alive. Much more likely is that the victim in this case was Prince Mpanza's mother; a natural choice in the circumstances.

Affonso began his reign as he meant to continue it. The church was as militant then as ever in its history and he fitted well into the pattern. He dealt ruthlessly with those who remained outside it, he destroyed fetishes and symbols of the old worship as far as his power stretched and supplied in their place images of saints, crucifixes, *agni dei*, and other sacred objects. He was also a great church builder and the capital soon earned itself another name, *Ekongo dia Ngunga*—Congo of the Bells. The first church had been built by his father, John I, but rather like John's own faith, had quickly crumbled. During Affonso's reign he built the Church of the Holy Cross before 1517, the church of São Salvador, the most important church in the town, and finally in 1526 the Church of Our Lady of the Victories, known to the townsfolk as *Ambila*, the 'church of the graves', because it was located near the sacred wood where the dead kings were buried. By the end of the century there were six churches in the capital to serve its ten thousand inhabitants. Some were stone-built, others simple affairs of mud and palm matting.

On the face of it, Affonso was behaving in a way his Portuguese advisers could not have hoped for in their most sanguine moments. He seemed to accept everything they told him. On their suggestion he 'ennobled', as his father had done, the principal men of the town, he adopted Portuguese dress and manners and, of course, religion. He sent his sons to be educated in Portugal and kept up a barrage of requests to Lisbon for teachers and artisans. He learnt to read and write Portuguese. He modelled his court after that in Lisbon, established a Portuguese secretariat and imitated Portuguese etiquette. But he was not entirely uncritical. Just as the Zulu kings were appalled at some of the harsh British laws of the nineteenth century, Affonso, who studied the Portuguese code, found that trivial offences often merited grim sentences and he jokingly asked a Portuguese envoy, 'What is the penalty in Portugal for anyone who puts his feet on the ground?'

Perhaps his greatest achievement was his education policy. By 1509 he had built his first school for four hundred pupils; by 1516 Rui d'Aguiar notes the presence in the capital of a thousand students, 'sons of noblemen', who were not only learning to read and write but were studying grammar and the humanities 'as well as the things of faith'. He also mentions schools for girls, a most surprising innovation in Africa, which were directed by a sister of the King.

All this needed organization and, above all, teachers, and much of the correspondence between Affonso and the kings of Portugal consists of pleas for more and more trained teachers. From the beginning of his reign he sent selected young men to be educated at the college of Santo Eloi in Lisbon. Some were his own relatives, some the sons of his new aristocracy. In 1512, for instance, nineteen young men left for Lisbon and in 1516 about the same number.

Not all these young scholars benefited by their new environment but two were to achieve fame. One was to become a professor and finally principal of a Lisbon college; the other, a son of Affonso, was to become a bishop. His name was Dom Henrique, he was eighteen years old and studying in Lisbon when his father decided that he wished to enter direct contact with the Vatican and not go through Portuguese intermediaries as had been the case until then. King Manuel of Portugal made no objection. He was aware that a certain glory would attach to Portugal, not only for discovering the Kingdom of Congo but for having 'civilized' its inhabitants to the point where such a meeting could be feasible; indeed, he went further, he helpfully suggested the protocol for the visit.

It was decided that Dom Henrique would lead the mission, that he would address the Pope formally in Latin and that King Manuel would ask the Pope to create the young Congolese a bishop. While these plans were being formed ships were arriving in the Tagus with ivory, rare skins and palm-cloth textiles for His Holiness and when they had been crated and packed, the strange mission set off across Portugal, Spain, France, over the Alps and slowly down northern Italy towards Rome where it arrived in 1513. Five years later, Dom Henrique was elevated to the rank of Bishop of Utica on the formal proposal of four cardinals, the Papal Bull published by Leo X beginning '*Vidimus quae super Henrici* . . .' Three years later, Henry of Congo returned to his homeland.

It was all very remarkable and in its way very modern; there was the education of students in Europe, the requests for technological aid by Affonso, the concentration on local education, the recognition that the Kingdom was a 'developing nation' and that the quickest way of entering Western trade and commerce was to ape Western methods. Of course the influences and pressures on the Kingdom were enormous. Several fleets set off from the Tagus from 1508 onwards and though many died of sickness aboard the caravels and others of malaria, blackwater and yellow fever once they reached Africa, there were still hundreds of white advisers, priests, artisans, printers, missionaries, teachers and colonial settlers in Mbanza Congo and the surrounding provinces.

In this first quarter of the sixteenth century the affairs of the Kingdom were at the flood. Never again would they be quite the same. The 'royal brothers' of Congo and Portugal treated each other on an equal footing, there was no colour prejudice in the Kingdom itself, the Bakongo yearned to be like their new white friends (not masters), a black king had become a benevolent despot, humane, learned and above all at that time, a devout Christian.

And yet a Roman Catholic missionary in the Congo can write in 1889, nearly four hundred years later: 'A Negro of the Congo knows the names of only three kings—that of the reigning monarch, that of his predecessor, and that of Dom Affonso I.' This is sometimes quoted to reinforce the stature of Affonso and certainly it does, but it poses some equally significant questions: What happened after Affonso? Why were the kings, whose line survived into the twentieth century, so unmemorable? It is as though the last king in French historical memory was Louis XII; in English, Henry VIII.

5

IN A SENSE the experiment in the Congo set a pattern for the future colonization of Africa, for the things that went wrong in the Old Kingdom in the sixteenth century kept going wrong in other parts of Africa until the middle of the twentieth century. Yet, during the reign of Affonso at least, the Portuguese were more humane, more benign, than almost any other Western power that came to occupy a part of Africa. So although much—one could say most—of the blame for what happens next can be attributed to the Portuguese, at least some must be borne by Affonso, who seems to have been a shade too credulous for the good of his own people. He is the kind of African leader one met in the last days of imperialism, the Oxbridge or Sorbonne-educated young man who returns to his people only to find that the gap between them is so wide that neither understands the other. To Affonso's subjects he was still Nzinga Mbemba, but to the Portuguese he was Dom Affonso I; he was the 'father' of his own people, but the 'brother' of King Manuel. It was a schizophrenic relationship.

One of the main reasons why the experiment failed was that Portugal attempted to ship out its institutions unchanged to the African bush. It has been written of the Bakongo that they saw themselves as the central race on earth, that it never entered their heads there could be better countries or better people. The same must hold true of Portugal. To the Portuguese their institutions—church, court, law, education—must have seemed the very best there were, why modify them for Africa?

Unhappily, while some of these institutions blossomed in the mild Atlantic breezes they could not stand the freedom of the boiling African bush. Take the mission of 1508: after sickness had culled the numbers, about fifteen priests, euphoric at being alive, reached Mbanza Congo and offered Affonso grandiose plans for the evangelizing of his people. Affonso was delighted. It was partially for this that he was to keep up his arduous correspondence with King Manuel. But, alas, the good fathers were soon buying and selling slaves, in some cases with funds solicited from Affonso, and setting up house with black mistresses.

Affonso complained to King Manuel and in 1512 received a reply which is one of the most interesting documents in the early history of black and white in Africa. This *regimento* consisted of four sections. In the first it was provided that the Portuguese should help Affonso in the betterment of his kingdom: teaching him how to make war Portuguese-style, instructing him in Portuguese law and court etiquette, and helping him build churches. It also enjoined the Portuguese themselves to act with tact and consideration, to offend no one, but wherever possible to help create an African equivalent of Portuguese society.

The second part was in direct answer to Affonso's complaint against the missionaries. Priests were to live together and were not to accept money from the Mani Congo and those who had behaved badly were to be sent home; any slaves they possessed were to be sent to Portugal at the owner's expense.

The last two sections were frankly commercial. It was pointed out to Affonso that it was not economic for vessels to bring goods to the Kingdom from Portugal and return with empty holds. It was made clear that what King Manuel did for the Congo he did out of love for his brother but at the same time he was not averse to seeing these empty vessels filled up with slaves, copper and ivory on their journey home. Finally, the leader of the Portuguese expedition was to undertake a complete study of the Congo—strength, resources, census—and report back to King Manuel.

In an appendix to the *regimento* the King suggested the titles and armorial bearings—containing among other symbols the famous flaming swords—which the King of Congo should adopt and bestow on his nobility: 'principes, ifamtes, duques, marquezes, comdes, bixcomdes, barões.' The chiefs of the six most important feudatories of the Mani Congo were to be dukes, lesser notables were to be marquises, counts and barons; the King's offspring were to be princes and princesses.

While this document is enlightened for the age—and would have been enlightened at any time during the next three centuries—it contained in it a series of time-bombs, the most important of which was that the local Portuguese were to have 'extra-territorial' rights and were placed under a *Corregedor* or magistrate who tried them according to Portuguese law. Offenders found guilty were sent back to Lisbon for punishment. And so, from the Bakongo point of view, the two most vital factors in law were absent, that justice should be the same for everyone and that it should be seen to be done.

In the event, no one paid much attention to the *regimento*, other than Affonso. Mbanza Congo was what these days would be called a wide-open town and the pickings were too good. Priests traded in slaves, Portuguese adventurers arrived, in spite of Affonso's protests African mistresses moved in with their white lovers and a revolt by a coffle of slaves being taken to Mpinda (the port of the Old Kingdom) caused a flare-up of smouldering resentment. Affonso appealed again to his 'brother' in Portugal.

More than twenty of Affonso's letters to King Manuel and his successor, King John III, survive, and very bleak reading they make. As with Theodore, Emperor of Abyssinia in the nineteenth century, whose letters to Queen Victoria were ignored for years at a time, so it was with Affonso and the Portuguese Court. But where Theodore reacted by imprisoning most of the missionaries and diplomats in his country, Affonso turned the other Christian cheek and sat down once more with secretary and writing materials to chide his brothers for lack of interest.

'Most high and most powerful prince and king my brother,' he wrote to King Manuel in 1517. 'It is due to the need of several things for the church that I am importuning. And this I would not probably do if I had a ship, since having it I would send for them at my own cost.'

The ship is a recurring request. Off the coast of Gabon was the Portuguese island of São Thomé which had been discovered in 1490 and which rapidly became a haven for remittance men, ex-convicts and adventurers. It also became a kind of central slave *entrepôt* and slaves were either shipped on from there or remained to work the island's sugar plantations. Its strategic position as a staging-post to the East, its safe anchorages and its prosperous sugar industry gave the island economic advantages which the Congo kingdom did not have, and Affonso soon found that he was not so much a partner of the Portuguese kings as a vassal of São Thomé.

Even Affonso's son, Dom Henrique, Bishop of Utica, first black bishop of the Kingdom, who had achieved so much simply by becoming a bishop, found his office shorn of authority. He became an auxiliary of the Bishop of Madeira and took his instructions through São Thomé. His life must have been bitter. He was ordered by his father to remain in Mbanza Congo where his false position drew laughter from a white priesthood, itself squabbling over slaving transactions and young black girls. Henrique died in 1535, having achieved almost nothing.

Again Affonso appealed to Lisbon, citing São Thomé's avarice. 'Most powerful and most high prince and king my brother, I have already written to you several times of my need for a vessel ...' But the São Thomé lobby at Manuel's court was too powerful and no ship was ever allowed to fall into Affonso's hands. At this time all slaves coming from the Congo provinces had to pass through São Thomé whose Portuguese governor, ruling the island like a Roman proconsul, seized a quarter of the slaves for himself. This meant that the financial return Affonso expected was much reduced. In desperation he wrote to King Manuel asking that São Thomé be given to him in fief. He also asked for more teachers and priests. The last lines of this letter read: 'And we beg your Highness not to leave us unprotected or allow the Christian work done in our kingdom to be lost, for we alone can do no more.'

Lisbon was amused at his unworldliness; the King did nothing. Interest was now beginning to swing away from the Old Kingdom and to centre on São Thomé, on the colonization of Brazil, and on the huge empire Portugal had built up after rounding the Cape of Good Hope. By the time King John III began to rule Portugal at the end of the second decade of the sixteenth century, interest in Congo had turned to apathy and the king left Affonso's requests for doctors and technicians unanswered from one year's end to the next.

6

THERE was one factor above all others that bedevilled relations between Affonso and Portugal, and that was slavery; not so much the act itself but the fact that a close connection grew between missionary and slaver, often fusing him into the same person. Africa was no stranger to slavery, in many parts it was indigenous and had been from time immemorial. New pools of slaves were created in familiar ways; by war, by raids and by breaking the laws of a tribe, but it was possible to sell oneself into slavery for strictly commercial reasons. If any slavery can be called benign, that which existed in Africa before the whites arrived could perhaps be so described, and it must have been somewhat similar to that which Wilfred Thesiger describes on the Trucial coast as recently as twenty years ago, where he found African slaves occupying places of great responsibility in the ruling hierarchy. That was all to change for the worse.

In 1442, at a time when the Portuguese were exploring the Atlantic coast of Africa, one of their captains, Antam Gonsalves, who had captured a group of Moroccans and brought them to Lisbon, was ordered by Prince Henry to return them to Africa. He received in exchange for them ten black slaves and a quantity of gold dust. From that moment the fate of millions of black Africans was sealed. Portugal immediately fitted out fleets of vessels, built forts on the West African coast and went into the business of slaving.

It is impossible to say how many blacks were shipped as slaves during the following four hundred-odd years but if one takes the numbers who arrived on the other side of the Atlantic and adds to that the estimates of those who died or were thrown overboard in the middle passage, and again adds the estimated number of Africans killed in slaving raids, the figure runs very high. In his book *Black Mother*, Basil Davidson writes: 'So far as the Atlantic slave trade is concerned, it appears reasonable to suggest that in one way or another, before and after embarcation, it cost Africa at least fifty million souls. This estimate may be about one fourth of black Africa's approximate population today and is certainly on the low side.'

As soon as the real business of slaving got under way, the slave himself became totally subhuman in the minds of the shippers. He was so much flesh and bone which had to occupy the smallest possible space on board ship. The view taken of him on landing was little different. He was a work cypher. This meant that the *kind* of slavery itself had changed: it was no longer the domestic slavery or vassalship understood in Africa, but the cold chattel slavery of Europe where a man was stripped of all his rights and property.

Most people—that is, of those who cared one way or the other—rationalized their guilt. We find that the character of the black man is attacked not only by lobbyists for the slave trade but by intellectuals. Blacks are turned into fiends— cannibalistic, subhuman, sexually gross—in order to 'justify' their treatment. Here is a Liverpool pamphlet of 1792: 'Africans being the most lascivious of all human beings, may it not be imagined, that the cries they let forth at being torn from their wives, proceed from the dread that they will never have the opportunity of indulging their passions in the country to which they are embarking?' There is a need to turn the black man into an *Untermensch* so that what happens to him is of less consequence. The next step is that all blacks are *Untermenschen* and we are racing full tilt towards racial discrimination and *apartheid*.

It did not take long, once the trade really got under way, to find these attitudes widely held. Father Cavazzi wrote in 1687 of the Kingdom of Congo: 'With nauseating presumption these peoples think themselves the foremost in the world ... They imagine that Africa is not only the greatest part of the world, but also the happiest and most agreeable ... '

After the middle of the seventeenth century, most people who were not making a profit out of the slave trade felt it to be morally wrong. Almost every European nation was engaged in it, each excusing itself by depicting the Africans as hopeless savages, at the same time blaming each other for treating them badly. The Dutch said the French were cruel, the French said the English were brutal and that the Portuguese were not only cruel but incompetent. The English made fun of the French for being excitable and of the Portuguese for baptizing whole shiploads of slaves before taking them to Brazil. Malcolm Cowley, in the introduction to his book, *Black Cargoes*, which he wrote with Daniel Mannix, says: 'In truth these wholesale baptisms must have been ludicrous affairs, yet they are not without meaning. They showed that the Portuguese at least regarded Africans as human beings with souls to be saved ...' He adds: 'In the end it is hard to assign the chief guilt to any national group. English, French, Dutch, Danes, Brandenburgers, Portuguese, Mandingos driving slaves from the Niger to the coast, the absolute kings of Dahomey, Yankee skippers, Congolese middle men, and Egbo merchants in old Calabar: the trade brutalized almost everyone who engaged in it. The guilt for it rests not wholly on the white race, or partly on the African kings and slave merchants, but beyond that on humanity itself, the same humanity that was responsible for Auschwitz and Mauthausen and, in its blundering fashion, for Hiroshima and for the next catastrophe; I mean on the apparently inexhaustible capacity for greed and numbness of heart and the infliction of suffering that survives in the nature of man.' The last sentence could be the epitaph for the Old Kingdom of Congo.

7

THE ECONOMY of the Kingdom was based partly on slavery, and the longer the Portuguese remained the more important it became. In the early years other sources of revenue—textiles, ivory and skins as well as dues and tolls—fortunately brought the kings of Congo a lively revenue. Without this money the Kingdom would not have reached the level of development it achieved during the sixteenth century. There was one other source of wealth which was a royal prerogative: the ownership of the source of all currency. They used seashells found on the island of Loanda, which the Portuguese called the *Ilha do Dinheiro* (Isle of Money). Women mined the shells and graded them into sizes with special sieves. All belonged to the King and much went into the pockets of the large numbers of clergy he supported, as well as his masons and artisans who, in fact, did little to earn it. Both sections used the shells to buy slaves.

In the early days of co-existence, the Kingdom's domestic market functioned well. The necessities of life were abundant and there were few manufactured goods that were not common to everyone. If they yearned after any single commodity it was salt and this they prized above most things and paid highly for it.

There was also a ready market for textiles, forged iron and necklaces, but this all changed when the Portuguese brought with them the results of their own technology. Soon red parasols, gilt mirrors, brass hairpins and a dozen other trinkets were displacing the familiar adornments which had suited the Bakongo for so long. They lusted after the new goods. But the Portuguese shipowners in Lisbon had no use for baskets of shells; they wanted 'hard' currency: slaves.

The slaves of Congo occupied much the same position as they did in other parts of Africa; they were workers and servers. But they were also what might now be described as secretaries and factors and in many cases had considerable freedom, journeying on trading missions into the interior on behalf of their owners. This was not what the Portuguese foresaw for their blacks and as their hunger for slaves increased—ironically whetted by Affonso himself, who had sent lavish gifts of slaves to the Portuguese court—the King became more and more isolated in his attitudes.

The export of slaves increased quickly. In the first hundred years of contact the Kingdom was drained of about half a million people. Almost all the Portuguese in the Kingdom were involved. They wanted to be in and out of Congo as fast as possible, they wanted 'instant' fortunes, for they knew that the longer they remained, the less their chances were of ever leaving the place. Here is a contemporary description contained in a letter: 'The climate is so unhealthy for the foreigner that of all those who go there, few fail to sicken, and of those who sicken, few fail to die, and those who survive are obliged to withstand the intense heat of the torrid zone, suffering hunger, thirst and many other miseries for which there is no relief save patience, of which much is needed, not only to tolerate the discomforts of such a wretched place, but what is more, to fight the barbarity, ignorance, idolatry and vices, which seem scarcely human but rather those of irrational animals.'

The traffic began to cause dissension and real fear of depopulation. Affonso must have considered a break with Portugal, but it was not really possible. His own throne was insecure. Several of his vassal states were on the edge of rebellion—largely because they too were being denuded of inhabitants—and it would only need Portuguese encouragement to push them over. Affonso would then have Portuguese arms and armour against him. He stopped short of a complete break and to protect his own people he set up a slavery commission in 1526 consisting of three chiefs to make sure that the coffles of slaves being herded to the coast in increasing numbers were really captives from the interior and not free Bakongo He also wrote another letter to Portugal, this time to King John III.

Manuel, big and brutish though he was, had shown some interest in the Old Kingdom; John III, whose reign began in 1521 and who was eventually to become completely dominated by his ecclesiastical advisers, cared nothing at all. The letter from Affonso took on a bitter note. He complained that traders had undermined his own monopoly on which rested much of his power. 'We cannot estimate,' he wrote, 'how great the damage is, because the merchants mentioned above capture daily our own subjects, sons of our noblemen, vassals and relatives . . . and cause them to be sold.' He complained of the depopulation of his country, of the corruption and licentiousness of the merchants, he begged again for priests and teachers, for wine and flour for the Holy Sacrament and made the emphatic statement, ' . . . it is our will that in these kingdoms there should not be any trade in slaves or market for slaves.'

Nothing could have been further from Portuguese ambitions and a later letter of 1539, a few years before Affonso's death, shows that nothing had changed for the better, only for the worse. Still believing in Portugal's institutions, he sent off five nephews and one grandson, two of whom were to be educated there, two in Rome and two prepared for minor holy orders in Lisbon. He begs his royal brother to 'give them shelter and boarding and to treat them in accordance with their rank, as relatives of ours with the same blood . . .' Then he asks after a group of twenty young students sent to Lisbon in 1516, ten of whom had been seized as slaves *en route*. 'But about them we do not know so far whether they are dead or alive, nor what happened to them . . .' It is callous enough for the Portuguese court to have remained silent about the young men but one also has the feeling that twenty-three years marks a certain dilatoriness on Affonso's part in asking after them.

The results of these appeals were not what Affonso had hoped: Portugal, to safeguard its source of slaves, began to make alliances with Affonso's neighbours, one of which was the country of Dondo to the south, which was ruled by the Ngola, a title which eventually became the name Angola. The Ngola, a tributary of the Mani Congo's, threw off the yoke in 1556, and fought a victorious battle against the Old Kingdom in which Portuguese settlers fought on both sides to defend their investments.

The last decade of Affonso's reign was marked by dissension and corruption. He was an old tired man, forgotten by Portugal, rotting away in the broiling sun of central Africa, surrounded by scheming immigrants who meddled and vied for patronage and favours, for although Lisbon had little thought for him he still exerted some authority in his own capital.

It is difficult to estimate the number of Portuguese resident in Congo in the 1530s. In his book, *Portuguese Africa*, James Duffy says there were 'never more than two hundred white men, enjoying an influence out of all proportion to their number. Their mulatto children became functionaries, agents of the slave trade, lesser members of the clergy. Children of two worlds, they paid allegiance to neither and were as responsible as their fathers for the constant turmoil that beset the Congo.'

This was the situation when, in the early 1540s, Affonso died.

8

ONE OF the many fascinations of the Kingdom of Congo is that one seems to be studying it by time-lapse photography; everything is accelerated. For the first fifty years the state flowered under its two Christian kings, then it began to wither, an infinitely longer and more squalid process. One can recognize the path trodden by so many other civilizations: the arrival of the founding fathers, the struggle to form the state, the sinewy young nation, the golden age of building and Christian conversion, the disenchantment, the corruption, the beginnings of decline, the invasion of the barbarian hordes, the temporary reunification, the longer decline, the attempt to re-create the golden age, the dismal descent into the dark ages ...

On the death of Affonso, there was a violent struggle for succession between two relatives of the dead king, Pedro and Diogo, which Diogo won. Pedro took sanctuary in a church and remained there until he died, twenty years later. Diogo ruled from 1545 and during his time Congo began its long slide into ruin. It was almost forgotten in Europe except as a place to procure slaves. The church, however, still made fitful attempts to cling to the souls of its inhabitants.

In 1548 the first Jesuits arrived, three priests and a lay preacher, and set about trying to put right the wrongs left by their secular and evangelical forerunners. At first their zeal was exemplary: 2,100 baptisms were recorded in four months, three churches were erected, one of which, dedicated to the Saviour, gave the capital a new name, São Salvador. The lay preacher, Diogo de Soveral, set up schools to cope with six hundred children. For a moment, things looked good. But even so coolly intellectual a group as the Jesuits were unable to withstand the temptations and sly corruptions of the hot land and soon they were buying and selling slaves; one priest, Father Jorge Vaz, collected sixty slaves in three years. Five years after their arrival the Jesuit mission departed wealthy failures.

While this was going on São Thomé was asking Portugal to

boycott Congo because, they said, Diogo was abusing the Jesuits as well as robbing slave caravans on their way to the coast. Diogo replied that the Jesuits were guilty of loose conduct and of calling him an ignorant dog (a serious insult). A second Jesuit mission arrived, but by this time Diogo had pushed his Christianity to one side, had taken on an entourage of concubines and was generally slipping back into pagan ways. He forbade his subjects to attend the missionary schools; there was nothing the Jesuits could do but return to Europe.

In 1561 Diogo died and the battle for succession was re-enacted, with different players. The reign of Affonso II, the heir apparent, was brief: he was murdered while at Mass. His murderer was his own brother, Bernardi, who now became king. He himself died in battle with a neighbouring king and was succeeded by Alvaro I, who ruled for nearly twenty years.

Alvaro's reign began on a not very optimistic note: the borders of Congo were suddenly breached by a tribe called the Jaga, whose ferocity and cannibalistic tendencies caused them to be held in terror. As they swept towards São Salvador, Alvaro, with his *duques* and *marquezes*, *bixcomdes* and *barões*, as well as the white population of the capital, fled to the Congo River and took refuge on an island in the middle of the stream, leaving the Jaga to lay waste the kingdom.

So far the story of the Kingdom of Congo has been pieced together from the writings of priests, missionaries and travellers, some with vested interests in promoting a point of view, most writing years after the events they describe. Now a plain English sailor comes on to the scene who, forty years after the Jaga invasion of Congo, was to fight alongside them and who has left a vivid description: *The Strange Adventures of Andrew Battell of Leigh in Angola and the Adjoining Regions* first appeared in the famous collection *Purchas His Pilgrimes* in 1613 and is an account of what happened to Battell in the years following his departure from England aboard a privateer.

He was born and lived as a child in Leigh near Southend when it was a flourishing port. In 1589 he sailed with Abraham Cocke for the Rio del Plata to prey on Spanish vessels engaged in trade with Portugal's growing colony, Brazil. It was a disastrous expedition and Battell was captured by the Portuguese with four others while foraging for food on an island off the South American coast. Of Captain Cocke nothing more was ever heard. Battell was first taken to Rio and then back across the Atlantic to Angola where he spent nearly twenty years, much of it in the service of his Portuguese masters trading up and down the Angolan coast. Twice he tried to escape and each time was recaptured and flung into prison.

On one of the trading missions in 1600 or 1601, a black chief called Mafarigosat prevailed on Battell and his men to help him in a tribal war. The traders agreed and with the help of their muskets the enemy was, not surprisingly, demolished. But when Battell and the Portuguese and half-castes of the trading mission wanted to return to their ship, the chief refused. He demanded that one of the whites remain until the remainder returned to help him in another war he was contemplating.

Here is Battell: 'The Portugals and Mulattos being desirous to get away from this place, determined to draw lots who should stay; but many of them would not agree to it. At last they consented together that it were fitter to leave me, because I was an Englishman, than any of themselves. Here I was fain to stay perforce. So they left me a musket, powder and shot, promising this lord Mafarigosat that within two months they would come again and bring a hundred men to help him in his wars and to trade with him ... Here I remained with this lord till the two months were expired, and was hardly used because the Portugals came not according to promise.

'The chief men of this town would have put me to death, and stripped me naked, and were ready to cut off mine head. But the Lord of the town commanded them to stay longer, thinking the Portugals would come.'

Battell took to the bush but was captured by the Jaga and taken to their main camp. Had he known who they were he might have considered himself out of a lukewarm frying pan into the blazing fire, for the word Jaga is a corruption of the Bantu word *a yaka* or *va yaka*, 'they fight'. He says he was taken to a place called Calicansamba, which he describes as a 'town' with avenues of baobab trees, cedars and palms. 'In the middle of the town there is an image which is as big as a man and standeth twelve feet high; and at the foot of the image there is a circle of elephants' teeth, pitched into the ground. Upon these teeth stand great store of dead men's skulls, which are killed in the wars, and offered to this image. They used to pour palm oil at his feet. This image is called Quesango, and the people have great belief in him and swear by him; and do believe when they are sick that Quesango is offended with them.'

The Jaga treated Battell well. They had never seen a white person before and of course had no knowledge of arms. He decided to live with them in the hope that their migrations would take them westward to the coast where he might possibly get a ship. But the Jaga were in no hurry. They remained where they were for the next four months, 'with great abundance and plenty of cattle, corn, wine, and oil, and great triumphing, drinking, dancing, and banqueting, with men's flesh, which was a heavy spectacle to behold'.

After more than a year of wandering, the Jaga, accompanied by Battell, did turn westward, attacked an Angolan chief and burnt down his town: 'Here we found great store of wild peacocks, flying up and down the trees in as great abundance as other birds.'

Once again they moved westward and attacked a chief who seven years before had routed a Portuguese–Angolan army of more than forty thousand led by Balthasar de Almeida. The Jaga laid siege to the town and during this time Battell managed to escape. He joined a caravan of slavers and finally reached his Portuguese masters.

In all he was with the Jaga for twenty-one months, living and fighting as one of them. His most valuable asset was his musket and, he says: 'I was so highly esteemed with the Great Gaga because I killed so many Negroes with my musket, that I had anything I desired of him.' His brief descriptions of Jaga social life and habits have stood the test of later scholars.

According to Battell they had a great predilection for palm wine and must have caused much devastation in order to get sufficient quantities, for he writes that they 'cut the palm trees down by the root, which lie ten days before they will give wine. And then they make a square hole in the top and heart of the tree, and take out of the hole every morning a quart, and at night a quart. So that every tree giveth two quarts of wine a

This engraving of São Salvador, capital of the Kingdom of Congo, shows in a somewhat idealized form the progress made by 1686.

The King of Congo, possibly Alvaro, receives a deputation of Portuguese visitors.

A Congolese aristocrat using hammock-men for a journey in the bush. Burton was to use a similar conveyance later in Dahomey.

The king's throne and insignia (in the foreground), as Dapper saw them late in the seventeenth century.

Dress and weapons used by the inhabitants of Congo in the eighteenth century.

day for the space of six and twenty days and then it drieth up.'

Here is his marvellous description of the 'Great Gaga' as he continues to call the Jaga chief, Calandula: 'The Great Gaga Calando hath his hair very long, embroidered with many knots of Banba shells, which are very rich among them, and about his neck a collar of *masoes*, which are also shells, that are found upon that coast, and are sold amongst them for the worth of twenty shillings a shell: and about his middle he weareth *landes*, which are beads made out of ostrich eggs. He weareth a cloth about his middle, as fine as silk. His body is carved and cut with sundry works, and every day anointed with the fat of men. He weareth a piece of copper cross his nose, two inches long, and in his ears also. His body is always painted red and white. He hath twenty or thirty wives, which follow him when he goeth abroad; and one of them carrieth his bows and arrows; and four of them carry his cups of drink after him. And when he drinketh they all kneel down and clap their hands and sing.'

One of the oddities of the Jaga was the practice of killing all their own children by burying them alive, while rearing those of their beaten enemies. There are echoes here of the Mamelukes of Egypt who preferred to train Georgian slaves as their successors rather than bring up their own children, of the *arioi* priesthood of Tahiti and even, in some respects, of the Turkish Janissaries who recruited only Christian children. Battell writes that when the Jaga took a town they kept the boys and girls of thirteen or fourteen as their own children.

'But the men and women they kill and eat. These little boys they train up in the wars, and hang a collar about their necks for a disgrace, which is never taken off till he proveth himself a man, and bring his enemy's head to the General (chief); and then it is taken off and he is a freeman, and is called *gonso* or soldier.'

A point on which there is a good deal of speculation is Battell's constant reference to cannibalism, for except in circumstances of great famine as occurred in Lesotho in the nineteenth century, cannibalism in Africa was mostly ritualistic. 'When the Great Gaga Calandola undertaketh any great enterprise against the inhabitants of any country, he maketh a sacrifice to the Devil, in the morning, before the sun riseth. He sitteth upon a stool, having upon each side of him a man-witch: then he has forty or fifty women stand round about him, holding in each hand a *zevra* (zebra) or wild horse's tail, wherewith they do flourish and sing. Behind them are great store of *petes*, *ponges* and drums, which always play. In the midst of them is a great fire, upon the fire an earthen pot with white powders, wherewith the man-witches do paint him on the forehead, temples, 'thwart the breast and belly, with long ceremonies and inchanting terms. Thus he continueth until sun is down. Then the witches bring his *casengula*, which is a weapon like a hatchet, and put it into his hands and bid him be strong against his enemies . . . And presently there is a man-child brought before him; two whereof, as it happeneth, he striketh and killeth; the other two he commandeth to be killed without the fort.

'Here I was by the man witches ordered to go away, as I was a Christian . . .'

In 1610, Battell returned to Leigh with, as his servant, a young boy who claimed to have been held captive by a gorilla. At that time a Reverend Samuel Purchas was Vicar of Eastwood, a village two miles north of Leigh, and it was he who worked with Battell on an account of his *Adventures*.

9

SUCH WAS the tribe which had sent Dom Alvaro I, the Mani Congo, fleeing to the island in the Congo River with his white advisers and his black noblemen.

The exact island, among the hundreds which turn the river into a watery maze, upon which the Bakongo were to spend about a year, is uncertain. It is sometimes referred to as the Isle of Horses, at others Hippopotamus Island or Elephant Island. We do know that it was small, a factor which was to aggravate an already horrific situation, for plague soon broke out.

The Kingdom itself was devastated. The Jaga entered São Salvador and burnt it, slaughtering anyone who survived. Their army then split into separate regiments and conquered the remaining provinces. Thousands of homeless wandered the roads, many of them dying eventually of starvation. On the island the plague grew worse and was accompanied by a shortage of food. King Alvaro sickened, not with plague, but with dropsy from which he suffered for the rest of his life.

As those on the island reached the edge of starvation slavers arrived from São Thomé with food. The traveller Lopez describes what happened next: 'The price of a small quantity of food rose to that paid for a slave, who was sold for at least ten crowns.

'Thus, forced by necessity, the father sold his son, and the brother his brother, everyone resorting to the most horrible crimes in order to obtain food.' The food was unloaded, the weak, half-dead sons and brothers of dukes and marquises and barons were transferred to rowing-boats and thence carried farther downstream to where the caravels from São Thomé were anchored. Yet even as the slaves were being sold both sides observed the letter of King Affonso I's slavery decree. Here is Lopez again: 'Those who were sold to satisfy the hunger of others were bought by Portuguese merchants ... the sellers saying that they were slaves, and in order to escape further misery, these last confirmed the story.' There can have been few sights in Africa sadder before—or since—than men and women pretending to be slaves so that those actually selling them could benefit by obtaining food.

As the weeks passed into months and things grew worse, King Alvaro turned in desperation to Lisbon. He sent an ambassador to young Sebastião of Portugal and for once a request from Congo was answered with speed. In 1570 Captain Francisco de Gouveia and six hundred soldiers and adventurers reached Congo. He was joined by Alvaro and his rump of courtiers, bodyguards and white settlers and in nearly two years of intermittent fighting, the combined force eventually broke up the Jagas and drove them out of the Kingdom. Afterwards Gouveia built a strong wall around the town of São Salvador. In gratitude for the restoration of his kingdom, Alvaro formally acknowledged vassalage to the King of Portugal and agreed to send annual tribute of one-fifth of the yearly collection of cowrie shells, which could always be exchanged for slaves. He then married, had four daughters and two sons, and an additional two daughters by one of his slaves. He is almost the last great figure in the story of the Old Kingdom.

The Jaga invasion had given the Kingdom a severe shock and once Alvaro regained his throne in São Salvador he was able to take stock of the future. It did not look promising. The Jaga had been defeated, not destroyed, and were perched on his frontiers ready to strike again. Angola, his great southern neighbour, was being opened up by the Portuguese and colonized. He must have felt caught between the two pressures which were to mark African history from that point on, the pressure from within—historically a fact of life and one with which all African kings had had to deal—and that from Europe unfamiliar and therefore frightening. He did what his predecessors had done, the only thing he could do: he appealed to Portugal and Spain (which had ruled Portugal since 1580) and he also appealed to the Pope. He asked for missionaries and artisans to help rebuild his kingdom. He also offered to hand over his copper and silver mines. For years Portugal had been certain that vast deposits of minerals lay in the hinterland of Congo, though no one had discovered them, least of all the kings, so that the mines which Alvaro generously offered to transfer only existed in the imagination.

Alvaro was unfortunate in his ambassadors. One was the Portuguese merchant Duarte Lopez. He left Congo in 1583 with a pouch of letters and a head full of careful instructions. But the ship in which he was travelling sprang a leak near the Cape Verde Islands and was blown by contrary winds to the West Indies. It finally sank off Grenada and the crew and passengers had to swim ashore. Lopez was marooned there for nearly a year before he could join a fleet sailing to Spain.

In the meantime Alvaro, having heard no news and fearing that the ship and his ambassador had been lost, sent off his prime minister, Dom Pedro Antonio, in another ship. This was captured by English pirates. A prize crew was put aboard and the ship sailed for England. As they were landing the ship was wrecked and Dom Pedro and his son, who had accompanied him, were drowned.

By the time Duarte Lopez had recovered from his ordeal and felt well enough to leave Spain and complete his mission to

Rome, King Alvaro I had died and had been succeeded in 1587 by his son, Alvaro II. He knew that his father had wanted to remove Congo from Portugal's tutelage and place it directly under the Holy See and he worked towards the same end. The pressures that Alvaro I had recognized had built up even further, and Alvaro II made repeated efforts to dissociate Congo from the Angolan territories which now were blatantly colonial and whose colonists were trying to nibble away at the borders of Congo. He appealed directly to the Pope, offering 'all the metal which will be discovered in the Kingdom' in exchange for protection against 'force and vexations'.

But poor Alvaro II had as little luck with his ambassadors as his father had. The envoy this time was Antonio Manuel who was robbed at sea by pirates and delayed both in Lisbon and Madrid. He reached Rome on January 3, 1608, four years after leaving Congo and so exhausted was he and so despondent—he had seen most of his embassy die *en route*—that two days after arriving and within hours of delivering his message, he too died. It is by the grandeur of his funeral, which was said to have been the equal of that of a former ambassador from France, that Congo was finally recognized by the Vatican as a Christian kingdom. The funeral was described as one 'almost befitting a king', and there is a fresco in the Vatican showing the Pope visiting Antonio Manuel on his death-bed. But for all the funeral pomp, little was achieved in the way of help for Congo and the following year Alvaro II died without achieving his greatest ambition, the disengagement of Congo from Portugal.

It would be tedious to enumerate the kings that followed him; their reigns were short, their lives filled with rivalry and intrigue. The swift turnover meant that some were only children, like Alvaro IV who came to the throne in 1631 aged thirteen and ruled only four years.

While the various factions were competing for power within the kingdom, great changes were taking place in the outside world. The southern Atlantic, which had for so many years been the private preserve of Portugal and Spain, saw the influx of France, England and Holland. The Dutch began settling in the province of Soyo and entered the slave trade. In Angola the Portuguese allied themselves with the Jaga and raided

Congo for slaves. Things became so bad that King Garcia II Affonso (1641–61) made common cause with the Dutch against the Portuguese and was able to gain some control of his country once more. But in 1648 the Dutch abandoned Angola. They already had their eyes on the Cape of Good Hope, which they were to colonize four years later; Congo was left to the tender mercies of the Portuguese once more.

The King was defeated, a treaty was signed containing punitive clauses, slavery was rife, everything was collapsing. In 1665 came the final ironic blow: two Christian armies, both marching under banners of the Cross, met on the field of Ambouila. One was a black army led by King Antonio I, the other Portuguese. The Bakongo suffered a total defeat and King Antonio was killed and decapitated.

10

A ND THAT is almost that. By 1667 the Portuguese had got all they could out of Congo and were abandoning it. A few years later, a bishop was to write of São Salvador that it was nothing but 'a den of savage beasts'. By 1701 a report stated: 'The news coming from the Congo is always worse and the enmities between the royal houses are tearing the Kingdom further and further apart. At present there are four kings of the Congo ... There are also two great dukes of Bamba; three great dukes in Ovando; two great dukes in Batta, and four marquises of Enchus. The authority of each is declining and they are destroying each other by making war among themselves. Each claims to be chief. They make raids on one another in order to steal and to sell their prisoners like animals.'

Almost, but not quite ... there is one surprise remaining which sounds an historical echo so loudly one might almost accuse the Old Kingdom of stage management. And yet it springs surely out of the misery and chaos that made up Congo at the end of the seventeenth and beginning of the eighteenth centuries. Out of the ashes of Christian teachings and the old fetish religion, was born a new cult which took for its banner the golden age of Affonso I; it was a religion born of nostalgia, of distaste and despair for the present, and in that sense it was as much a political revolutionary movement as it was evangelical. The new cult started when a young woman professed to have seen the Virgin and to have learnt of Christ's indignation at conditions in Congo. There is a strong relationship between this revelation and those made to Joan of Arc in France in the fifteenth century and to a Xhosa maiden in south-eastern Africa in the middle of the nineteenth century, which we shall deal with later. The three occasions coincided with periods when the nations to which the mystics belonged were threatened by overwhelming pressures. According to this woman, the Virgin asked her to recite the Ave Maria three times and ask for Divine Mercy three times each evening. A young man took this slightly further by announcing that in his revelation a warning was given that the people of Congo would be punished unless they rebuilt São Salvador. Next an old woman said she had found the head of Christ which had been disfigured by man's sins. This turned out to be a stone brought up from a river. She also claimed to have had a vision of the Virgin.

These were no more than the stirrings of a new religious feeling. The true Joan of Arc figure and the founder of the Antonian sect, which was to sweep the Old Kingdom with the promise of a golden future in the shape of the past, was a young girl of noble birth named Kimpa Vita, who called herself Dona Beatriz. Like Joan, she took up the task of wiping out the evils besetting her country. Here is a description of her by Father Laurent de Lucques, a Capuchin who was to fight her and her new religion with great ferocity. 'This young woman,' he wrote, 'was about twenty-two years old. She was rather slender and fine-featured. Externally she appeared very devout. She spoke with gravity and seemed to weigh each word. She foretold the future and predicted, among other things, that the day of Judgement was near.'

By 1704 her teachings were spreading outwards and she was gaining disciples all over the land. Even what was left of the nobility in São Salvador, where she later preached, gathered to her, touching her and being touched, giving her their cloaks to cover her head, fighting over food or drink which she had touched. When she travelled, the paths were cleared ahead of her by a group of women disciples. When she walked along these paths it was said that twisted trees grew suddenly straight. The word went out that at long last God was coming to the aid of the anguished Kingdom and that Dona Beatriz was His representative.

Father Bernardo de Gallo, another Capuchin, described an interview he had with her in which she revealed the miraculous beginnings of her conversion from heathenism. He wrote: 'She said it happened this way. She was lying ill unto death when a brother dressed as a Capuchin appeared to her. He told her he was St Anthony, sent by God to restore through her the Kingdom, to preach to the inhabitants and to chastise severely those who opposed it.' Thereupon she died but revived when St Anthony entered her body. She told her parents what had happened and set out on her great mission to the capital where she claimed St Anthony was the 'second God' and that he held the keys to Heaven. The sect took its name from him.

According to M. Balandier, in his book, *Daily Life in the Kingdom of the Kongo*, she succeeded in combining the religious tradition of Congo with Portuguese Christian tradition; St Anthony, deeply revered in Portugal, was one of the three saints worshipped in the Old Kingdom. Balandier describes how she tried, symbolically, to revive the beginnings of Christianity and bring about its rebirth. She imitated the death of Christ each Friday, went up to Heaven where she dined with God and pleaded the cause of Congo and was born again each Saturday. She imitated the Virgin and longed to give birth, by immaculate conception, to a new Saviour. And when she did have a son she said to Father de Lucques, 'I cannot deny that he is mine, but how I had him I do not know. I do know, however, that he came to me from Heaven.' Simple words, one might think, even touching, but given the religious fanaticism of the times, deadly.

Dona Beatriz was a revolutionary who would have found a place in any one of several black movements today. Some of her teachings are bizarre enough, but beneath them one can find the first stirrings of *négritude*, of black power, of the belief that black is beautiful. She emphasized the differences between black and white rather than the similarities. White people, she said, came originally from a kind of clayey rock, while black people sprang from the wild fig tree. Her preachings were part prophecy, part political doctrine. She taught, for instance, that Congo was the true Holy Land and that the founders of Christianity were black. She said that Christ was born in São Salvador and was baptized at Nsundi and that the Virgin Mary was the daughter of a black *marqueze* and a concubine. She predicted a golden age when São Salvador would be rebuilt and repopulated and would be filled with 'the rich objects of the whites'. She foretold that the roots of fallen trees would change into gold and silver, that fabulous mines would be discovered containing metals and gems. To be part of this wonderful future all one had to do was believe.

Father de Gallo and Father de Lucques fought her influence by every means at their disposal. Father de Gallo in particular denounced her 'frauds' and said that to lend credence to her powers of divination she had parcels of cowrie shells buried in different parts of the ruined cathedral, then publicly revealed the location of the caches.

But Dona Beatriz was hard to fight because she had modelled herself closely on the missionaries themselves. She preached against vice, superstition, the old fetish religion and in general against the same sins as the good fathers. She adapted the *Ave Maria* and the *Salve Regina*. She established her own church, sent out disciples to proselytize those who lived in the distant areas of Congo and even set up a nunnery. She soon began to be regarded by her black flock as a saint.

While she accepted and preached many of the Christian precepts, she was solidly against the missionaries and their white religion. Her people were told not to worship the Cross because it had caused Christ's death. She rejected the Catholic form of baptism, its confession and prayer, and made polygamy 'legal'. Foreign priests were threatened, discomfited, and accused of opposing the work of salvation of the 'black saints'. As her religion grew, so did nationalist sentiment: Antonianism gave expression to the need of many Bakongo to rebuild their society.

All this was watched with the gravest concern by the Capuchins. They saw Antonianism as a force which would weaken and finally destroy Catholicism in Congo as well as the link between Congo and Europe which was now more than two hundred years old. Since Antonianism was more than simply a religion—it was belief in the future of the nation itself—it was hard to fight. Here is Father de Gallo again writing of the time when Dona Beatriz journeyed to São Salvador: 'Thus it came about that São Salvador was rapidly populated, for some went there to worship the pretended saint, others to see the rebuilt capital, some to see friends, others attracted by the desire to recover their health miraculously, others still out of political ambition and to be the first to occupy the place. In this manner the false saint became the restorer, ruler and lord of the Congo.' Antonianism was all things to all men, but the one thing it did not do was make Dona Beatriz ruler of Congo, as Father de Gallo suggests. Had it done so she would have been safe.

The Capuchins could no longer stand by and watch the erosion of Catholicism by a quasi-religious, nationalistic movement, so they began to put pressure on the Mani Congo, King Pedro IV. For a time the King was unmoved but then, when it became plain to him that his own situation was being weakened by pretenders who were using the new cult against him, he acceded to the Capuchins and had Dona Beatriz arrested. It was within the King's power to have her executed for committing the heresy of claiming her child was Heaven-sent, but he hesitated, the current of popular sentiment was running strongly in her favour. He seriously considered allowing her to escape to her followers. But the Capuchins sensed his indecision and, motivated 'solely by zeal for the glory of God', as Father de Gallo has it, exerted more pressure. The King gave in and his royal council passed a sentence of 'death by fire on the false Saint Anthony and his guardian angel'.

The sentence was carried out on July 2, 1706, and here is Father de Lucques' eye-witness report on the death of Dona Beatriz, for which he shared responsibility: 'Two men holding bells ... stood in the midst of this huge throng and gave a signal with their bells, and at once the crowd fell back and in the midst of the empty space the *basciamucano*, the judge, appeared.' According to de Lucques, he was dressed from head to toe in a black cloak and wore a hat on his head of a black 'so ugly that I do not believe its like for ugliness has ever been seen'. Dona Beatriz, carrying her baby son, was led before him. She appeared to be very frightened. They sat down on the hard ground and waited for the sentence to be carried out.

'We understood then that they had decided to burn the

child along with his mother,' says Father de Lucques, allowing himself a flash of pity. 'This seemed to us too great a cruelty. I hurried to speak to the King to see whether there was some way to save him.'

The judge made a speech which had nothing whatever to do with the matter in hand, being a eulogy of the King, at the end of which he pronounced the sentence against Dona Beatriz, saying that 'under the false name of St Anthony she had deceived the people with her heresies and falsehoods. Therefore the King, her Lord, and the Royal council condemned her to die at the stake together with her child.'

Father de Lucques describes how she made every effort to recant but without success. 'There arose such a great noise among the crowd that it was impossible for us to be of help to the two condemned persons. They were quickly led to the stake . . . For the rest, all we can say is that there was gathered there a great pile of wood on which they were thrown. They were covered with other pieces of wood and burned alive. Not content with this, the following morning some men came again and burned the bones that remained and reduced everything to very fine ashes.'

Antonianism did not die suddenly, but lingered on in the shadow of its first martyr. 'Relics' were collected, places at which she had taught were considered holy. For a time there was hope of the kingdom recovering its national vigour. But it was not to be. The pressures had been too great, the greed too widespread; and the Old Kingdom of Congo slipped out of men's consciousness into an age of darkness.

By the end of the eighteenth century São Salvador was a ruined city, its churches tumbling down, its walls open to any marauder. A priest who made the long journey from the coast wrote to the Bishop of Angola that he found only an agglomeration of untidy huts behind a palisade, nothing more. 'It has passed away like the torrential rains which simply moisten the surface and leave the subsoil dry and sterile.' Some years later the Old Kingdom became part of Angola. The last half of the nineteenth century saw a great influx of missionaries in Africa and once again the Old Kingdom seemed profitable ground, this time to the Baptists, who set up a mission at São Salvador in 1878.

In the 1950s São Salvador was visited by F. Clement Egerton, who says in his book, *Angola in Perspective*: 'It has completely lost any romantic character it ever had, and is now no more than a straggling village. The walled cities have disappeared and the eleven churches with them. What is left of the Cathedral is unimposing, just the chancel arch and some low remains of chocolate-coloured walls. It is surrounded by the unkempt grass which is everywhere to be seen in the dry season; and the graves of the early kings of the Congo, rough, obelisk-like monuments in an untidy churchyard, look unkempt and neglected also.'

He spoke to an old man of nearly seventy who sported a magnificent white moustache and who called himself Dom Pedro VII, the last king of Congo, but there were rumours that he was an impostor. He lived near the ruins of the cathedral in an unpretentious house around the walls of which hung copies of paintings of Portuguese royalty.

Egerton was shown the 'regalia' which he describes as 'a royal robe trimmed with white fur, which looked more like rabbit than ermine, a silver crown, a sceptre, and miscellaneous utensils, none of which looked more than a hundred years old. It was rather pathetic.' This old man, who died in 1955, was given a small subsidy by the Portuguese authorities which he increased by growing a little coffee and rice.

Since Egerton's visit a great deal has happened in Angola and much of the country has been convulsed by civil war. On the night of March 14, 1961, a Bakongo terrorist organization called the União das Populacãoes Angolanas (U.P.A.) crossed the northern border of Angola into what had been the Old Kingdom and slaughtered more than two thousand Europeans, half-castes (whom they ceremoniously beheaded) and black contract workers who had come north to work in the coffee plantations. (It was this operation which began the Angolan emergency, the conduct of which was radically affected by the 1974 left-wing *coup* in Lisbon.) The group of terrorists was led by Holden Roberto, who had been educated by the Baptists at São Salvador and who saw himself as the modern king of Congo, before opting for fervid pan-Africanism on the Nkrumah pattern. It has been estimated that most of the deaths in the slaughter that followed were among the contract workers. These came from a people called the Ovimbundu, of whom the Jaga once formed a part. After the massacre, about twenty thousand refugees fled south, many dying of hunger and thirst on the way. It was several years before they gradually returned to their homes.

São Salvador has changed since Egerton's visit. There is a splendid Franciscan mission in the village with a school holding five hundred children as well as a teachers' training college. In 1971 there were four white bishops in Angola, one half-caste, one Goan—and one black. . . .

PART TWO

'The King's Head Thing'

'It is no mere lust of blood nor delight in torture and death that underlies the rite (human sacrifice) in these lands. The King has to perform a disagreeable task over his ancestral graves, and he does it; his subjects would deem it impious were he to curtail or to omit the performance, and suddenly to suppress it would be as if a European monarch were forcibly to abolish prayer for the dead.'
—Sir Richard Burton

Regiment of Dahomey Amazons in action

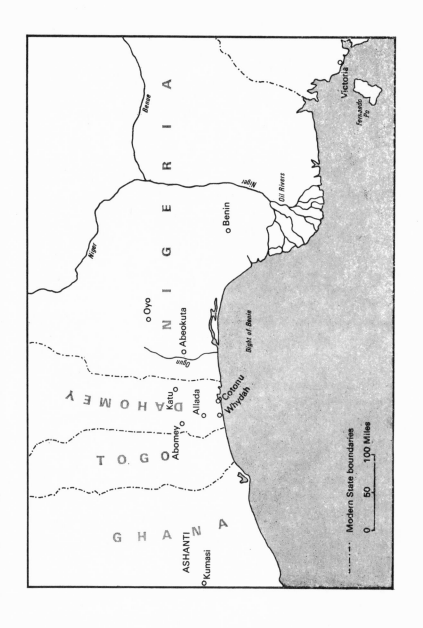

1

U NLIKE THE Old Kingdom of Congo, Dahomey made an impact on the world from an early stage in its development. In an area of Africa which was the very heartland of the slave trade, Dahomey was among the most notorious of all the black slaving nations; and among a group of peoples who practised ritual murder, it was Dahomey which became the most infamous. Of its culture, of its unique dualistic bureaucracy, little was reported and less cared about. While slavery was what might now be called a growth industry, Dahomey was wooed by every white slaving nation; when at last the conscience of the world was aroused, Dahomey was vilified, blockaded and put under pressure to stop the flow of slaves. It can perhaps be said that Dahomey was created by external pressure and finally weakened by external pressure. But unlike the Kingdom of Congo it had an internal strength, a recognition of its own destiny that has assured its survival, true in a different political body, until today. The great difference between the two kingdoms as far as the life-force is concerned is that Dahomey was built by black people while much of the Kingdom of Congo was created by whites.

The beginnings of the Dahomean nation-state are lost in mists and myths. At the start of the seventeenth century there was no such place as Dahomey and it seems to have emerged between 1620 and 1630 when the Fon, a race who lived inland behind the Slave Coast, drew together in self-defence against the slave-raiding of their eastern neighbours, the Yoruba of Oyo and the coastal kingdoms of Whydah and Allada. So in the beginning Dahomey was forced to protect itself against precisely the sort of depredations it was later to practise on others with such economic success.

One other major factor affected the country's growth: its geographical peculiarity. Today its shape is roughly that of a thick but stunted tree which sprouts on the coastline of the Bight of Benin and grows due north into the bulge of Africa between Togo and Nigeria. Its littoral is only sixty miles wide, its length at best four hundred and fifty miles and its widest point about two hundred miles. Until well into the eighteenth century it was much smaller, consisting only of the area around the old capital of Abomey, which lies about fifty miles inland, and it had a population of about two hundred thousand. At that time the Dahomeans, like their inland neighbours, were terrified of the sea; it was tabu. However, unlike their neighbours whose lands were bounded by swamps, mountains, rain forests and wide rivers, the young Dahomey was an almost featureless area of bush country difficult to defend without superior arms, and the most superior arms were flowing into Africa from Europe as payment for slaves. They could only get arms by going to the coast for them. So it was that in spite of this tabu, in 1727 Dahomey broke through to the coast, taking as it did so the small independent statelets of Whydah and Allada which, until then, had refused to allow it to sell its slaves except through them. They were helped by a natural phenomenon called the Gap of Benin, a break in the forest zones lying on either side of Dahomey, which connects the hinterland with the coast giving the country a different climate from that of its neighbours. It is a *lusus naturae*, a freak of nature which is called by the French 'the hole'. Along several thousand miles, from Senegal to the Niger, the hinterland of West Africa is approachable from the sea only at the mouths of rivers, but once through the rough surf off the coast of Dahomey a traveller could walk the short distance to Abomey with relative ease. From the moment they established themselves on the coast, the Dahomeans' power and reputation began to grow. It is also from this period that the world began to notice Dahomey.

As an introduction to the long association of European slavers with the country, one can do no better than quote a letter from the splendidly named Bullfinch Lamb which was written from Abomey in 1724, three years before the breakthrough to the coast. Captain Lamb, an agent of the English African Company, had been captured by the Dahomean monarch, 'Trudo Audati, King of Dahomey and Emperor of Popo' when Dahomey overcame the town of Jaquin, and was taken to the King's court, where he became a much-favoured prisoner. His letter is to his superior in Whydah, Mr Tucker.

From the Great King Trudo
Audati's Palace of Abomey,
in the Kingdom of Dahomey.
Nov. 27, 1724.

Sir,

About five days ago, the king of this country gave me
yours of the 1st instant, and immediately required me to
answer it in his presence, which I did, though in a very
indifferent manner: so that if I do not recall it, I hope you
will excuse that as well as this.

As to the late conference I had with his majesty on
receiving your letter, I think he does not want to make a
price to let me go; for when I pressed him much to tell
me on what terms he would send me away, his answer was,
he did not want to sell me, I was not a black man; but upon
my again pressing him, he made a sort of jesting demand to
the sum of I think 700 slaves, about £10,000 or £14 a head.
Which strange ironical way of talking, as I told him, made
my blood run cold in my veins . . . he is prodigious vain and
proud, but he is withal, I believe, the richest king and
greatest warrior in this part of the world; and you may
depend on it, in time will subdue most of the countries
round him. He has already set his two chief palaces round
with men's skulls, as thick as they can lie on the walls, one
by another, and are such as he has killed in war; each of
which palaces are in circumference larger than St James's
Park, about a mile and a half round.

After a plea that something be done so that he was not
forced to spend his youth 'as it were for nothing in this cursed
place', Lamb goes on to say that he is being treated well, that
he has been given male and female servants and a constant
supply of food and drink to maintain both himself and his
staff and that 'if I loved brandy I might soon kill myself,
having enough of that'. This is a recurring theme. Many of the
travellers who reached Abomey in the following 150 years had
to wait months before permission was given to leave, and they
record a constant intake of rum, brandy, gin and claret by
which they cushioned themselves from the heat, frustration
and terrors of the court.

Whenever the King walked in public Lamb was ordered to attend, often having to sit for hours in the harsh sun, though being allowed a 'kidey-soll or umbrella' to prevent sunstroke. For such attendance the King often gave him a reward of cowrie shells, 'two, sometimes three or four grand cabess'.[1]

Lamb became something of a gentleman-in-waiting to the King and whenever His Majesty rode abroad he was ordered to accompany him. He was given a horse but lacked saddlery and in his letter he asks for 'horse furniture' to be sent from the coast both for himself and the King 'as it is very uneasy to ride a bare horse'. He rather touchingly suggests that the company charge him for these things as well as one or two other objects like 'a little English dog' and a pair of shoe buckles which the King needed.

In case the English African Company felt that he was worrying too much about his own fate, Lamb suggested that Mr Tucker send him money so that he could promote the company's interest by trading for slaves while still a captive. He went on:

> Most of the ink you sent me being unfortunately spilt I beg you will send me a paper of ink-powder. His Majesty has likewise got from me the greatest part of the paper, having a notion in his head of a kite, which, though I told him it was only fit for boys to play with, yet he says I must make one for him and I to play with; so I beg you will send two quires of ordinary paper and some twine for that use, and a score of match, His Majesty requiring me sometimes to fire his great guns, and I am much in fear of having my eyes put out with the splinters.

He asked for any prints, pictures or books which Mr Tucker might have handy, for the King had a delight in looking at things like that and often carried a Latin mass-book which he apparently consulted whenever he had decided *not* to grant Lamb a request. Then a most surprising request: 'If there is

[1] The existing exchange rate was four boges to one tokey; five tokeys to one gallina; twenty gallinas to one grand cabess, which equalled one pound sterling.

any cast-off woman,' Lamb wrote, 'either white or mulatto, that can be persuaded to come to this country, either to be his wife or to practise her old trade, I should gain His Majesty's heart entirely by it and he would believe anything I say about my going and returning again with more white men from the company.'

He described the battle in which he was captured. The house where he had been staying in Jaquin had been one of the first fired by the attacking Dahomean army. He had lost all his possessions but had managed to get clear and watch the remainder of the assault. He was then captured and taken to the Dahomean general who, 'though he was in a great hurry and flushed with victory took me very kindly by the hand and gave me a dram, which was some comfort to me, though I knew not who he was . . . .' He accompanied the general through the streets of the town where 'there was scarce any stirring for bodies without heads, and had it rained blood it could not have lain thicker on the ground.' Lamb remained in the town for two more days and then was carried by hammock-men into the interior.

Having seen so many cruelties committed on the bodies of old men and women, also on such as were not able to travel by reason of their wounds and burns, etc, I could not choose but labour under dismal apprehensions, particularly the first morning when they led me out, as I imagined to sacrifice me, with a drum beating a sort of dead march before me, and many hundreds gathered about me, jumping and tearing, enough to rend the very skies with such a noise as would fright the devil himself. Many had drawn swords and knives in their hands, which they flourished about me, as if ready for execution. While I was calling on God to have mercy upon me, the general sent orders to the petty captain of war to bring me to him, being retired about two miles out of the camp. His orders were quickly obeyed, and I brought to him, which put an end to my fears.

I should have given you an account of my introduction to the king had not His Majesty sent this minute in a hurry to me for this letter, which I cannot have time to copy or correct, as I intended. I therefore beg you will pardon

tautology and all other faults. Being, with hearty service to all the gentlemen, Sir, Your most obedient humble servant,
Bullfinch Lamb.

Eventually Lamb was given permission to leave Abomey and he returned to Britain a much richer man than he had left. The King of Dahomey had given him a parting gift of 320 ounces of gold and eighty slaves, as well as an interpreter called Tomo who had also been captured at Jaquin. Two reasons have been advanced for the King's munificence: firstly, that he wanted to open communications with King George I of England and discover as much about Britain as he could; secondly, he hoped to try and prevail on Whitehall to stop exporting slaves to the colonies but instead to buy them and keep them on the Guinea Coast to work at European-supervised plantations.

Before Lamb left he was required by the King to take a most solemn oath to return, but unlike Diogo Cão, whose honour is one of the small bars of sunshine in the story of the Old Kingdom, Lamb never did. Nor did he send Tomo back to report on life in Britain. Instead he went off to Barbados and sold Tomo to an American. This breach rankled with the King and it did not incline him to think well of Europeans after that. It is possible that the incident was kept fresh by the keepers of the tribal memory for when Richard Burton visited Dahomey in 1863 he was fulfilling a promise to return made a year previously during a brief visit to Abomey. The fact that Burton kept his promise caused the then King, Gelele, to treat him with exaggerated respect.

There were relatively few European visitors to Abomey before or after Burton; had foreigners been allowed to wander freely about the countryside there would have been many more. But the virtue of having a capital a good few miles inland meant that any potential traveller had first to get in touch with the King's viceroy at Whydah on the coast and apply for permission to visit Abomey. A few travellers and slavers, among them the Englishmen Robert Norris, Frederick Forbes, Eardley-Wilmot and J. A. Skertchly, did receive permission and each wrote an account of the visit. But by far the most important traveller to reach Abomey was Burton. He was a man with a trained mind, a brilliant linguist, and a writer with endless patience for whom no detail was too small or insignificant. In her essay *Richard Burton: The African Years*, Caroline Oliver writes: 'The most important result of Burton's visit was the book[1] he wrote. It is the best description of Dahomey written while the monarchy was still a living force. It is also probably his best African book, because his interest in, and understanding of much of his subject often surmounts the impulse to jeer. He describes Fon culture and religion, the Dahomean constitution and the sacrificial rites with objective authority, and as usual the detail is astonishing. During the five-day ritual at Abomey, he recorded every dance movement, the pattern of every one of hundreds of decorated umbrellas and every ceremonial wiping of the royal nose and face. As the record of a visit of little more than two months it is a great achievement.' And for all his outlandish statements on race, his rash temperament and his open dislike of Negroes he seems able, in his book, to divorce the scholar from the bigot and gives us the clearest as well as the most detailed picture of the Kingdom of Dahomey at almost the height of its power.

Yet if Dahomey was strong, it had now reached a critical period in its history. After an existence of nearly two and a half centuries in which it had emerged as one of the most powerful kingdoms in Africa, it was, only thirty years after Burton's visit, to be gobbled up by the French Colonial Empire. From early in the eighteenth century Britain had been exerting growing pressure on the Dahomean kings to stop slaving and put an end to the 'Annual Customs', during which Abomey, the capital, reeked with the blood of human sacrifice. It was the British Government, in the shape of Burton, which arrived in Dahomey in 1863 to exert yet more official pressure. To appreciate the meeting between Burton and Gelele, the last of the great Dahomean kings, it is necessary to discover who they were and what had produced them.

[1] *A Mission to Gelele, King of Dahome.*

2

RICHARD BURTON was born in 1821 in England, but a few months later his family moved to central France, and from then on he saw little of England until he was old enough to go to Oxford. His was a remarkable childhood. In an age when children were strictly controlled, he and his younger brother Edward grew up in an atmosphere of such freedom that their self-willed behaviour became a scandal wherever their father settled.

At nineteen, Richard went to Oxford. He was a tall muscular young man with a fierce, drooping moustache and a manner not calculated to bring out affection in his elders and betters. Indeed by the time he was sent down for disobedience, his intellectual arrogance had developed to a point where he was roundly disliked by his professors. He was by this time a steady drinker, a massive smoker, including the occasional pipe of opium, a fine swordsman and a precocious sensualist. He had also developed the passion for languages which was to dominate his life. At Oxford he questioned his tutors' pronunciation of Latin and German, and it is typical of him that when he did at last go to Dahomey, he wrote of it as Dahome, its people, the Fon, as the Ffon, and its capital Abomey as Agbome.

From Oxford he joined the Bombay Native Infantry, as a result of which he spent nearly seven years in India, very few of which were actually occupied in soldiering. He worked on a geographical survey of Sind (which he spelled Scinde), and took part in the regimental sports of boxing, cock-fighting and pig-sticking. Gradually he became so proficient in a few chosen tongues that he found it amusing to disguise himself as a Moslem and wander in places where no ordinary white man would have dreamed of going. He became fascinated by the sexual practices of the Orient, and produced a report on homosexuality in Karachi which he presented to the Commander-in-Chief of the Army, Sir Charles Napier. Later this was forwarded to Bombay where its pornographic details so horrified officials that

Burton became dubbed 'the white nigger', a calumny in his eyes, since he despised Negroes. He was socially ostracized and nearly dismissed the service. All prospect of promotion vanished.

He was bitterly disappointed. Weak from cholera, and suffering from ophthalmia, he sailed for England on extended sick leave, where he launched himself on his literary career with several books on India and Goa. In one he suggested that suitable punishments 'for controlling the natives of Central Asia' might be flaying the men alive, chopping them in two vertically, stoning them to death, impaling them and cutting off their limbs. He also favoured flogging instead of imprisonment, and in this at least he shared an African philosophy; from Gelele in the north-west to Shaka in the south-east, African kings professed astonishment at the cruelty of the prison system practised by the whites.

The next ten years contain everything that made Burton famous in his lifetime. In 1853 he journeyed to Mecca and Medina in disguise; the following year he visited the closed city of Harar where, as in the earlier journey, one false step would have brought instant death. There was a spell in the Crimea from 1855–56 and then came his great Central African journeys: the discovery of Lake Tanganyika, the endless marches, the recurrence of ophthalmia, fever, the conflict with Speke. Once again, by the time he left Africa early in 1859, his health was in ruins.

By 1861, Burton had also visited America and after a stormy courtship of ten years, at last got married. Once more he was short of money, so he began looking round for employment. He decided on the Foreign Office and in particular, fancied the position of consul at Damascus. But his reckless arrogance was beginning to pay reverse dividends. There were too many people in high places who had suffered from him over the years to acquiesce now in his desires. Instead, he was offered the consulship on the tiny island of Fernando Po in the Gulf of Guinea at a salary of £700 a year. It had the reputation of being the graveyard of the consular service. Burton wrote to the Foreign Office accepting the post and the army happily eliminated him from its ranks.

So, at the age of forty, without financial reserves or the

prospect of a pension, he began a new career in Africa, at the bottom of the diplomatic ladder.

* * *

The island of Fernando Po lies off the West African coast less than five hundred miles from Dahomey and Burton was in no hurry to reach it, which was just as well, since the captain of his steamer was on salary-and-commission and the commission was based on the amount of coal he saved each voyage. The result was that the vessel pottered slowly south, first to Madeira and the Canaries, which Burton did not care for, then a succession of West African ports which he cared for even less. The basic reason was that they were inhabited by black Africans and he was not a lover of the Negroid races. His previous experience of Africa was mainly that of the east–central regions, of relatively unsophisticated savannah tribes whose contact with Europeans was limited and in some cases non-existent. In the lake regions it was earliest morning in the relationship between white and black and there was still a pristine quality about it; in West Africa it was late afternoon, and a pretty dismal and tarnished afternoon at that. The blacks on the littoral had been selling their inland brothers for hundreds of years. Sierra Leone was partly populated by freed slaves; so was Monrovia. There was very little you could tell either side about each other they didn't already know.

Burton was shocked when at Sierra Leone a porter demanded double pay for carrying his bag because he would be 'breaking the Sabbath'. He writes dryly: 'I gave it readily and was pleased to find that the labours of missionaries had not been in vain.' And he reflected on 'how much better is the heart of Africa than its epidermis'.

Farther down the coast he was incensed to learn that the term 'nigger' had been outlawed and was equally upset when a few blacks rode as first-class passengers between the ports. 'It is a political as well as social mistake to permit these men to dine in the main cabin which they will end by monopolizing. A ruling race cannot be too particular about these small matters.'

Here is Burton the philosopher on the subject of race: 'I

believe the European to be the brains, the Asiatic the heart, the American and African the arms, and the Australian the feet, of the man figure. I also opine that in the various degrees of intellectuality, the Negro ranks between the Australian and Indian—popularly called red—who is above him. From humbly aspiring to be owned as a man, our black friend now boldly advances his claims to *egalité* and *fraternité*, as if there could be brotherhood between crown and clown! The being who "invents nothing, improves nothing, who can only cook, nurse and fiddle", who has neither energy nor industry, save in rare cases that prove the rule!—the self-constituted thrall, that delights in subjection to and imitation of the superior races ... And yet we—in these days—read such nonsense pure and simple as "Africa for the Africans".' It may have been as well for Burton's choler that he did not know the Dahomean kings considered themselves so superior to Europeans that they did not deign to shake their hands.

He reached Fernando Po on September 27, 1861, and felt 'uncommonly suicidal' on the first night he spent there. It is hard not to feel sympathy for him. The island had been discovered by the Portuguese in the fifteenth century but ceded to Spain in 1778. First attempts to develop it failed and, with Spain's consent, the administration was taken over by Britain who used it as a base for her West African Squadron which was engaged in suppression of slavery. The main industry was the palm oil trade, the climate was hot and sticky and the coastal regions malarial; yellow fever ravaged the island from time to time; it was not the most salubrious spot.

Burton began the years of Foreign Office employment as he meant to continue them: absent without leave. He was only in the Fernando Po office a week before he was off to inspect the Oil River ports in the Niger delta. Back for another week and then off again, this time with the commander of the West African Squadron, to Nigeria, the Cameroons and Lagos, whence he visited the town of Abeokuta, the capital of the Egbas, the implacable enemies of Dahomey. During the trip into the West African hinterland he must have made his secret trip to Dahomey. It had to be secret because he had applied to the Foreign Office for permission to visit the kingdom and had been refused.

On his return to Lagos he went off to Victoria in the Cameroons where he organized a small mountaineering party and he was so delighted with the trip that he reported back to England on the healthiness of the country; suggesting its suitability for hospitals in which white administrators could recover from fevers and tropical diseases. Actually the Cameroons, with its high rainfall, would have killed them off in shoals. He visited Gabon looking for gorillas, then went to England on home leave, returning to West Africa in 1863. Fernando Po seemed more congenial to him on his return because he moved away from the coast into the hills. Even so he did not stay long but was soon off to explore the Congo estuary, Luanda and parts of Angola. Each of his West African trips resulted in a two-volume book. Apart from *A Mission to Gelele*, he wrote *Abeokuta and the Cameroons Mountains*, *Wanderings in West Africa* and *Two Trips to Gorilla Land and the Cataracts of the Congo*.

It was when he returned from the Congo that the British Government entrusted him with a mission to Dahomey.

3

THE HISTORY of Dahomey has close links with and indeed runs parallel to the expansion and subsequent falling away of the slave trade. By the time the Fon came down through the Gap of Benin to capture the coast towns, Whydah was already established as one of the busiest and cheapest slaving ports; Dahomey had a ready-made business. All it needed was slaves, but no African community sold its own people into slavery unless they had committed serious crimes. So the raiding system began, with the result that nations rose and fell in proportion to their ability to wage war on their neighbours. The long war of attrition between Abomey and Abeokuta, for example, shows first one side in the ascendancy, then the other.

To withstand these attacks, a people needed weapons, to obtain weapons they needed slaves, to raid for slaves they needed weapons: it was a terrible spiral maze through which no nation of the Slave Coast was able to escape. Huge quantities of firearms were poured into West Africa. One estimate gives the number of guns manufactured in Birmingham alone at the height of the slave trade as between 100,000 and 150,000 a year. The saying was: one gun, one slave; though Basil Davidson points out that this was on the optimistic side, since African traders were seldom willing to sell a captive for a gun alone but demanded other goods as well.

The European traders on the coast, who lived in the shadow of forts built by their respective countries to safeguard national slaving interests, might well have regretted the huge inflow of guns, for it strengthened the bargaining power of the African slavers and their factors, the *mongos* and *cha-chas*. But there was nothing they could do about it. They were caught in a dilemma of their own making; they had to have slaves, and to get them they had to pay with guns.

In all this turmoil, one surprising fact emerges and that is the internal stability of Dahomey once it had achieved its enlarged borders. There can be few black states—or white, for that matter—whose kings reigned as securely or for such lengthy periods as those of Dahomey. Gelele, for instance, whom Burton came to visit, was the ninth king of the Alladahonu dynasty at Abomey which had begun just over two hundred years before. If one accepts the kingdom's dates as being from 1650 to 1889 then there were only ten kings and their average reign was twenty-four years. This contrasts with Dahomey's neighbours. At Porto Novo, for instance, the average reign was less than nine years. One of the ways in which the ruling clan of Dahomey managed to avoid the parricide and fratricide that occurred wherever kingdoms flourished was to exclude male descendants of recent reigning kings from important offices and to use the females of the royal household as administrators. The King was always chosen from the ruling clan and his name was given out to the people before his father's death. Long reigns meant late successions for many of these rulers, which in turn eliminated much of their issue from a chance of succession. Brothers were also, in theory, refused succession rights, which helped to reduce the number of candidates intriguing for the throne. Succession disputes did occur in Dahomean history, but were infrequent by comparison with many other African races. Dahomey grew stronger and stronger, until it became a child of its own military power.

* * *

Bullfinch Lamb gives one the feeling that the Kings of Dahomey were little worse than kindly eccentrics. Forty-eight years later there had been a change, described by Robert Norris in his book, *Memoirs of the Reign of Bossa Ahadee, King of Dahomey*. Norris, a trader, had hardly landed in Whydah when he came upon a tragedy which underlined that change. He visited the market and found the viceroy passing sentence of death on a middle-aged woman, who was on her knees before him. 'I requested her life might be spared', he wrote, 'but I was disappointed: He told me the king himself had considered the offence, and decreed the sentence; which was "that her head should be cut off, and fixed upon a stake" which was lying by her, and which she had been compelled to bring with her from Abomey for that purpose.

'During this conversation a little girl prompted by curiosity, and ignorant of what was doing, made her way through the crowd; and, discovering her mother, ran to her mother to congratulate her on her return (from Abomey). The poor woman, after a short embrace, said, "Go away, child, this is no place for you", and she was immediately conveyed away. The viceroy proceeded in his sentence, which the poor wretch heard with seeming indifference, picking her teeth with a straw which she took up from the ground. When the viceroy concluded his charge to the spectators, of obedience, submission, and orderly behaviour, which the king required from all his people, the delinquent received a blow on the back of her head, with a bludgeon, from one of the executioners which levelled her to the ground; and another severed it from her body with a cutlass. The head was then fixed on a pole in the market place, and the body was immediately carried to the outside of the town and left there to be devoured by wild beasts.' Her crime had been that of accidentally setting fire to a neighbour's hut.

Norris was to see many such sights in Abomey at the time of the Annual Customs but retained a cool enough head to report in detail on whatever he saw. Not long after he arrived there, he was sent for by the King. He unpacked his presents, 'a handsome sedan chair and a chamber organ' and went off to the palace gate. 'On each side of it was a human head, recently cut off, lying on a flat stone with the face down, the bloody end of the neck towards the entrance. In the guard-house were about forty women (these were some of the famous Amazon brigade who guarded the King) armed with a musket and cutlass each; and twenty eunuchs, with bright iron rods in their hands.' Norris was led through two courtyards where more severed heads were on display. He then passed through a third door and found the King seated 'on a handsome chair of crimson velvet, ornamented with gold fringe, placed on a carpet, in a spacious cool piazza, which occupied one side of the court. He was smoking tobacco, and had on a gold-laced hat, with a plume of ostrich feathers; he wore a crimson damask robe, wrapped loosely around him; yellow slippers and no stockings: several women were employed fanning him, and others with whisks to chase away the flies: one woman, on her knees before him, held a gold cup, for him to spit in.'

Norris presented the King with his gifts. The King appeared to be delighted with both, especially the sedan chair, and he spent a happy hour being carried round and round the court. Almost as an afterthought, Norris added: 'In the evening I purchased thirty-two slaves, which finished the business of the day.'

Norris, who was in Abomey in the early months of the year, experienced another of the country's unique aspects, the strange wind that blows from the north-east called the *harmattan*. He wrote: 'It comes on indiscriminately at any hour of the day or night; at any time of the tide, or at any period of the moon's age; and continues a day or two; sometimes five or six; once I knew it to continue a fortnight; and there are generally three or four returns of it every season.

'The wind is always accompanied with an unusual gloominess and haziness of the atmosphere; very few stars can be seen through the fog; and the sun, concealed the greatest part of the day, appears only for a few hours about noon, and then of a mild red, exciting no painful sensation in the eye. No dew is perceived during the continuance of this wind; nor is there the least appearance of any moisture in the atmosphere. Salt of

Tartar, dissolved in water, so as to run upon a tile, and exposed to the *harmattan,* even in the night, becomes perfectly dry again in a few hours. Vegetables of every kind suffer considerably from it: all tender plants, and seeds just sprouting above the earth are killed by it: the most flourishing evergreens feel its baneful influence; the branches of the lemon, orange and lime trees droop; the leaves become flaccid, and wither . . . the grass withers and dries like hay. The covers of books, shut up closely in a trunk, and protected by lying among clothes, bend back as if they had been exposed to fire: the panels of doors, window shutters, etc, split; and the joints of a well-laid floor of seasoned wood, will gape so wide that one may lay his finger in them: the sides and decks of ships, become quite open and leaky and veneered work flies to pieces from the contraction of the wood in different directions.' Norris found that the air temperature dropped by as much as ten or twelve degrees when the wind sprang up and that if it blew for several days at a time he suffered, like the Dahomeans, from chapped lips and nostrils; if it blew for more than five days, large areas of skin sloughed away. But, like many other winds, this was alleged to have medical benefits: it was supposed to cure sores and cuts, help the fever-stricken, stop epidemics like small-pox, and ameliorate the flux. In April the rains began and the *harmattan* ceased to blow. It was during the *harmattan* season that most travellers journeyed to Abomey. It was also during that season that the King of Dahomey often honoured his ancestors with the Annual Customs which were to become so widely known. Norris was a witness to them, so was Burton.

4

BY THE beginning of 1864 West African slavery was in the last stages of decay, except in Dahomey. The trade's decline had been brought about by many factors, not the least of which was a more humanitarian spirit in the world. But there were more particular reasons, like the presence of the West African Squadron and the fact that American ships would no longer participate in slave transport.

Slavery itself had been changing in the past thirty years and

Bound and gagged, victims of the 'King's Head Thing' are brought into the royal presence before being executed.

The King of Dahomey being drawn to a state ceremony in a carriage he received as a gift from Europe.

A Dahomean victim after execution is hung upside down outside the palace.

Dahomean Amazons. They were often used as shock troops in the wars with neighbouring states.

Richard Burton as he was when he made his famous visit to Dahomey.

The Royal Navy gunboat Teaser *captures a slaver off the African coast in 1857. More than 230 slaves were found in its stifling hold which measured 50 ft. × 20 ft. × 3 ft. 6 in.*

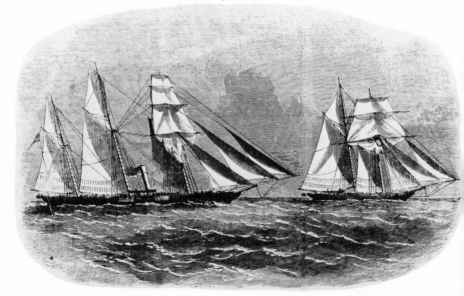

the days had long since gone when vessels could arrive on the African coast, fill up with slaves, and ply their peaceful passage back to America or Brazil. Britain abolished slavery in 1808 and from 1817 various countries, including Spain, Portugal, the Netherlands, Sweden and France granted her the right to stop and search their ships for slaves. But because America was not a signatory to the agreement—instead she sent a small squadron of her own to police American shipping—Britain's task became highly complicated. The case of the *Illinois* illustrates this: In 1843 the *Illinois* was discovered at the Dahomean slave port of Whydah by a British cruiser. The Royal Navy boarded her and discovered that she had American papers, which meant she could not be seized. She took aboard 430 slaves and set sail. She encountered the same British cruiser, which was lying off shore. But the captain of the *Illinois* thought the British cruiser had sailed off down the coast and that the vessel sighted was an American frigate. Immediately, he hoisted the Spanish flag. Spain had been a signatory to the British agreement so the British cruiser set off in pursuit. The *Illinois* saw her mistake, hauled down the Spanish flag and raised the American. Once again the British cruiser was helpless.

This sort of thing went on for some years and it became common for the captain of a slaver to 'sell' his vessel to a member of the crew whose nationality precluded the vessel from being searched since his government had signed no agreement. Finally it reached a point where something had to give. It did so in 1845 with the case of HMS *Wasp*. The *Wasp* had captured two Brazilian slavers, the *Felicidade* and the *Echo* off the coast of Africa and had put prize crews aboard. The *Echo* was carrying four hundred slaves and, while the *Felicidade* was empty, she was fully equipped for the trade. The prize crew on the *Felicidade* consisted of Midshipman Palmer and nine seamen. They were attacked by the Brazilians and knifed to death. The ship then hoisted her colours and sailed to the Slave Coast. There she was stopped and boarded by HMS *Star*. The boarding party found bloodstains and a Negro servant told them what had happened. Ten of the Brazilians were implicated in the murder and taken to Britain for trial.

The court ruled that since the *Felicidade* had no slaves on board and since Brazil had not signed a clause covering equipment, the original capture of the vessel had been illegal. The defendants were acquitted and sent back to Brazil.

As a result of the *Wasp* case, the attitude of British seamen on the Slave Coast hardened. Officers led boarding crews with the watchword, 'Remember the *Felicidade*!' There was no mercy for those who resisted. The crews of slavers were now often marooned on the coast to die of fever or by African spears, instead of being taken to Sierra Leone for trial.

At the end of the 1840s, Brazil, in spite of signing treaties outlawing the trade, was still the richest transatlantic market for slaves, taking fifty and sixty thousand a year. Britain lost patience and in 1849 despatched a squadron under Admiral Reynolds with orders to break up the Brazilian trade. Reynolds sailed into the harbour of Rio de Janeiro and burnt three slavers at their moorings. He then sailed along the coast seeking out slavers in every river and creek and destroying what he found. Brazilians were outraged. But their Foreign Minister, Paulino, could only reply, 'When a powerful nation like Britain is evidently in earnest, what can Brazil do?'

This sort of harassment eventually began to pay dividends in terms of West Africa. Those slavers who wanted to continue the trade began to search for ports in the Indian Ocean. The African states on the west coast—except for Dahomey—began to capitulate to pressure and, in some cases, more than pressure, for the abolition of slaving was used as an excuse by the great powers to colonize large sections of Africa. This meant that the West African Squadron could now give all its attention to Whydah.

5

IN THE 1860s Lagos was annexed by Britain and the presence of English missionaries in Abeokuta, where they were in constant danger from Dahomean attacks, added a political incentive for the British Government to bring pressure to bear on Dahomey. Invasion was discussed and, naturally, supported by Burton, but the Admiralty held back, unwilling to add to its responsibilities on the west coast. The only alternative was a diplomatic mission. In 1862 Commander Eardley-Wilmot, Officer Commanding the Squadron, went to Abomey to feel out King Gelele on an anti-slavery treaty. He seems to have been rather taken in by the King, for he left—*he* also promised to return but never did—naïvely confident that conditions were favourable for negotiation. When his naval duties kept him elsewhere, Burton was chosen for the return visit.

He received his orders in a letter from Lord Russell, the Foreign Secretary. After telling him to make certain that a proper reception was accorded him in Abomey, Russell went on: 'You will, on your arrival, inform the King, that the many important duties which devolve on Commodore Wilmot . . . have prevented him returning in person to confirm the good understanding which it is hoped has been established between the King and Her Majesty's Government by the Commodore's late visit . . .

'With regard to the question of the export of slaves from his territories, you will not fail to impress upon the King the importance which Her Majesty's Government attach to the cessation of this traffic.

'Her Majesty's Government admit the difficulties which the King may find in putting a stop to a trade that has so long existed in his country and from which his ancestors have derived so much profit, but his income from this source must be very small compared with that of former kings, and it will be to his interest to find out some other form of revenue, before that which he now derives from the sale of his fellow men to the slave-dealers is entirely put a stop to. You will remind the King that he himself suggested to Commodore Wilmot that if we wished to put a stop to the Slave trade, we should prevent white men from coming to buy them, and you will state that Her Majesty's Government have concluded a treaty with the United States Government which will prevent, for the future, any American vessels from coming to ship slaves.

'With regard to human sacrifice, I rejoice to find from Commodore Wilmot's report, that the number of victims at the King's Customs has been exaggerated.

'It is feared, however, that much difficulty will be

experienced in prevailing upon the King to put a stop to this barbarous practice, which prevails more or less openly along the greater part of the Western African coast.'

According to Russell, King Gelele had told Wilmot he would welcome English traders at Whydah and would help to rebuild the English fort there which had fallen into decay. Burton was to point out to Gelele that there should be a 'sufficiency of lawful trade to induce them to do so'. Russell continued: 'English merchants cannot take slaves in return for their goods, they must have oil, ivory, cotton, and such other articles as the country is capable of producing. The King will see, therefore, that it must depend very much on his own exertions, and those of his subjects, whether it will be worthwhile for British merchants to settle at Whydah.'

He pointed out that the presents for the King were those Gelele himself had asked Wilmot to get for him 'with the exception of the carriage and horses, and with respect to these you will explain to the King, that in the first place it would be a difficult matter to get English horses out to the Coast, and even supposing they arrive safely at their destination, it would be very doubtful from the nature of the country and climate, whether they would long survive their arrival.

'If, however, the future relations with the King should be of a nature to warrant such a proceeding, Her Majesty's Government would not hesitate to comply with his wishes, by sending him an English carriage and horses.'

The presents which Burton was to take with him comprised: 'One forty feet circular crimson silk Damask Tent with pole complete (contained in two boxes). One richly-embossed silver Pipe with amber mouthpiece in morocco case. Two richly embossed silver Belts with Lion and Crane in raised relief, in morocco cases. Two silver and partly gilt Waiters. One coat of Mail and Gauntlets.' One wonders what either the King, or the Foreign Secretary, had in mind for the Mail and Gauntlets. At most times of the year they would have induced heat-stroke. Perhaps sometime someone might consider a monograph on the diversity and number of useless presents sent to Africa by European governments in the eighteenth and nineteenth centuries. High on the list must come the mail and gauntlets as well as Norris's chamber organ which would have been wrenched out of tune the moment the *harmattan* began to blow. The Foreign Office must have had a long-lasting musical tradition for in the mid-nineteenth century we find a British consul carrying a box organ all the way from London to Abyssinia for the Emperor—who was incensed at the absurdity of the gift and gave it to a missionary.

Much of Burton's previous wandering had been done either incognito or as a private citizen. Now he was to travel in style. On November 29, 1863, he boarded the *Antelope* and sailed to the echoes of a seventeen-gun salute, landing at Whydah a few days later, where he spent five days. He found the town 'not exceedingly unhealthy, despite its extreme filth', but complained that there was no society left. 'The old days of sporting, picnics and processions, of dancing, loving, drinking and playing, are gone, probably never to return,' he wrote. 'The place is temporarily ruined and as dull as dull can be, except when the occasional breaking of the blockade gives a kind of galvanic life.' Two months before, a steamer had reached the open sea with nine hundred slaves aboard. Those in Whydah with an interest in slaving had celebrated the occasion with a banquet and, according to Burton, 'even the non-slaving traders and others were there drinking pro-slavery toasts . . . All here is now in transition state. Slave exporting is like gambling, a form of intense excitement which becomes a passion; it is said that after once shipping a man, one must try to ship another. And the natives of Whydah give the licit dealer scanty encouragement. Having lived so long without severer toil than kidnapping, they are too old to learn labour, they allow their houses to fall, their plantations to become bush, their streets to be half grown with rank grass, and their swamps to reek undrained.'

He visited the English fort—in fact, Burton was the kind of traveller who saw *everything* and one must picture him out early in the morning until late at night with note-book and sketch pad; he was a man with an enormous appetite for work.[1] He found the building almost falling down and in the compound

---

[1] In 1878 when Burton was in Trieste a journalist found him at work on eleven different projects; each had its own room.

a fetish figure 'throned amid a mass of filth—yet the people wonder that they suffer from smallpox and measles'. He described another fetish figure which he saw in the town as 'squat, crouched, as it were, before its own attributes, with arms longer than a gorilla's, huge feet and no legs to speak of. The head is of mud or wood, rising conically to an almost pointed poll; a dab of clay represents the nose, the mouth is a gash from ear to ear, and the eyes and teeth are of cowries, or painted ghastly white. Legba is of either sex, but rarely feminine. Of the latter I have seen a few . . . the breasts project like the halves of a German sausage and the rest is to match.'

The picture that emerges of Whydah is that of a decrepit tropical town decaying in the heat and humidity, its alleys and roads choked with grass or mud, its houses built away from each other, some collapsing, some only made of mats, and over everything the brooding presence of carrion crows, vultures and marabou storks.

Fourteen years before Burton's visit Commander Frederick Forbes visited Dahomey on an anti-slaving mission and in his book *Dahomey and the Dahomans* he wrote of Whydah: 'The principal building is the cha-cha's (King's agent's) house, a large ill-built erection of no particular form, occupying one side of the principal square; and, as nothing can be cleanly in Africa, opposite, occupying a side of the square, is a corral for cattle, seldom cleaned except by the animalcula of the exuviae that decay breeds.'

Having applied for and received permission to travel to Abomey, Burton set off on December 13 at the beginning of the *harmattan* season. His party consisted of John Cruikshank, a naval surgeon, the Reverend Peter Bernasko, described as a 'native assistant missionary', his son Tom, who was eleven, and several interpreters, even though Burton had already begun a study of the language. Some idea of the size of the operation might be gained from the fact that this group was attended by fifty-nine porters, thirty hammock-men to carry them, and sundry cooks and flag carriers, making a caravan of ninety-nine people. When Commander Forbes took the same road in 1849 his smaller party still needed twenty-six hammock-men, and thirty-six porters, twenty of whom were women. And there were an additional five women whose only function was to carry Forbes's money: he had changed fifty dollars into cowries and was faced with the staggering prospect of having to take 100,000 shells wherever he went.

As Burton's safari wound on its way, royal messengers began to arrive from Abomey. Each carried a carved stick which served as his credentials. They inquired solicitously after Burton's health and stayed to drink a glass of rum, of which he had a large supply.

The principal members of his party adopted the local form of transport, the hammock. Burton found it a 'not unpleasant conveyance, especially when the warmed back is a time cooled by walking. These barbarians, however, have not, like the Hindoos, invented a regular four-in-hand; two men are easily tired, especially by standing still, which is wearisome to them as to loaded camels. When they reach a rough place another pair, diving in between the usual number, roughly clutch the cloth at the rider's shoulders and heels, bumping, if possible, his pate against the pole.'

On the journey he met four of the famous 'Amazons', the Household Brigade of Abomey, whose duties were to guard the King, often to sleep with him, and in war to be used as an assault force. On Burton's secret visit to Dahomey he had been made a sort of Honorary Colonel-in-Chief of one of the Amazon troops; notwithstanding that, he did not care for them. 'The four soldieresses were armed with muskets, and habited in tunics and white colottes,' he wrote, 'with two blue patches meant for crocodiles (insignia). They were commanded by an old woman in a man's straw hat, a green waistcoat, a white shirt . . . a blue waistcloth, and a sash of white calico. Two of the women . . . were of abnormal size, nearly six feet tall, and of proportional breadth.' Contrasting the Amazons with the men, whom he found rather effeminate, he said, 'Such, on the other hand, was the size of the female skeleton, and the muscular development of the frame, that in many cases femininity could be detected only by the bosom.'

The idea of a tribe of ferocious fighting women has fascinated the world for thousands of years, and the word 'amazon' (lit. 'breastless') dates from ancient Greece. It was first used to describe a legendary race of female warriors said to have come from beyond the Caucasus and to have settled in Asia Minor.

They were governed by a queen, and according to some authorities the female children had their right breasts cut off in order to facilitate their use of the bow. Once a year the tribe cohabited with men of a different race and the resulting female children were trained in war; the male children were destroyed. Amazons frequently recur in Greek literature from Homer onwards and were believed to have invaded Attica in 1256 B.C.

The Dahomean Amazons certainly did not have their breasts cut off but in some other respects seem to conform to their legendary precursors. They were formed by King Agaja in about 1727 from a group of female elephant hunters. In his *History of Dahomy* published in 1793, Archibald Dalzel describes how Agaja 'armed a great number of women like soldiers, having their proper officers, and furnished like regular troops with drums, colours, and umbrellas, making at a distance a very formidable appearance.' With these shock troops he attacked and defeated a combined army made up of soldiers from Whydah and Popo.

To the Dahomean people the Amazons were known as 'mothers' and held the centre position, the most honoured, in battle. Forbes described the result of rivalry between the Amazons and the male soldiers: 'The amazons are not supposed to marry, and by their own statement, they have changed their sex. "We are men," say they, "not women." All dress alike, diet alike and male and female emulate each other: what the males do the amazons will endeavour to surpass. They all take great care of their arms (these were usually long-barrelled Danish muskets) polish the barrels, and, except when on duty, keep them in covers.' Forbes visited Abomey during the reign of King Gezo, Gelele's father, who, according to Burton 'ordered every Dahoman of note in the Kingdom to present his daughters, of whom the most promising were chosen, and he kept the corps clear of the servile and the captive. Gelele, his son, causes every girl to be brought to him before marriage, and, if she pleases, he retains her in the palace ... these girls, being royal wives, cannot be touched without danger of death ...'

Although the Amazons were supposed to remain celibate, Burton was soon to come across a large number who were pregnant and suggests that only about two-thirds of the women were virgins. Forbes ascribed their ferocity to their way of life. 'The extreme exercise of one passion,' he wrote, 'will generally obliterate the very sense of the others; the Amazons, whilst indulging in the excitement of the most fearful cruelties, forget the other desires of our fallen nature.' Burton demurred. All passions are sisters, he said and went on: 'I believe that bloodshed causes these women to remember, not to forget LOVE ...' He saw troops of Amazons marching and said they were 'remarkable for a stupendous stratopyga, and for a development of adipose tissue which suggested anything but ancient virginity—man does not readily believe in fat "old maids".'

He described the Amazons as 'an evil' in the Dahomean empire. Wherever he went he remarked on the sparseness of the population and blamed much of this on the Amazons as an institution. 'The women troops, assumed to number 2,500, should represent 7,500 children; the waste of reproduction, and the necessary casualties of "service", in a region so depopulated, are as detrimental to the body politic as a proportional loss of blood would be to the frame personal. Thus the land is a desert, and the raw material of all industry, man, is everywhere wanting.'

On the march to Abomey he was also to encounter a facet of Dahomean life which irritated almost every traveller: whenever either the King's wives or the Amazon's slavewomen walked abroad no man was allowed to look at them. Their presence was heralded by a bell. J. A. Skertchly, the English zoologist who visited Abomey eight years after Burton and who was kept there by Gelele, a virtual prisoner, for nearly nine months, was rudely dumped by his hammock-men who fled into the tall grass at the side of the track when the bell was heard. Skertchly watched as five women filed past with water jars on their heads. The leading woman had a bell round her neck. He said: 'No man is permitted to meet them, while, if the tinkle of the bell is unheeded, they will stop and rattle it in high dudgeon until the baneful male scampers into the bush.

'This institution is one of the greatest nuisances in the country, for in the capital there are so many of these bands journeying from one of the royal palaces to another, that a straightforward progress of twenty yards is scarcely practicable.' Clearly Burton found this onerous too and often did not give way, especially when out shooting in the early morning. He recounted how the women said, 'He is a white and knows no better.' At other times he would take out pencil and paper and pretend to sketch them. This caused them to flee.

6

K ING GELELE met Burton in the town of Kana which lay just outside Abomey and was the site of the King's country palace. Here Burton experienced something that was to weary him throughout his stay: the need to dress up in his best uniform and wait in the sun, sometimes for hours, for the appearance of the King; the 'penance of reception', he called it. Skertchly's experience of the formality was so formidable that he broke into italics at the memory; Burton took a loftier tone. He was sent for at 10 a.m., but said he knew from experience that such ceremonies never took place until the afternoon so did not make an appearance until 1 p.m. when he and his party were shown a programme of dancing and singing. They had no sooner taken their seats than an old card table arrived—a present from Commander Wilmot to Gelele—on which were set bottles of rum, gin and wine. Burton had earlier decided to try and avoid the rough spirits in favour of Muscadel, but found this difficult in the face of repeated messages sent by the King urging him to drink up. At 2 p.m., to the sound of an occasional cannon shot, they were led to the palace and were allowed to enter once they had removed their ceremonial swords and closed their umbrellas, neither object being allowed to appear before the King. They were then guided through a courtyard and found King Gelele sitting in the shade on an 'earthbench' covered in red, blue and striped cotton cloths. Burton described him as being between forty and forty-five, tall and with an athletic body, broad-shouldered, muscular, with well-turned wrists, neat ankles, 'but a distinctly cucumber-shaped shin'. The face was jowly but strong and though his expression was hard, Burton found it open and not at all bad tempered. He wore his finger nails very long and Burton suggested that

African kings must show the talons of meat eaters to make it plain they do not live on 'monkey-food'—fruits and vegetables. His teeth were strong and white but some of the surfaces were covered with tobacco tar. His eyes were red and inflamed and Burton put this down to a variety of things: the glare, the wind, too much fornication; but mostly he blamed smoking; the King apparently smoked continuously.

The pipe was an institution in Dahomey. Norris remarked on it during his visit. Clay pipes from Europe were much in vogue and there was also a minor pipe-making industry in Abomey. The King's pipe was highly decorated and chased with silver and was put away in a special case when not needed. Burton says his tobacco pouch was 'nearly the size of a modern carpet bag. The Dahomeans, even the King, use Brazilian roll and American leaf; a few prefer the worst kind of cigars.'

Gelele's face was pitted by small-pox scars and his skin was not so much black as reddish-brown; there were rumours that his mother was a mulatto from the Whydah. His dress on this occasion was simple, a plain white cotton body-cloth edged with watered green silk, drawers of purple flowered silk reaching to mid-thigh and Moorish sandals embroidered in gold. For jewellery he wore bracelets, an armband, a single blue bead and a fetish charm in the shape of a human incisor that hung round his neck and was supposed to ward off illness.

At this first meeting Burton began to get some idea of the veneration in which the Dahomeans held their kings. Gelele was looked upon as a god, his word was final, his power absolute. This had its snags since the power and divinity overshadowed the man, which meant that it was almost impossible for Gelele to institute changes—in the Annual Customs, for instance—without weakening his own position.

He was surrounded by wives and Amazons. Through open doorways Burton could see slave girls peering out at him. None appealed to him physically, but they atoned for their home-liness by their extreme devotion to the King. 'If perspiration appears upon the royal brow it is instantly removed with the softest cloth by the gentlest hands; if the royal dress be disarranged it is at once adjusted; if the royal lips move, a plated spittoon, which, when Mr Norris wrote, was gold, held by one of the wives, is moved within convenient distance; if the King sneezes, all present touch the ground with their foreheads; if he drinks, every lip utters an exclamation of blessing.'

After grasping Burton's hand and 'snapping fingers' the King inquired after the health of Queen Victoria, the state of the Foreign Office and of the British people and when Burton had reassured him on all three points they sat down in an atmosphere of great goodwill. Gelele could not get over the fact that Burton had returned as promised and remarked on this more than once. As they raised their glasses to toast Queen Victoria the visitors received a shock. The King suddenly wheeled round and two of his wives raised a screen of white calico between him and the others so that no one might see him drink. Each time there was a toast—and there were several, including one to Burton—the same ritual was observed, and each time there was a prodigious outburst of noise: guns were fired, Amazons rang their bells and high officials bent to the ground clapping their palms. When the toasts were done, salutes were fired, the first for royalty, then eleven guns for Commander Wilmot and nine for Burton. This did not suit him at all and he demanded the same number as his predecessor. Despite the fact that his interpreter 'turned blue' with apprehension Burton insisted he tell the King, who quickly apologized and ordered two more guns fired. Honour satisfied, the visitors left the presence.

It was during this time that Burton saw several decorated skulls said to have been those of the most important chiefs Gelele had killed. He was surprised at how well kept they were. This was part of Dahomean tradition. Norris was told by King Adahoonzou II that if he, the King, fell into the hands of his enemies he wished to be treated 'with that decency of which I set the example'. Burton noted that one of the skulls was that of Akia'on, chief of Attako near Porto Novo, who was taken by Gelele three years before. 'Beautifully white and polished, it is mounted in a ship or galley of thin brass about a foot long, with two masts, and jib-boom, rattlings, anchor, and four portholes on each side . . . when King Gezo died his successor (Gelele) received a message from this chief, that all men were now joyful, that the sea had dried up, and that the world had seen the bottom of Dahome. Gelele rejoined by slaying him, and mounting his skull in a ship, meaning that there is still water enough to float the kingdom, and that if the father is dead the son is still alive.'

Burton also saw the ritual observed by even the most important people of the land when they came to greet the King: they rubbed themselves on the ground and threw handfuls of dust on their arms and shoulders. This offended him as it had done Forbes, who described the ritual compliments Dahomeans paid the King as 'filthy praise'.

On December 20, Burton entered Abomey. The King and his suite followed the next day. Gelele was detained at Kana because 150 of his Amazons were found to be pregnant: 'So difficult is chastity in the Tropics,' wrote Burton. Several of the women were sentenced to death with their lovers, the men being saved up to die at the Customs, the Amazons to be executed in the privacy of the palace which Burton found 'more civilized than Great Britain, where they still, wondrous to relate, "hang away" even women, and in public.'

* * *

Abomey, rainbow's end for a traveller from the coast, was no great hidden city of grandeur and wealth, but a big rambling place of mud houses built behind mud walls, parts of which were crumbling. Dalzel described the central area as 'an assemblage of farmyards with long thatched barns', from which Burton did not dissent. Forbes wrote, 'The city is about eight miles in circumference, surrounded by a ditch about five feet deep, filled with prickly acacia, its only defence. It is entered by six gates, which are simply clay walls crossing the road, with two apertures, one reserved for the King, the other a thoroughfare for his subjects. In each aperture are two human skulls . . .' Inside the city walls was a great deal of wasteland as well as many cultivated small-holdings. It was an easy place to get lost in. There were no regular streets and all the houses were surrounded by high red clay walls which also enclosed banana and orange trees. Water was a problem. The nearest supply was five miles away and every drop had to be brought in by hand.

Skulls and the larger human bones still ocupied places on the walls when Burton entered the city. He also noted skulls hanging from several doors as he passed. He was taken to a hut which was to be his lodging and described it as a barn forty-five feet long and twenty-seven feet wide, roofed with heavy thatch that came down to within five feet of the ground. The rooms were dark and close and he had a hole knocked through the wall of one to let in more air. He made a shutter for the opening from a claret case and turned the place into a 'tolerable study'.

The next day he visited the main palace. He travelled by hammock and on the way there saw a man standing, gagged, in front of a drummer. Burton was told that he was a criminal awaiting execution at the forthcoming Customs. The gag was a ferocious instrument, a Y–shaped stick, the sharp end of which was wedged against the palate while the fork held down the tongue. The gag was used in case the man managed to speak to the King when, according to Dahomean custom, he would have to be pardoned.

At the palace Burton's party was kept waiting for three hours for the ceremony which would mark the arrival of Gelele. But the old card table was set up before them and Burton passed the time sampling the liquors—he tried to stick to the Muscadel but boredom and frustration gave him a harder head and he drank the trade gin and the rum as well as some liquor he had brought along himself. He was gradually joined by other *caboceers* (dignitaries or headmen) such as Buko-no, a fetish man who owned the house in which he was staying, and Prince Chyudaton, a Dahomean aristocrat, who arrived 'riding a little nag, as if on side saddle, and shaded by an umbrella hat of worn palm leaves'. The prince was sucking a lettuce leaf. For further entertainment an Abeokutan prisoner-of-war danced for them and Burton made the point that not all such captives were killed or sold. In mid-afternoon the King arrived at last. A long line of flags and umbrellas— multi-coloured parasols and umbrellas were *de rigueur* in Abomey—were seen coming in the gates of the palace. With thudding drums and the firing of muskets the procession paraded around the courtyard. There were thirty-three different groups of *caboceers*, royal relatives, fetish men and other important folk. Last of all came King Gelele with five hundred musketeers, a skull standard, bobbing umbrellas, swaying flags, drums, rattles and horns. The king himself rode in a carriage pulled by men and was shaded by four white umbrellas. Behind him came a crowd of slaves carrying chairs, boxes, baskets and cowrie shells, bottles and other valuables. In the midst of the din and dust, Gelele was carried ten times round the courtyard in a bath-chair—a present from England —while he covered his mouth to keep out the dust. Burton noted that he looked weary and cross, 'an expression not unfrequent upon the brow of royalty in all lands'. The male soldiers retired and the Amazons gave a display of dancing and singing to the *obbligato* of musket fire. They were accompanied not only by the usual coloured umbrellas and flags but also by platters of skulls, women carrying weapons like long cut-throat razors, rattles, cymbals and drums. Twelve of the women then proceeded to carry the King round the yard in a hammock of yellow silk.

The colourful ceremony was punctuated every now and then by presents of more liquor from Gelele. Perhaps it was the drink, perhaps the riotous display, perhaps both: in the event, Burton retired 'with the usual finale to a Dahomean parade—a headache'.

The following day he presented the official gifts to the King, and made the mistake of giving him not only those sent by the Foreign Office but also the gifts he had brought himself. He assumed that his munificence might result in his being able to deliver his message from the British Government at the very start of the visit so that he would be able to leave Abomey at any time he wished thereafter. Had he kept back some of the gifts he might have been able to bargain for an audience. But subtlety in dealing with people in powerful positions had never been one of Burton's points. He regarded the gift ceremony as a trial, so the sooner it was over the better. And this turned out to be so. The main present, the 'forty feet circular crimson silk Damask Tent with pole complete ...' was found to be too small. Burton and his party were obliged to pitch it themselves and found it complicated. The tent pegs were made of wood and, of course, would not have lasted long in a land where white ants are endemic. It was apparently quite pretty when they finally got it up (more so than anything belonging to the King, Burton thought), yet the only part of it admired was the gingerbread lion on the pole-top. Of the other presents: the pipe was never used because Gelele liked his old one better; the belts caused disappointment because apparently Commander Wilmot had been asked, not for belts, but for bracelets; the silver waiters were much admired but no one knew what they were for; the gauntlets were too small and the coat of mail was too heavy. Burton imagined it would be hung up and used for target practice, but he was wrong. It was still there when Skertchly visited Abomey. Gelele showed it to him and then made one of his wives put it on, commenting that the English must be very strong to fight encumbered by such a weight. It was clear that apart from the waiters the presents had been a disappointment. The King constantly pressed for the horses and carriage. 'I vainly, for the dozenth time, explained the difficulty of sending them. It was disposed of at once with consummate coolness. Carriages had been brought, and could come again. If the horses died upon the beach at Whydah, no matter. King Gezo, after obtaining an equipage, had taken the strong name Nun-u-pwe-to, and the son burned to emulate the sire.' Clearly annoyed at the reception of the presents Burton, in the voluminous daily diary of his mission, had some scathing suggestions for gifts that *would* be appreciated: '. . . children's toys, gutta-percha faces, Noah's Arks; in fact, what would be most acceptable to a child of eight—which the Negro is.'

The King remained silent throughout the presentation. But 'his disappointment soon pierced through his politeness, which was barely retained by a state of feeling best expressed by our popular adage, "Better luck next time," especially in the matter of an English carriage and horses'. Burton then asked whether he could deliver his message but was told that he would have to await another opportunity. He was dismissed with a decanter of rum and a bottle of Médoc, which had gone sour.

7

T O   T H O S E   emissaries like Forbes and Burton who came with the express purpose of delivering a message from Her Majesty's Government, the time spent at Abomey awaiting the King's pleasure must have seemed frustrating. But if Gezo and Gelele had seen them on their arrival and sent them off the following day we would have been denied many facts about the life of the Dahomeans in Abomey.

Skertchly has inveighed against Gelele for keeping him at Abomey for so long, but his book is a record of that period. It not only demonstrates his prejudices but also confirms many things that Burton had written. Skertchly was on less certain ground when he wrote in *Dahomey As It Is* of things of which he had no experience like 'buffalo-eating pythons', which he described as 'occasionally to be met with on the plains'. He passed some of his time by pretending to doctor the locals. A man was brought to him whose arm had been shattered by a bursting musket. Skertchly refused to help him. He saw that the man was seriously injured and tried to excuse his callousness by saying that if the man had died he would have been accused of killing him. Dwarfs, hunchbacks, palsied old people, men with withered arms, the blind, the deaf, the dumb and the lame, all came to Skertchly for help. He related with amusement how he gave them a mixture of curry powder, carbolic acid and camphor.

Burton was a different person entirely. Although he affected irritation, boredom and a generally patronizing attitude, he was a scholar and spent his life in search of facts, even if he sometimes got them wrong. For instance, he only spent two months in Dahomey yet he pried the secrets of Afa divination from Buko-no; learned the complex organization of the Dahomean government; studied the funeral, marriage and religious customs of the people and learned all he could about human sacrifice and the Amazons. Most important of all, by the time he left he could carry on a conversation in the Fon language. He followed his usual practice of study, helped by his extraordinary memory (at one time he could recite a quarter of the Koran by heart). In languages with written grammars he would first buy a simple textbook and vocabulary and underline the words and rules he felt should be memorized. He carried these books with him everywhere and studied them whenever he had a spare moment during his working day. By this method he learned on average three hundred new words a week. When he had acquired a basic vocabulary, he chose a simple story book and read it, marking with a pencil any new words he wanted to remember. Then he went on to a more difficult book. When he came across a new sound not found in any other language he trained his tongue by repeating it hundreds of times a day. In the case of Fon, he probably made his own vocabulary and grammar through notes of his conversations, recording new words and phrases. His facility gave him a supreme advantage in communication over other travellers in Dahomey.

Until his book was published the world looked upon the country as a kind of charnel house. There were stories that the King walked to his throne along a pathway ankle-deep in human gore, that he paddled about in a canoe in a tank of human blood, that he sacrificed two thousand people in a single day. It is interesting to contrast these stories with the conclusion of the French historian E. F. Gautier who, in 1935, called the old Dahomean monarchy the most advanced form of political organization in the black world.

There is no doubt that a great deal of cruelty existed but there was much else besides. One of the main virtues of the people was their diligence. While numerous famines are recorded in the Niger region to the north there is scarcely any record of famine in Dahomey. According to the economic historian Karl Polanyi, it is this diligence that made a success of the Dahomean agricultural policy, a fact made more remarkable when one remembers the drain on manpower caused by constant warfare. A 'Minister of Agriculture', the Tokpo, had responsibility for administering the policy of the country. He and his officials decided where certain crops were to be grown, for instance, millet near Abomey, maize and manioc between Whydah and Allada. Conservation was practised from early times. The output of palm wine was safeguarded by the King's ruling that no palm wine could be made except from trees growing wild in the bush. A census was taken each year at the end of the rainy season. This was much more exhaustive than anything done today. A total count was taken of the population and of the numbers of cultivators, weavers, potters, hunters, blacksmiths, slaves, etc. Then the food stocks throughout the kingdom were measured; a check was made on the number of palm trees, cattle, sheep, poultry and manufactured goods. Taxes were assessed on the basis of these totals. The total population figure was a state secret, known only to the King, and any village or provincial chief who disclosed the figures for his group would have been killed.

There was taxation. Pig farmers, for instance, paid one pig a year. Cattle, sheep and goat farmers were taxed once every three years, when up to an eighth of their herds was taken. Only wealthy people owned horses. Each horse was rated at four thousand cowries annually. Every trade or craft was liable for taxation. Internal trade was also taxed. A 'passport' system was used to keep count of porters who carried goods through tollhouses and there was a tollhouse at the entrance to every town. There was also a tax on inheritance. Forbes said that everything was taxed and the tax went to the King. 'If a cock crows near the highway, it is forfeited to the tax gatherer and, consequently, on the whole distance from Abomey to Whydah, the cocks are muzzled.' He also commented on the severity of the law: treason, murder, adultery, cowardice and theft were punishable by death. Although the King was generous in his gifts of hard liquor to the whites who came to his court, drunkenness was frowned upon among the Dahomeans and the King kept his own drunkard. He fed him on rum, exhibiting him at the Customs so that his pitiful condition might serve as a warning. The King also had his own 'smoker', not this time to serve as an awful example but in fact the occupier of a much-favoured office. Burton described him as one of the true African fantasticals. He carried a long-stemmed pipe and was supplied from the King's pouch.

Prostitution existed and was controlled by the King. The prostitutes were known as 'public women' and were sent to live in various parts of the country. At first, payment for their services was twenty cowries, but inflation raised this fourfold. According to Dalzel the women were appointed as a precaution by the Government to prevent the peace of private families being violated, and this was perhaps more necessary in Dahomey than in any other state, as adultery was 'severely punished and every indiscretion of gallantry exposes the delinquents to death or slavery . . .' There was also the fact that many Dahomeans were required to abstain from sex while their wives suckled an infant—usually three years—because it might cause sickness in future children.

The centre of the Dahomean universe was the royal household: here State and King combined. For instance, the King's wives, estimated at two thousand, were expected to play their part in the administration of the State. Others were employed at various crafts. Some of the King's children acted as special messengers and performed other duties in the King's service. And although such people as ministers, tax collectors, auditors and the like lived in their own houses, they were supplied with food from the palace. The actual palace building was large. Each King built a gateway of his own which consisted of a gap in the wall closed by rough wooden doors. A long barnlike structure was erected near the gate and here the King, with his court around him, would dispense justice and perform his royal duties.

The most interesting aspect of Dahomey's governing tradition was its 'doubling' of people in key jobs. The administration was known for its honesty and reliability and Gautier rates its excellence beyond that of any other African state. One of the ways in which this came about was to create a female counterpart to every male official. This duality went right through the nation, even to the King.

The female doubles were called 'mothers' and within the palace the King had a complete counterpart of the administrative apparatus throughout the kingdom. It was the duty of each woman to know intimately all the administrative affairs of her male counterpart and keep a constant check on his operations. So whenever an official reported to the King on any matter, the *naye* (mother), his double, was there to give her version if it differed. Dualism also existed in the army, which was divided into a right and left wing. Each wing was split into a male regiment and a female regiment. Every male, from the highest-ranking officer down to the last soldier, had his female counterpart. The right wing was commanded by the *mingan*, the

Prime Minister, and his counterpart was the 'she-*mingan*' who, according to Burton, took precedence. Burton himself had a 'mother' in Abomey, who was assigned to him by the palace. This was the custom for all visitors to the capital and it was her duty to look after his needs during his stay; she was present at all audiences with the King.

Dualism found its strangest manifestation in the kingship: Gelele was two kings in one, the Town King and the Bush King. The Town King lived in the palace in Abomey; the Bush King, *Addo-Kpon*, had his palace at Kana. Each had its own complete establishment. Skertchly says the reason was that the office of kingship in Dahomey was so great that the King could never soil his hand by commercial dealings; but since the wealth of the country depended upon the sale of slaves and oil—the former being an exclusive royal monopoly, and the greater part of the oil exported from the country also from the King—how could these be sold without reducing the monarch to the position of a petty trader? 'There was the rub. Gezo surmounted this difficulty by the invention of the bush King, who could take all the onus of ignoble trade, leaving the true monarch to rule over his subjects and spend his revenues . . . All the oil and palm kernels sold at Whydah are the produce of *Addo-Kpon*'s plantations, but Gelele buys the rum, powder and cloth; a very convenient way of getting a good name for spending money . . .'

* * *

'At Benin . . . they crucified a fellow in honour of my coming— here nothing! And this is the bloodstained Land of Dahome!!' Thus Burton in a letter to his friend Monckton Milnes. And, in what is described by his biographer Byron Farwell as 'in the same light vein', he had promised to send another friend, Fred Hankey, a human skin stripped from a living human victim, preferably a woman. This is typical Burton bravura, re- miniscent of the attitude which, when he was a small boy in France and had witnessed a guillotine execution, had led him to adapt the idea for a new game at school. Never squeamish about violence he had also, at Oxford, attempted to call out a fellow-student who had remarked derisively on his impressive moustaches. Luckily, the young man had had the wit to apologize. In Dahomey Burton had, in fact, sent a message to the court that he officially objected to being present at any human sacrifice and suggesting that animals be substituted. He threatened to leave at once, with or without permission, if any death took place in his presence. Having made his official position clear it seems reasonable to assume he would privately have been fascinated. However, though he was there for the period of the Customs, he saw no one actually killed.

For some days after the giving of the presents he was aware of growing nervousness and excitement in the Abomey air and *caboceers* began to arrive from outlying districts. He celebrated Christmas first in a hot rain, then in a *harmattan*. Three days later the Customs began.

Human sacrifice was not uncommon in West Africa among the tribes of the littoral and the forests, and according to some scholars it was not necessarily a matter of terror or dismay. Royal wives, relatives, and servants expected to die when the King himself died, how else would they gain honour among those on the other side? Those who were close to the King may simply not have wished to live without him. In some states human sacrifice grew in a reverse ratio to the decline of the slave trade.

Basil Davidson writes, 'What seems to have happened in some of the states that were profoundly affected by the coastal trade was that the custom of human sacrifice became increasingly distorted, both into a means of "conspicuous consumption" by display of wealth in slaves and, as time went on, into an instrument of political repression. Certainly the distortion grew worse. Its occasional terror reached a climax in the years of acute commercial insecurity that followed on the abolition of the slave trade. Then, with the mainstay of these societies cut suddenly away, superstition sank to gruesome depths . . . '

In the mid-seventeenth century Dapper was writing of Benin, 'No person of rank or wealth dies there unaccompanied by bloodshed.' But as a later writer pointed out, servants often begged to be allowed to die with their master, indeed in some cases only a favoured few, those best qualified to serve him, were despatched. But by the mid-nineteenth century the killings had accelerated in Benin into a kind of generalized mayhem. A European missionary has left an account of what occurred after the death of King Eyamba V at Old Calabar in 1847: 'Eyamba had many wives of the best families in the country, as also many slave concubines . . . Of the former, thirty died the first day. How many by the poison ordeal, under imputation of witchcraft against his life, we never knew. Those who were honoured to accompany him into *Obio Ekpu*, or Ghost Land, were summoned in succession by the message, once an honour, now a terror, "King calls you". The doomed one quickly adorned herself, drank off a mug of rum, and followed the messenger. Immediately she was in the hands of the executioners, who strangled her with a silk handkerchief . . .' The killings continued each evening, some victims were taken to the river and drowned, others beaten to death. After the holocaust the missionaries tried to get laws passed forbidding human sacrifice but it was not until a revolutionary secret society group called the Blood Men—whose object was to save, not shed blood—was formed that the massacres ended.

During Burton's visit the Annual Customs in Dahomey resulted in eighty deaths; all of the executed were either criminals or captive war prisoners. The Customs themselves formed a part of the very essence of monarchical rule. The King was looked upon as divine, the link between the people and the deified ancestors. He was also the guardian of the people's livelihood. The two functions came together at the Customs which was the principal event in the annual economic cycle and the time when some of the Kingdom's wealth was redistributed. During the Customs the King received gifts, payments and tributes; he then gave back part of them to the crowd. On the economic aspect, Polanyi wrote that it may be analysed as 'a move of goods and money towards the centre and out of it again, that is, redistribution. It was the main occasion of building up the finances of the royal administration and of distributing cowries among the people.' Its religious aspect was expressed by Melville J. Herskovits, who was one of the first to bring the complexity of Dahomey's culture to the attention of the world. Writing in the 1930s, he said: 'In the life of every Dahomean his ancestors stand between him and the gods . . . the respect and worship of the ancestors may then be thought of as one of the great unifying forces that, for the Dahomean, give meaning and logic to life.'

Burton felt that the Customs had been thoroughly misunderstood in Europe. The King took no pleasure in the tortures and deaths, nor in the sight of blood. 'The two thousand killed in one day, the canoe paddled in a pool of gore, and other grisly nursery tales,' he put down to the romantic lies of slave-traders in Whydah who probably invented them to deter people from visiting the King. Whatever the reasons, he felt it was hypocritical to lay any blame on the Dahomeans when 'in the year of Grace 1864 we hung four murderers upon the same gibbet before 100,000 gaping souls at Liverpool, when we strung up five pirates in front of Newgate . . . and when our last Christian King but one killed a starving mother of seventeen with an infant at her breast, for lifting a yard of linen from a shop counter. A Dahomean visiting England but a few years ago would have witnessed customs almost quite as curious as those which raise our bile now.' Burton believed that the African victims were killed without cruelty: '. . . These negroes have not invented breaking on the wheel or tearing to pieces their victims . . .'

He thought Dahomey showed up rather well in comparison with Abeokuta, Ashanti and Benin. When he visited Benin in 1860 a sacrifice had just been performed. At Komasi a man was sacrificed every day except on Wednesdays which were the King's birthdays, and the death of any important person was followed by a minor blood-bath. By contrast, in Dahomey only a single slave was killed on the death of the Prime Minister or his 'double'. But so ingrained was human sacrifice he felt that to abolish it would mark the end of Dahomey itself. 'The practice originates from filial piety. It is sanctioned by long use and custom, and it is strenuously upheld by a powerful and interested priesthood. That, as our efforts to abolish the slave export trade are successful, these horrors will greatly increase, there is no room to doubt. Finally, the present king is for the present committed to them; he rose to power by the goodwill of the reactionary party and upon it he depends.'

There were two forms of Customs. The first was the Grand Customs, 'The King's Head Thing'. which took place on the death of a King. Burton, though he never witnessed a Grand

Customs—fortunately, perhaps, for it was a fearsome time—wrote: 'Human sacrifice in Dahomey is founded on a purely religious basis. It is a touching instance of the King's filial piety, deplorably mistaken, but perfectly sincere. The Dahoman sovereign . . . must enter Deadland with royal state, accompanied by a ghostly court . . .'

One of the earliest brief accounts of a Grand Customs comes from Dalzel, who ended his *History* thus: '1791. In the months of January, February and March, the solemnization of the Grand Customs, and of the King's Coronation, took place; the ceremonies of which lasted the whole three months, and were marked almost every day with human blood. Captain Fayrer, and particularly Mr Hogg, Governor of Apollonia, were present; and both affirm that not less than 500 men, women and children, fell as victims to revenge and ostentation, under the shew of piety: many more were expected to fall; but a sudden demand for slaves having thrown the lure of avarice before the King, he, like his ancestors, showed he was not insensible to its temptation.'

Of the Annual Customs, 'The Yearly Head Thing', Burton said they were first heard of in Europe in the days of King Agaja, in the early eighteenth century, though they had doubtless been practised many years before him. They were an extension of the Grand Customs and their function was to supply the departed monarch with fresh attendants in the shadowy world. For Burton, they began on December 28, 1863.

The day opened with a volley of muskets after which Burton received a message from the King saying that the Customs had begun and that they were expected at the Palace. About noon he went, with his party, to the market place and the first thing he saw was the victim shed. From a distance it looked like an English village church—a barn and tower. It was about one hundred feet long, forty feet wide and sixty feet high and it held twenty victims. Each man was sitting on a stool close to one of the supporting pillars to which he was tied in a complex series of loops, one of which passed round his neck. But Burton said the confinement was not cruel; each victim had an attendant next to him to keep off the flies, all were fed four times a day and at night they were untied and allowed to sleep. They were dressed in the garb of state criminals, white shirts with scarlet trimmings and a blood-red heart sewn on to the left breast. On their heads they wore long white hats like dunces' caps. Burton felt that under similar restraint European prisoners would probably have tried to escape and probably have succeeded: 'These men will allow themselves to be led to slaughter like lambs.' He went on: 'I imagine it is the uncertainty of their fate that produces this remarkable *nonchalance*. They marked time to music and they chattered together especially remarking us. Possibly they were speculating on the chances of a pardon.'

Skertchly also noticed this seeming lack of worry when he attended the Annual Customs a decade later. He disagreed with Burton's theories, saying he had seen men laughing 'who knew their heads would be stuck at the palace gate within five minutes'. His thesis was that 'the dull brain of the negro is too sluggish to permit any future fate to influence his passions for good or evil'. Perhaps it was his enforced stay at Abomey which gave him such abrasive opinions of the blacks; whatever the reason, Burton sounded like a pink liberal by comparison.

The Customs at which Burton was to be a spectator were called the 'So-sin Customs' ('the house-tie thing') and took a total of five days to perform. They took their name from the fact that the Captain of the King's House, the *Sogan*, confiscated all houses from their wealthy owners, who were obliged to redeem them after a few days with bags of cowries.

Once again Burton and his party were seated in a good position to view the proceedings and they had not been sitting long when a cannon, fired inside the palace, announced that royalty was on its way. A corps of Amazons formed two lines outside the palace gate and down it stalked Gelele, accompanied by a group of his wives, on his way to perform a fetish ritual so that the proceedings could start. While he was doing this Burton noticed more victims in a second shed and his description is uncharacteristically compassionate. 'I counted nine victims on the ground floor and ten above . . . They resembled in all points those of the market shed, and looked wholly unconcerned, whilst their appearance did not attract the least attention. Yet I felt haunted by the presence of these

morituri, with whose hard fate the dance, the song, the dole
(grief) and the noisy merriment of the thoughtless mob
afforded the saddest contrast.' Near the victims sat the fetish
men who stared at Burton and his party with a 'not over-
friendly eye'. It is no great wonder, for wherever Burton went
he ostentatiously used his notebook and sketch pad and these
were regarded with the gravest suspicion. When the King
finished his ritual, he and Burton snapped fingers and asked
after each other's health and then the King went to lie on a
couch strewn with cloths and shaded by umbrellas. Burton
estimated there was a crowd of two thousand five hundred
which included about three hundred children.

After some preliminary dancing, Gelele stepped forward to
make a speech, the burden of which was that his father, Gezo,
had improved the Annual Customs when he was King, as
Gelele was trying to do in his turn. And he piously hoped that
his children would do as much in his memory. At the end of
his speech he retired behind a curtain to refresh himself, then
reappeared to sing and dance for his people, at which he was
assisted by two 'leopard wives', the youngest and prettiest of
his harem who were dressed in white waistcoats and striped
loin-cloths. Before sitting the King wiped the sweat from his
forehead and, with a jerk, scattered it over the delighted
group nearest him. Gelele finally settled down to listen to
praises of himself before rising once more to reward publicly
several captains in his army by promoting them to higher
ranks. Later in the day he came over to the visiting party,
which consisted of Burton, Dr Cruikshank and the Reverend
Bernasko, and said he was expecting them to dance, sing and
drum. Dr Cruikshank and Burton agreed to dance because they
knew it was expected of them, but Gelele postponed this trial,
saying that when he did call them he would make it in the cool
of evening as the sun did not suit white men.

Late in the day Burton left, but not before he had sent a
second message to Prince Chyudaton officially objecting to
being present at any human sacrifice. He was reassured. In
fact, there were no plans to execute any of the victims before
the end of the So-sin Customs. In hindsight Burton dismissed
the day's proceedings as poorer than those of any hill rajah in
India. 'All was a barren barbarism, whose only "sensation" was

produced by a score of men looking on and hearing that they were about to die.'

* * *

During the Customs, Burton wrote, ' . . . the labour of pleasure in Dahome is somewhat hard.' After the first day the Reverend Bernasko had to go to bed with 'a harmattan'. Burton does not explain what this mysterious ailment was and one is left with the impression of the good clergyman drying up and splitting like wood. They begged off and the King postponed the Customs for that day. On December 30 the Customs were revived and Burton and his party took their places in the afternoon. They had to wait two hours before the King made his appearance, but it was worth waiting for. He arrived wearing a skull cap of straw decorated with a brilliant striped cloth riding side-saddle on 'a little dingy nag'. Behind his lion-umbrella and parasol came a group of singing Amazons carrying seven skulls mounted on fancy flags. They were followed in turn by a dozen 'leopard wives' and a rearguard of old women and small girls.

The King mounted a platform and took off his clothes, keeping on a pair of shorts made of dark satin with yellow flowers. From his left shoulder hung a long sash of crimson silk and a short, silver-mounted sword. He put on a toga of a kind of green mosquito netting and took in his right hand what looked like a large bright billhook. He formed an effective figure against the glowing western sky. He then treated them to a series of dances, all in what Burton describes as the 'decapitation style'. After each dance he would rest and take some rum and occasionally would send some over to Burton. Once, indeed, sending over one of the brass-mounted skulls to be used as a drinking cup. By the end of the afternoon he had danced thirty-two times and began to give away decanters of rum which, Burton said, was a sure sign he was weary of pleasure.

The third day of the Customs was given over to the distribution of money to his people. The Dahomeans knew exactly what was to come and prepared for it. The King mounted his platform on which a great number of cowries had been placed;

his people, in Burton's words, 'removed their ornaments and girt their loins'. It was, apparently, tradition to fight for the royal largess. 'No notice is taken if a man be killed or maimed in the affair; he has fallen honourably fighting for his sovereign. Some lose eyes and noses . . . I have seen a hand through which teeth met . . . We speedily withdrew our chairs.' The King took strings of cowries and threw them high in the air. The bundles were torn to pieces in a moment, so were the strings, and some times a serious fight would break out over a single cowrie shell. The King, surrounded by his guard, then walked around the square, still throwing strings of cowries into the crowd and gradually a cloud of dust obscured almost everything, so great was the scramble and the fighting. The point of all this was that Dahomey knew no credit. In the markets payment for goods was by cash only. This form of annual distribution, eccentric as it might have appeared, did put money into circulation.

Later Burton himself was summoned by the King and he and his party had to scrabble like children in the dust as the King hurled strings of cowries at their feet. After a series of dances performed by hunchbacks Gelele walked to the victim-shed and slowly paced the length of it among the *morituri*. Every now and then he would throw two or three heads of cowries to one of the victims and these were gathered up and placed on their caps. He then joined Burton and gave him a hint that if he pleaded on behalf of the victims it was possible that some might be spared. Burton had been expecting this and co-operated, saying that mercy was the great prerogative of kings. This seemed to please Gelele for on his orders nearly half the prisoners were untied, brought before him and made to crouch on all fours to hear the royal lips utter the reprieve. He then gave Burton two decanters of rum, which meant that they had their 'pass' or permission to leave the presence.

The Customs continued their merry way with dancing, singing, parading, feasting and drinking, a good share of the latter partaken by Burton. But there was much more: it was a time when all great palavers were settled, when wrongdoers were punished and rewards were conferred on those who merited them. It was a time when the spoils of the previous war were divided up, when officers were promoted in the army, when the King gave some of his Amazons as wives to favoured officials, when new laws were passed, old ones repealed.

Although Burton did not see human sacrifice, the beating of the death-drum at night left him in no doubt about what was happening and on his way to take part in the fifth day of the Abomey Customs he witnessed the results. The first change he noticed when he reached the palace square was that one of the victim-sheds was empty. Then he saw a grotesque sight: four corpses, in their red-heart shirts and dunces' caps, were sitting in pairs on wooden stools, kept upright by a double-storeyed scaffold about forty feet high, made of roughly trimmed beams. A short distance away on another double scaffold two victims were hanging, one below the other. Between these was a gallows about thirty feet high from which one corpse was hanging upside down. Farther on, two corpses were tied horizontally along the cross-bar of a gallows. Burton saw no signs of violence on the naked bodies, though they had been mutilated after death 'in respect of the royal wives'.

He went on and found the second victim-hut empty too. On both sides of the entrance lay a dozen heads. 'They were in two batches of six each, disposed in double lines of three. Their faces were downwards, and the cleanly severed necks caught the observer's eye.' Around each heap was a raised rim of white ashes. Within the palace entrance were two more heads, making a total of fourteen. After viewing the corpses Burton and his party took their seats, 'enjoying the fine Harmattanish weather, and were greeted by sundry nobles, who politely thanked us for honouring the day with our uniform'.

This was the day on which the King displayed his wealth. It was a unique exhibition. Forbes, with a meticulousness for detail that for once even outdoes Burton, takes an appendix of thirteen pages to list what he saw. He begins with the procession of women. They numbered nearly two thousand and marched past the King in single file carrying, among a multitude of other things, a carved sheep, a 'horseman clock', glass chandeliers, a silver ostrich with a silver egg under each wing, and one gilt chair. Then came a procession of men who displayed, among other things, a tray containing three human skulls, the King's bath-tub, a live ostrich, a 'large box on four wheels', a landau (English), an umbrella ornamented with eighty human jaw bones, a large wooden horse on wheels, a green chariot, a 'native' sofa and various skulls, jawbones, muskets, banners and umbrellas. After the last lines of men had passed the King it was the turn of the women again and apart from wives, Amazons, etc., who were also part of the King's wealth, Forbes noted 'an English wheeled-chair of the time of Elizabeth', a glass coach, 'Dahomey make', an English family coach, a sarcophagus on wheels, two wooden mounted horsemen on wheels (English made), one head wife, one otto-man of deer skin, six ladies of the chamber, fifty-two chamber utensils 'more useful than ornamental', hundreds of varying-coloured bottles and vases, one washing-pan, dozens of harem-women, one grandmother 'in scarlet and gold' and two women each described as 'another King's widow'—perhaps the skulls of their husbands had preceded them.

Burton spent several hours watching similar processions, but where Forbes had been impressed, he was irritated and wrote that 'almost any pawn-broker's shop could boast a collection more costly'. Yet he found interest enough to make lists nearly as long as Forbes's and among the strangest of the King's possessions listed 'a huge battle-axe perforated like a fish-slicer', two American trotting wagons with leather hoods, a male slave carrying a long blue pole, topped with an imita-tion knife, stained red, and 'a fat sheep with a necklace of cowries and a cloth over its hinder parts', as well as the usual complement of wives, Amazons, soldiers, slaves, skulls, guns, banners and umbrellas.

At the end of the ceremony Burton once more tried to de-liver his message, and once more the King put him off. The bodies were still in place as he made his way back to his house. The heat was already beginning to affect them.

* * *

Burton was allowed a day's rest, then he was plunged into the Customs for the Bush King, *Addo-Kpon*. These were much the same as for the Town King and were held at *Addo-Kpon's* palace about six miles south-west of Abomey. Gelele wanted Burton to fight again for cowries. On the first occasion he had taken the King's invitation seriously and had knocked over the Reverend Bernasko in his eagerness, and it was this diverting spectacle that the King wished to see repeated. Burton refused. However, on the second day Gelele was adamant that the white men do something towards the entertainment and held Burton to his promise of a dancing exhibition. Unabashed, Burton collected his party, tapped out the rhythm he wanted to the Dahomean drummers and performed what he describes as a *'Hindostani pas seul'* which apparently drew tremendous applause. Then the King indicated it was the turn of the Reverend Bernasko to entertain them. It had been agreed that a man of the cloth did not have to dance in a public place so Mr Bernasko devised a different form of entertainment: he conducted a short religious service—a 'God-palaver', as Burton had it. He had a concertina and accompanied himself in hymn-singing for half an hour. One of the hymns, whose irony considering the occasion seems to have been lost on him, was 'All people that on earth do dwell'. A short distance away those in the victim-shed would not be dwelling there very long.

When he had finished the King requested a grand exhibition with Mr Bernasko playing and singing while Mr Cruikshank and Burton danced. 'It was almost too ridiculous,' Burton wrote. 'But we complied for a short time.' He was lucky he only had to dance. John Duncan, an earlier traveller to Dahomey, had to dance before King Gezo and play the Jew's harp at the same time. Burton then danced a second solo which drove the crowd wild with delight and several *caboceers* came to dance around his party. In the midst of all this dust and confusion the Reverend Bernasko, apparently carried away by the moment, was heard to recite:

> 'O let us be joyful, joyful, joyful,
> When we meet to part no more.'

That night was a second *Nox irae*, as Burton called it, when the victims were despatched to the noise of death-drums and musket fire. Again he did not witness any killing. But Skertchly did. He was an enforced guest at the bush King's Customs in

1871. This was the infamous *Attoh* Customs which used a platform about 100 feet long by 30 feet wide built outside the palace. Skertchly says that when he attended the Customs there were twenty-six men in the victim-shed bound *à la mode* and sitting on large flat baskets. The ceremony was heralded by a solemn procession of fetish priests and priestesses. 'In the middle was a native of Katu, gagged and bound to one of the baskets in common use by porters, and behind him, lashed to similar baskets, were an alligator, a cat, and a hawk. These were borne on the heads of some of the inferior priests, and a band of horns and drums played a kind of knell in staccato time, something after the fashion of a bell tolling— a few quick notes and then a pause. This sad procession slowly paraded three times round the market . . .

'At the end of the parade they formed before the platform, and cowries, cloth, powder and a gun, were dashed (given) to the victim who, together with the three animals, was then placed upon the heads of some of the Amazons and carried to the platform. A speech was made giving the reason for the forthcoming killing; the man would go to the dead men, the alligator to the fish, the cat to the animals, and the hawk to the birds—to tell of the great things done by Gelele.

'The basket with the unfortunate man upon it was then toppled over the edge of the platform, the poor wretch falling on the hard earth at the foot with a force that, let us hope, stunned him. The basket was then upended, and the executioner for the nonce commenced his horrid work.

'The knife was light, short, and without edge, and after three chops at the neck of the victim without separating the vertebrae, he put the bloody weapon between his teeth and borrowed another heavier knife from a bystander, and with it completed his barbarous work. Sickening as was the spectacle, I was not able to discover the least sign of pity, horror, or disgust on the faces of any of the throng; the monarch alone turning his head away from the fearful sight.' Over the next few days Skertchly was to see this repeated again and again.

Burton did, once more, see the results of the killings for when his party went back to the palace in Abomey the following day the original corpses, which had been badly torn about by buzzards, had been replaced by newly dead bodies. Four were hanging head down, two were lashed in a sitting position and two others in a horizontal state. Burton was assured, as he had been the first time, that these men were criminals and captives. The two corpses lying horizontally had had salt bags forced over their heads as a punishment for stealing the King's salt. In the ground at each side of the palace gate four fresh heads were hidden by little fences of grass.

During the tail-end of the Customs he tried several times to see the King but each time he was put off. 'Time slips easily away at Agbome,' he wrote. 'Rising with the dawn, we set out as soon as the hammockmen can be collected, and walk till nine a.m. Refection follows till eleven, and my lesson in Fon outlasts the noon. If we visit the Komasi Palace the rest of the day will be blank; the brain becomes so weary that work in the evening is impossible. If we avoid it the afternoon is an inverted copy of the forenoon.' It was not until February 20, nearly two months after their arrival, that the King finally saw Burton on his mission. The reason may have been that Dahomey had declared war on Abeokuta and Burton, who had visited the town, was asked to draw its defences; or perhaps it was because he threatened to leave Abomey whether he was 'passed', i.e. given permission to leave, or not.

The meeting was unlike any previous one. Most white people had been in awe of the Dahomean kings; Burton was in awe of no one. They talked for several hours in a room in the palace and although both were polite, neither minced words and each went through a phase of anger, a 'stirring of the mind', in the Fon phrase. Burton began by complaining that he had been kept waiting for two months; the King replied that he had been busy with his Customs. Burton complained that he had not been allowed to move freely about Dahomey or journey to the Makhi mountains for sport and recreation. The King asked whether roaming around Dahomey and enjoying sport and recreation in the mountains were contained in his orders from the Foreign Office. When Burton admitted that they were not, the King assured him that if he had been ordered to move about freely he would have been allowed to do so. Burton must have experienced a 'stirring of the mind' just then for he says that Gelele waited until his brow cleared before asking him to read the message. This was largely the same as all the others sent over the years by the British Government: Would the King please stop slavery and end the ritual killings. And the King's reply was equally old: he said that the slave trade was an ancestral custom established by white men to whom he would sell all they wanted. In any case the traditions of his kingdom compelled him to make war; and unless he sold off the prisoners he must kill them: would the British Government like that any better? Of the sacrifices he said that he only killed criminals or war captives who, if they could, would do the same to him. He asked for Burton's comments on these matters and was told that nude and mutilated corpses were a disgusting sight and that Burton would advise all Englishmen who wished to avoid 'tickling of the liver' (nausea) to keep away from Dahomey. This apparently stirred the King's mind and he complained bitterly about the Royal Navy interfering with his shipping. They had reached an impasse and one imagines them glowering at each other in silence with the Reverend Bernasko, who had accompanied him, caught in the middle and fearful for his life.

Abruptly, the King said the meeting was over. Burton wrote: 'He told me that if my mind was no longer stirred we might drink together. I again denied personal bad feeling towards him . . . (we) drank gin and liqueur. The King then arose to conduct us outside the palace. The inner doorway being too narrow for two abreast, I fell back a little, and he asked the reason, through the interpreter. My answer was, with us crowned heads always walk first; whereupon he shook hands cordially, told me that I was a "good man, but", rolling his head, "too angry". At the distance of 200 yards he stood, shook hands, snapped fingers, and bade us adieu, exhorting a speedy return.

But Burton never did return. The following day he left for the coast where a cruiser was waiting to pick him up.

8

ON THE day Burton left Abomey, the Dahomean army, led by Gelele, marched on Abeokuta. It took them twenty-two days—on twelve of which they marched from 6 a.m. to 2 p.m., on ten of which they rested—to cover the 120 miles between the two capitals. They marched in four battalions, the total force being estimated at between ten and twelve thousand, and were almost starving by the time they reached the Ogun River. On March 15, 1864, they crossed the river near Abeokuta, floating three old cannons—one bore the legend, 'Mexico, 1815'— with them. Though it was early in the morning and foggy, they were soon spotted by the Egbas and a warning cannon was fired to wake the town. When the Dahomeans came in sight of the walls they found them lined with muskets and the Egbas awaiting the attack unafraid. The Dahomeans came on, making for the gate at which King Gezo had been beaten back in an earlier war but the Egbas had dug a series of tunnel defences and now four hundred young warriors poured out through these passages on to the plain and barred the Dahomeans' path. The Dahomeans altered course and reached a point about two hundred yards from the walls of the town when the battle began. The Dahomeans charged the walls but were stopped by musket-fire from above, and many took cover in the dry moat. Amid the smoke and flying ball the Amazons stormed the walls in a furious charge, only to be dragged over the top by the defenders and cut to pieces. Some crept through the tunnels but were decapitated by the waiting Egbas. It is said that one Amazon, who had lost an arm in the escalade, shot an Egba with the other before being speared to death. Three other Amazons were cut down and their heads and hands exhibited on poles.

The battle lasted for about an hour and a half when the Dahomeans withdrew. They had lost between eighty and a hundred soldiers on the walls, the Egbas fifteen. The long march, the lack of food and the powerful Egba defences combined to demoralize the Dahomean army and they began to retreat on the Ogun River valley. The Egbas came after them and soon the retreat became a rout. All cohesion was lost. Order was replaced by chaos. Officers could no longer control their men or women. Battalions split up into small groups which were hunted down mercilessly by the Egbas. What made everything worse was that it was the end of the dry weather and none of the small streams contained water. The Dahomeans fled through the bush, many dropping from hunger and thirst. Between four and five hundred Dahomean prisoners were butchered by the Egbas on the spot because they were too weak and exhausted to travel back to Abeokuta. Many had walked and run more than thirty-five miles by nightfall. The Dahomean loss was fearful. One estimate put the total number of dead at more than six thousand, which was half the Dahomean army. The Egbas cut all the bodies to bits. It is said that every Egba, man and woman, who passed a Dahomean corpse, slashed or stoned it. Commenting on the defeat, Burton wrote: 'According to the latest accounts, the incorrigible king at once bought a number of slaves and returned to his capital a conqueror.'

* * *

The Reverend Bernasko reported that Gelele once said that 'his father was a king of blacks and a friend of whites; but himself is a king of both'. Burton would never have agreed. He despised Gelele as he did all blacks and often disparaged his actions, especially his defeat at Abeokuta which he compared unfavourably with the much braver stand—though it also ended in defeat—by his father Gezo in 1851. And it is true that Abeokuta was Gelele's Moscow. He tried another attack in 1871 and took another beating. But Abeokuta was the exception; apart from that he was a most successful warlord and one scholar has estimated that of thirteen expeditions against a total of fifty-three towns and villages he captured 5,800 prisoners and 2,300 heads. In the pantheon of Dahomean kings he is one of the best-remembered, both for his success in war and for his skill in allegory and metaphor, and as late as 1911 his sayings were still employed by the Fon people as the best means of illustrating their history.

It was Gelele's misfortune that his reign coincided with an awakening world conscience and also, of course, with the scramble for Africa. By 1863 the French had obtained protectorate rights on Porto Novo. In 1868 they signed a treaty with Gelele's viceroy in Whydah which ceded them the beach at Cotonu. There was pressure from the Portuguese to get a toehold on the coast. Everyone wanted a share of the palm oil trade. It is hardly surprising that there were conflicts of interest between whites and between whites and blacks. In 1876 the first dispute arose with the Europeans. A group of chiefs arrested the Whydah agent of the English firm of Swansea and Company after a quarrel over certain goods. Although he was soon released he informed the Royal Navy, which took an extreme imperialistic view of the case and demanded from Gelele heavy compensation in palm oil for insulting an English subject. The King refused. The Navy blockaded the coast and trade suffered. Gelele, brooding in Abomey, said that he had no need of European goods anyway and threatened to block the roads to Whydah, thus wrecking trade entirely. The white traders on the coast became fearful of being ruined financially and after seven months of blockade they themselves paid the compensation and the blockade was lifted. But the lesson was clear. Big commercial concerns had invested too much in Dahomey for their governments to take this sort of thing casually. Portugal abandoned any claim on Dahomey. The French signed more treaties with the viceroy. The country began to split in two: the chiefs on the coast dealt on the spot with white commercial interests, signing away land and rights; the King in Abomey, not comprehending the nature of the treaties, was unwilling to allow their implementation. It is basically the same story as occurred elsewhere in Africa. The whites, because of their philosophy on property and ownership, failed to comprehend that the land was not divisible, could not be shared out or sold or lent; it belonged to the people in the symbol of the King. So when the French prepared to assert what they thought were their rights at Cotonu and suggested that Gelele give up certain dues and accept a pension, he told the French representative that he would never give up his rights at Cotonu, that the *yegovan* (viceroy) and the *caboceers* who had signed the treaties had had their heads removed and that he recognized no treaties he had not signed himself.

The French decided to send a mission to Abomey to treat with the King. When it arrived Gelele was ill and he died on December 31, 1889—with nothing agreed. With him, for all intents and purposes, died the Dahomean monarchy. He was succeeded by Behanzin, who also refused to surrender what he regarded as his inalienable rights over Cotonu. There were skirmishes between Dahomeans and French. Then Behanzin, in keeping with Dahomean war tradition, attacked a group of tribes which the French considered were in their sphere of influence. They told Behanzin to keep off. The King described their letter as an insult. Dahomean soldiers next fired on a French river steamer without orders from the King. The French mustered an expeditionary force. Behanzin tried to parley, but his letters were ignored. On August 10, 1892, the French bombarded Whydah and several other towns and advanced on Abomey. The Amazons fought tigerishly but the French were too well armed. However, the female battalions managed to delay the advance long enough for Behanzin to burn down Abomey and his palace with it so that it would not fall into French hands.

The expeditionary force camped near the ruins of the town while negotiations proceeded with Behanzin. At last, on January 25, 1894, the King gave himself up after the French had accepted a puppet king called Ago-li-agbo, who was to rule under their authority. Dahomey thus became part of the French colonial empire until it was granted independence in 1960. It is an independent republic, which would have depressed Burton were he alive now. For he was intransigent to the last. Writing about the defeat of Gelele at Abeokuta, his book ends:

'Many years must lapse before Dahome [sic] can recover from the blow, and before that time I hope to see her level with the ground.' If losing her freedom to French colonial interests meant being 'level with the ground', he must have been well satisfied. But it is odd to reflect that had Burton been black, he would probably have ruled Dahomey precisely as Gelele had done, if not more ferociously. Indeed, it would have been impossible to do otherwise: the mould had been formed hundreds of years before when the whites put pressure on Africa, the black mother, for her children.

PART THREE

'The Lice in the Queen's Blanket'

'Whoever feels for the native and cares for his future must wish a fair chance for the experiment now being tried in Basutoland, of letting him develop in his own way, shielded from the rude pressure of the whites.'
—James Bryce. *Impressions of South Africa.* 1898.

Basuto warrior dressed for battle

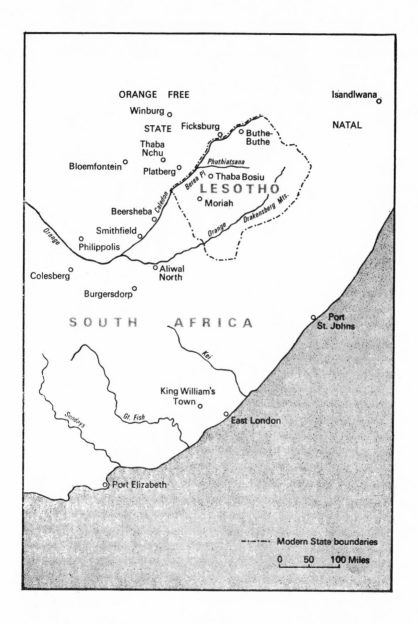

ORANGE FREE

Winburg

STATE   Ficksburg   Buthe-
                         Buthe
Thaba
Nchu
Bloemfontein   *Phuthiatsana*
        Platberg   *Berea Pl*
                    Thaba Bosiu
                  LESOTHO
                     Moriah
    Beersheba
                              Drakensberg Mts.
Orange Smithfield
    Philippolis   *Orange*

Colesberg   Aliwal
                  North
    Burgersdorp

S O U T H   A F R I C A
                              Port
                              St. Johns
                  Kei
         King William's
            Town
Sundays *Gt. Fish*
                  East London

        Port Elizabeth

Isandlwana

NATAL

— · — · — · — Modern State boundaries

0   50   100 Miles

1

IN THE early 1820s a catastrophe fell upon a large part of southern Africa. From the east coast of what is now Natal across the high central plateau of the country to the edge of the Kalahari Desert, inter-tribal warfare broke out on a scale never experienced before; twenty-eight tribes were wiped out, others were fractured into family units and absorbed by other tribes. Villages were burnt and crops and cattle looted to feed rampaging armies. In a few years the countryside became a tawny wasteland over which moved a host of broken men in search of food. Cannibalism, almost unknown in these regions, became rife: husbands ate their wives, mothers their children.

This was a purely black phenomenon and the few whites who had penetrated thus far into the interior by that time, missionaries and traders, a few hunters, were the only foreign witnesses. No one knows how many people died during the years that followed, but one historian puts the figure at two million. The shock of the period on those involved was so great that it caused the very roots of black society to wither. Yet, out of this chaos only a few years later was to emerge a unique black kingdom which still exists. Extraordinary as these two factors are in themselves, what is almost beyond credibility is that Lesotho, or Basutoland as it was called in the colonial period, should exist how and where it does: an independent black state lying in the middle of South Africa.

It owes its existence in the main to one black man, one white man and a not-very-impressive hill. The black man, the father of the Basuto nation, was called Moshesh,[1] the white man was a French missionary, Eugene Casalis, and the

---

[1] The spelling of Bantu names has undergone changes in recent years. Moshesh is now spelt in a variety of ways, Mosheshwe or Moshoeshoe being the most common. The name means 'the shaver', i.e. the man who shaves his neighbours clean—of cattle. I have kept to the simple spelling forms wherever possible. Lesotho is the name of the country, Basuto the people, Mosuto a single person and Sesuto the language they speak.

hill was—and still is—called Thaba Bosiu, the Mountain of Night.

Lesotho is a long way, both physically and emotionally, from the banana trees and hot savannahs of Dahomey, and the fever valleys of the Old Kingdom. Here are no coloured 'kidey-solls', no courtly pageantry, no Annual Customs, no slavery, no furs and tippets from Portugal, no black dukes or bixcomdes. They are two different worlds. Though Lesotho lies to the south of both, it is in a sense a more 'northern' country than either.

It is a land of snow-capped mountains, of bleak, treeless uplands, of savage winters and unpredictable summers where snow has been known to fall on Christmas Day. It is about the size of Belgium but the country it has most often been compared to is Switzerland. There is a similarity, but with a Switzerland of the past: of lost and isolated valleys and of endless mountains—the highest in southern Africa—rising and falling in waves of brown winter grass. Its people dressed themselves in animal skins and furs and lived in small villages of mud and thatch. They spent much of their time in summer attempting to steal their neighbours' cattle, and much of the winter crouched over eye-watering fires of dried dung.

As the Bushmen had found years before when they were hunted from their lairs near the Cape of Good Hope, it was a good country for hiding in. Even today many of its valleys are almost inaccessible, its mountains are often natural fortresses with flat tops guarded by steep cliffs; there are caves everywhere. In a sense Lesotho is itself a fastness, a fortress, a land–island towering out of the plains of South Africa. It was towards this fastness that thousands of homeless refugees made their way in the late 1820s. Until that time it had been almost uninhabited, there was no Basuto nation.

Moshesh was in his late thirties by the time the tribal wars —the *difaqane* or 'forced migrations', as the period is known— began. He came out of nowhere. His father, Mokachane, was a simple village headman. In his youth and early manhood Moshesh gave little evidence of the man to come. He was a cattle reiver in the tradition of his people, but slightly more daring than his contemporaries. Because of this he attracted a small following. At this time the Caledon River Valley, where he had been born, was comparatively thickly populated by small clans of Basuto, each governed by a chief who was constantly contracting alliances with or fighting against one or other of the neighbouring clans. There was no overall power and a 'war' between two clans was little more than a raid which, though it might result in the loss of large numbers of cattle, did not cause much loss of life.

Moshesh was pursuing this mode of life with a future no more or less bright than any other petty headman's son, when he underwent a seminal experience: he met a chief called Mohlomi, who had garnered a wide reputation as a philosopher, wandering prophet, rainmaker and benign wizard. He was also what one historian has called a 'practical polygamist', who married into ruling families wherever he went, settled cattle on his bride and went on his way. Mohlomi was uncharacteristic of his place and time, for he practised as well as preached a wide tolerance, showed goodwill to all, detested war and constantly inveighed against it. Some time before his death he completely converted Moshesh, a considerable feat, for the size of a chief's following depended upon the amount of food he could provide, which in turn meant his success as a raider. It is a measure of Moshesh's genius for compromise that he was able to graft Mohlomi's new concepts on to the traditional Basuto way of life, yet still win an increasing number of followers. By the year 1822 when the *difaqane* began, he was a minor chief ruling a small clan in a part of the world few, if any, white men had penetrated.

Less than two hundred miles to the north-east another minor chief had gathered a following and was committed to expanding his vassalage and his territory. This was the Zulu king, Shaka, an almost exact contemporary of Moshesh's. The date for Shaka's birth is given as 1787 and that for Moshesh as about 1786. The effect of Shaka's rise to power on Moshesh was to be enormous.

Shaka had become the Zulu king in 1817 by means of treachery and murder, and immediately began to reorganize this small and insignificant east-Nguni tribe. By the time he had finished it had become the most famous fighting machine in the black world. Shaka dispensed with the long throwing spear that was most commonly used in battle and introduced the short stabbing spear. This meant a fundamental change in battle tactics. Instead of facing an enemy on a long front and throwing missiles at him, the Zulu army now attacked at close quarters, using a pincer movement that was likened to the head and horns of a bull, the head containing the shock troops who bore the brunt of a frontal attack, the horns closing around the flanks of the enemy and preventing his escape. With these tactics Shaka's *impis* proved unstoppable. What happened when the Zulus exploded from their small tribal area in search of *Lebensraum*, cattle and new citizens had the most profound effect on millions of blacks who had never even heard his name. It was like dropping a stone into the centre of a pond; but here the outward-flowing ripples overtook each other. Tribe after tribe fled from the Zulus, each in turn falling on a neighbouring tribe, that tribe on the next, the next upon the next, and so on across South Africa: the 'forced migrations' had begun.

One of the most infamous hordes produced by these swelling circles of destruction was the Mantatees.[1] They comprised portions of several clans but mainly those of the Batlokwa (the People of the Wild Cat) who had fled westward over the Drakensberg Mountains. This horde, swollen to about fifty thousand, rolled across the country, killing and looting until they reached the fringe of the Kalahari Desert near the Batlapin town of Litakun. Here they were faced by a small force of one hundred well-armed and well-mounted Griquas, and five hundred Batlapin warriors.

The Reverend Robert Moffat, a missionary at Kuruman, has left an account of this meeting. He was riding with a reconnaissance party of ten Griquas under their chief Waterboer when they came in sight of part of the huge horde—about fifteen thousand—in a ravine near Litakun. The remainder, about thirty-five thousand, had occupied the town itself. Not all of these, of course, were fighting men, for the Mantatees marched much as the Persians had marched under Darius and Xerxes, with their women—and in this case children as well.

[1] They took their name from their formidable leader, a woman called MaNantatisi who was said to have only one eye in the middle of her forehead and whose warriors were said to suckle at her huge, pendulous breasts.

When the battle was joined the Griquas employed tactics that the Voortrekkers were to use successfully a few years later against attacks by Bantu armies: with the advantage of being mounted they were able to advance to fire, and retire to reload, and yet remain all the while outside the range of the spears. For several hours this one-sided warfare continued. The Griquas were using heavy muskets and each ball fired into the densely packed throng would have injured more than one person. The Mantatees, unable to get to grips with the elusive Griquas, set fire to Litakun and began to move out of the town. It must have been a wild sight: the flames leaping up from the burning thatch of the huts, the black smoke rising in pillars, the great clouds of dust set up by thousands of bare feet, and the Griqua horsemen riding the perimeter, firing at will. The two sections of Mantatees now joined together forming a host five hundred yards long and one hundred yards wide. As they retreated, the Batlapins, who had taken little part in the battle, swooped down from the neighbouring heights and fell like wolves on the wounded, the women and the children, hacking some to pieces with their war axes to get at bangles and ornaments.

Moffat wrote: 'The wounded and dying did not manifest those signs of sensibility which the situation was calculated to draw forth. The cries of infants who had fallen from the arms of their flying or slaughtered mothers, were distinctly heard; but the others seemed but little affected by their woeful situation. A ferocious thirst for vengeance seemed to reign paramount in the breasts of the dying warriors. Several times I narrowly escaped the spears and battle axes of the wounded, while engaged in rescuing the women and children. Men, struggling with death, would raise themselves from the ground, and throw their weapons with the utmost fury at any one of us who approached them. Their vengeful spirit seemed to be subdued only when life was extinct. Instead of laying down their arms, and suing for quarter, some actually fought on their knees, their legs being broken!

'Many of the Mantatees, especially the women and the infirm, appeared to be suffering dreadfully from famine. Most of the prisoners were much exhausted, and exceedingly ravenous for food; and the dead warriors looked lean and gaunt, though in battle they had displayed amazing agility and swiftness. About five hundred bodies of the enemy lay scattered over the field of battle—so destructive had been the Griqua muskets; while on our side not one man was killed and only one slightly wounded. One Bechuana (Batlapin) lost his life, being slain (a fate richly merited) by one of the wounded whom he was plundering.'

The Mantatees journeyed back across the High Veld the way they had come, resumed their old name of Batlokwa and settled near Moshesh. At that time his stronghold was a steep-sided hill near Buthe-Buthe in the Caledon Valley. MaNantatisi settled her people just north of the river near the present town of Ficksburg. Her policy was to gather as many people under her leadership as she could and extend her territory as far as possible. But that was also Moshesh's policy and he was in her way. Her army, under the leadership of her son, a young but brutal warrior called Sikonyela, began to harass Moshesh, whose store of food in his hill fort dwindled to a dangerously low level. In desperation he sent out runners to find a stronghold farther away from the Batlokwa. When they returned they described a hill about sixty miles to the south-west which stood in an isolated valley and which, though it was not very high, appeared to be strong enough to withstand an attack. Moshesh moved his whole tribe, now about two thousand strong, with their cattle, by a circuitous route through remote valleys eluding the Batlokwa outposts. But the mountains were infested with cannibals and several of the tribe who could not keep up were attacked and eaten, including Moshesh's own grandfather, Peete. Moshesh finally reached his destination late one afternoon and by nightfall the entire tribe with its cattle were on the hilltop. This has been advanced as the reason the hill was called Thaba Bosiu—the Mountain of Night.

There can be few mountains which have played so vital a role in the history of a people as Thaba Bosiu—one thinks of Masada on the Dead Sea or Magdala in Ethiopia. Had Moshesh had the choice of any hill in southern Africa he could not have done better. It is insignificant when one first sees it. It lies on the Phuthiatsana River and is only about 350 feet at its highest point. The top, which is almost completely flat, is some 150 acres in extent and has an abundant spring of water. The whole flat area—good enough grazing for short periods of siege—is guarded by cliffs which drop away just below the summit and completely surround it. There are six fissures which give access to the top but of these only three might be considered possible by an attacking army. They are called the Khubelu, the Mokachane and the Raebe passes. Moshesh built his own huts above the first and placed those of his father, Mokachane, above the second. The Raebe Pass was suitable for launching rocks, so great piles were gathered near the top, some of which still remain. The hill was a natural fortress, better than a Crusader castle; it could withstand a siege in conditions far less insanitary and therefore less liable to disease. Today Thaba Bosiu is deserted. It is the burial mound of the Basuto kings and as such it is a sacred place.

By the beginning of 1827, three years after the move to the new fortress, Moshesh's tribe had expanded to about three thousand, part living on the top of the hill and part around the base. Like Shaka, MaNantatisi and several other chiefs, Moshesh had given succour to many refugees. He was prospering. He was far enough away from the Batlokwa to feel reasonably safe. His most dangerous enemy, Shaka, died about this time, murdered by his half-brother, Dingane, to whom Moshesh paid a tribute of young maidens, skins and feathers in exchange for peace. For a while the peace endured, but no one expected it to last for ever.

The first of many attacks on Thaba Bosiu came not from either the Zulus or the Batlokwas but from a tribe of Zulu origin called the Amangwane who had landed up on the Caledon River as a result of the *difaqane*. Moshesh was already paying tribute to their chief, Matiwane, but it is said that Matiwane objected to the Basutos paying tribute to the Zulus as well. This may have only been an excuse, for Moshesh's cattle had been increasing even faster than his tribe, and cattle were wealth. Whatever the reason, Matiwane decided to attack Thaba Bosiu in July, 1827. The Amangwane approached the fortress from a high plateau called the Berea from which one can actually look down on Thaba Bosiu. Then they had to descend the plateau and cross the Phuthiatsana

River before reaching the base of the hill. The Amangwanes, fielding six divisions and greatly outnumbering the Basutos, attacked in almost complete surprise. But two of the Basuto 'war doctors' were just in time to confine them to a comparatively narrow front by bewitching several of the river crossings which the superstitious Amangwane then refused to use. Moshesh at first attacked the enemy below Thaba Bosiu, causing severe damage. When other elements of the Amangwane tried to storm the heights they were destroyed by a shower of rock avalanches. In the midst of this Moshesh ordered a counter-attack. It was too much for Matiwane's forces, who began streaming back up the Berea plateau, passing caches of beer which they had brought to celebrate their anticipated victory.

Four years later, Moshesh faced another critical challenge: he was attacked by Moselekatze and his highly trained Matabele *impis*. Moselekatze, a Zulu clan chief, had broken with Shaka and fled from Zululand nearly ten years before. During that time he had outdone his former master in acts of cruelty. He had crossed the Drakensberg westward and cut a bloody swathe through what is now the Transvaal. When Shaka pursued him he began a scorched earth policy that laid waste hundreds of square miles and aggravated the existing famine. After a while he swung south and on a day in March, 1831, Moshesh, standing on Thaba Bosiu, saw the approaching regiments. He knew that these Matabele warriors were veterans, battle-trained and battle-hard, and wisely decided to fight them from a defensive position and not take his army down on to the plains. The Matabeles topped to rest on the banks of the Phuthiatsana River, sharpening their spears and seeing to their feathered head-dresses. Moshesh used this time to build up huge mounds of rocks at the top of his hill passes.

The Matabele attacked twice up the steep fissures and each time were driven from the slope by plunging boulders. It was a form of warfare they had not encountered before and for which they had no answer. After bitter recriminations and allegations of cowardice they began to drift away to the north. Now Moshesh showed the qualities that were to distinguish him throughout his life, qualities that any international statesman might have envied. He sent a herd of cattle down to Moselekatze with the message that these were for his men so that they would not be hungry on their long march back to the Transvaal. Moshesh was never again attacked by the Matabele, but that did not mean his Basuto were to be left in peace.

From 1830 they had to contend with a different kind of enemy, the Koranas, a tribe of Hottentot blood who, though professing Christianity, lived by the booty they could collect plundering weaker tribes. Like their cousins the Griquas who had fought so well against the Mantatees, the Koranas, though few in number, were well armed and well mounted. Most were first-class shots. Acting in small bodies they would leave their huts, cover forty or fifty miles in a night, dismount at dawn outside one of the Basuto villages that were now being built farther and farther from Thaba Bosiu as the population increased, shoot down the warriors, who could not reach them with their assegais, kill the women, drive off the stock, and leave. Their weakness was liquor: they drank it wherever they found it and they often found it in these villages. It was usually a heavy beer made from local millet and it was because of the Koranas' predilection for this beverage that the Basutos had their first successes against them. They would wait until the Koranas were stupefied by drink, kill them and then watch their horses for hours until they were sure that the explosion of the muskets had not come from these strange beasts, which they have never seen before.

The Koranas were no real threat to Moshesh but their tactics set him thinking. He had seen how impotent his warriors were against the musket and the horse and decided never to be at such a disadvantage again if it could be avoided. It would be difficult to overemphasize the importance of this decision. It made the Basuto, certainly as far as horses were concerned, unique among Bantu tribes so that when they were later to meet the armies of white nations they could do so on some level of equality. This could not even be said of the Zulus—in spite of their victory at Isandlwana—for they kept to the old weapons and old ways which had stood them in good stead against their black neighbours but which had little relevance to the increasingly sophisticated weapons of the whites. Until the Basuto captured horses from the Koranas, their warriors had gone to war on foot dressed in a leather kilt, a brass gorget round the neck and a ball of feathers on the head. For arms they used shields of hardened leather, spears and light throwing axes. It took several years before they had a nucleus of horses to breed from. When they did a new type of horse, the famous Basuto pony, emerged. It was small but it was able to endure hardship and in the mountains it was as sure-footed as a goat.

But this was in the future and for the moment Moshesh and his tribe had to endure on their hilltop surrounded by thousands of starving people, many of whom had turned cannibal.

Moshesh was as much to blame for this state of affairs as anyone, and he knew it. In 1843, in the presence of a group of cannibals led by a bushy-browed giant called Rakotsoane— the very group that had eaten Moshesh's grandfather, Peete— he said, 'We, the masters of the country, did drive you to live on human flesh for men cannot eat stones. You ate my father but before that I had eaten yours.' (Meaning all their means of subsistence.)

Cannibalism, according to a French missionary, the Reverend D. G. Ellenberger, spread from the Orange River to the Vaal, depopulating the land and stopping all friendly intercourse between tribes and villages. Murder and robbery were rife, people only dared to move in large armed parties. How easy it was to change the nature of people to whom cannibalism was quite foreign was shown by what happened to a tribe called the Bafokeng. Once a powerful people, the forced migrations had left them frail and frightened. Moshesh in a moment of weakness gave in to pressure from his brother Mohale and allowed him to raid the Bafokeng for whatever cattle they had left. Mohale took everything and the Bafokeng were left utterly destitute. They adopted cannibalism as the only means of saving themselves, killing and eating any travellers they could ambush. In each case, they flayed the victim and dressed the skin as they might have done an animal hide, then made clothing for the women and breech-cloths for the men.

Moshesh's people were one of only three Basuto clans who

did not become cannibals and the other two saved themselves either by moving into the Cape Colony or being lucky enough to live in an area so remote as to be inaccessible.

Mr Ellenberger, who made a special study of cannibalism in Lesotho, wrote: 'It must be remembered that in the early days the staple food of a pastoral people was milk supplemented by grain. Therefore when the invasions came, and the cattle were captured by the enemy, people had to fly from their homes and fields, cultivation ceased, and they were in grievous case. Even the game, which had been abundant, disappeared before the invading hordes, but the beasts of prey remained, and throve exceedingly on the liberal diet so lavishly provided for them. Women with babies on their backs, dragging little children along with them when flying before the enemy, have testified how they had to abandon their offspring to wild beasts, or wilder men, when they were unable to follow any longer; and how they themselves escaped at the cost of cruel sufferings, subsisting for weeks on water and roots, if on nothing worse. One wretched woman, when converted, sobbed, "I am indeed a murderess, for I have eaten the fruit of my own womb."

'Cannibalism as practised by the Basuto was indeed a madness. All human instinct, all reason, fellowship, intellect, everything in fact which raises the human being over the brute beast, became extinct or obliterated. They practised cruelty for its own sake and the pleasure it gave them, torturing their victims in a fiendish manner before despatching them. Children were butchered or roasted alive under the eyes of their parents, or vice versa; women in the presence of their husbands. They would bind the hands of captured people, and drive them before them as they would cattle. If any one resisted, he was killed and eaten at once, to save the trouble of driving him. The women of the cannibals were just as blood-thirsty. They would frequently accompany their husbands on the man-hunt, so as to miss no part of the feast.

'When, as it sometimes happened, many victims were captured at one time, the fattest was eaten first, and the lean ones were forced to eat the flesh in order to fatten them. Sometimes a young woman would be spared for sexual purposes. One such, a tall, thin woman, lived to relate her experiences. She was captured with some others near Teyateya-neng, and driven to a cave near Cana, where all who were in good condition were devoured that evening. She, however, was spared for the purpose stated, and later on escaped. If no victims were forthcoming, wives and children were eaten, but, owing to superstition, not as a rule by their own husbands or fathers. It was thought better to exchange them for others. But this was not always possible; and, if he were hungry, the scruples of the cannibal would speedily be overcome, whether the victim was wife, child, or comrade.'

During the 1830s a French missionary estimated the number of practising cannibals between the Orange River, the Drakensberg and the Vaal at between seven and eight thousand. Ellenberger put the figure low at four thousand and estimated that if each one ate one person a month it would make a total of forty-eight thousand eaten during one year. During the six worst years from 1822 to 1828 this would mean that more than a quarter of a million were eaten.

Cannibalism not only devastated the land but also produced difficulties of a more domestic nature. For instance, when Moshesh's eldest son reached the age of seventeen, it was high time that he was circumcised but it was not possible for him to undergo the rite while his grandfather's grave (he had been eaten) remained in a state of defilement. Moshesh put his agile mind to work and came up with a solution. He summoned Rakotsoane and his cannibals and caused all of them to be rubbed with a special mixture which would purify them. In other words, he was treating them all, for the purposes of the purification ceremony, as the tomb of the departed. At the time several of his chiefs urged him to kill Rakotsoane and his cannibals. Moshesh refused, replying, 'I must consider well before I disturb the sepulchre of my ancestor.'

This, then, was the state of affairs in a country which as yet had no name and no geographical boundaries—the defining and keeping of which was to cause almost all the future trouble—when a man arrived with two companions to preach the gospel to the Basuto. His name was Eugene Casalis and he had been sent out to South Africa by the Evangelical Missionary Society in Paris. It is doubtful whether any nation has been as lucky with its missionaries as the Basuto were with these Frenchmen who followed each other from Paris over the next fifty years. Unlike the perfervid monks and friars who arrived in the Old Kingdom to proselytize with one hand and slave with the other, whose legacy was the horrible irony of a black puppet king executing a black woman and child for committing a heresy against a white religion; unlike Burton, whose contempt for King Gelele and all things negroid was to entrench the very customs he had been asked to try to change—and unlike so many priests, missionaries, immigrants, hunters, farmers and prospectors who tried to shape the country to their own needs—the members of the Paris Evangelical Mission came to Africa wanting nothing from her in exchange for what they hoped to give. The fact that they were Protestant missionaries, themselves a persecuted race in Roman Catholic France, almost certainly gave them a quality in dealing with blacks in Africa that no other missionaries possessed. In his book, *The Rise of the Basuto*, G. Tylden flatly states: 'It is hardly possible to overestimate the value of the work of the mission in Basutoland . . . the Basuto owe to it in no small measure their place in the world, their language, their literature, the preservation of their tradition and history, their share in the education they so much desire, and an example of everything that should make up the life of the tribe.'

It was, perhaps, the very best time for missionaries. The anti-slavery movement was in full flood; men's consciences had been stirred. While missionaries were often unpopular in the countries to which they were called they retained a firm grip on the liberal mind in Europe. No one, least of all politicians, could afford to offend the all-powerful Aborigines Protection Society which actively supported the Protestant missions. Neither governments nor their army commanders could any longer ignore missionary opinion. Moshesh was soon to have access to this powerful group in Europe through the French missionaries in his country, and especially through Casalis, who has often been called his 'foreign minister'.

2

EUGENE CASALIS wrote two books about his years in Lesotho; both are classics of their kind *The Basuto*, is the most important early work on the people and country. The other, *My Life In Basuto-land*, is a personal portrait of a young man transparently idealistic, deeply religious, easily touched, very emotional, with a great need to love and be loved—and yet possessed of a streak of French bourgeois toughness without which he could never have survived in Africa.

He was born in the town of Orthez in the Basses Pyrénées in south-western France in November, 1812, of a comfortably-off Protestant family whose ancestors had lived through the dangerous times following the Revocation of the Edict of Nantes. His grandfather, a man of deep convictions, had used his house as a refuge for the 'pastors of the Desert', the Protestant ministers who in the time of Huguenot persecution travelled secretly around France holding illegal services. His grandmother had been taken from her parents when she was seven by a *lettre de cachet* and shut up in an Ursuline convent at Pau until she was eighteen. She reverted to Protestantism and also took up the dangerous business of helping to keep the faith alive.

It is not surprising in view of this romantic background and of the extreme piety in which Casalis was reared that he should have been drawn to the Church, although he quite candidly stated that his very first leaning towards religion, when he was seven, was because he dreaded death and hell.

He was not much older when he realized there were people in the world with black skins. He wrote, 'Already there began to show itself in me that love for the coloured races that seemed almost innate. When I saw a negro or mulatto, which, indeed, rarely happened, I felt towards him a lively sympathy. I wanted to stop him, to get him to seat himself by me and tell me his history. This taste seemed the more remarkable as these people, at that time so little known in our small provincial towns, were the objects there of a special repugnance.

I attributed my feelings towards them to the emotion which had been awakened in me by reading a history of the conquest of Mexico. A missionary's romance, entitled *Gamul and Leria*, had also made me shed tears over its description of the sufferings of two little Africans, and over the picture it gave of their happiness after they had become converted.'

He studied classics and theology with a tutor in Bayonne and then joined the Evangelical Missionary Society in Paris when he was eighteen. So far he had led a somewhat sheltered life. This changed in Paris. Cholera, which had been creeping across Europe from Asia, finally reached the city in spite of a *cordon sanitaire*. One Saturday evening rumour spread through the streets that a cook had died of the disease. The following day Casalis, an apprentice, was preaching a sermon when a member of the congregation collapsed. 'I descended precipitately from the pulpit', wrote Casalis, 'and held him in my arms. His vomitings covered my clothes. We carried him away. A doctor was sent for. Two hours later poor Postry (his name has always remained with me) was no more; and the next day when I conducted his funeral, his coffin was laid in the midst of twenty others.

'In the course of some weeks we saw thousands fall at our right hand and our left; but at the Mission House not one was touched. Every evening as we went to bed in the dormitory, we embraced each other as though for the last time.' When the epidemic diminished, Casalis and a co-missionary, Arbousset, with whom he was to go to Africa, slogged over the country roads of France carrying the Protestant message to remote villages and cut-off communities. It was hard work struggling through mud and often snow but it was to stand him in good stead for the trials to come.

In 1830 France had conquered Algiers and Casalis and Arbousset were set to work to learn Arabic. Then suddenly the Cape of Good Hope began to be discussed. Casalis was not pleased. 'We had very comfortably settled down to the idea of a field of labour whose distance from home was an affair only of hours,' he wrote. They started to learn Dutch. Soon Casalis went to Orthez to spend two months with his family before setting off. His father had what they thought was chronic gastritis—he was, in fact, dying of stomach cancer—and the eight weeks were fraught with the unspoken spectre of parents and child never seeing each other again. Casalis vividly described the final leave-taking.

'A moment after we were in the saddle, and had gone some steps, I heard my father calling me back.

'"Descend," said he; "I must embrace you once more."

'"No, I beseech you. We shall lose what little strength we still have left."

'"I command you!"'

'I threw myself again into his arms, and he clasped me to his breast in a convulsive embrace, gasping in a broken voice, which went to my heart, 'I shall never see you again here below!"' It was two hours before Casalis could stop sobbing.

He and Arbousset were ordained in 1832 and immediately set off for London where they were joined by M. Gossellin, a stone-mason from Amiens who was to accompany them as an 'artisan missionary'. They sailed from Gravesend in November. Casalis was nineteen years old.

*   *   *

In 1832 the Cape Colony was on the threshold of huge physical and emotional changes. It had been in British hands since 1806 and during that time the white population had greatly expanded. The interior of the country was little known by the outside world. A few farmers had settled just north of the Orange River, hunters and missionaries somewhat farther. On the eastern side of the country farmers of Boer and British stock confronted the southward-moving Xhosa pastoralists, both sides laying claim to areas of good grazing land. Already there had been wars between black and white, and there would be more to come.

The event which was to change everything was still two years off: the emancipation of all slaves in the British Empire was scheduled for 1834 but was casting a long shadow. Farmers in the Cape were worried about labour shortages and were incensed that the British Government had agreed to pay compensation to slave owners only if they came to London to collect it. The way in which emancipation was carried out was one of the main causes of what became known as the Great

Trek, in which hundreds of Boer families crossed the Orange River to put themselves beyond British sovereignty and in so doing opened up the country and created their own republics.

Casalis landed in Table Bay on February 23, 1833, after a voyage of just over three months, and hated Cape Town on sight. It was a natural reaction; he was far from home and in an alien society. But he soon recovered in the warm summer weather surrounded by all the colour and liveliness of a multiracial seaport where he mixed with Malays and Hottentots, English clerks and Dutch farmers, where the profusion of fruit reminded him of Provence and the Languedoc.

He and his two companions were staying with Dr Philip, the superintendent of all the London Missionary Society's stations in the colony and one of the most famous missionaries in the history of the country—he was constantly vilified for his liberal views of blacks—when they heard that their destination, an Evangelical mission station even deeper in the African interior than the Reverend Moffat's at Kuruman, had been destroyed by tribes during the *difaqane* and no longer existed. The incumbent missionaries had fallen back on Moffat's station and Casalis decided to join them there. The three of them sailed to Port Elizabeth and journeyed through the Zuurveld and the Karoo, going from one mission station to the next, until they reached the L.M.S. station at Philippolis. 'Without knowing it,' Casalis wrote, 'we had reached the place and the hour where God was about to reveal the field of labour He had destined for us.'

At Philippolis, Casalis met a coloured farmer called Adam Krotz, who had a curious tale to tell. At that time the whole of the central plateau stretching north-east from Philippolis into Natal was *terra incognita* to most cartographers. In fact a map which Casalis had bought in Paris before leaving simply described it as 'sandy and desert plains', than which nothing could be further from the truth. From time to time small parties of starving Basuto had drifted down to Philippolis and Krotz had settled some of them on his farm. When they had learnt enough Dutch to be able to communicate with him they described their country, waxing particularly eloquent about the amount of wild game to be hunted. Krotz had decided to explore it.

'While I was carrying on my hunting at a place eight days' journey from here,' he told Casalis, 'a chief sent two men to beg me to visit him. I took with me as interpreter one of the natives of the country whom I had received on my farm. He conducted me to a mountain where this chief had fixed his residence and who was, for this reason, called the Mountain Chief. His true name was Moshesh, son of Mokatchane.

'He told me that for several years past he had been the victim of incessant attacks, by which three-quarters of his subjects had been destroyed or dispersed. He had asked me there to know if I could give him any good advice, if I could show him any means of securing peace for the country. I thought at once of the missionaries; I spoke to him about Moffat and about our own men (i.e. those at Philippolis). I tried to make him understand the services which such men could render him.

'The idea of having near him permanently wise men, friends of peace, disposed to do all in their power to aid him in his distress, pleased him greatly. He wanted to have some at once. "Do you know any?" he said to me, "who would be disposed to come?" I replied that such men sometimes came our way. "Oh, I beseech you, tell the first you meet to hasten here. I will give them the best possible welcome. I will do everything they advise me to do." I promised him not to forget his prayer.

'Shortly after my return home I found that he, in doubt whether I should have the means of fulfilling my promise, had sent me two hundred cattle, in order that I might procure him in exchange at least one missionary. But they had been intercepted and captured *en route* by the Koranas.'

Krotz, who was keen on another hunting expedition, offered Casalis his services as guide. There was no question in Casalis's mind that this was a call, and he accepted it.

Instead of the ten days which the journey should have taken, they were in their wagons for three weeks as Krotz and several hunting companions made detours in search of springbok, wildebeeste and eland. Their route took them over a series of high plains that rose in steppes to the line of black mountains that was their final destination. Wherever they came in sight of a village the population fled in terror and

Casalis was later told that the hunters' guns had caused the villagers to think they were Koranas.

They reached the Caledon River in June, midwinter in these latitudes, and Casalis was immediately struck by the attributes of the first Basuto clans he met. He wrote: 'Their skin was soft, bronze rather than black in colour, their limbs robust and well-modelled. Their average height was the same as our own. We were struck by the dignity of their bearing, the grace of their movements, and the deference and cordiality which characterized their manner of address. The mantles made of the skins of animals, with which they covered their shoulders, the huts in which they lived, and the pleasure they took in anointing their limbs with oil, seemed the only things that assimilated them to the savage, such as we are accustomed to conceive him.'

As they drew nearer to Moshesh's country they found ample evidence of the *difaqane*. 'Almost everywhere were human bones,' Casalis wrote. 'In some places the number indicated battle-fields. Broken earthenware, fallen walls overgrown with brambles, the easily recognized boundaries of fields formerly cultivated, revealed to us frequently that we were on the site of a once populous village. There were still some left which were inhabited, but they were much smaller and on almost inaccessible heights.'

They sent a runner to Moshesh telling him that they were near, then they crossed the icy waters of the Caledon and made camp. The following morning they were roused by Moshesh's two sons, Letsie and Molapo, who came riding down on the camp like Assyrians. 'Entire novices in the art of riding,' wrote Casalis, 'they came down on us with a rush almost without warning, at the risk of upsetting everything. It would be impossible to imagine anything more grotesque than the aspect of these young madcaps, mounted bareback, their naked legs striking the steaming flanks of their steeds like flails. The panther (leopard) skins which floated over their shoulders did not improve them. Certainly the nude is nowhere more out of place than on horseback.'

Casalis must have been relieved to discover through Krotz's interpreter that this exuberant exhibition was no more than an expression of welcome and he was told that they were not only expected, but impatiently so. Casalis at once saddled up and with Krotz and the interpreter crossed the Phuthiatsana River and began climbing Thaba Bosiu. As they followed the narrow pathway to the summit Casalis looked up and saw a long line of people forming on the edge of the rocks above, whom he at first took to be crows. The path became too steep for horses so they dismounted and walked the remainder of the slope. The moment they reached the top there was a general rush in their direction and they were surrounded by hundreds of inquisitive Basuto.

'Suddenly,' Casalis wrote, 'a personage attired in the most fantastic fashion advanced, a long wand in his hand, growling and snapping like a dog. At his appearance everybody retreated and fell into line, making in this way an immense semi-circle behind a man seated on a mat. "There is Moshesh," said Krotz to me. The chief bent upon me a look at once majestic and benevolent. His profile, much more aquiline than that of the generality of his subjects, his well-developed forehead, the fullness and regularity of his features, his eyes, a little weary, as it seemed, but full of intelligence and softness, made a deep impression on me. I felt at once that I had to do with a superior man, trained to think, to command others, and above all himself.

'He appeared to be about forty-five years of age. (He was, in fact, forty-seven.) The upper part of his body, entirely naked, was perfectly modelled, sufficiently fleshy, but without obesity. I admired the graceful lines of the shoulders and the fineness of his hands. He had allowed to fall carelessly around him, from his middle, a large mantle of panther skins as lissom as the finest cloth, and the folds of which covered his knees and his feet. For sole ornament he had bound round his forehead a string of glass beads, to which was fastened a tuft of feathers, which floated behind the neck. He wore on his right arm a bracelet of ivory—an emblem of power—and some copper rings on his wrists.

'After we had looked an instant at each other in silence, he rose and said, *Lumela Lekhoa*, "Welcome, white man!" and I replied by holding out my hand to him which he took without hesitation.'

* * *

132

Like the arrival of the first Portuguese mission in the City of Congo, this one had begun auspiciously. It would seem that from the very first moment of their meeting a friendship developed between Casalis and Moshesh that was unusual for its time and place; one detects an almost paternal feeling, for Moshesh was twenty-seven years older than Casalis. Whatever the root, their relationship is like no other of the period.

Having greeted each other, Moshesh took Casalis to his principal wife, Mamohato, some distance away, and the missionary was able to inspect the village. It was nothing like the City of Congo or Abomey, but simply a mass of low thatched huts built so close to each other that the thoroughfares were no more than narrow lanes and even these were encumbered by people, for most of the work, such·as the preparation and cooking of food, the making of clothing, and the repair of arms, was done outside in fine weather. In the middle of the village was a huge cattle kraal, rather like a medieval bailey, where the herds were penned at night for safety. They paused at the doorway of Moshesh's main house. 'Before entering it,' Casalis wrote, 'he caused to pass before me his inferior wives, to the number of thirty or forty, not suspecting, poor man, what I thought of polygamy, nor the blows I was meditating against it.' In Mamohato's hut Casalis was given a pot of milk and what he described as a loaf of *sorgho* (sorghum) of the size and form of a cannon ball.' He sat looking helplessly at the food until one of the servants, more observant than the rest, hurried off and found him a spoon made of horn.

While he ate, he studied Moshesh's queen. She was, he says, of a somewhat ripe age, but not unattractive. She watched him with an expression that 'seemed to say that she found me very.young, and that she was happy to mother me a little'. While Moshesh played with one of his young sons, Casalis finished his meal. Soon Krotz came to collect him and they descended the hill and rejoined the others at its foot. It had turned bitterly cold, which came as a shock to Casalis, who had only experienced hot weather until then, and it began to snow.

In spite of the weather, Moshesh followed them down to inspect their tents and gear and one has the impression that, just as he had shrewdly summed up what he needed from the Koranas, he was now, at the beginning of his relationship with white men, judging their culture and technology from the artefacts they had brought with them: it is a keynote of Moshesh's character that he was always willing to learn. The following evening the missionaries invited him to dinner. None had any idea of cooking and the King ended up with hashed mutton and pumpkin served on a saucepan lid. He did not mind—the mission in Paris was later to be shocked at this lack of respect—being much taken instead with a sweet white sand called sugar. The others ate directly from the saucepan itself since their plates had not been unpacked. The easy informality of the relationship between Moshesh and the missionaries is striking compared with that of the court in Dahomey and Congo. By the time the evening ended, Moshesh had invited them to remain in his country and had offered to help them get started. In return they were to pass on their knowledge to his people. A week or two later, after surveying much of the surrounding countryside, the three missionaries decided to settle in a valley they called Moriah, which is now known as Morija. It was a fair distance from Thaba Bosiu— about twenty miles—but seemed to contain everything they needed: water, wood for building and firing—lack of wood was the main reason they had not settled closer—and fertile land for growing the seeds they had brought with them.

3

AT THIS time Lesotho was untainted by any contact with outside civilization and was in that sense like the Old Kingdom before Cão's arrival. But the Basuto were an even simpler people. There was no palm-tree culture, for instance, and no coinage. Their economy was based upon cattle, the raiding of which from other clans and tribes formed their main preoccupation. Cattle were woven into the very fabric of Basuto society.

By comparison with many tribes the laws which governed them seem far from harsh and many have a Solomon-like ring. Every man was responsible for the good behaviour of his

Moshesh in 1833, just before the Boers and the British began to exert pressure on him.

Joseph Orpen

Eugene Casalis

Sir George Grey

President Boshoff

Sir George Cathcart

Sir Harry Smith

Adam Kok

President Hoffman

Thaba Bosiu, the Mountain of Night, which saved the Basutos from defeat on several occasions.

Moshesh and his advisers in 1860. The man with his hand on the king's shoulder is his brother, Mopedi.

neighbour and he was liable to be punished for a crime committed by his neighbour if he failed to report it to the chief. A father was responsible for all the members of his family until they married. A village was collectively responsible for each of its inhabitants. If the skin of a stolen animal was found in a village, or the spoor traced to it, and the thief not caught, the village had to compensate the owner. This attempt to make everyone share in the responsibility of keeping the society stable is clearly shown by another law which stated that if a man saw two others fighting and made no attempt to stop them he was held jointly culpable if either was hurt.

Their sexual customs naturally seemed permissive to a succession of missionaries—who tried to change them. For example, any man who seduced or tried to seduce an unmarried girl had to pay two head of cattle; if she became pregnant, six head. Adultery, which was punished by death in some other tribes, drew a fine of two or three cows from the guilty male, also a fine of one cow from the woman's family. Meddling with a chief's wives was much more serious and anyone seducing his principal wife was either driven from the community or strangled.

The death penalty was used sparingly. Ellenberger says that the 'national sense' was always against it. This may have led to a freer society compared with many other African peoples and it is possible that the tolerance of the Basuto allowed Moshesh room for manoeuvre in his later dealings with his white neighbours, unlike the kings of Dahomey, who were caught in the chains of rigid conservatism and were unable to change even though they may have wished it, without the fear of disrupting their society.

It must be remembered that Ellenberger was a missionary and missionaries are never the most reliable judges of sexual matters. Casalis does not even comment on sexual customs. In his anthropological study of the Basuto, Hugh Ashton says that according to information he collected in the 1930s and 1940s relations between boys and girls in the old days used to be entirely innocent. So pure were the youths and maidens that they even bathed naked together and yet remained chaste. Ashton said, 'It is difficult to say how true these reports really are, and one is tempted to discount them against the familiar "things-are-not-what-they-were-when-I-was-a-child" attitude of older people. But there is no reason to suppose, as is so often done in South Africa, that Africans are "naturally" immoral and promiscuous and that therefore such chastity was improbable if not impossible.

'The general attitude still is that boys and girls and unmarried young men and especially women, should be chaste, and this is still strong enough to cause considerable individual variation. Many do keep chaste and a doctor of many years' gynaecological experience considers that an appreciable proportion of unmarried girls are virgins. On the other hand, many Basuto allege and deplore that nearly everyone has premarital love affairs: there is good evidence that some children's sexual experience begins even before puberty.'

From the first the Basuto seem to have been agriculturists, herdsmen and hunters. They had rudimentary farm implements and men, women and children worked in the fields. The men built the huts, which were made of thatching grass, and they were also the tailors, shoemakers, dressmakers, woodcarvers and implement makers. They were able to work in metal and made wood axes and battle axes, assegais and knives. The women prepared and cooked the food, were able to make and bake pottery in open-air fires of dried cowdung, a very skilled occupation, wove sleeping mats of rushes and in general managed the house and children. They made fire by rubbing hard wood on soft and lamps by using a small pot filled with fat containing a fragment of charcoal.

Their food was plain but wholesome. They ate a porridge of ground maize or kaffir corn boiled in water, pumpkins, beans and sugar cane; bread was made from kaffir corn and they grilled meat over open fires. One of their main staples was thick milk which was kept in skins until it curdled. They made beer from the local corn. This simple diet and open air life resulted in people reaching great ages and old folk of 100 or 120 years were said not to be uncommon. They had no written language but loved to spend time listening to and telling stories, posing riddles, inventing aphorisms and proverbs, and listening to the panegyrics of their bards which told of great deeds in hunting and war.

They sound very much like 'noble savages'. And after listing some of their virtues such as energy, resolution, enterprise, cheerfulness, frankness, kindness, etc., Ellenberger turns them into human beings with the sentence, 'But they had their bad qualities as well.' And we find that they were often selfish and jealous, were given to lying and cheating, frequently stole things and enjoyed illicit sex—which went to show that they were no better and no worse than anyone else.

4

IT took Casalis, Arbousset and Gossellin almost three years to settle into their new life and although Casalis put a brave face on things in his books, it is not difficult to read between the lines. At times he suffered terribly from loneliness and a mind-sapping *ennui* which he considered the particular burden of Frenchmen who are transported to alien lands. At times he was on the edge of suicide, at others, the celibacy he was forced to endure seemed to have a deleterious effect on him.

Three days after they had decided to make Moriah their base, Krotz and his hunters began the long trek back to Philippolis and, with only a tent, a wagon and a few belongings, Casalis and his friends were left utterly alone in so wild a landscape that not even the great herds of antelope appeared to have seen human beings before. 'They did not seem to trouble themselves about our presence,' Casalis wrote.

They started by building a rough cabin of tree-trunks comprising three small rooms, one in front which served as a sitting-room, a second which was the bedroom and a third in which they kept their equipment. There were no proper windows or doors but they left a few holes which allowed enough light to read by day and which at night they stuffed up with clothing. They killed a sheep or antelope once a week and hung its carcass from one of the roof-beams. It was an uncomfortable house but it only took a week to build and was not meant to be more than a stop-gap until Gossellin built their permanent home of stone.

Six weeks later Casalis made the long journey to Philippolis to buy tools and livestock. He also brought back slips of peach, apricot, fig, apple and quince trees. He bought a herd of heifers at seventeen shillings and sixpence a head, sheep at three shillings and several horses. Like all true Frenchmen, he suffered agonies because they had no flour for bread, so he brought back wheat as well as vegetable seed and potatoes. It was a hazardous journey. The country was infested with lions, but he reached Moriah in safety. A small colony had grown up around the cabin. Moshesh's son, Molapo, and a group of young men had built grass huts near by and were, on the King's orders, to help the missionaries start their farm.

Soon Casalis settled into the routine of building. 'The labours of the first three years were extremely fatiguing,' he wrote. 'The hardest came first; those demanded by the preparation of materials of construction. During entire months we were doing nothing except hewing stones, working lumps of clay for bricks, with our trousers turned up to the knees, cutting down trees and sawing them into beams and planks. Of all our work nothing was so trying as this last. ... At times one might have seen us all three stretched on our backs, exhausted, quite out of breath. ... The natives would look at us with open mouths, seeking vainly to comprehend the view of life which could lead men to kill themselves to provide so simple an affair as a shelter from the sun and rain.'

Although they were cut off from the society of other white people by the vast distances, they managed to send and receive letters, in spite of the fact that the nearest post office was at Graaff-Reinet, about three hundred miles away. Almost a year passed before they received letters written by their parents just after they had left France. Post would simply lie in Graaff-Reinet until a traveller, black or white, was going in their direction. No letters were ever lost. Later the missionaries were able to organize a postal route which speeded things up slightly; a reply from Europe now only took an average of ten months to reach them. 'In such conditions,' Casalis wrote, 'correspondence is a trial rather than a consolation.'

This feeling of bereftness, of being cut off in the midst of southern Africa, began to get him down. He started 'in [his] secret heart to nourish the unworthy hope that my life would not be a long one'. To make matters worse, he received news that his father had died. 'In the first burst of my grief there was mingled a feeling akin to remorse. It was this element which gave it its bitterest pang. I seemed to myself to have killed my father.'

He was lucky that Gossellin was a practical man not given to fancies. One evening as they were seated outside the cabin, Gossellin pointed out a strip of turf under some young olive trees and offered to dig one shovelful of earth from it each day. When Casalis asked the reason Gossellin replied, 'When the hole is finished you will be just ready to be put into it!' He continued, 'Family affection is no longer a benediction when it unmans the heart, instead of fortifying it. You, so young, and yet to be thinking of ending. Why, we haven't begun yet!' Casalis said that these words were just enough to make him pull himself together.

His father's death proved to him that they were no longer regarded as strangers, for when the news got about people arrived from all sides. Moshesh sent a deputation to offer his sympathy and Casalis broke down. When he recovered he told them that his father had gone to Heaven. This confounded them for, according to their beliefs, the dead travelled in the opposite direction, sinking into the bowels of the earth.

The bereavement also had the effect of convincing the Basuto that the missionaries were not simply going to disappear one day. They had fully expected Casalis to return to France to take possession of property which they felt his father must have left him. Once they realized that the missionaries were a permanent fixture, more and more Basuto began to build huts near by and soon, under the command of another of Moshesh's sons, Letsie, there was a community of between three and four hundred people

* * *

The stone house at Moriah began to take shape; vegetables grew, and so did wheat; the fruit trees put on leaf. Slowly the mission was coming to grips with the country and the people and more time could be given to the original reason for coming to Africa. The missionaries realized that twenty miles from Thaba Bosiu was too great a distance and decided that someone must settle there if the mission was to be a success. Casalis volunteered. But the stock of furniture and utensils

was only sufficient for the mission house so once more he had
to make the long journey into the Cape Colony and back again.
When he came to leave Moriah there were touching scenes,
for although he would not be going far, the missionaries knew
they would seldom see each other. Gossellin came with Casalis
to help build a small shack on a hillock below Thaba Bosiu,
then he returned to Moriah.

'Then commenced for me,' Casalis wrote, 'a kind of life
which was the quintessence of all the difficulties and all the
vexations which I had known up to then, but of which I had
before borne only a third. *Vae soli*! "Woe to the solitary!"
I experienced in its every phase, from the time of my waking
till the hour of sleep, and during the watches of the night, the
terrible truth of that word.' He tried to counteract his loneliness by work; he started a small school, he visited the huts,
he preached, he helped to improve agriculture, he advised on
the construction of bigger dwellings. But gradually the panacea
itself began to overwhelm him. 'When was I to find time for
it,' he wrote, 'obliged as I was to prepare as well as I could,
my own meals, repair my clothes and linen, and keep up a
measure of order and decency about me?'

He spent a great deal of time brooding about this question
and realized that if he had no help he could not go on. He
needed a companion. Marriage! The very thought, he said,
made him tremble. 'I, who was already more than half a
savage . . . where and how to find the other?' But clearly the
need for a wife had been in his mind for some time for he had
already written to the Society in Paris as well as to his
mother to get their permission. So he set off on his travels
once more, this time a horse-back journey all the way to Cape
Town, where he found a wife, Sarah Dyke, whom he married
in April 1836, returning with her to Lesotho after two months.
They spent some time at Moriah, then moved to Thaba Bosiu.
Casalis's unique position among the Basuto might have suffered had they taken a dislike to his wife. As it was, he could
hardly have done better. Mrs Casalis, with her blue eyes and
fair skin, was at first an object of wonder, then, as she nursed
the sick and worked tirelessly among children and old people
she was taken into the Basuto family like her husband and
given the name 'Ma-Eugene' after the birth of her first child.

These years were vital for the Basuto, in view of what was to come. It is quite possible that if Casalis had delayed going to Thaba Bosiu for a few years he might never have been allowed to settle there, for, by the 1840s, white pressure on the Kingdom was enormous and the elders of the Basuto people might well have persuaded the King not to allow white people—including the French missionaries—to settle anywhere near them. But he was in time. And although he never succeeded in making a Christian out of Moshesh, and although Moshesh did not always take his advice, Casalis's influence on the development of Lesotho was very great.

However, before these political crises followed each other, he had begun his mission work at Thaba Bosiu, actively assisted by Moshesh. Whenever he wished to preach, Moshesh ordered his public crier to call everyone together, including the women and children. The tribal elders at first did not care to be humiliated by the presence of females, but Moshesh was firm. When the women, fearful or embarrassed at what might happen, sent their children in their places, Moshesh would call out, 'Where are the women?' Then, when they had shuffled forward and squatted down in shy groups, the King would turn to Casalis, standing on a specially built platform, and say, 'They are here. Begin.'

Often at night Moshesh would invite Casalis to one of his huts where they would talk. Sometimes the King's advisers would be there as well and they would discuss their different ideas of the world, humanity and the Creation. One night Casalis promulgated the doctrinal thesis that God created Man of one blood.

'What?' cried one of the tribal elders. 'That can never be. You are white; we are black: how could we come from the same father?' Moshesh turned on him, pointing out that in his herds there were white, red and spotted cattle. Did they not all come from the same stock and belong to the same master? On another occasion when Moshesh was discussing his basic belief in the unity of mankind he made one of those remarks that come ringing down the years. 'Black or white,' he said, 'we laugh or cry in the same manner; what gives pleasure or pain to the one race, causes equally pleasure or pain to the other.'

A great friendship grew up over the years between the two men and Casalis became one of the most powerful figures in the Kingdom. Moshesh called him 'my white man' and would send for him at any time to ask his advice or just to chat. The King seems to have been something of an insomniac for he would often take Casalis into an empty hut at night and they would talk for hours on end, sometimes until the first rays of dawn. He would then rise, go to the door of the hut, call out, 'Ah! Dia ha!' ('I have seen the light'), and return to his hut and go to sleep, leaving Casalis to go wearily off about his business. Casalis was told that this unfailing cry of joy at the first hint of dawn was a daily reminder to Moshesh of the time when, hemmed in by enemies, he went to sleep each night with the thought that he would be killed before morning.

The most serious division between the two was over the vexed question of polygamy and Casalis chipped away at the King over the years, without success. 'The subject often came up in our conversations. We (the missionaries) never introduced it in a special or direct manner in our preaching because we well knew that a reformation in this matter could only be the natural and spontaneous fruit of a cordial adoption of the great Christian principle. But Moshesh made no difficulty about discussing it with us.

'"You are right", he would say. "Even with us there have been, in all time, men here and there who were content with one wife, and, far from blaming them, they have always been cited as models. Since we do not admit that one woman has the right to several husbands, one does not see why a man should have the right to several wives. And then if you knew what these women make us suffer by their quarrels, and the rivalry which they foment amongst our children! . . . With all my herds and my stocks of grain, there are days when I am in danger of dying of hunger because all my wives are sulking with me, sending me from one to the other. . . . Our women age quickly, and then we cannot resist the temptation of taking younger ones. Amongst the older women there are some who become idle and they are the first to advise us to take another wife, hoping to make a servant of her."'

Moshesh described polygamy as a strong citadel and feared

that neither Casalis nor his colleagues would be able to shake it, and he pointed out that it took a long time to get white people to content themselves with one wife. 'We will talk of this again,' he would say, leaving the subject wide open. 'It is certainly annoying there should be this difference between you and us. Without that we should soon be Christians.'

5

WHILE MOSHESH was testing his dialectic in these sessions with Casalis, and while the mission at Moriah was gradually expanding and extending its influence, things were happening beyond the encircling mountains that were going to have a profound effect on Lesotho; it was about to be dragged, however unwillingly, into the arena of white power politics. As scheduled, the slaves had been freed and as foreseen the way it had been done had caused widespread dissatisfaction, setting off the Great Trek.

In 1836 hundreds of farmers of Dutch and French extraction left British authority and crossed the Orange River into what they considered was no-man's-land and is now known as the Orange Free State, Natal and the Transvaal; some pressed farther and farther into the interior, others decided to settle as soon as they were beyond British jurisdiction. However, under a scheme put forward by Dr Philip, Casalis's friend and mentor at the Cape, the Cape Colony was now ringed by statelets ruled by the Griqua chiefs Adam Kok and Andries Waterboer, and a third by Moshesh. When the Griquas tried to enforce their rule on the trekkers they were ignored. But Moshesh could not be ignored. In the early 1840s his tribe was estimated to be between thirty and forty thousand strong; he had the ear and the sympathy of his missionaries—more stations had been founded by both French and Wesleyan missions—and he watched the settlement of farmers near his borders with displeasure; he himself was planning to expand his territory and increase the size of his nation.

Events to the north and north-east of him had conspired to make this dream a possibility. Moselekatze and his Matabele had been defeated by the Boer trekkers and driven across the Limpopo River into what is now Rhodesia and, closer to home, Dingane, Shaka's heir, was defeated by the Boers at Blood River. All the shattered tribes which had been living from hand to mouth since the *difaqane* now came out into the sun once more. From his eyrie in fortress-Lesotho, Moshesh watched this particular change thoughtfully. The two most powerful black leaders in southern Africa had been eliminated and he had the whole field to himself. The historian George McCall Theal, who had no love for blacks, wrote, 'This is crediting him [Moshesh] with powers of observation greater than those of all the officers of the Colonial Government and of all the missionaries with the different tribes. But it is no more than his due. For ages the Bantu have been developing this peculiar kind of intelligence, and Moshesh was the cleverest man that the race has produced in modern times.'

His general unease at the arrival near him of white trekkers was intensified by several incidents, two of which left lasting impressions. In the first, one of the trek leaders, Piet Retief, managed by trickery to handcuff Sikonyela, now chief of the Batlokwa. He was told he would only be released when disputed cattle were returned. That a chief could be so treated had a great effect on the Basuto and in the future it provided Moshesh with an excuse on several occasions not to meet white officials. When he did meet them he almost always insisted that Casalis or another of the missionaries go with him.

The second incident concerned one of the ablest of the trekker leaders, Andries Willem Pretorius, who tried and executed an envoy from Dingane. This act, which Theal describes as 'a great mistake and a great crime', horrified the Basuto even more. It was one of their most sacred laws that an ambassador was sacrosanct. Casalis quoted this in his book, *The Basutos*: 'The person of a messenger is inviolable. This principle has passed into a proverb: *Lengosa ga le molatu* (a delegate can have no fault).' What particularly appalled the Basuto was that the whites were Christians yet they respected neither the person of a chief nor the life of a chief's messenger.

Much of the history of South Africa is the story of boundary and border disputes, from the time of the first settlement when the Hottentots, the original people of the Cape of Good

Hope, found themselves excluded from certain areas by decree of the Dutch East India Company, to the mid-nineteenth century when there were constant border disputes between Bantu and British, Bantu and Boer, Bantu and Bantu, and British and Boer. A series of Xhosa wars was fought on the eastern frontier in which the names of boundary rivers —the Kei, the Keiskama, the Great Fish, the Sundays—pass like signposts in a colonial nightmare. The history of these border disputes, and their manifold results, is so complex as to make even the most political of historians blench.

What happened is what had already happened in the Old Kingdom of Congo and in every other black kingdom where whites had arrived; two irreconcilable philosophies had met head on: the black and white conception of land-holding. As has already been said, the black view was that the land belonged in perpetuity to the tribe which held it, it was indivisible. This clashed violently with the white philosophy of private ownership and the sanctity of property. What made it worse was that while the whites wanted everything down on paper, exact definitions, exact boundaries, the black kings consciously tended to leave them vague.

By the beginning of the 1840s things were building up to the first disputes between Moshesh and the Boers who had settled along the lower Caledon River. Some were beyond even the most shadowy of his boundaries; others were well within. At the beginning they were received by Moshesh on terms of friendship and allowed to build houses, plant crops and graze cattle. It was a vast, underpopulated landscape and there was plenty of room for everyone. But the Boers were 'settlers'. The very act of building a house and planting crops meant they were staking their claim to the land, they were putting down roots. In Moshesh's view they were simply occupying the land at his pleasure; neither he nor anyone else could divide it up for private ownership. It was not long before cattle thefts began to disrupt the early harmony. The same thing was happening in the two Griqua states but on a much greater scale. However, most of the Griqua clans were under the protection of the powerful London Missionary Society. The Society put pressure on the British Government and Britain warned the emigrant farmers not to interfere with the Griquas or the Basutos. This meant that the Boers had no rights of protection in these territories, something that added fuel to the anti-British feeling many of them had nurtured since birth.

In 1843 Moshesh signed a treaty with Britain by which he was to receive £75 a year either in money or arms, in return for holding his part of the frontier of the Cape Colony against all comers; to surrender all criminals and fugitives; and generally to act as an ally of the Cape Administration. The treaty also made an attempt at defining what these borders were but since they had been neither surveyed nor discussed Moshesh was placed, for an annual pittance, in a difficult situation. There were immediate protests by the Wesleyan missionaries at Thaba Nchu who suddenly found themselves part of Moshesh's territory when they had considered the huge tracts of land surrounding their mission to be held by them on behalf of their Baralong and Griqua flocks. Letters of protest and explanation began to fly between the Cape Government and the Orange River area.

Beyond Moshesh's boundaries, tension was growing between the Boers and Adam Kok's Griquas. There were disputes, then incidents. A Boer force took the field, a British flying column raced up from the Cape and dispersed it. This column, small though it was, had a great influence on Moshesh. It consisted of two squadrons of the 7th Dragoon Guards wearing brass helmets and red coats and carrying rifles as well as the traditional swords; two guns, six-pounders of the Royal Artillery; two companies of the 91st Regiment (1st Battalion of the Argyll and Sutherland Highlanders), and two troops of the Cape Mounted Rifles, which was a mixed force of whites and Hottentots. All the men were well-armed and well-mounted and the sight of them reinforced Moshesh's early decision to concentrate on cavalry and guns in his own army.

Speeches were made, a shaky peace established, boundaries were marked and a small detachment of fifty-eight troopers under Captain (late Major) Warden were left to keep the peace in an area of about fifty thousand square miles. Encroachment continued, so did cattle-reiving by both white and black, with the resulting recovery raids. The country was in an uproar. On the Cape Colony's eastern border, British troops were engaged in a seemingly never-ending series of wars, the Kaffir Wars, with Bantu tribes. In the midst of this Moshesh was expected, without help, to maintain his boundaries and keep his country stable.

It was at this point that a new figure entered the history of Lesotho. He was Sir Harry Smith, a soldier's soldier who exploded on to the veld like a firecracker. He gave the impression of never being still, never weary, always in motion. Major-General Sir Harry George Wakelyn Smith, to give him his full title, was born in 1787 and by the time he entered Moshesh's life had served in South America, had fought in the Peninsular War and at Waterloo, and had earned the title, the 'Victor of Aliwal' after his famous victory in 1846 when he defeated a Sikh army at the village of Aliwal in the Punjab. A portrait of him painted in 1856 when he was sixty-nine shows a man still young-looking for his years, with the face of a country squire who might have been found galloping through the pages of Surtees. There is also a look of the Duke of Wellington about him, big-nosed and long-faced.

As a dashing young captain, he had been at the siege of Badajoz in Spain in 1812. When the town fell, British troops ran amok. In his book, *The Age of Elegance*, Sir Arthur Bryant described what happened:

'The men, separated in the darkness from their officers, parched with thirst and half-mad from the fury of the attack, broke into the cellars and wineshops. By dawn they had become a mob of fiends. They had been promised, in accordance with the rules of war, that if the garrison resisted after the breaches had been made, the city would be given up to sack . . . Women were dragged screaming from hiding holes and raped, wine casks were broached in the streets, and satyrs with blackened faces drank till the liquor ran from their mouths and ears. No officer could control them . . .

'Down at the camp below the town, where the British wounded lay in thousands, two young officers, standing at their tent door on the day after the attack, saw two Spanish ladies approaching, the elder of whom, her ears torn and bleeding from the grasp of drunken savages, confided to their protection her sister, a girl of fifteen. Such was her faith in the British character, she declared, that she knew the appeal would not be in vain. "Nor was it", wrote one of the officers. "Nor could it be abused for she stood by the side of an angel— a being more transcendently lovely than any I had ever before beheld. To look at her was to love her—and I did love her, but I never told her my love, and in the meantime another and a more impudent fellow stepped in and won her!" Two days later Juanita Maria de los Dolores de Leon was married to Captain Harry Smith of the Rifles. The Commander-in-Chief gave her away, and she became the darling of the Army, henceforward sharing all its adventures and hardships. Many years later, when her husband, the Victor of Aliwal, had become the hero of Victorian England and Governor of the Cape, she gave her name to a South African town destined to become the scene of another famous siege.' This was Ladysmith which was besieged for 130 days in the Boer War.

Sir Harry was just the sort of person the Cape colonists loved: he had fought in the war of 1835 and now, at sixty, he was back in the country as Governor and High Commissioner, having gone on record as guaranteeing he would finish any future Kaffir War in three weeks at the most. Unhappily, while he knew the old trade of warfare, he knew little or nothing about civil administration. That did not deter him. In January, 1848, he rode north with only his personal staff to see what chance there was of bringing the trekkers back into the British fold. It was plain there was none. So instead he proclaimed 'the Sovereignty of Her Majesty the Queen of England over the Territories north of the Great Orange River, including the countries of Moshesh, Moroko, Moletsane, Sikonyela, Adam Kok, Gert Taaibosch, and other minor chiefs as far north as the Vaal River, and east to the Drakensberg . . .' This meant that the trekkers had to become British subjects or move on once again. And, while Sir Harry disclaimed any intention of increasing British territory, his proclamation was, in effect, one of the largest annexations in South African history.

The declaration of the Sovereignty was made in the small trekker village of Winburg in February. Moshesh was there, so was Casalis. Casalis wrote: 'His Excellency [Smith] was very gracious, spoke to me in French (very well); recalled the Pyrénées and the Battle of Orthez, at which he had been present; complimented Moshesh on his skill in horsemanship; told him that he knew him well, and had often heard him spoken of; made him a present of two new saddles of the latest make, of a marquee tent, a gold watch (all this whilst cantering for half an hour); asked him if the country of Winburg belonged to the Basutos to which Moshesh replied in the affirmative ... We entered the village under a fire of musketry.' Sir Harry told Moshesh that although the muskets made the sound of war they were being used now as a sign of peace to which Moshesh replied in his most pious voice, 'Peace is the mother of nations.' They spent some time talking together in Sir Harry's tent and Moshesh mentioned the disputes existing between himself and several other chiefs including Sikonyela and Moroko. 'Trust me,' said Sir Harry, 'and no one will dare to raise his hand against the Great Chief of the Basutos.' Then, according to Casalis, he raised his right hand about a foot above the desk and said, 'Moshesh is like this.' Then, raising his left hand another foot above the right he said, 'But Her Majesty is as this!...'

Soon afterwards he called a meeting with the Boers and presented Moshesh to them. Holding him by the hand he told them they were indebted to Moshesh for the peace they had enjoyed. He said: 'Let no man move from his place on which he is, and let no man presume to encroach upon Moshesh.' If they spoke of revolt and were determined to recommence their oppressions in other parts he, the Governor, would 'follow them' up, even though it were to the gates of the infernal regions!

Before Sir Harry dashed back to the Cape, he and Moshesh exchanged letters denouncing the farmers. They were published and gave the trekkers further cause for disenchantment. A bare six months later, the farmers were once more in arms, this time having called on their compatriots north of the Vaal to come to their aid. Major Warden and his small body of men were no match for them. The Boer leader Pretorius forced him to cross the Orange River under a safe conduct but not before Warden had sent a letter to Moshesh apprising him of the situation. Moshesh had been waiting for what he called the fight between the two 'white bulls' and he now lay low, watching and waiting. Sir Harry, on the other hand, went off like a rocket. On July 29 he and his staff left Cape Town in three horse-drawn wagons and, travelling at six miles an hour, they reached Colesberg, 615 miles to the north, on August 9. By the 27th he and his mixed force of regulars and Griquas numbering about five hundred was across the Orange River and marching towards Bloemfontein. The two forces met at Boomplaats, and Sir Harry won an easy victory. Once again he disappeared south, leaving Warden and his small force to rule the Sovereignty.

Moshesh had been watching the events with troubled interest and drew two conclusions: he was certain now that of the opposing white races the most powerful, and therefore the one with which he would side, was the British. But they had a habit of vanishing south leaving him to defend his own lands, so it seemed only prudent to increase his strength as much as he could. The Basuto were ordered to find horses and guns any way they could; by working for white farmers or by stealing them if necessary. Gun-running had started on the borders of the black states and the Basuto welcomed unscrupulous white dealers. Since the Napoleonic wars, most of the world's active armies had been re-armed with percussion-lock muskets and there were hundreds of thousands of obsolete flintlocks lying about the Continent and Britain. A fair proportion found their way into Lesotho in exchange for cattle, and in a few years Moshesh was able to field a force of about seven thousand men, well-mounted and adequately armed.

6

'FOR some years,' Casalis wrote, 'the incessant pressure of the whites appears to have opened the eyes of the natives: their attention was more drawn to whatever affected their common interests: the chiefs became more indispensable to their subjects and the idea of a general confederation of the tribes formed for the purpose of making headway against a foreign race seemed to grow every day.'[1]

[1] This vital passage, as Tylden points out, appears only in the original French version of *Les Bassoutos* and was never, for some reason, translated.

It is likely that the growing unease among the tribes was the start of an anti-white feeling. Tylden wrote: 'However much Moshesh might profit by his association with white people, and there is no doubt he did profit and fully realized it, there was much to cause him serious uneasiness. As time went on that uneasiness grew.' What particularly worried him was the off-hand manner and lack of dignity with which the British had been treating tribal chiefs who expected and received immense respect not only from their own people but from all other tribes. Moshesh's network of messengers going backwards and forwards across the Drakensberg into Natal and the Eastern Cape brought him similar stories from all parts of the country. Nor could he understand how the British (i.e. white people) could take the side of groups of Hottentots, whom Moshesh considered treacherous, against the trekkers, who were also white. Another difficulty for Moshesh was the religion which Casalis and Arbousset had brought to his country. They had preached peace on earth. Yet he had only to look around him to see that all the whites were at least as warlike as the Bantu themselves. Moshesh's fertile mind evolved a philosophy to capitalize on the situation. In general he wanted a confederation of black tribes to counteract white pressure and, in particular, as a backstop, so to speak, in case this did not work, an alliance with Britain. But the alliance was proving difficult because of the Basutos' desire to run with the hare and hunt with the hounds. While proclaiming friendship with Britain, they, at the same time, ignored Warden and his boundary—the Warden Line—between Boer and Basuto and continued their depredations in the Sovereignty. Indeed, two of Moshesh's sons, Letsie and Nehemiah, who had been educated at the Cape, returned to Lesotho and immediately began raiding cattle. In one raid against Sikonyela, the Basutos, according to Major Warden, lifted 73 horses, 6,303 cattle, 2,470 sheep and 2,966 goats. They did so with Moshesh's connivance, for cattle-raiding was in the direct Basuto tradition of proving one's manhood; it was the way Moshesh had proved his own, the way he had gathered his power. Complaints reached Warden, who wrote to Sir Harry.

'It is evident to me,' Sir Harry replied, 'that Moshesh is acting dishonestly and that the ambition of his sons has prompted him to the improper line he has pursued. Your suggestion therefore that this Chief must be humbled ... must be carried out ... If Moshesh shuts himself up in his mountain ... I believe some howitzer shells may be thrown upon him ...' Sir Godfrey Lagden, who was High Commissioner in Lesotho later on, says in his book, *The Basutos*, 'In these words are to be read the first rumblings of the wars to follow later. Sir Harry Smith had clearly flung away the scabbard.'

Moshesh quickly became the focus of Major Warden's displeasure. After a Basuto attack on Chief Moroko near Thaba Nchu, Warden wrote to Sir Harry, 'The Basuto people are proud and insolent towards their neighbours ... the time is not distant, I imagine, when it will be necessary to place them under restraint. ... The Basuto require humbling ...' To Moshesh Warden wrote, 'Depend upon it that however strong you may imagine yourself to be, there is a stronger hand ready to punish the wicked doings of a people ten times more powerful than the Basuto.' Moshesh ignored him and during the months that followed the cattle raiding increased. Warden became more and more angry, and it is easy to see why. He had an impossible job trying to police an area of fifty thousand square miles where the blacks and half-castes were natural cattle-reivers, the whites were natural land-grabbers and Moshesh, sitting like some great spider in his web of mountains, must have seemed the worst of all with his pious replies to letters of accusation, his clever French missionaries, his reluctance to come off his mountain for meetings and his willingness to sign papers agreeing to boundaries he had no intention of keeping. In June, 1851, Warden wrote to him demanding six thousand 'good cattle' and three hundred horses in fines and reparations. He ordered them to be delivered within ten days—an impossible demand. By the time Moshesh received the letter a mixed force of about a thousand comprising, British, Griquas, Baralongs and some Boers who did not mind in whose company they fought as long as it was against Moshesh, was perched on his borders. Warden had had enough. 'Prosecute the war ...' Sir Harry had written, and this he was doing. But Moshesh had long been prepared for such a contingency.

When the combined column advanced they were attacked by a vassal tribe of the Basutos, the Bataung, from the steep-sided heights of Viervoot Hill. Warden ordered Major Donovan, who had command of the troops, to storm the heights. But neither of the two six-pounder guns could be man-handled up the seven-hundred-foot slopes. The British and Boers halted at the top. The Baralong advanced, chasing away a few Bataung cattle guards and reached the nearest village. There they found beer. In a short time most were too drunk to fight. The battle had begun at seven in the morning, by eleven the Basuto force arrived. One of the guns was nearly captured and was hastily withdrawn. The Boers were set the task of trying to extricate the Baralong. By mid-afternoon the combined force, which had lost 152 killed, was in retreat. The humiliation was completed and the Sovereignty lay open to whatever Moshesh might do against it.[1]

Here again he showed his diplomatic skill. He made no move; he had previously warned the farmers not to join Warden's force—most had not served—and he now contented himself with minor raids on those who had been unwise enough to fight him.

The battle of Viervoot had widespread repercussions. The French missionaries wrote a memorial to the British Government in which they not only gave an eye-witness account of the fight but the reasons leading up to it. 'We think', they wrote, 'there has been an unwarrantable disregard of the rights, the past history, the different habits, the relative position and the respective wants of the native population. This had led the natives to suspect the Government of a disposition to *divide in order to reign* ... Natural rights, past grievances, past benefits, past engagements and treaties, feudal allegiances, kindred ties, family bonds, have been discarded and overlooked.

'Moshesh has been placed on a level with chieftains whom he had received in the land ... This astounding mode of

---

[1] Curiously enough, a black writer, S. M. Molema, gives a different outcome. In his book, *The Basuto Past and Present*, published in 1920, he wrote, 'In the interests of the Orange Free State they [the British] reinforced by the Thaba Ncho Baralongs *attacked* [his italics] Moshesh and defeated him at Vierfirt [*sic*].'

government has been crowned by employing one tribe against another ... A chief who would have had no objection to meeting the British Resident (Warden) personally is filled with indignation by the prospect of finding himself surrounded by men with whom he has been at war in bygone days and who are ready to exult in his humiliation ... Limits have been made in the very centre of the territory of Moshesh (the Batlokwa had been settled nearer him) contrary to the solemn promises made to him in conferences with the highest English authorities ... nothing less than the prospect of irretrievable ruin could prompt us to speak as we do this day. The perversion of the feelings of the people is already frightful. War will drive them completely back to barbarism. No resource remains to them if vanquished than to take refuge in the recesses and strongholds of their mountains. This once accomplished, it may be safely predicted, that the Sovereignty will be untenable for civilized men during many years.'

The memorial was undoubtedly partial but its weight, coming on top of pressure by the London Missionary Society, made an impression on the British Government, and the Colonial Secretary, Lord Grey, wrote that 'the ultimate abandonment of the Orange Sovereignty should be a settled point in our policy'. The British Government had never wanted the Sovereignty, indeed, they did not even want South Africa, except for the Cape Peninsula as a revictualling stop on the voyage to India. 'They were weary of kaffir wars,' wrote the historian Eric A. Walker, 'which only seemed to benefit land speculators and shop-keepers who naturally liked a large garrison; the Sovereignty was worthless in their eyes ...'

There was a flurry of activity: Sir Harry Smith was recalled; a two-man commission, Major Hogge and Mr Owen, was sent to the Sovereignty and signed the Sand River Convention with the Boers declaring that Britain had no interest in and would not attempt to rule the land across the Vaal River. This meant a further exodus of farmers away from the Sovereignty, away from British rule, to the present Transvaal. In the Sovereignty the commissioners dismissed a few officials, and condemned the Warden Line as unjust to the Basutos, but demanded huge reparations from Moshesh for earlier crimes. Warden himself was replaced.

But nothing changed. The cattle-raiding by both sides on the border grew worse. Something final had to be done to bring about peace. A new man was sent out from Britain. He was Sir George Cathcart who replaced Sir Harry Smith. Following Smith's policy, he had ended the latest Kaffir War—which had been fought on the eastern coast of the country near the present towns of East London and King William's Town—and now he could turn his attention to the Sovereignty. In December, 1852, he mobilized 2,500 men at the village of Burgersdorp in the north-east section of the Cape Colony.

Lieutenant-General Sir George Cathcart was a very different man from Smith. Unlike Sir Harry, who always looked upon himself as a plain soldier, Cathcart was the son of an earl. During his army career he had seen service in 1813 in Germany and 1814 in France, and had become a favourite of the Duke of Wellington, whose influence had secured him the governorship of the Cape. His portrait shows a man of imperious bearing with a determined mouth but sensitive eyes. The historian Cory describes him as 'tall and slim and one of the kindest and gentlest of men'. He was predisposed in favour of the blacks—which was just as well since the British Government's policy was one of *rapprochement* with the tribes—and ended up with no great opinion of the white colonists, a feeling that was reciprocated in some quarters. He was in favour of abandoning the Sovereignty, but first he, too, considered that Moshesh needed to be taught a lesson.

'There yet remained one rankling sore to be healed before it could safely be said that all was peace and that the maintenance of a large force could safely be dispensed with,' he wrote to the British Secretary of State. 'I allude to the protracted state of petty warfare which exists in the Sovereignty between the dependents of the paramount Basuto chief, Moshesh, and a portion of the burgher (farmer) population bordering on his territory.'

And again: 'If I make war on Moshesh, it must be on good grounds and a well-established *casus belli*, and then it must be no small war.'

He also decided that he would use only regular troops and would not ask white farmers, Griquas, Koranas or Baralongs to help him. His force comprised two thousand infantry, five hundred cavalry and two guns. He thought it perfectly adequate. Now he only needed the *casus belli*. From his encampment at Burgersdorp he crossed the Orange River in very hot weather and arrived at the Wesleyan mission of Platberg a few miles north-west of Thaba Bosiu on December 13, 1852. The following day he sent a letter to Moshesh demanding, in reparation for previous raids, a total of ten thousand cattle and one thousand horses. This was somewhat less than Hogge and Owen had asked for but Cathcart demanded that they should be delivered *in three days*. The following day Moshesh arrived at the British camp with Casalis and a number of counsellors. Hundreds of Basuto who had tried to accompany him were driven back by the King with his riding-crop. Moshesh was dressed in a blue jacket, gold-laced trousers and a cap. The Governor and his staff were also splendid in gold braid and stood outside a marquee to greet Moshesh. The Basuto delegation were led to three tents where food and drink awaited them. When they had refreshed themselves the conference began, Casalis and his brother-in-law, Dyke, acting as interpreters. It was, by any standards, a remarkable confrontation and an official minute exists. After the briefest of pleasantries they got down to business.

GOVERNOR: I will not now talk much, but wish to know whether you received my message yesterday, in which I made the demand for cattle and horses. I have nothing to alter in that letter.

MOSHESH: Do you mean the letter I received from Mr Owen?

GOVERNOR: Yes.

MOSHESH: I received that letter, but do not know where I shall get the cattle from. Am I to understand that the ten thousand head demanded are a fine imposed for thefts committed by my people, in addition to the stolen cattle?

GOVERNOR: I demand but ten thousand, though your people have stolen many more, but consider this a just award, which must be paid in three days.

MOSHESH: Do the three days count from yesterday or today?

GOVERNOR: Today is the first of the three.

MOSHESH: The time is short and the cattle many. Will you not allow me six days to collect them?

GOVERNOR: You had time given you when Major Hogge and Mr Owen made the first demand and then you promised to comply with it, but did not.

MOSHESH: But I was not quite idle. Do not the papers in the Commissioner's hands show that I collected them?

GOVERNOR: They do. But not half the number.

MOSHESH: That is true, but I have not now control enough over my people to induce them to comply with the demand, however anxious I may be to do so.

GOVERNOR: If you are not able to collect them, I must go and do it; and if any resistance be made it will then be war, and I shall not be satisfied with ten thousand head, but shall take all I can.

MOSHESH: Do not talk of war, for, however anxious I may be to avoid it, you know that a dog when beaten will show his teeth.

GOVERNOR: It will therefore be better that you should give up the cattle than that I should go for them.

MOSHESH: I wish for peace; but have the same difficulty with my people that you have in the colony. Your prisons are never empty, and I have thieves among my people.

GOVERNOR: I would then recommend you to catch the thieves and bring them to me and I will hang them.

MOSHESH: I do not wish you to hang them, but to talk to them and give them advice. If you hang them, they cannot talk.

GOVERNOR: If I hang them they cannot steal, and I am not going to talk any more, I have said that if you do not give up the cattle in three days, I must come and take them.

MOSHESH: I beg of you not to talk of war.

But Cathcart had come to do nothing else, and by giving Moshesh only three days to deliver ten thousand head of cattle—an almost impossible task—he had manufactured his own *casus belli*.

The dialogue between the two men sounds neutered, set down in the formal phraseology of Government minutes. There is another source. Sergeant James McKay of the 74th

157

Regiment (2nd Battalion Highland Light Infantry) was on guard that day. He recalled heated words and fists slamming on tables, the Governor springing to his feet saying that he would give Moshesh four days to bring in the cattle and horses (this was a late concession). And then, thumping the table again to emphasize his point, 'If they don't bring them, I will go and fetch them!' And Moshesh replying strongly, 'Well, your Excellency, you know that when a dog is kicked he generally turns and bites!'

The concession of the extra day did not, in the event, matter: the Basuto were never going to hand over ten thousand cattle. But days of grace had been offered and days of grace were taken; the troops sat down to wait. Besides the Royal Artillery, the force with Cathcart consisted of two squadrons 12th Royal Lancers, two companies Cape Mounted Rifles, four companies of the 2nd Queen's (the West Surrey Regiment), three companies of the 43rd Regiment (1st Battalion the Oxford & Bucks Light Infantry) and 73rd Regiment (2nd Battalion the Black Watch), four companies 74th Regiment (2nd Battalion the Highland Light Infantry) and one company of the 1st Battalion the Rifle Brigade. The officers and men were all veterans of the Kaffir Wars on the eastern frontier of the colony. The Rifle Brigade and a few specialists in other companies carried rifles which far outranged the Basuto muskets; but the rest of the force were armed with smooth-bore muskets not much better than the Basuto flintlocks. The Basuto, of course, could make no reply to the howitzers and rocket tubes.

The wait could not have been too arduous for the troops for it was typical High Veld summer weather of warm sunny days and afternoon thunderstorms which cooled the air and settled the dust. They were extremely well victualled. Their supply train comprised 164 wagons—the entire column occupied six miles on the march—and to their surprise they had been able to buy such luxuries as Crosse and Blackwell's pickles, and bottles of Bass's India Pale Ale in the village of Burgersdorp.

On December 17 Cathcart broke his resolve not to use tribesmen. He sent guns and ammunition to Sikonyela's Batlokwa, Moshesh's most uncompromising enemies, and demanded their help if there was fighting. He also called on Moroko to place his Baralongs along the road to Bloemfontein to protect his line of communication. On the 18th, Nehemiah, one of Moshesh's sons, drove three thousand five hundred head of cattle, some in poor condition, into Cathcart's camp. They were escorted by five hundred mounted men and the British troops were able to view their enemy. The Basuto were described as being well mounted, riding on primitive saddles which hurt the backs of their ponies and using leather thongs for stirrups. They carried assegais in leather quivers on their backs, held a musket in one hand and many had a light battle-axe, the national weapon, tied to the saddle. On their heads, they wore balls made of ostrich feathers, jackals' tails and wildebeeste manes. With reason, they were described as 'wild-looking'. One of the French missionaries arrived to beg for more time, but no answer was given. Early on the morning of the 20th the British force crossed the Caledon River into Lesotho; what was to become officially known as the Affair at the Berea had begun.

7

BEREA MOUNTAIN, NAMED after a mission at its base, is really a high plateau with steep sides that made ascent difficult; such flat-topped plateaux and smaller hills—Thaba Bosiu itself, for instance—are not uncommon in southern Africa and are often to be seen rising out of bare plains. The Berea lay directly between Platberg mission and Thaba Bosiu and overlooked Moshesh's stronghold. Several precipitous paths led to the top where there was excellent grazing and springs of good water, ideal pasturage, easily defended. As Cathcart approached the plateau he saw herds of cattle on the top and since the capture of cattle was one of the objects of the expedition here was an opportunity not to be missed; he decided to take the Berea.

He split his force into three divisions, one under his own command, one under Colonel Eyre, which consisted mostly of infantry, pack mules and a few rockets; and a third, the mounted men, under Colonel Napier, Cape Mounted Rifles.

The plan was that Eyre should ascend the plateau, round up the cattle, drive them down the paths and join up with Napier, who was to circle the plateau's northern end, and the Governor, who would circle it to the south, on the plain before Thaba Bosiu. Both Eyre and Napier had orders not to fire unless fired upon. But when Napier's cavalry saw the cattle they could not resist them.

Tylden described what happened next: 'There is a fairly obvious and not very steep way up, and Napier, sending a troop from each regiment as advance guard, followed them on to the tableland. There were only cattle guards in front of him and these fired from behind a stone wall and were charged and dispersed by the advance guard. The top of the Berea is rolling country with dead ground everywhere and the cavalry soon found themselves galloping in scattered formation trying to collect cattle. The cattle, excited by the herds' calling and whistling, were half frantic and in one place it was only by shooting an ox and blocking a footpath off the hill that they could be stopped. At nine a.m. Casalis and Dyke at the mission at Thaba Bosiu were watching the Lancers up on the Berea firing their pistols at the cattle herds. By midday, Napier had begun to move off down his track of the morning with four thousand head of cattle. Major Tottenham, 12th Lancers, with thirty of his regiment, was acting as rearguard, and away to his proper left nearer the Berea mission was a party of both regiments. Molapo (another of Moshesh's sons), with his own men and some Bataung, about seven hundred men in all, had come up close to the rearguard and were waiting to attack. He put in a party of footmen from the nearest villages and then moved forward. He outflanked Tottenham and drove him off the plateau and also pushed the mixed detachment of both regiments away from the rearguard and off the hill. The best Tottenham could do was to rally at a wall half-way down the slope. Here he was reinforced by men collected by Napier and halted Molapo's advance. The Lancers had lost twenty men and were hard pressed. The Basuto swerved off to their right around the flank of the captured cattle and were charged by a troop of Lancers at the foot of the Berea, suffering casualties.'

Molapo had killed and wounded about fifteen per cent of Napier's force but had not managed to recapture the cattle.

He had, however, put Napier's men—who retired to the Caledon River camp—out of the fighting. Meanwhile Eyre had scaled the cliffs as ordered, but not without needless bloodshed. Before they started the climb his infantrymen had come upon a Basuto village and had killed several women and young girls: it is said in mitigation that the soldiers were used to fighting against the coast tribes on the eastern frontier who always evacuated non-combatants from the villages; whatever the excuse, the damage was done.

When Eyre reached the top he found himself, in his turn, among the cattle escaping from Napier's men. They managed to get together a herd of about fifteen hundred. While they were doing so a handful of Basuto wearing the white-covered undress caps and carrying lances of the 12th Lancers looted from the men who had been killed, infiltrated Eyre's troops. A Captain Faunce of the 73rd and three soldiers were unlucky enough to be taken prisoner. They were forced down the cliff path towards the Basuto village and there butchered by a hunch-back dwarf as a reprisal for the deaths of the women.

On the plateau Eyre had to face Molapo and the Basuto horse but by extending his men in a semi-circle and using his rockets he was able to hold on to the cattle. In the early afternoon heavy thunderstorms swept the Berea, causing the Basuto to seek shelter. About 4 p.m. Eyre was able to bring the cattle down and rendezvous with Cathcart on the plain. His losses had been slight.

Cathcart had marched south round the Berea without meeting any serious opposition and halted between the plateau and Thaba Bosiu. There he was joined by Eyre and, when the rain stopped, by about five thousand Basuto horsemen. They would not close but kept circling and wheeling as the howitzers dropped shell among them. Only a few casualties were inflicted. With evening drawing on Cathcart considered his position too exposed and he and Eyre fell back on a small village where they were able to pen the cattle in stone-walled kraals. Cathcart blamed Napier and Eyre for the setback. In despatches he complained of being left in the lurch while they had 'run wild after cattle', which he said did not accord with his orders. 'They are both fine fellows,' he wrote, 'but soldiers

161

will easily see that the fault is not mine that we did not make a better job of it.'

As darkness deepened the Basutos closed in, shouting and singing to the cattle. There were some racing oxen among them trained to obey calls and these became restless.[1] About 8 p.m. they communicated their unease to the rest of the herd and four hundred frantic beasts burst out of the kraal and got away. All that night the troops stood to their arms but no further attacks were launched.

When morning came, there was not a Basuto in sight yet the threat of their presence was enough to force a decision on Cathcart. In his despatches he compared them to Circassians and Cossacks and the possibility that they might come riding down on him again caused him to move back to the camp on the Caledon River. The British had lost thirty-eight killed and fourteen wounded; the Basuto twenty dead and twenty wounded. It was during Cathcart's retreat that Moshesh produced one of the great diplomatic masterstrokes of African history. Not long after the British column had reached the river camp an envoy arrived with a letter which Moshesh, Casalis and Nehemiah had composed the previous night.

From the CHIEF MOSHESH to the HIGH COMMISSIONER.

Thaba Bosigo,
Midnight, 20 Dec. 1852.

Your Excellency,

This day you have fought against my people and taken much cattle. As the object for which you have come is to have a compensation for Boers, I beg you will be satisfied with what you have taken. I entreat peace from you—you have shown your power—you have chastised—let it be enough I pray you; and let me be no longer considered an enemy to the Queen. I will try all I can to keep my people in order in the future.

Your humble servant,
(Signed) MOSHESH

[1] This was a popular Basuto sport. The oxen would come to a call, a whistle, or to a particular chant and race riderless several miles to the home kraal. Pots of beer would be wagered on the outcome.

Why had Moshesh decided to turn victory into defeat, at least on paper? There is no doubt that the Basuto themselves were exhausted by the previous day's fighting and that he dreaded the renewal of hostilities. But above all he was a pragmatist, and Lagden, who lived in Lesotho for sixteen years, wrote: 'The fact was that both Generals (Cathcart and Moshesh) were sincerely anxious to find a way out of their dilemma and an excuse to call it "Peace". Moshesh had spent a miserable night. He was conscious of victory and dreaded its consequences more than defeat. Every time he saw one of his warriors decked in the garments of a Lancer it must have sent a pang through him, for he knew that the memory of the dead soldiers on the mountain, mutilated probably by his wild people against his wishes, would assuredly yield a harvest of vengeance from all white people, who abhorred the idea that blacks should prevail against whites. Yet, it was a fair enough fight to which no exception was or could be taken. Still, the Chief was stirred with the instinct that nothing but an heroic measure could save him from retribution at the hands of the British with whom at all times he wanted to be friendly, for he believed they meant well enough, though their methods were strange. In the dead of night he roused his missionary, M. Casalis, in whose presence he ordered his educated son, Nehemiah, to write down the inspired words of the letter. The inspiration was that he should accord to General Cathcart the honours of the day, admit chastisement and render homage.'

Cathcart quickly accepted Moshesh's offer. While the envoy waited he wrote a letter to the King in which he said, among other things, 'The words are those of a great chief. But I care little for words, I judge men by their actions. I told you if you did not pay the fine I must go and take it; I am a man who never breaks his word. I have taken the fine by force and I am satisfied ... I now desire not to consider you, chief, as an enemy of the Queen, but I must proclaim martial law in the Sovereignty ... for though you are a great chief, it seems that you either do not or can not keep your own people from stealing ... now, therefore, Chief Moshesh, I consider your past obligation fulfilled.'

When Cathcart's reply and his attitude to Moshesh became

known in the camp there was considerable dissatisfaction. He was urged by his senior officers to return. For all his talk of war and the threat to take three times the number of cattle demanded as a fine, the force was now retiring with fewer cattle than had been demanded.

On December 22 Cathcart issued an Order of the Day in which he said, 'The Commander of the forces conveys his thanks to the Army engaged against the Basutos at the Berea on the 20th instant for their gallant conduct, and his admiration of their steadiness and discipline, by which an overwhelming host of Basutos and Bataungs were defeated, during a contest which lasted from early in the morning until 8 p.m. when the enemy, with a force of not less than six thousand well-armed horsemen, under considerable organization, after repeatedly assailing the troops at every point, was driven from the field with such severe loss as to compel him to sue for peace.' But no one was taken in. No matter how often Cathcart proclaimed victory, the men knew they had lost and were humiliated.

Moshesh, too, was in no doubt as to who had won and he made sure that the black peoples of South Africa learnt the truth. So rapid was communication between Moshesh and other tribal chiefs that King William's Town learnt the news of the Berea—the real news—two days before official despatches arrived.

In 1853 Moshesh turned on Sikonyela and his Batlokwa and drove them out of Lesotho. There were no reprisals. Moshesh was then sixty-seven. He was at the height of his power. He had defeated a British army and, with the possible exception of the Zulu king Mpande, he was the most powerful chief in South Africa. But he still had to face the Boers.

8

ALTHOUGH CATHCART had threatened martial law in the Sovereignty, it was an empty gesture. Just over a year after the Berea, a special commissioner, Sir George Clerk, signed the Bloemfontein Convention with the frontier farmers—much like the Sand River Convention—

this time stating that H.M. Government had no treaties with any chief other than Adam Kok and had no intention of making any that would hurt the farmers of the new 'Orange Free State'. With that the British marched away, pleased to be shaking the Free State dust from their boots. So the frontiers were now wide open—as they had been during the Sovereignty. The Free Staters set about the business of creating a State. A Volksraad (Parliament) was formed and in September, 1854, J. P. Hoffman was elected President. The cattle raiding on the Lesotho borders went on unchecked.

In Lesotho itself an event occurred which plunged the whole country into grief. Mrs Casalis—Ma-Eugene—died on June 17. Casalis described how chiefs and their councillors rode in from remote villages to pay their respects; many had been preceded by runners asking Casalis to delay burial as long as possible since they wished to see her once more. 'The bounds prescribed by my reverence for the dear remains were already past, while still others came to press kisses, bathed with tears, upon her forehead and all this passed in a land where the terrors inspired by death were such that one would have believed a house rendered forever uninhabitable, if in taking out a corpse it was not carried through a breach made at the end opposite the door!'

Two years later, in 1856, Casalis was recalled to take over the Mission House in Paris. By the time he wrote his moving account of life in Lesotho the Paris society had celebrated fifty years of field work there. During that time they had created schools, churches, an industrial college, a theological school, installed a printing press, built agricultural establishments, taught the Basuto how to cultivate wheat, potatoes and other vegetables; they had introduced the plough, had improved the strain of horses, sheep and bullocks and had seen Lesotho reach a point where it had a small export trade in cereals, wool and cattle.

In 1854, too, Cathcart left South Africa and was replaced by Sir George Grey. He had also been an army man but had resigned early and explored the coast of Western Australia before becoming governor of South Australia and later of New Zealand. He had earned a considerable reputation as an administrator, which was just as well, for one of the strangest and most pitiful chapters in South African history was about to be written; good administrators would be sorely needed.

In 1856 the Xhosa nation, one of the main Bantu tribes of South Africa, who lived on the eastern frontier of the Cape Colony several hundred miles to the south-east of Lesotho and who had been intermittently engaged in a series of exhausting wars—the Kaffir Wars—with British and Boer forces for more than thirty years, began to commit mass suicide. The tragedy has come to be known as the 'Cattle Killing' because much of the stock owned by the Xhosas was slaughtered on the advice of wizards. Its result was to have a profound effect on the economy of the Colony and was, overnight, to create a poverty-ridden slum where the Xhosas lived.

Moshesh has been held either wholly or in part responsible for the disaster. Short of any proof, one has to rely on theory and one such theory holds that Moshesh engineered the tragedy for two reasons. The first is that it was in line with his plan for a confederation of black against white and that it would unite the blacks once and for all. The second was that he now faced pressure from the Boers of the Orange Free State and as Professor Walker wrote, he 'proposed to keep the Colonists from helping the Republicans by giving them something to occupy themselves on their own borders'. If Moshesh was responsible, the deviousness of the scheme was in character for he was still keeping his options open as far as Britain was concerned. Had the confederation worked he would probably have been its leader, but he was realistic enough to recognize that it might not: in which case he wished to be allied to the strongest white group, the British.

In March, 1856, a seer called Mhlakaza and his daughter, Nonqause, began preaching to the Xhosas a doctrine of resurrection. Nonqause said she had spoken to the shades of old tribal heroes who pointed to the decay of their race through the oppression of the whites. They could no longer be silent spectators and it was their intention to rise again and save the Xhosas from extermination. However, there was a condition. They would only return if the entire Xhosa nation killed off all its cattle, leaving only horses and dogs. All grain was to be thrown away and no fields were to be cultivated. When these conditions had been fulfilled a great whirlwind would blow across the land and sweep away all Xhosas who had refused to obey. Only then would the great warriors of the past rise up to take over the nation's destiny.

The news of the vision swept through southern Africa like a brush fire. Some whites refused to take it seriously. But one person was totally convinced that an enormous tragedy was brewing if nothing could be done to stop it. He was the Reverend Charles Brownlee, a missionary and administrator among the Gaikas, one of the tribes that made up the Xhosa nation. He worked tirelessly to damp down the spreading hysteria. He and his wife were later to write the only full accounts of the disaster.

Mrs Brownlee wrote, 'At first the kaffir nation was stunned. The sacrifice seemed too great. Tidings of the marvellous sights witnessed near Mhlakaza's village filled the country. The horns of oxen were said to be seen peeping from beneath the rushes which grew around a swampy pool near the village of the seer; and from a subterranean cave were heard the bellowing and knocking of the horns of cattle impatient to rise . . . There were those who said they had actually seen the risen heroes emerge from the Indian Ocean, some on foot, some on horseback, passing in silent parade before them, then sinking again among the tossings of the restless waves. Sometimes they were seen rushing through the air in the wild chase as of old. Then again they were seen marshalled in battle array. The horrors to befall the unbelievers were enlarged upon. White men would be turned into frogs, mice, and ants.

'One can imagine the effect of all this upon an intensely superstitious people.'

Brownlee used himself unsparingly. For months he spent almost every day in the saddle riding from village to village, reasoning, pleading and warning. Whenever they told him of the wonderful things that had been promised he always gave them a simple answer: 'Napakade' (never). He said it so many times that this became his name in Xhosa. In June 1856, he wrote to Colonel Maclean, his superior, saying among other things there was a rumour that 'Black Russians' had arrived. Rumours of the Crimean War had been current among the Xhosas from 1854 and they were convinced that the Russians were black people like themselves and that having fought the English in the Crimea they were coming south to fight them again and drive them into the sea. This rumour was given a certain credence when a rowing-boat was washed up on the coast containing a naval cap decorated with gold braid. The Xhosas assured themselves that the Russians had killed the British crew.

Brownlee was worried that violent incidents involving white people might occur and wrote that travellers should take the utmost precaution. 'I do not think any solitary or unprotected traveller is safe and it would be well for traders and others who cross the Kei, to travel under the protection of some influential Kaffir.' But for all his efforts the killing of cattle and the destruction of stored grain began.

Mrs Brownlee wrote of the delusion: 'Wonderful reports were constantly in circulation. Armies were seen reviewing on the sea, others sailing in umbrellas; thousands of cattle were heard knocking their horns together and bellowing in caverns, impatient to rise, only waiting until all their fellows who still walked the earth were slain; dead men years in the grave had been seen, who sent pathetic appeals to their kindred not to delay their coming back to life by refusing to obey the prophet. Cattle were then killed, feasting was the order of the day, but it was impossible to consume all. Dogs were gorged on fat beef, vultures were surfeited, whole carcasses were left to putrefy, the air became tainted with corruption. Alas! Later on it was the carcasses of men and women, young men and maidens, children and infants that strewed the wayside. Oh, the sadness of it all.'

The Brownlees bought one thousand bags of maize to store at the then price of about five shillings a bag. As famine gripped the area the price rose to two pounds and three pounds a bag and even at those prices it was often impossible to find it.

Brownlee had been desperately working on the Gaika chief Sandile and early on managed to restrain him from ordering his people to destroy their food stocks, in spite of pressure on him by his mother, who is reported as sending him a message stating, 'It is all very well for you, Sandile. You have your wives and children, but I am solitary. I am longing to see my husband; you are keeping him from rising by your disobedience to the command of the spirits.'

In January, 1857, ten months after the beginning of the delusion, Nonqause ordered that all cattle be killed within eight days. 'It was a week of painful anxiety,' wrote Mrs Brownlee. 'I feared for my husband's life, as many of the evil-disposed were very bitter against him, and they believed it was his influence that kept Sandile from obeying the prophet.'

In expectation of the start of a millennium the Xhosas cleaned out their empty cattle kraals and corn pits, enlarging them and making them stronger to hold the coming bounty. Many huts were re-thatched and strengthened to resist the expected whirlwind.

'The eighth day came on which the heaven and earth were to come together amid darkness, thunder, lightning, rain, and a mighty wind, by which the Amagogotya (unbelievers) together with the white man would be driven into the sea,' wrote Mrs Brownlee. 'At the dawn of the great day a nation, many of whom had doubtless not slept, rose joyfully, decked themselves with paint, beads and rings, to welcome their long-lost friends. One of the saddest sights was that of an old woman wizened with age, and doubly wrinkled by starvation, decked out with brass rings jingling on her withered arms and legs. They had kept on their ornaments hoping against hope, till too weak to remove them. The sun rose and made the circuit of the heavens closely watched by expectant hosts in vain. He set in silent majesty in the west, leaving the usual darkness over the earth, and the black darkness of a bitter disappointment in the hearts of thousands.' Within days people began to die. Food, anything edible at all, was at a premium.

Not every Xhosa had destroyed his cattle and grain. All of one Sunday the Brownlees watched herds being driven past their house by Xhosas wishing to put as many miles and a military post or two between themselves and the starving thousands.

Those who had destroyed their property soon weakened and sat all day in their villages. Each morning they would walk or crawl to the cattle kraals and corn pits hoping to see them full. Each morning they were disappointed. Bones which they had thrown away in days of plenty were now gathered and gnawed. Women and children wandered across the veld digging for roots—so assiduously that the whole area became pot-holed and unsafe for riding. Messengers were sent to the worst-affected areas telling the people they could get food either on farms owned by whites or in the nearest towns, but many still hung on and it was not until hundreds had died that the movement towards the Colony began. 'Those who reached us were most pitiable figures,' wrote Mrs Brownlee. 'Breathing skeletons, with hollow eyes and parched lips. The innocent children looked like old men and women in miniature, some only a few days old.' The land was covered with dead and dying. It was summer and the possibility of disease was real. The Government gave half a crown to anyone who found a body and buried it. Soup kitchens were set up, corn and meat were distributed, but for many the help had come too late.

It is not easy to give exact figures, but the most likely estimates are that between a hundred and fifty and two hundred thousand cattle were killed. This led to a death rate from famine and disease of between twenty and thirty thousand people. The population of certain chiefdoms between the Kei and Fish Rivers was estimated to have dropped from 104,721 in January, 1857, to 37,697 in December—a loss of over sixty-seven thousand. Of this total about thirty thousand moved into the Colony for employment. Some went as migrant labourers and later returned. Others settled on farms in the eastern Cape and their descendants have remained there as farm servants ever since.

In recent years another theory has been advanced for the catastrophe—that the Xhosas acted as they did in expectation of the millennium. In his book, *The Trumpet Shall Sound*, a study of millenarism, and in particular the 'Cargo Cults' of Melanesia, Peter Worsley wrote: 'The basic condition (for the emergence of a millenarian movement) is a situation of dissatisfaction with existing social conditions and yearnings for a happier life ... It is no accident that the millenarian idea, when introduced into suitable situations in societies where the idea itself was previously absent, has flourished like the bay tree.' And again: 'There is (another) type of social situation in which activist millenarian ideas are likely to flourish. This is when a society with differentiated political institutions is fighting for its existence by quite secular military–political means, but is meeting with defeat after defeat. One may cite the case of the rise of the prophet Nonqause at a time when the Xhosa people were beginning to realize that they were losing the long-drawn-out Kaffir Wars.'

The most obvious parallels are the two great waves of Ghost Dance among the American Indians in 1870 and 1890, when prophets promised the return of the dead if people would abandon sin and adopt the cult. The Sioux, who had suffered severely from the loss of tribal lands and the disappearance of the buffalo, emberked on this with such fervour that the massacre at Wounded Knee resulted, in which 300 out of 370 Sioux were butchered by machine-gun fire. There are also parallels among the 'Cargo-Cults' where property is destroyed in expectation of the return of dead heroes. And there is a ringing echo of Dona Beatriz in the Old Kingdom, whose way to a Golden Age also lay in invoking the past. She, however, foresaw the future in terms of a new religion, not as an age built on a framework of self-destruction. The parallels go further; the Old Kingdom was in a state of disorder and decay brought on largely by white pressure. The Xhosas, who had fought a series of losing wars over a long period, had seen their tribal lands diminish, and had become more and more densely packed as their area of land grew less.

Millenarism may have been partly responsible for the 'Cattle Killing', but several major historians nominate Moshesh as the villain. Cory states flatly: 'War, due to the Basutos stealing Free State cattle and the farmers' retaliations, was always impending . . . And it was noticed that when war . . . became more imminent, activity in the cattle killing became more intense. When in August (1858) the Free State Boers made an expedition against a robber chief Witzie, in which Moshesh was in no way involved . . . there was such a lull in cattle killing that it appeared . . . (it) had quite died down . . . But when Moshesh expected attacks prophecies were most abundant. Moshesh therefore must have been acting either directly or indirectly with Mhlakaza . . .'

9

MOSHESH was growing old; at the time of the Cattle Killing he was seventy, and was vulnerable to his family now that Casalis had gone. He had had a series of wives over the years, and some of his own children were younger than some of his grandchildren. His sons were proud. They had seen a British army advance on their country and go away defeated; they had seen their tribe's fame act as a magnet to other tribes; alliances had been made, knees bent, vassalage acknowledged. The Affair at the Berea had given the Basuto a new stature: Moshesh's sons became conscious of their power and arrogantly raided into the Free State. There were constant forays in search of easy pickings and the infant Boer state grew more and more apprehensive. As Tylden said, 'There was no real safety for either life or property (in the Free State) and the extent of a man's holding was usually little more than the range of his gun or rifle.' From this period dates a story which has been retold, changing only its locale, in every African emergency since. A farmer's wife asked her Basuto servants if, in the event of war, they would kill her and her children. She was told that their job would be to kill the neighbouring family, whose servants would perform the same office for their employers. Jan Fick, one of the best-known and toughest men in the Winburg district was quoted as saying, 'I have been fighting kaffirs since I was eleven years old, when my father's house was burnt down in a kaffir outbreak and we had to fight for our lives in the veld.' The result was that in 1857 when a permanent executive was set up in the Orange Free State and a constitution adopted, one of the provisions was that there would be no equality in Church or State between black and white.

Like Lesotho, the Free State had its renegades and adventurers, and the executive was unable to do much to restrain them. There were no real prisons and it was difficult to bring offenders to justice. The position of the Landdrosts (magistrates) was so precarious that they feared to hand down corrective sentences on whites who might have influence behind them. The Landdrost of Winburg was savagely attacked by a white farmer when he gave judgement against him. The farmer felled him with a blow from the butt of his horse-pistol then tried to strangle him.

In an attempt to keep the peace, President Hoffman, who was living on a farm given him by Moshesh, had sent as his first ambassador to the Court of Thaba Bosiu, Joseph Millard Orpen, a man of integrity who was farming in the Free State. Orpen, an Irishman born in Dublin in 1828, eventually became one of the Basuto's most ardent champions, married twice—both times into French missionary families—and died aged ninety-seven in 1925. He succeeded in maintaining the *status quo* for a year or two but things were gradually accelerating towards a confrontation.

One of the most arrogant of Basuto cattle raiders was Moshesh's brother, Poshuli. In February, 1858, on the pretence of hunting, he and a large party made a showy display in a disputed area and ejected a Boer family from their farm. This had immediate repercussions: the Free State seethed with rumours, alarmist reports were sent to Bloemfontein, and the farmers took their families into laagers—the traditional fortified wagon camps which the Voortrekkers had used so successfully in times of attack. Attempts were made on both sides to take the heat out of the situation but they were unavailing. The weeks dragged by. The laagers became dirty and insanitary. There was fear of disease. A state of war existed without the war itself.

Lagden wrote: 'The two races were on the brink of war. It was not that they hated each other so much as that they were the victims of much misunderstanding, partly due to the vagaries of British policy, partly to the scheming of land-grabbers and adventurers who too often got the approval of Major Warden and other officials for occupying ground which the natives were forbidden to expropriate and the Government had no power to give away. A succession of governors made treaties, laws, boundaries and pledges which were alternately confirmed and disallowed. Inspired by the best intentions they created problems and pirouetted around them.'

On March 11, 1858, the first Boer–Basuto war broke out, called the Month's War. The President of the Free State, then Boshoff, made a formal declaration claiming the Warden Line. About a thousand men were put into the field armed with percussion-cap smooth-bore guns and seven small pieces of ordnance of which little use was made. The force split into two columns, one under Commandant Senekal entering Lesotho from the north, the other under Commandant Weber from the south. Senekal tried to cross the Caledon River where the British had crossed four years previously, at Cathcart's Drift, but his force was faced by six thousand Basuto who attacked unrelentingly for forty-eight hours, killing seventeen Boers and hurling them back across the river. They finally moved downstream to link up with the southern column.

Weber had had an equally disastrous start, disastrous in the sense that what he had done would from then on be stigmatized a Boer atrocity: he had attacked the French Protestant Mission of Beersheba on the farm Zevenfontein which had been established twenty years before on land given by Moshesh himself. The attack came as a shock to French and Basuto alike for the Boers were known to be a devoutly Christian people, puritan and Calvinistic. But they disliked missionaries. They considered that the London Missionary Society in particular, and missionaries in general, tended to take the side of black against white and that those blacks who had lengthy contact with missionary stations became insolent, lazy and so made unattractive labourers. Naturally there are two accounts of what happened. According to the Boer version the station was considered a menace to Weber's lines of communication and a force under a man called Sauer, who was the Smithfield magistrate, surrounded it at daylight and called on the residents four times in the space of two hours to surrender their arms. The Basuto inmates refused, became hostile; the Boers opened fire, killing thirty and capturing three thousand head of cattle. In the version of M. Rolland, head of the mission, one summons was given to surrender with a time limit of only five minutes. He stated he was still trying to get together the arms to hand over when the building was hit by a hail of bullets. Ten people who fled from the mission and stumbled

174

into a ravine for shelter were hunted down and shot. The station was then pillaged. Whichever version was preferred, what is important is the fact that a French Protestant mission was attacked at all. The French missionaries had achieved a unique relationship with the Basuto and had the sympathetic ear of both the French and British Governments; it was something the Boers never seemed to realize, something that eventually would work against them.

Moshesh did not move. He sat on the top of his mountain and let the two forces come towards him, drawing them farther and farther from the Free State. Then, at a place called The Hell because of its brooding ugliness, an element of Weber's force foolishly went after a decoy herd of cattle. Moshesh's son Letsie cut them off, surrounded them and attacked them with the terrifying Basuto throwing axe. Although the Basuto lost more than sixty men in the skirmish and the Boers only fifteen the *pro rata* loss to the Boers was the more serious for they had no reserves to draw on. On 25 April, 1858 the north and south columns met and moved towards Thaba Bosiu under Senekal's overall command. When they reached Casalis's first mission station at Moriah, a terrible sight confronted them; they found the mutilated corpses of their comrades who had been killed at The Hell. The bodies had been badly hacked about and portions were missing. It was Basuto custom to remove parts of their dead enemies to make a strengthening medicine for their own men. Under the circumstances it is not surprising that the mission was sacked. Again there are two versions: the Boers said that Arbousset, Casalis's original companion, and several English traders had helped the Basuto and encouraged them. Arbousset, on the other hand, claimed that he and the traders had taken refuge in a cave and had had no part in the fighting.[1]

The Boer force, numbering only about nine hundred men because of desertions, moved on Thaba Bosiu. They found

[1] Appealed to by the French mission, the British Government refused compensation on the ground that the war had nothing to do with Britain, but the Free State Government eventually paid £100 towards the construction of a new school building.

every pass blocked and defended. Moshesh now counter-attacked by sending raiding parties into the Free State where they wrecked farmsteads and drove off cattle. It was what the Boers had feared most. More began to desert. There was a proposal to storm Thaba Bosiu. It was refused. Men drifted away, fearful of what was happening to their families. The force became weaker and weaker. On June 1 the Free State president had no option but to ask Moshesh for an armistice.

Once again, as with the outcome of the British attack, the resultant propaganda was wide of the truth. Rumours of victory swept across the Free State; some claimed that the Boers had achieved what they had set out to achieve: they had captured great herds of cattle and chastised the Basuto. Moshesh wrote a letter to the Free State president when the Boer desertions were at their height that is a classic of African satire. It began:

Good Friend,

I, Moshesh, do greet you, Boshoff, my chief and master. Your messenger came in last night with a letter, in which your Honour begins to speak of peace. I am sorry that you ever spoke of war. It is not Moshesh who began the war, and I must add that I have not fought any battle as yet.

It is a very long letter and must have made excessively irritating reading for the Free State president. Moshesh was quite agreeable to overtures of peace, but he was not going to be done out of his lecture. He took Boshoff to task on the grounds of cowardice as well as the professed Christianity of the Boers, both bitter pills to swallow. Another section reads:

Oh, my good chief Boshoff, call in the captains of your late commando, and rebuke them much, for they have done you much harm in their march through my country.

You style yourself a Christian in your last letter to me. I knew long since that you were a Christian, but the captains of your warriors are not, for if you persisted in saying that they also are Christians, we would immediately conclude that there is no God. What! Does their Christianity consist in destroying Christianity?

Another section reads:

As the winter is drawing near, I wish that your deputation would soon come, because in case we could not agree, we must go on with the war, for the sooner we fight the better for all parties, in order that after the great battle is over we may retire into some winter quarters ... The reports of your commandos and correspondents which are published in *The Friend* (a Bloemfontein newspaper which still exists) are wonderful inventions, and therefore they are utterly false.

However, some burghers of the Free State might take them to be faithful and trustworthy statements, and taking for granted that we have been greatly and easily defeated, they might in succeeding years be inclined to incite wars against us, perhaps for very specious reasons. Moreover, these statements have hurt the feelings of our warriors, whom I had great trouble to keep within bounds during the present struggle.

The English know that we are no cowards and we would like the Boers to learn that we know how to fight for our rights ... and then perhaps peace would be a little more sincere on the part of the Boers.

In his reply, Boshoff made no reference to the true state of affairs, but there is an illuminating letter from him to the resident magistrate of Aliwal North in which he said: 'The Boers, by their unaccountable sudden break-up, have brought me in such a fix as I never yet was in all my life. They imagine that they have given Moshesh such a licking that he will keep quiet for many a day, poor fools.'

10

ANOTHER GOVERNOR; another boundary conference; 1864. This time the new British Governor was Sir Philip Wodehouse, and there was a new president of the Orange Free State, an extremely able man, Jan Hendrik Brand. And, of course, Moshesh. As in Greek drama, the myth remains constant, the end never varies, only the actors change. A new border was defined, more paper was signed, more promises were made—and broken. The difference this time was that the Basuto considered themselves hard done by and another war became inevitable. However, before it broke out, Moshesh passed a law which was one of the cornerstones on which Lesotho was built and to which the country in great measure owes its present existence. It is known as 'The Law for Trade' and once and for all sums up the attitude of a black African king towards the land of which the kingdom was composed: 'I, Moshesh, write for any trader, whoever he may be, already in my land, and for any who may come to trade with the Basutos; my word is this: Trade to me and my tribe is a good thing. I wish to promote it. Any trader who wishes to establish a shop must first obtain permission from me. Should he build a house, I grant him no right to sell it. Further, I do not grant him liberty to plough the fields but only to plant a small vegetable garden. The trader who fancies that the place he is sojourning in belongs to him must dismiss the thought, if not, he is to quit; for there is no place belonging to the whites in my land; and I have granted no white man a place, either by word, or by writing.' When Britain eventually took over Lesotho as a protectorate she based her informal policy on this philosophy.

But at the time the immediate future of Lesotho was dominated by the desires of her white neighbour. Brand was elected president of the Free State in 1864 and inherited a country torn by dissension and restlessness. It has been said that he foresaw a new war against the Basuto as the only way of uniting his people; if that is so, his ideas on statecraft seem to run parallel with those of Moshesh. He also foresaw the difficulty of bringing a country to economic maturity without a port; his munitions, for instance, had to come up all the way from Port Elizabeth, a British-controlled port, by ox wagon. If he could launch a sudden attack on fortress-Lesotho, take its rich lands, he might then be able to roll down towards the coast, opening up a Boer corridor to Port St Johns. It was an imperial dream. On May 29, 1865, he tried to turn it into reality.

To the Basuto the second war with the Free State is known as the 'War of the Noise of Cannon'. To the Free State, 'The Great War'. This time the white republic was better prepared:

her army varied between two thousand five hundred and four thousand men with mercenary detachments of Hottentots and Bantu hostile to the Basuto. The Boers had replaced their muskets with rifles and were magnificent shots; they also had a number of field guns but were as yet unsophisticated in their use. The Basuto on the other hand were less militarily efficient than they had been eight years before. Their most obvious disadvantage was Moshesh's age: he was nearly eighty and was slipping away. The Black Confederation had come to nothing and he had transformed his allegiance totally to Britain. His great desire—one he had had all his adult life—was still to be taken under her wing and it had now become an obsession. However, Britain had no plans to add Lesotho to the Empire. Only a few years before, Moshesh had maintained to Orpen that Queen Victoria would not desert her children, thereby putting himself in a totally false position, for while she had black 'children' in many parts of the world, Moshesh was still unadopted. He always said he wanted to be her soldier, and to have her represented at Thaba Bosiu. His sons did not share his feelings and because they no longer felt his grip they did more or less what they pleased. The land was not united under a single hand any longer. Still, it was a formidable nation; it could put between ten and twenty thousand mounted warriors into the field and though they were less well-armed than the Boers, they outnumbered them at least five to one. And they had made reasonable preparations; a number of fortified mountains were stocked with grain, and cattle had been hidden in the high valleys.

Once again the attack was made by two columns, one led by Jan Fick, the second by Louw Wepener and after one or two minor skirmishes they joined up before Thaba Bosiu having 'annexed' portions of Lesotho on the way. It was one of the consistent weaknesses of Boer armies that the men were highly individualistic, untrained in the acceptance of orders, and prone to group loyalties. This time there were many in Wepener's column who resented the overall command going to Fick, and things were made worse by the fact that the two commanders did not like each other. Once again the magic of Thaba Bosiu began to work. As they laagered below it, a superstitious depression swept the Boer rank and file. The

179

Mountain of Night had never been taken: would it again prove too much for them? On August 8 Fick ordered Wepener to attack the Raebe Pass on the southern face. After the Boer cannon had silenced Moshesh's artillery Wepener and a thousand men assaulted the mountain. But half way up he committed a fatal error; he changed his plan of attack. The men faltered, some retired. Others stayed where they were. Only eight men reached the top and they had to scramble down to safety when they discovered that no one was willing to support them. Six days later, Wepener led another attack, but morale had suffered in the interim. Of the six hundred men who were to follow him, only three hundred actually did so and some of these stayed behind at the foot of the hill.

This time there was no rush to the top but a steady advance from rock to rock, bush to bush, firing, reloading, firing, reloading. The fissure up which the Boers were advancing became narrower as it neared the summit, which meant that the men had to bunch together. Stones and boulders began to crash down on them and by afternoon only about one hundred men were left unwounded. But they were doing well. The fissure had been blocked by three stone walls, two of which had been taken. The third was held by one of Moshesh's sons and some of the best warriors. At 5 p.m. Wepener climbed out on to a flat rock near this wall to open his field of fire, and was shot dead by a volley from the Basuto. Wessels, the second-in-command, then tried to force the wall and he, too, was shot. The Basuto counter-attacked and the disheartened Boers surged down the fissure in a panicky horde. Wessels, badly wounded, managed to get clear with difficulty. Of the three hundred stormers who had started with Wepener, eleven had been killed and nine seriously wounded. The Basuto losses were light.

Although, in the years to come, the Free State developed new tactics and acquired more powerful weapons, they never again tried to capture Thaba Bosiu. It was one of the mountain's ironies that its reputation outstripped reality. Had the Boers known what panic their attacks caused they might have renewed them with success. Letters from French missionaries described the conditions on the mountain during the following days as deplorable. Moshesh had collected a vast herd of cattle on the top, thinking his people would forget their divisions and fight for the common wealth of the nation. Thaba Bosiu was soon in a fearful state. The springs were unable to cope with the demand and the cattle, maddened by hunger and thirst, died in thousands, their dead bodies being used as barricades. With the summit one stinking mass of decaying flesh—four thousand carcasses were counted later—and the probability of disease, Moshesh wrote to the Free State president suggesting that Sir Philip Wodehouse be called in as mediator. The president seemed to think that the Free State had won the battle, for the terms he demanded were extraordinarily harsh. Forty thousand head of cattle, five thousand horses, and sixty thousand sheep, to be delivered in four days; the land which Wepener and Fick had 'annexed' to go to the Free State; a Boer magistrate to sit at Thaba Bosiu; all arms and ammunition to be given up; and two of Moshesh's sons to be sent as hostages until the peace treaty was signed.

It was impossible for Moshesh to comply. In a letter to Wodehouse in which he criticized what he called unreasonable conditions there was the following paragraph: 'Another condition imposed upon me is that I must become subject to the Free State; but I will never do so. I consider myself subject to the British Government and I hope Your Excellency shall take interest in my cause, and come to establish peace as soon as possible, as I am determined the Government of the Free State will never have my country. I am, therefore, giving myself and my country up to Her Majesty's Government under certain conditions which we may agree upon between Your Excellency and me.'

While Moshesh awaited a reply from Cape Town—it was unfavourable, for the British Government did not wish to increase its holdings in South Africa at the time—the Transvaal entered the war on the side of the Free State and the laagers at the foot of Thaba Bosiu were disbanded. But this time the Boers did not go home. Instead they split up into commandos and began a series of *chevauchees*, quartering the country, rounding up its cattle, fighting wherever an enemy force showed. In April, 1866, a kind of peace was signed but only so that both sides could get the harvest in, and by

February, 1867, Moshesh and his sons felt themselves strong enough to renew the struggle to regain land they had lost. By July, Free State commandos were again in the field and what was known as the 'Little War' began. These commandos harried the Basuto much as the Koranas had done; they burnt crops, drove off cattle, made lightning raids on villages. The Basuto became refugees in their own country. Those who could, travelled to the mountain fortresses for safety. Hunger, the old enemy, returned and with it cannibalism. Moshesh for once had no answer. Though there was food in various parts of Lesotho there was no means of distributing it. People began to die of starvation. Moshesh, in despair, began bombarding Wodehouse with requests for help.

Wodehouse was sympathetic. For some time he had been in favour of Lesotho's annexation by Britain and, indeed, had requested it. So, too, was the British Civil Commissioner at Aliwal North, Mr John Burnet. Two years previously, at the end of the 'Great War', he had visited Thaba Bosiu and had written to Wodehouse, 'Moshesh is done mentally. All is disorganization and jealousy among the greater Chiefs, who as well as the petties find the reins slipping from their hands. The great mass of the people are tired, worn out by the oppression and bad government of the Chiefs; and I am persuaded that the whole of Basutoland is ripe, rotten ripe, for falling into the hands of the Queen's Government if a plan could be found.'

In one last desperate appeal to Wodehouse for annexation by Britain, Moshesh described himself and his nation as being 'the lice in the Queen's blanket'. Again Wodehouse pressed the British Government and in January, 1868, received a document from the Duke of Buckingham and Chandos, Secretary of State for the Colonies, authorizing the annexation of Lesotho to the British colony of Natal—not the Cape, as Wodehouse had hoped. But it was enough. Wodehouse told the Free State president that hostilities would now cease. The annexation was only just in time. The Boers had done what they had never managed before: by their guerrilla tactics, they had almost conquered Lesotho. The rugged land had been reduced by perpetual harassment but the symbol of its identity, Thaba Bosiu, still stood like some Krak de Chevalier, when all around the people had been defeated. On March 12, what Moshesh had so fervently wished occurred. Wodehouse issued the following proclamation:

> Whereas with a view to the restoration of peace and future maintenance of tranquillity and good government on the north-eastern Border of the Colony of the Cape of Good Hope, Her Majesty the Queen has been graciously pleased to comply with the request made by Moshesh, the Paramount Chief, and other Headmen of the tribe of the Basutos, that the said tribe may be admitted into the Allegiance of Her Majesty; and whereas Her Majesty has been further pleased to authorize me to take the necessary steps for giving effect to Her pleasure in the Matter:
>
> Now, therefore, I do hereby proclaim and declare that from and after the publication hereof the said tribe of the Basutos shall be, and shall be taken to be, for all intents and purposes, British subjects; and the territory of the said tribe shall be, and shall be taken to be, British Territory. And I hereby require all Her Majesty's subjects in South Africa to take notice of this my Proclamation accordingly.
>
> God Save the Queen!

Although in the years ahead Lesotho was also to be ruled by the Cape Colony before coming under direct British rule this was the beginning of the country's long journey to its present unique position, that of an independent, multi-racial black kingdom poised in the very heart of a country whose policies are diametrically opposed.

But Lesotho had paid a heavy price; thousands of Basuto had been killed in the fighting, some had died of starvation, tens of thousands of cattle had been lost. In one sense a certain justice had been meted out for their years of border raiding. Their morale as a nation was temporarily shattered. On April 15 Wodehouse held a *Pitso*, a national assembly of the Basuto nation, about twenty miles from Maseru, where Moshesh made his unequivocal surrender to Queen Victoria. 'The country is dead', the old man said. 'We are all dead, take us and do what you like with us.'

In the Free State, the farmers were bitter. A whole new country had lain open before them; now it was closed for ever.

It was as though Moshesh had willed himself to live until the future of his country was secure, for once Wodehouse made his proclamation Moshesh's strength began to fail and he declined rapidly. He found it difficult to remain awake and would often fall into a doze even when guests were present. Once when Wodehouse visited him, the King told him he expected to die soon and was glad to know his people were safe. Wodehouse was greatly affected by the old man's frailty. Moshesh asked him to describe the new boundaries of the kingdom but fell asleep as he was doing so.

The months passed. Moshesh spent much of his time dozing beneath a pile of skins. When important visitors arrived at Thaba Bosiu he made an effort to gather what strength he had left; with their departure he would slip more deeply into lassitude and senility. As he approached his death, he became obsessed by a need to embrace the Christian faith. He decided to be baptized by the missionaries and March 12, 1870, was chosen. A huge platform was built at his insistence so that everyone might witness the event. For days beforehand, thousands of Basutos made their way along the mountain tracks. Two days before the baptism was due, Thaba Bosiu was thronged by people. But Moshesh died in his sleep on March 11, simply slipping away in the early dawn in the presence of two of his sons. Those who had come to rejoice with him stayed to mourn his passing. He is buried on Thaba Bosiu. Tylden wrote a fitting epitaph: 'Since his death he has become to the Basuto the incarnation of all their most cherished traditions and most of their characteristics, as well as the originator of their prosperity.'

* * *

The story of Lesotho does not end with the death of Moshesh, nor was its future a path strewn with roses.[1] But it is the

[1] The Cape Government took over Lesotho in 1871 and in 1880 tried to disarm the people. The Basutos rose in rebellion and what has come to be called 'The Gun War' ensued, which lasted for about a year. In 1884 the country was transferred directly to the Crown and came under the authority of the Colonial Office.

watershed. There was a saying among the Boers during the 'Little War' that it was 'a rifle and a bush and a range of six hundred yards that beat the Basuto'. Looking back now, one does not see things in those simplistic terms. While Moshesh lived on his mountain, the Basuto were never beaten. By the time he died he had, in effect, passed the paramountcy of his people to the fierce old Queen across the water—whom no one beat. Moshesh and Casalis had stood together for a long time, but finally it was only Moshesh who was left to withstand the pressure. Unlike the Old Kingdom of Congo, which opened its arms to the white man too widely, unlike the Kingdom of Dahomey, which shut its doors too firmly, Moshesh was a man who understood whites; they were, in the long run, no different from himself. But he also had luck; there was Casalis and there was the length of his own life. It seems unlikely that, had he died at three score years and ten, his sons could have saved their country. And so, one might say that it was a mountain and a man who beat the Boers.

11

MOSHESH'S GREAT-GRANDSON, Moshoeshoe II, is the present King of Lesotho. He is in his thirties, a slender, good-looking man with his forebear's aquiline features. He was educated in Britain and now lives in the former British residency. He has a passion, like many Basutos, for racehorses.

When Lesotho became independent in 1966 King Moshoeshoe left Oxford in the midst of his studies and returned home to lead his people. But things had changed since his great-grandfather's day. Politicians had taken over the old functions of village headman and court adviser, and he found himself isolated from the people he wished to lead. He persisted in his endeavour, provoked a trial of strength between himself and the politicians and soon found himself in exile in Holland. There he finally acknowledged that the role of kingship had changed and was allowed to return to Lesotho as a constitutional monarch.

The country itself is ruled by the Basotho National Party,

but in effect by the King's uncle, Chief Leabua Jonathan who, as Prime Minister, seems at the time of writing (1974) to be redesigning the structure of Lesotho politics into a one-party state.

The future of the country is uncertain. One view holds that it is a land of vanishing freedoms, that law and order will eventually break down and that it will become a black slum more and more dependent upon South Africa, where ninety per cent of its able-bodied men presently find employment. A more optimistic assessment suggests that it is on the point of a great leap forward. Seven new luxury hotels are planned to cope with an expected tourist boom. De Beers, the diamond giant, has bought a twenty-five per cent holding in a new diamond mine in the north. A huge dam is planned to enable Lesotho to sell water to the thirsty industrial areas of South Africa.

Neither view is much in evidence to the casual traveller in Lesotho today. I first visited the country more than twenty years ago, when it was ruled by young men of the Colonial Service. The capital, Maseru, which lies about fifteen miles from Thaba Bosiu on the Caledon River, was a hamlet with dusty, rutted streets; what buildings existed were constructed of dressed mountain stone and red corrugated-iron roofs. It had not changed much since the Earl of Rosslyn stayed with Sir Godfrey Lagden—commissioner for sixteen years—during the Boer War. In his book, *Twice Captured*, the Earl described the Residency as 'a nice comfortable little bungalow', and said, 'the Government offices are also worth looking at, but I cannot claim any desire to live there for sixteen years . . .'

In those days there were less than a hundred whites in Maseru, today there are several thousand in Lesotho, many of them traders, but also a significant group of diplomats and representatives of United Nations organizations. Maseru still has an impermanent frontier look. Its main street—there are few others—is lined with a mixture of old and new buildings, none more than two or three storeys, and it is easy to pick out the solid structures of the colonial period. Basuto horsemen wrapped against the mountain cold in coloured blankets, still ride their ponies into town and tether them along the main street in grassy vacant lots which, according to the roadside signs, are eventually to be developed as the headquarters of this or that ministry.

Down a side road is a brash American hotel, part of a worldwide chain, that is the centre of Maseru's social life. It stands above the Caledon River, a glass and concrete structure, new, raw, but already exerting an influence that has spread beyond the borders of Lesotho. Here one can buy porno bestsellers and girlie magazines, banned in South Africa, see the latest movies uncut by a South African censor, play roulette and blackjack and, in the darkened American bars, pick up black girls. Across the river in South Africa such practices are not only illegal but, if pursued, would carry gaol sentences.

It is instructive to watch *apartheid* break down under these pressures. Each weekend the hotel is filled with Moshesh's old enemies, Free State farmers. The magazines and books disappear from the racks, the casino is packed with whites jostling the local blacks for a place at the tables, assignations are quickly made. (When I was there a new rule was made banning single women from both the casino and the bars.)

While Maseru must act as a kind of pressure valve to frustrated South Africans, the sight of whites throwing their money about, dominating the fruit-machines and the gaming tables, racing down the newly tarred roads in their big American and German cars, has produced the opposite effect among the Basuto. The country is one of the ten poorest on earth and it is not surprising that the wealth of its surrounding neighbour has activated feelings of envy and dislike even above the natural dislike of its *apartheid* philosophy.

One is aware of a sense of uneasiness among whites either living or touring in Lesotho. Many traders employ nightwatchmen to guard their homes from burglars; shop assistants, hotel receptionists, government civil servants all made one feel barely tolerated. Herd boys on lonely country roads offer black power salutes to whites driving by.

But these are pinpricks that will resolve themselves in time, and time is on the side of the Basuto. The royal house, if subdued, is healthy; the state exists and, with luck, will become more viable, and it is in South Africa's interest to help where it can.

The abiding impressions one carries away are of the beauty

of the country itself: smoke rising from a hillside village as the evening cooking fires are lit; golden yellow cliffs glowing in the early sunshine; blue-black thunderstorms sweeping across the Berea plateau at noon; and, as one crosses the narrow bridge that takes one into South Africa and sees the first 'Whites Only' notice on the customs post, the impressions give place to a simple feeling of wonder—that Lesotho has survived at all.

SOME SOURCE BOOKS

The Kingdom of Congo

Armattoe, Dr R. E. G. *The Golden Age of West African Civilization* (Lomeshie Research Centre, 1946)

Axelson, Eric *Congo to Cape. Early Portuguese Explorers* (London 1973)

Balandier, Georges *Daily Life in the Kingdom of the Kongo* (Trans. Helen Weaver, London 1968)

Boxer, C. R. *The Old Kingdom of Congo*, in *The Dawn of African History*, edited by Roland Oliver (London 1961)

Bush, M. L. *Renaissance, Reformation and the Outer World* (London 1967)

Childs, G. M. *Umbundu Kinship and Character* (London 1949)

Davidson, Basil *The African Awakening* (London 1955) *Black Mother* (London 1961)

Duffy, James *Portuguese Africa* (London 1949)

Egerton, F. C. *Angola in Perspective* (London 1957)

Eppstein, John *Does God Say Kill?* (London 1972)

Lopez, Duarte *see* Pigafetta

Parry, J. H. *The European Reconnaissance* (New York 1968)

Pigafetta, F. and Lopez, D. *A Report of the Kingdom of Congo* (trans. and ed. by M. Hutchinson, London 1881)

Ravenstein, E. G. *The Strange Adventures of Andrew Battell* (Hakluyt Soc.)
The Voyages of Cão and Bartholomew Dias 1482–88 (Geographical Journal, London 1900)

Wheeler, D. L. and Pelissier, R. *Angola* (London 1971)

The Kingdom of Dahomey

Akinjogbin, I. A. *Dahomey and its Neighbours 1708–1818* (London 1967)

Argyle, W. J. *The Fon of Dahomey* (London 1966)

Burton, Sir R. *A Mission to Gelele, King of Dahome* (London 1966)

Dalzel, Archibald *The History of Dahomy* (London 1793)

Farwell, Byron *Burton* (London 1963)

Forbes, Frederick E. *Dahomey and the Dahomans* (London 1851)

Greenidge, C. W. W. *Slavery* (London 1958)

189

Herskovits, M. J. *Dahomey. An Ancient West African Kingdom* (New York 1938)

Mannix, D. P. and Cowley, M. *Black Cargoes* (London 1963)

Newbury, C. W. *The Western Slave Coast and its Rulers* (London 1961)

Norris, R. *Memoirs of the Reign of Bossa Ahadee, King of Dahomey* (London 1789)

Oliver, Caroline *Richard Burton: The African Years* in *Africa and its Explorers* ed. by Robert I. Rotberg (London and Harvard 1970)

Polanyi, Karl *Dahomey and the Slave Trade* (Washington 1966)

Pope-Hennessy, James *Sins of the Fathers* (London 1967)

Skertchly, J. A. *Dahomey As It Is* (London 1874)

Wilson, J. Leighton *The British Squadron on the Coast of Africa* (London 1851)

The Kingdom of Lesotho

Arbousset, T. *Narrative of an Exploratory Tour to the North East of the Colony of the Cape of Good Hope* (London 1852)

Ashton, Hugh *The Basuto. A Social Study of Traditional and Modern Lesotho* (London 1967)

Becker, P. *Hill of Destiny* (London 1969)

Brownlee, the Hon. Charles *Reminiscences of Kaffir Life and History* (Lovedale, South Africa 1896)

Bryce, James *Impressions of South Africa* (London 1898)

Casalis, Eugene *The Basuto* (London 1861)

My Life in Basutoland (London 1889)

Cory, G. E. *The Rise of South Africa* (London 1921)

Ellenberger, D. F. *History of the Basuto Ancient and Modern* (London 1912)

Lagden, Sir Godfrey *The Basutos* (London 1909)

Molema, S. M. *The Bantu* (Edinburgh 1920)

Oxford History of South Africa Vol. 1 (London 1969)

Rosslyn, Earl of *Twice Captured* (London 1900)

Theal, G. M. *Basutoland Records* (Cape Town 1883)

History of South Africa Vols III, IV and V (London 1889, 1893)

Thompson, George *Travels and Adventures in Southern Africa* (Cape Town, 1967)

Tylden, G. *The Rise of the Basuto* (Cape Town 1950)

The History of Thaba Bosiu (Maseru 1945)

Walker, E. A. *The Great Trek* (London 1934)

A History of South Africa (London 1928)

Worsley, P. *The Trumpet Shall Sound* (London 1957)

Index

History of Dahomy, 78
Hoffman, J. P., 165, 173
Hogge, Major, 154, 156, 157
Holland, 185
Hostages, 8
Hottentots, 146, 151, 179
Human sacrifice, 92, 95

Jaga horde, 33ff
Jonathan, Chief Leabua, 186
John I, King of Portugal, 6, 7
John II, King of Portugal, 14, 15
John III, King of Portugal, 27, 28, 33
John I, King of Congo, 12, 13, 18, 19
John, Prester, 6, 7

Kalahari Desert, 113, 116
Kaffir Wars, 147, 155, 158, 166, 171,
Kei River, 168, 170
Khubelu Pass, 119
Kingdom of Congo, economy, 14; sexual practises in, 16, 17; climate, 32, 134, 145, 185
King William's Town, 155, 164
Kok, Adam, 143, 146, 148, 165
Koranas, 121, 130, 134, 182
Krotz, Adam, 129–33, 137
Kuruman, 116

Lagden, Sir Godfrey, 152, 163, 173, 186
Lagos, 72
Lamb, Bullfinch, 56–60
Lancers, 158, 160, 161, 163
Lesotho (Basutoland), physical description, 114; 125, 134, 140, 141, 144, 150, 152, 163–6, 172, 174, 178, 179, 182–8
Letsie, 131, 139, 151, 175
Limpopo River, 144
Litakun, 116, 117
'Little War' 182, 185
London Missionary Society, 129, 145, 154, 174
Lopez, Duarte (with Pigafetta), 12, 15, 19, 41, 42

Maclean, Colonel, 168
Mamohato, 133

Mannix, Daniel, 31
Mantatees, 116–18, 121
MaNantatisi, 116, 118, 119
Manuel, Antonio, 43
Manuel I, King of Portugal, 15, 23
Maseru, 183, 186, 187
Matabele, 120, 121, 143
Mbanza Congo *see* São Salvador
McKay, Sergeant, 158
Melanesia, 171
Memoirs of the Reign of Bossa Adahee, 68
Mhlakaza, 166, 167, 172
Millenarism, 171
Moffat, The Reverend, 116, 117, 130
Mohale, 122
Mohlomi, 115
Mokachane, 119, 130
Mokachane Pass, 119
Molapo, 131, 138, 160
Molema, S. M., 153
Moletsane, 148
Moriah (Morija), 134, 137–40, 143, 175
Moroko, 148, 149, 152, 159
Moselekatze, 120, 121, 143
Moshesh, 113, 114; birth, 115, 118, 120, 121, 124, 125, 130, 131; meets Casalis, 132; physical description, 132, 133, 134, 139, 141–59, 162–6, 171–83; death of, 184; 185, 187
Moshoeshoe II, 185
Mpande, King, 164
Mpanza, Prince, 18, 19
My Life in Basuto Land, 126

Napier, Colonel, 160–2
Natal, 129, 143, 151, 182
Nehemiah, 151, 159, 162, 163
Nonquase, 167, 169, 171
Norris, Robert, 60, 68, 69

Ogun River, 106
Oliver, Caroline, 61
Orange Free State, 143, 149, 150, 165, 166, 172–8, 180–4, 187
Orange River, 122, 124, 128, 151, 153, 156
Orpen, Joseph, 173, 179
Orthez, 126, 148
Owen, C. M., 154, 156, 157

PERCEIVING ENVIRONMENTAL QUALITY

Research and Applications

Environmental Science Research

Editorial Board

A Continuation Order Plan is available for this series. A continuation order will bring
delivery of each new volume immediately upon publication. Volumes are billed only upon
actual shipment. For further information please contact the publisher.

PERCEIVING ENVIRONMENTAL QUALITY

Research and Applications

Edited by

Kenneth H. Craik
University of California at Berkeley

and

Ervin H. Zube
University of Massachusetts at Amherst

PLENUM PRESS · NEW YORK AND LONDON

Library of Congress Cataloging in Publication Data
Main entry under title:

Perceiving environmental quality.

(Environmental science research; v. 9)
Bibliography: p.
Includes index.
1. Environmental indexes—Addresses, essays, lectures. 2. Geographical percep-
tion—Addresses, essays, lectures. 3. Human ecology—Addresses, essays, lectures.
I. Craik, Kenneth H. II. Zube, Ervin H. III. Series.
GF23.I53P47   301.15'43'30131   76-13513
ISBN 0-306-36309-7

Preface

The purpose of this publication is to report on a series of research workshops which examined the place of environmental perception in a comprehensive system of indices for assessing and monitoring trends in environmental quality. The specific objectives of the workshops were to: (1) define the state-of-the-art in research on perception of environmental quality and identify salient conceptual and methodological issues; (2) delineate potential uses of perceived environmental quality indices (PEQIs) and related issues regarding ways in which PEQIs might enhance implementation, revision, or refinement of policy orientations; (3) identify the types of research which would assess adequately the efficacy of the development and the application of PEQIs; and (4) outline a realistic, pragmatic research strategy that relates to potential uses and identified policy issues.

The workshops were supported by a grant from the National Science Foundation, No. GSOC75-0782, and were held during the spring and summer of 1975 in Amherst, Massachusetts, and New York City. Contributed chapters for this volume were commissioned with funds from the Institute for Man and Environment, University of Massachusetts.

Scientific contributors to the understanding of environmental perception have increased substantially over the last decade, along with recognition that this realm of knowledge is crucial for an informed perspective on the impact of man on the environment. At the same time, there exists general consensus that the field remains diffuse and uncoordinated (Lowenthal, 1972b). Consideration of the practical use of PEQIs raises a number of issues that can give direction and focus to research in this area while serving the primary goal of clarifying the feasibility and appropriate conditions of employing PEQIs in (1) preparing environmental impact statements, (2) conducting follow-up evaluations of environmental projects, and (3) monitoring and communicating trends in environmental quality to decision-makers and the general public.

Three workshops were organized around the distinctive environmental contexts of: (1) scenic and recreation environments, (2) residential and institutional environments, and (3) air, water, and sonic environments. A fourth workshop was organized to review critically the preliminary findings from the first three. Workshops were limited in size to approximately a dozen persons. Participants were selected with the aim of including both leading researchers in environmental perception within the respective environmental contexts and potential users of PEQIs. The potential users represented state and federal agencies and private consultants and practitioners.

The workshops had three goals: review of methodological issues, analysis of policy and procedural issues, and examination of research needs. Each of these concerns was addressed initially by invited researchers for each environmental context. Three individuals were commissioned for each environmental context, through funds provided by the Institute for Man and Environment, University of Massachusetts, to prepare state-of-the-art review papers which served as the basis for discussions. The papers are also presented in this volume.

One outcome sought from the workshops was a broader and better integrated perspective upon present evidence and needed research on the role of extraenvironmental factors in perceptions of environmental quality, on the development of standard, comprehensive PEQIs for various environmental contexts, and on the impact of the use of PEQIs upon decision-making processes and outcomes. Following the review of methodological issues, analysis of policy and procedural issues, and an examination of research needs, round table discussions were held to suggest research strategies and priorities in research goals for the near future.

We want to acknowledge the substantive contributions made by each of the authors and round table participants. The mix of researchers and users proved valuable and stimulating. Participants in the first workshop on scenic and recreational environments included: Robert O. Brush, U.S. Forest Service; Terry C. Daniel, University of Arizona; Hugh C. Davis, University of Massachusetts; Julius Gy. Fabos, University of Massachusetts; Kenneth P. Hornback, U.S. National Park Service; Peter House, U.S. Environmental Protection Agency;

Rachel Kaplan, University of Michigan; George L. Peterson, Northwestern University; and Elwood L. Shafer, U.S. Forest Service. Participants in the second workshop on residential and institutional environments included: John Baird, Dartmouth College; Robert B. Bechtel, Environmental Research and Development Foundation; Charles Warren Callister, Callister, Payne & Bischoff; Gary Evans, University of California, Irvine; Arnold Friedmann, University of Massachusetts; John K. Holton, National Bureau of Standards; Norton Juster, Juster and Pope; Florence Ladd, Harvard University; Robert W. Marans, University of Michigan; Lester W. Milbrath, State University of New York, Buffalo; Daniel Tunstall, U.S. Office of Management and Budget; and Robert Wehrli, National Bureau of Standards. Participants in the third workshop on air, water, and sonic environments included: Mary Barker, Simon Fraser University; Robert Coughlin, Regional Science Research Institute; F. Peter Fairchild, New England Consortium on Environmental Protection; Charles H. W. Foster, University of Massachusetts; Thomas Saarinen, University of Arizona; Richard C. Smardon, Commonwealth of Massachusetts, Executive Office of Environmental Affairs; John D. Spengler, Harvard University; and Neil Weinstein, Rutgers University.

A fourth workshop was organized to provide a consultative review for the editors on the materials contained in the final chapter of this volume. Participants were invited from each of the three previous workshops. We extend our thanks to the individuals who participated in this repeat session—John Baird, Terry C. Daniel, Florence Ladd, Thomas Saarinen, Daniel Tunstall, and Neil Weinstein—but at the same time accept full and sole responsibility for the final chapter. We also wish to thank the University of Massachusetts graduate students who served as recorders for the workshop sessions: Marion Brown, Stephanie Caswell, James Palmer, and Craig Zimring. We are indebted to Christine Delsol for her editorial review, to Ann Dressler for assistance with graphics and for typing several drafts of the manuscript, to Gail Hammel for assistance on typing the final draft, to Judy Epstein for assistance with references and bibliography, and to W. R. Derrick Sewell for his consultation in planning the third workshop. We extend a note of thanks to Alice Klingener for assistance in the organization and administration of the workshops and are especially grateful to Helen Swartz for her assistance in both the organization of the workshops and the production of this manuscript.

ORGANIZATION OF THIS VOLUME

The volume is structured in five sections. Section I presents an introduction to environmental quality indices in general and to Perceived Environmental Quality Indices (PEQIs) in particular. Sections II, III, and IV are devoted to scenic and recreational environments; residential and institutional environments; and air, water, and sonic environments, respectively. Each section consists of the prepared review chapters and a summary of the workshop discussions, including a list of nominated research needs. Section V integrates the overlapping research needs emerging from the three workshops and offers a scientific and management program for the development and validation of PEQIs and for their application in environmental monitoring, impact assessment, and postconstruction evaluations.

K.H.C.
E.H.Z.

Contributors

Dr. Mary L. Barker
Department of Geography, Simon Fraser University, British Columbia, Canada

Dr. Robert B. Bechtel
Environmental Research Development Foundation, Kansas City, Missouri

Robert O. Brush
USDA Forest Service, Northeastern Forest Experiment Station

Dr. Robert E. Coughlin
Regional Science Research Institute, Philadelphia

Dr. Kenneth H. Craik
Institute of Personality Assessment and Research, University of California, Berkeley

Dr. Terry C. Daniel
Department of Psychology, University of Arizona

Dr. Florence C. Ladd
Department of City and Regional Planning, Graduate School of Design, Harvard University

Dr. Robert W. Marans
Institute for Social Research, University of Michigan

Dr. George L. Peterson
The Technological Institute, Northwestern University, Evanston, Illinois

Dr. Neil D. Weinstein
Department of Human Ecology and Social Science, Cook College, Rutgers University

Dr. Ervin H. Zube
Institute for Man and Environment, University of Massachusetts, Amherst

Contents

I. Environmental Quality Indices

II. Scenic and Recreational Environments

III. Residential and Institutional Environments

IV. Air, Water, and Sonic Environments

I
Environmental Quality Indices

The Development of Perceived Environmental Quality Indices

KENNETH H. CRAIK AND ERVIN H. ZUBE

The assessment of environmental quality can serve many useful purposes, by (1) clarifying the goals of environmental policy, (2) judging the effectiveness of environmental protection programs, (3) gauging the environmental impacts of proposed public and private projects, and (4) communicating trends in environmental quality to public officials, citizens, and decision-makers. For example, federal, state, and local governments have formulated environmental protection programs which may involve the commitment of billions of dollars; objective, quantitative procedures and indices for assessing environmental quality can be used to monitor the effectiveness of programs and assure a systematic form of accountability. As a recent Library of Congress report on environmental quality assessment observes: "The concept of environmental indices is not a product of academic whim; it evolved from a recognized need by policy makers" (Library of Congress, 1973, p. 2).

The term *index* has usually been used in reference to an aggregation of individual indicators or measurements which collectively convey information about the quality of some complex aspect or component of a condition, property, or phenomenon. For example, unemployment

DR. KENNETH H. CRAIK • Institute of Personality Assessment and Research, University of California, Berkeley, California 94720.   DR. ERVIN H. ZUBE • Institute for Man and Environment, University of Massachusetts, Amherst, Massachusetts 01002.

rates, average income levels, and years of formal education have been used as "social indicators" to convey information to decision-makers and the public about the social well-being of different metropolitan areas, states, and nations (U.S. Office of Management and Budget, 1973; Sheldon & Parke, 1975). Currently, indicators are used to monitor the magnitude of change over time in selected components of the social system and physical environment. When indicators or measures are converted to indices, a complex and challenging task, subjectively based weighting factors are often used to designate the relative importance of each indicator to the aggregated qualitative assessment.

In this country, the current impetus behind efforts to assess environmental quality flows quite directly from the National Environmental Policy Act (NEPA) of 1969. This act created the Council on Environmental Quality (CEQ) within the executive office of the president and requires the president to transmit an annual environmental quality report to the Congress. Section 204 of the act directs the CEQ to "gather timely and authoritative information concerning the conditions and trends in the quality of the environment," while sections 102(B) and 102(C) direct all agencies of the federal government to identify and develop methods and procedures "which will insure that presently unquantified environmental amenities and values may be given appropriate consideration in decision-making along with economic and technical considerations" and to prepare a detailed statement on the environmental impact of any proposed action "which may significantly affect the quality of the human environment."

All these purposes of NEPA entail methods and indices for assessing environmental quality and monitoring trends and changes in it. By early 1973 "approximately 4,000 federal environmental impact statements (EISs) had been prepared in response to the National Environmental Policy Act of 1969" (Twiss, 1974 p. 5). Many subsequent state laws, such as the California Environmental Quality Act of 1970, have markedly extended the domain of actions that require EISs. The urgent need for improved quantitative and objective processes for developing EISs and assessing impacts upon environmental quality has been thoroughly documented (Dickert & Domeny, 1974).

A critical review of the situation has been issued recently by the Environmental Studies Board of the National Academy of Sciences-National Academy of Engineering (NAS-NAE, 1975). The report finds that despite strong statements of need by all three branches of government and the scientific community, progress toward the development of environmental quality indices (EQIs) has not been satisfactory. The availability of competing physical indices characterizes the assessment of air quality (e.g., the MITRE Air Quality Index—MAQI; Extreme Value Index—EVI; Oak Ridge Air Quality Index—ORAQI) and water quality (e.g., Prevalence-Duration-Intensity Index—PDI; Water Quality Index—WQI), while even the conceptual issues involved in assessing the quality of land use remain unclarified (Thomas, 1972). The relatively more refined monitoring systems and indices are public health oriented and physically based. Air quality, for example, is assessed by indices such as those derived from ambient air levels of carbon monoxide, sulfur dioxide, nitrogen dioxide, and particulate matter.

POTENTIAL CONTRIBUTIONS OF PEQIs

A truly comprehensive assessment of environmental quality would include an appraisal of the quality of the *experienced* environment. Thus, observer-based evaluations of the everyday physical environment constitute an array of monitoring indices that could parallel and complement the physically based system of indices now under development. As the NAS-NAE report on environmental quality indices notes: "One approach which can improve our understanding of land use as well as other environmental areas is the measurement of people's perceptions of environmental quality" (NAS-NAE, 1975, p. 42).

Four principal uses of Perceived Environmental Quality Indices (PEQIs) are worth noting. First, PEQIs might be developed to assess aspects of environmental quality that intrinsically involve the interplay between the human observer and the environment (e.g., noise pollution, scenic quality). A comprehensive set of land use indices, for example, could include such measures of perceived environmental quality as the public appraisal of visual–aesthetic quality in the urban environment and scenic quality of landscape in the nonurban environment. Standard, quantitative techniques could be applied to the development of such PEQIs, which would be especially useful in monitoring aspects of environmental quality for which physical indices are unavailable.

Second, PEQIs might serve as criteria for establishing physically based EQIs. Thus, physical EQIs can be derived by first identifying urban areas perceived by residents as being high and low in environmental quality and then searching for physical attributes that differentiate them (e.g., Appleyard & Carp, 1974). Similarly, the hunt is on for attributes of land form and land use that will predict observer evaluations of landscape quality (Craik, 1972a). Although the success of current efforts is impressive (Zube, Pitt, & Anderson, 1974), there is potential hazard in employing physically derived indices prematurely as surrogates for observer-based evaluations. Statistically derived combinations of physical measures are likely to yield substantial but far from perfect predictions of PEQIs. Thus, there is the danger that these imperfect surrogates will become embedded and enshrined in standards and guidelines that abstract only a partial set of components of environmental quality. Their widespread application in the field may systematically and relentlessly eliminate essential elements of environmental quality not captured in the statistical equations.

A third use of PEQIs appears in efforts to gauge the extent of congruence between perceptions of environmental quality and physical EQIs (e.g., Jacoby, 1972). For example, the relation between on-site public perception of air quality and MAQI or ORAQI readings must be determined. Discrepancies between the two forms of appraisal might suggest: (1) eventual problems in the credibility and consequent public acceptance of physically based EQIs; (2) problems of misunderstanding and misperception, calling for programs of public environmental education; (3) limitations and inadequacies in the EQIs; and, without doubt, (4) a challenge to scientific understanding.

A fourth potential use for PEQIs is for conducting person-centered EQ assessments as well as the traditional place-centered EQ appraisals. In the latter case, PEQI readings from a sample of observers would be averaged to obtain an index for a locale (e.g., a neighborhood, a watershed). In contrast, person-centered PEQ assessments would identify and survey an individual's personal environment (e.g., residence, workplace, transportation system, recreational environment, public environment) and appraise the PEQ of that particular set of environments. "Citizens who perceive their air as clear; their water as clean and palatable; their landscapes as scenic; their residential and work environments as safe, attractive and functional, and their auditory environments as pleasant rather than noisy, enjoy an enhanced sense of environmental well-being (EWB)" (Craik & McKechnie, 1974). Thus, by aggregating PEQIs for each individual across the various environmental categories, a goal index is available for gauging the impact of environmental policies, programs, and projects upon a directly relevant facet of human welfare. In addition, the comparison of levels of EWB among subgroups of the general public can serve to gauge the degree of social equity attained in the provision and attainment of a sense of environmental well-being. Because of differences among individuals in home range and accessibility to environmental setting in a region, it is difficult to infer the EWB of various population subgroups on the basis of place-oriented EQ appraisals alone.

This fourth, person-centered application of PEQIs in the development of environmental well-being assessments is akin to the current efforts to devise a standard array of social indicators and quality of life indicators (U.S. Office of Management and Budget, 1973; Campbell, Converse, & Rogers, 1975). A recent panel at the Eighth World Congress of Sociologists ("Perceptions of Environmental Quality and Measuring the Quality of Life") dealt in part with this fourth potential use of PEQIs. The report by the U.S. Office of Management and Budget, *Social Indicators, 1973,* was organized around eight areas of social concern: health, public safety, education, employment, income, housing, leisure and recreation, and population. Thus, there is both a conceptual and a substantive relationship between the notion of PEQIs and social indicators or quality of life measurement. The focus of the research workshops, however, was not primarily on this area of common ground. It is important to note that the first three uses of PEQIs have a more direct bearing upon the function of environmental perceptions in monitoring trends in environmental quality, preparing environmental impact statements, and conducting follow-up evaluations of built environments and environmental transformations.

The concept of environmental well-being, however, does serve to emphasize that physical EQIs have stressed the negative role of environmental quality, as if "health" were simply an absence of "pathology." However, appraisal of the perceived sonic environment, for example, would attend not only to noise pollution, but also to pleasant sounds, not just to the whine of sirens, but also to "the music of rivers" (Leopold, 1949; Southworth, 1969). EWB indices also directly gauge the attainment of an environmental goal. Often, quite strained efforts are made to use public health impacts to justify environmental policy goals. A straightforward assertion might be more defensible and gain wider support, namely, that when citizens look and move around their environment, use it, listen to it, smell it, they should be able to evaluate their environment favorably.

Unfortunately, few, if any, PEQIs have achieved the status of standard, reliable measures. However, the attainment of adequate and useful indices may be feasible within the context of current methodology. Perliminary work has been conducted on: perception of air, noise, and water pollution; perception of landscape and scenic resources; perception of urban residential quality; perception of the quality of outdoor recreation facilities; perception of the quality of transportation systems; and perception of the quality of work and institutional environments (e.g., factories, hospitals, schools). For reviews of this research, see Craik (1970, 1971, 1973); Goodey (1971); Jacoby (1972); Kates (1970); Lowenthal (1961, 1972b); Saarinen (1969); Sewell & Little 1973).

The NAS-NAE critical review of environmental quality assessment (1975) has urged a state-of-the-art appraisal "to establish criteria for developing standard PEQIs; to identify the properties of the observer-as-environmental-quality-appraisal-instrument; to review the conceptual and methodological issues in using PEQIs in conjunction with physical environmental indices in policy and decision-making; to ascertain their role in communicating with the general public, and to consider the specific PEQIs that could be appropriately aggregated into an index of environmental well-being" (pp. 43–44).

SCIENTIFIC AND POLICY ISSUES

There are several disciplinary approaches to the study of man–environment relations as indicated in Figure 1 (Column 1). Within each discipline, a variety of research paradigms and areas of concern can be found, as Column 2 illustrates for environmental psychology. Furthermore, the study of environmental perception, itself, subsumes an array of substantive issues (Column 3). The distinctive feature of this volume is its concentration upon one of these issues, namely, the perception of environmental quality and, particularly, the potential role of environmental perception measures as environmental quality indices in policy formation and decision-making settings.

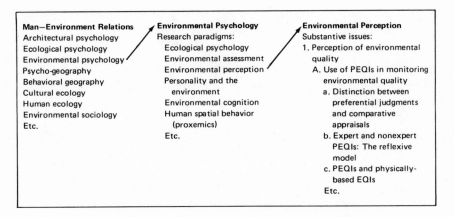

Man–Environment Relations	Environmental Psychology	Environmental Perception
Architectural psychology	Research paradigms:	Substantive issues:
Ecological psychology	Ecological psychology	1. Perception of environmental
Environmental psychology	Environmental assessment	quality
Psycho-geography	Environmental perception	A. Use of PEQIs in monitoring
Behavioral geography	Personality and the	environmental quality
Cultural ecology	environment	a. Distinction between
Human ecology	Environmental cognition	preferential judgments
Environmental sociology	Human spatial behavior	and comparative
Etc.	(proxemics)	appraisals
	Etc.	b. Expert and nonexpert
		PEQIs: The reflexive
		model
		c. PEQIs and physically-
		based EQIs
		Etc.

FIG. 1. Scientific context and focus of the PEQI research workshops.

METHODOLOGICAL ISSUES

One obstacle to the development and use of PEQIs is the widespread assumption that observer-based appraisals of environmental quality necessarily entail pervasive individual and group variations among observers; engage only the personal tastes, inclinations, and biases of observers; and express merely their idiosyncratic likes and dislikes. In this view, PEQIs must inevitably fail to approximate the level of reliability and generality required to environmental quality indices and presumably attained by physical indices. However, the evidence to sustain or refute these assumptions has never been critically examined, and an agenda of needed research on these issues has never been systematically organized.

For example, the possibility of establishing a robust and meaningful distinction between preferential judgments and comparative appraisals has important implications for the development of PEQIs. Preferential judgments express an entirely personal, subjective appreciation of (or repugnance for) specific environments, while comparative appraisals judge the relative quality of specific environments against some implicit or explicit standard of comparison (Craik & McKechnie, 1974). If a panel of observers examines 20 suburban residential communities, the members may differ widely in their personal preferences and in their likes and dislikes. However, when asked to appraise the communities comparatively against the standard of "an excellent suburban development," they may very well display greater agreement. The conceptual criteria for establishing the distinction can be readily specified, for example: Preferential judgments and comparative appraisals constitute distinct, nonredundant measures; greater consensus among observers is displayed in comparative appraisals than in preferential judgments; preferential judgments reflect a wider range of observer characteristics and predispositions; and greater agreement between experts and nonexperts is found in comparative appraisals than in preferential judgments. However, the pertinent research evidence regarding the perception of environmental quality in various kinds of environments has not been marshaled in light of this distinction.

The distinction between preferential judgments and comparative appraisals simply illustrates one facet of the role of extraenvironmental factors in perceptions of environmental quality. The range of concerns with methodological issues for selected environmental context (e.g., air quality, scenic quality, residential quality) encompasses the following points:

Identifying the properties of the observer-as-environmental-quality-appraisal-instrument:

1. Is there evidence on the viability of the distinction between preferential judgments and comparative appraisals?
2. Is there evidence on the degree of consensus among individuals and groups in appraising environmental quality?
3. Is there evidence on the degree of agreement between experts and laypersons in their appraisals of environmental quality?
4. Is there evidence for other extraenvironmental, observer-related correlates (e.g., familiarity, social class) of variations in environmental quality appraisals?
5. Is there evidence on the degree and kinds of relationships obtaining between observer-based appraisals of environmental quality and pertinent physical environmental quality indices?
6. Is there other evidence that bears upon the feasibility of developing standard PEQIs?

POLICY AND PROCEDURAL ISSUES

The development of a PEQI operational system involves not only the quantitative measurement of perceived environmental quality but also the development of a policy and institutional framework for application, the training of persons in operational techniques, and the development of criteria and guidelines for their use. An essential task, therefore, is to consider the practicality and consequences of these applications of PEQIs, including the following points:

What criteria are appropriate for the development of standard PEQIs within the specific environmental contexts:

1. What research is available or needed to afford a standard set of comprehensive, sensitive instruments for use by observers in appraising degrees of environmental quality?
2. What research is available or needed to specify the optimal modes of presentation and selection of observers in observer-based appraisals of environmental quality (e.g., user panels vs. site-visit panels; expert vs. lay panels; direct vs. simulated presentations)?

What conceptual, methodological, and policy issues are entailed in using PEQIs in environmental policy formation and decision-making:

1. Are there instances in which PEQIs for a specific environmental context have been used in preparing environmental impact statements, conducting follow-up evaluations of environmental projects, or communicating trends in environmental quality to decision-makers and the general public?
2. Is there evidence on whether these applications of PEQIs are feasible and effective in decision-making and policy formation?
3. What guidelines can be offered for the use of PEQIs in these applications?
4. What research is needed to increase our understanding of the function of PEQIs in policy-formation and decision-making settings?

TERMINOLOGY, WITH ILLUSTRATIVE CASE EXAMPLES

An effort to organize and discern directions in a sprawling, multidisciplinary endeavor requires attention to terminological usage. Indeed, the workshop discussions generated novel terms, while revealing considerable confusion about certain terms having prior currency.

In our workshop summaries and conceptual overview, we will strive for consistency in the use of key terms. These terms, and a better sense of what they might mean, emerged in part from the workshop discussions. We have not attempted to impose these usages retroactively upon the prepared chapters. The alert reader may detect some variations, but internally consistent ones, in those sections of the volume.

Inevitably, the acronym for Perceived Environmental Quality Indices (PEQI) took on folklore status itself, with the prevailing pronunciation tending, justifiably or not, toward: pee-kwee. Nontheoretical imagery surrounding the term had its referent appearing in two forms: (1) as a small furry creature (a photograph of such a creature appeared in our mail with the query: Might this be a PEQI?), and (2) as an Indian tribe (provoking queries along the line: Who is the chief of the PEQIs?). It is perhaps not accidental that the attribute of elusiveness is common to both metaphors.

To acquaint the reader with key terms and concepts, we will review two case examples: the impact of a major new transportation system upon perceived residential quality in the areas through which it runs, and the appraisal of scenic quality for sites in the Connecticut River Valley.

THE BART RESIDENTIAL IMPACT STUDY

In 1972, the Bay Area Rapid Transit system (BART) began operations in the San Francisco region, the first new metropolitan transit system to be constructed in the United States since 1908 (Appleyard & Carp, 1974). Eventually, the system will link three counties (San Francisco, Alameda, and Contra Costa) through its 34 stations and 75 miles of track. In addition to its primary function as a transportation system, the complex network of tracklines, moving vehicles, stations, tunnels, and so forth will have important impacts—benign and detrimental, intended and unintended—upon residential quality along its domain of influence. In an effort to monitor the impact of BART upon residential quality, Appleyard and Carp (1974) undertook an extensive investigation of the residential environment along the BART route (Table I). The study included an analysis of perceived residential quality at the preoperational (but postconstruction) stage in the system's development. The research design calls for subsequent analyses of perceived residential quality to monitor impacts over a period of time.

In the preoperational stage, a representative sample of residents 18 years and older who live within one mile of the BART route was interviewed ($N = 2541$). In addition, 25 sites along the route were selected for more detailed analysis. They were defined spatially as one-quarter mile along the route and one-quarter mile on each side of the tracks; 11 of the sites included BART stations within their boundaries. The research program also included a survey of physical environmental characteristics of the sites, including statistics on traffic flow and land use, and an array of descriptive indices based upon field observations.

TABLE I. Dimensions of Residential Quality[a]

Dimension label
Aesthetics of the residential area
Feelings about living in this area
Noise disturbing outdoor activities
Traffic safety
Noise from sources outside own and neighbors' homes
Safety of self and property
Noise disturbing indoor activities
Noise from sources in own and neighbors' homes, except aircraft and trains
Characteristics of people in the area
Air quality
Maintenance (by residents) within own block
Nonautomobile mobility
Maintenance services (other than by residents)
Solicitors
Privacy
Automobile mobility
Noise from aircraft and trains
Animal nuisance
Alienation among residents
Environmental correlates of alienation

[a] Adapted from Carp, Appleyard, Shokrkon, and Zawadski, (1973).

Two control sites, located beyond the BART impact zone, were studied by similar techniques.

APPRAISAL OF SCENIC QUALITY IN THE CONNECTICUT RIVER VALLEY

The Connecticut River watershed extends over more than 11,000 square miles from near the Canada–New Hampshire border through four states to Long Island Sound. Scenic quality is regarded as an important resource throughout the entire valley, and its present condition and preservation are receiving regional attention by current environmental policy, management, and research (Ertel, 1975).

In 1973, Zube and his associates (Zube et al., 1974) conducted a study of the perceived quality of landscape for 56 sites located in the southern Connecticut River Valley. A diverse sample of valley residents ($N = 307$) served as observers. The landscape scenes were presented in the form of wide-angle color photographs (5 × 7 in.). Participants described and evaluated the scenes in several ways, including the procedure of sorting the photographs into seven categories ranging from "the highest scenic quality" to "the lowest scenic quality." A primary intent of the investigation was to examine the relationship between the perceived quality of landscape and the physical characteristics of the sites. For this purpose, physical properties of each site were measured (Table II).

KEY TERMS AND CONCEPTS

The two case examples will illustrate the following terms and concepts.

Place-Centered Appraisals and Person-Centered Assessments

In *place-centered appraisals,* the reports of a sample of observers regarding perceived environmental quality are combined to obtain an

TABLE II. Landscape Dimensions

Land form	Land use contrast
Relative relief ratio	Height contrast
Absolute relative relief	Grain contrast
Mean slope distribution	Spacing contrast
Topographic texture	Evenness contrast
Ruggedness number	Naturalism contrast
Spatial definition index	Water
Mean elevation	Water edge density
Land use area	Percentage water area
Land use diversity	View
Naturalism index	Area of view
Percentage tree cover	Length of view
Land use edge	Viewer position
Land use edge density	
Land use edge variety	
Land use compatibility	

index for a locale or site. By this means, the appraisals of residents in each of the 25 BART research sites provide the basis for obtaining PEQIs for each locale, and the scenic quality sortings made by observers can yield an average value, or PEQI, for each of the 56 Connecticut River Valley landscapes. Indeed, both investigations primarily entail place-centered appraisals. The unit of analysis is the site or place and the resultant PEQIs offer a basis for comparisons among locales and comparisons of the same locale over time. *Person-centered assessments* identify and survey an individual's personal environment (e.g., residence, workplace, transportation system, recreational environment, public environment) and evaluate the perceived environmental quality of that individualized set of environments. Analysis might focus upon a single environmental domain (e.g., residential) or it might aggregate readings across the individual's entire personal environment to gain a composite index. In either case, the unit of analysis is an individual rather than a site, and the intent is to learn something about persons, not places. In the BART study, for example, person-centered assessments of perceived residential quality might be related to socioeconomic status, length of residence, and other individual characteristics of research participants that might influence, in various ways, their current sense of environmental well-being.

Comparative Appraisals and Preferential Judgments

The instructions employed when observers are asked to record their perceptions of environmental quality can evoke various cognitive sets and orient them to perceive and judge in different ways (Leff, Gordon, Ferguson, 1974). Two instructional sets received attention in the workshop discussions. *Preferential judgments* (PJ) express an entirely personal, subjective appreciation (or repugnance for) specified environments, while *comparative appraisals* (CA) judge the relative quality of specified environments against some implicit or explicit standard of comparison (Craik & McKechnie, 1974). In the BART residential impact study, for example, participants might have been asked, "On a completely personal basis, how much do you like your neighborhood?" (preferential judgment), or, "Setting aside your personal feelings now, how do you compare your neighborhood with other neighborhoods in the Bay Area?" (comparative appraisal). Of course, both instructional sets might be employed in the same analysis of perceived residential quality.

Composite versus Global Indices

The scenic quality index in the Connecticut River Valley study, as well as the instructional sets just illustrated, represent global appraisals of perceived environmental quality. In contrast, the BART residential impact study asked participants to evaluate a wide array of residential features which could be assumed to represent constituent elements for a *composite index* of perceived residential quality (e.g., personal safety, privacy, attractiveness, maintenance). The global indices are directly derived from the overall evaluations rendered by observers. When constituent elements of perceived environmental quality are evaluated, a *weighting scheme* is required to derive a single index. Constituent elements can be granted equal weight in the final index, or the elements can be assigned differential weights, based upon some criterion of relative importance.

Monitoring Operations: On-Site Users versus Touring Panels

In place-centered appraisals, observers can have varying relationships to the locales being studied. Places can be appraised by their residents and other on-site users, or one or more places can be appraised by a *touring panel*. The composition of the touring panels can be representative of the general public or can be composed of persons designated by some criterion as experts. Thus, in the BART residential impact study, the primary observers are on-site residents, while the study of scenic quality in the Connecticut River Basin employed local residents, individuals from the wider general public, and experts (e.g., landscape architects, regional planners).

Monitoring Operations: Direct versus Simulated Presentations

In place-centered appraisals, observers can be presented with the research sites *directly* (e.g., through looking at, walking around, visiting, or living in them) or *environmental simulations* can be used (e.g., sketches, drawings, models, photographs, films, videotapes). The on-site residents in the BART impact study, of course, were directly presented with their own residential environments. The primary medium of presentation in the study of scenic quality was photography. However, in a substudy of eight sites, this form of environmental simulation was compared to direct field trips (Zube et al., 1974; see also Appleyard & Craik, 1974; McKechnie, 1976).

Types of PEQIs

During the workshop discussions, various species of PEQIs made their appearance from time to time. Three attributes offered promising and recurrent bases for a PEQI taxonomy: focus, instructional set, and variability of the obtained index (Table III). The first and second attributes appeared especially important to researchers, for they

TABLE III. Attributes of PEQIs

Focus	place-centered	person-centered
Instructional set	comparative appraisal	preferential judgment
Variability	high consensus	low consensus

represent important choice-points at the *outset* of PEQI surveys. Investigators must decide whether to focus upon an array of places or a sample of persons as the primary unit of analysis. They must employ clearly formulated instructional sets: either comparative appraisals or preferential judgments, or both. The third attribute, variability, concerns a property of the *obtained* indices and appeared especially consequential to decision-makers. If a PEQI displays low variability, then decision-makers can act upon this evidence of broad consensus in formulating policy or justifying decisions. If great variability among observers' judgments is shown, decision-makers must be aware that any action on the basis of the average reading of the index may represent the perceptions of only a minority of their constituency.

The implications of consensus in place-centered appraisals was vividly conveyed by Tunstall during workshop discussions:

> You know the French have the Michelin Guides, and they list 4-star views, 3-star views, and 2-star views—and almost everyone agrees. Maybe you could disagree now and then with Michelin, and you could write in and say, "That's not a 4-star view, that's a 3-star view." How did they decide one was a 4-star view of Notre Dame, and another side of Notre Dame was only a 3-star view or a 2-star view? Surely, a few people decided, but over a long term, over a couple hundred years that's been fairly well agreed upon, and the amazing thing is that it's cross-cultural. Americans arrive on their first day in Paris, and take a look and say, "Yes, this view is more interesting, or more monumental." And you tend to agree. I guess it's that part that I think you wanted to get at in the comparative appraisal. If over time we could do that, not 200 years with the Michelin Guide elitist approach, but within a few years, with a social science approach, then that's going to give it more substance in speaking to policy issues. You say, we need to protect this view for this reason because so many people agree it is such an important view.

The appraisal of scenic quality of landscapes appears to constitute a highly consensual PEQI. For the 56 Connecticut River Valley scenes, the Q-sortings for scenic value displayed noteworthy agreement. And in a later study, extending the sample of research sites to 217, (Anderson, Zube, & MacConnell, 1976) it was demonstrated that the composite appraisals made by a randomly selected panel of only 5 observers (drawn from the total sample of 30) would be expected to correlate +.99 with the composite appraisals of the total sample. As Brush notes (Chapter 3), similar findings of consensus in the perception of landscape quality have been generally reported. Whether similarly high agreement occurs for indices of perceived residential quality remains to be determined. It should be cautioned that comparisons of PEQIs on variability must be alert for methodological artifacts and should be based upon maximally similar measurement procedures (e.g., regarding type and size of observer samples; instructional set; judgment procedure and reporting forms; analytic steps in calculating the index).

In conjunction, the three attributes of PEQIs generate an 8-cell typology (Table IV). Peterson (Chapter 4) initiated typological references in his distinction between two forms of PEQI (p. 60): place-centered, based on comparative appraisals, and person-centered, based on preferential judgments. The notion of PEQI-Is and PEQI-IIs carried forward, through the first and subsequent workshops discussions. However, the meaning of the distinction shifted frequently. Clearly, PEQI-Is tended to be place-centered with high consensus, based on comparative appraisals (but possibly on preferential judgments also) (i.e., cells 1 and 2). But PEQI-II tended to refer variously and unsystematically to any or all of the remaining six cells of the taxonomy. The simple distinction between PEQI-Is and PEQI-IIs served a provocative and ultimately clarifying function, but workshop participants showed marked consensus in suggesting that its usefulness would not extend beyond this report. Certainly, the eightfold array is a more adequate PEQI typology.

The two case examples also serve to illustrate the uses of PEQIs. Place-centered appraisals of perceived environmental quality (PEQ) offer a potentially useful array of monitoring indices. Thus, they permit comparisons among the 25 residential sites in the BART impact study and among the 56 landscapes of the Connecticut River Valley study; and they afford a means of following trends over time. Both studies are also designed to permit a search for physical *environmental attributes* that correlate with observer appraisals of perceived quality and yield a basis for design standards and management guidelines. In addition, the place-centered PEQIs would contribute baseline data concerning current conditions, thus providing a useful context for gauging the effectiveness of policies and programs affecting the sites. The scenic survey of the Connecticut River Valley illustrates a method of monitoring the effec-

TABLE IV. A PEQI Typology

		Place-centered appraisals	Person-centered assessments
High consensus	CA	1	5
	PJ	2	6
Low consensus	CA	3	7
	PJ	4	8

tiveness of various subregional planning and management policies over time, although a more systematic sampling of sites than took place in the Connecticut River survey would be required for this purpose. Similarly, the BART impact study demonstrates an approach to identifying the effects of a major transportation project upon perceived residential quality. Finally, person-centered appraisals of perceived environmental quality can serve to estimate the degree of social equity attained in the provision of a sense of environmental well-being (e.g., among age groups throughout the BART impact region or in the Connecticut River Valley).

SUMMARY

The concept of PEQIs has apparent merit when viewed within the context of its potential application to real-world problems, for use in environmental policy formation and decision-making. The NEPA provides one institutional framework of direct relevancy. Potential applications for PEQIs include: monitoring trends in environmental quality, preparing environmental impact statements, and conducting follow-up evaluations of construction projects and environmental transformations. The step from concept to operational PEQI system, however, requires a careful identification and analysis of salient methodological issues for each environmental context and a definition of relevant policy and institutional frameworks for its application.

II
Scenic and Recreational Environments

The Constructs of Perceived Quality in Scenic and Recreational Environments

The functions of the environment are many and diverse—some general and some specific; some biological, physical, and social; and some psychological. As a source of aesthetic satisfaction—for example, as scenery—the environment can contribute to one's perceived sense of well-being. The general environmental function is that of a source of information, of a psychological stimulus. The perceived quality of the scenery is a function of the interaction of man and the environment. In contrast, as a source of outdoor recreation and satisfaction, the environment functions both as psychological stimulus and as a setting for social interaction. Except for a few solitary recreational pursuits, most recreational activities involve interactions with both the social and the physical environment. The perception of the quality of the recreational environment, therefore, may be as much a function of the interpersonal activities as of the physical setting which accommodates them.

Peterson (Chapter 4) suggests, for example, that social carrying capacity or the level of crowding is an important dimension of the perceived satisfaction of wilderness recreation. This is an aspect of a particular environment and of specific types of people and recreational purposes. It is also an example of the interaction of social and physical milieus in the perception of the quality of recreation environments.

Conceptually, scenery is a characteristic of all environments. It is the general appearance of places and the aggregated features which help to define the character of these places, both natural and urban. Recreational environments, however, are more readily defined in terms of discrete places. The environmental function of many of these individual

23

recreation places (e.g., parks, playgrounds, hunting areas) tends to be specific rather than general.

Brush (Chapter 3) notes that there is little in the literature on user evaluations of recreational environments. He speculates that the highly personal and subjective nature of leisure activities may mitigate against indices of quality for recreational environments that would be valid across large segments of the population. But for the scenic quality of nonurban landscapes, he finds evidence of a considerable degree of agreement across population segments. This consensus across populations also encompasses laypersons and professional environmental designers. In addition, he finds some support in reference to scenic quality for the distinction between preferential judgments appealing to personal tastes and predispositions, and comparative appraisals appealing to a widely held standard.

The conceptual and empirical distinctions, identified in the chapters, between scenic environments and recreation environments suggested to workshop participants the possibility of two kinds of PEQIs. The first, place-centered appraisals are environmentally focused, describing general attributes that are stable across population segments, and consensually used by most people. The scenic quality research findings reported by Brush tend to support this concept. Workshop discussion suggested that place-centered appraisals would have potential utility for monitoring regional changes in scenic quality, for evaluating alternative sites for large-scale projects, and as a component of a broad-based, aggregated, quality-of-environment or quality-of-life index.

Person-centered assessments were defined as more specific and observer focused. It would show intergroup differences; it would be specific for particular groups and decisions. It would also appear to be more consonant with the conclusions drawn from recreation-oriented research by both Brush and Peterson. Person-centered assessments would have potential utility for gauging environmental impacts and for postconstruction evaluations from the vantage points of specific user groups.

Peterson also suggests a possible relationship of these PEQIs to the notion of comparative appraisals and preferential judgments. Place-centered appraisals with an environmental focus are obtained from either comparative appraisals or preferential judgments, while person-oriented person-centered assessments are derived solely from preferential judgments. In both cases the observer is the measuring instrument, and in both cases the need for an experiential basis for the PEQI is recognized.

Both Brush and Peterson conclude that research is considerably more advanced on the scenic environmental domain, a point which was reinforced in the round table discussion. Peterson discusses a range of factors which are potentially important to the conceptual analysis of recreational environments and also presents a strong case for a careful analysis of the concept of quality as it relates to various environmental domains.

The development of standard PEQIs for scenic and recreational environments raises the pragmatic issue of what is to be measured and the subsequent evaluative concerns of reliability and validity. The domain of what to measure is perhaps least clearly provided by the current constructs of recreational quality.

Daniel (Chapter 2) observes that the selection of the relevant dimension, as in the case of landscape beauty, is not too great a problem, but that its unambiguous specification to an observer can be more difficult. In the case of the recreational environment, as indicated by Peterson, this problem is confounded by the difficulty of qualitative discrimination between the activity and the supporting environment. While the observer–participant activity is reasonably well described from scenic environments (i.e., seeing or viewing) and is also constant across all settings, such is not true for recreational settings. Activities vary from passive and sedentary to active and highly mobile and are dependent in part on the physical attributes of specific settings. Both Peterson and Daniel imply that the identification of what to measure might be facilitated by a perceptually defined landscape taxonomy that would attempt to identify and describe—not evaluate—environments and related activities which are perceived to be similar in nature. Such a taxonomy might be particularly helpful in dealing with the recreational environment. In other words, a set of standard environments or components would be identified and described for use in the development of scenic and recreational PEQIs. Whether the assessment of quality would be facilitated by the identification of standard environments or environmental components is conjectural. Intuitively, however, the concept has appeal and appears commonsensical.

In the following chapters, Daniel reviews the measurement requirements and criteria for a sound and effective index; Brush surveys empirical research on the factors affecting perception of scenic and recreational quality, and Peterson offers directions for research and development guided by a conceptual model of the process of environmental perception and appraisal, illustrating some of the practical questions of recreational and resource management which a PEQI measurement system might usefully address.

2

Criteria for Development and Application of Perceived Environmental Quality Indices

TERRY C. DANIEL

To develop a method for measuring or indexing environmental quality, some conception of what determines the quality of the environment must be established. What combinations of features or characteristics distinguish a "poor quality" environment from one of "mediocre quality" or "excellent quality"? If only an indication of the minimal requirements for the support of human life were desired, perhaps a set of features could be identified and assessed rather directly. However, the requirements for the support of an individual human life hardly approximate the level of environmental quality required to support, now and in the future, man living in complex, interrelated societies. Even if minimum subsistence levels were established, they could provide no more than an "absolute zero" for a scale of environmental quality. Environmental quality assessment (happily) can, for the present at least, be concerned with the identification and gauging of environmental features that are required to maintain a "quality of life" that is substantially above bare subsistence or survival levels.

DR. TERRY C. DANIEL • Department of Psychology, University of Arizona, Tucson, Arizona 85721.

The basic conceptualization of environmental quality that seems to underlie current assessment efforts may be termed *analytic*. That is, to determine general environmental quality, the quality of a set of individual elements or components is assessed, essentially independently, and these individual measurements are then combined, perhaps by some weighted averaging method. Several lists of the separate determinants or components of environmental quality have been developed, for example, the National Wildlife Federation's Environmental Quality Index (Kimball, 1972), but there is hardly complete agreement on the specific set of elements that should be included. While the rationale for including some elements seems reasonably clear and generally accepted (for example, air, water, and soil), the bases for including other constituents are less well defined and are more controversial (for example, wildlife). It is not the purpose of this chapter to develop a list of essential or desirable determinants of environmental quality. However, it is important to recognize that the analytic conceptualization assumes that measures of the quality of individual components can eventually be combined to yield a general indication of environmental quality. In addition to the obvious difficulties of identifying and weighting components of environmental quality, systems for measuring the quality of each component must be developed that will yield indices that are at least compatible with those for other components.

MEASURING ENVIRONMENTAL QUALITY

Measurement of the more "tangible" environmental elements has in many cases been approached directly; air quality, for example, has been indexed in physical–chemical terms as parts per million of various pollutant elements. While such direct physical measuring systems may provide very precise, reliable indices of the forms and amounts of environmental components, they cannot by themselves indicate the *quality* of the component. Some additional process must be employed to determine what forms and what amounts of an environmental component are required to achieve "acceptable" or "desirable" or "optimum" quality levels for that component. In the case of air quality, for example, the physical measures have been supplemented by (expert) medical judgment translated into legal minimum standards. Thus, a minimum "healthy" standard is established with regard to the concentrations of various pollutants (for example, carbon monoxide, sulfur dioxide) and any given body of air can be measured against that standard. A basic assumption seems to be that, in general, the lower the concentration of the designated pollutants, the "better" the air.

The established minimum standard, however precisely stated, only represents the current best medical–political judgment, and there are no clear indications of how this standard should be used to determine "air quality." How much reduction in which pollutants produces the best or highest quality air? How are the individual pollutant concentrations to be weighted? What are the implications of possible synergistic (or antagonistic) relationships among target pollutants and/or other, nontarget pollutants? Availability of direct (physical) measures of environmental quality determinants is certainly an important asset, but it does not by any means assure a valid index of the *quality* of that component.

Assessment of other, often designated "intangible," environmental quality components has necessarily been approached indirectly. The aesthetic components, for example, have not generally been assessed by any direct measurement device. Rather, quality is assessed indirectly, in terms of human experiences and judgments. In this case, the question of appropriate quality standards may be included (covertly or overtly) in the measurement itself. Human observers may be asked to judge the "quality" of the aesthetic experiences provided by their environment (or some component thereof), presumably basing their judgment on their own standards of quality.

Alternatively, they may be asked to provide comparative judgments ("Which of these alternatives is the best?") or to judge environmental quality relative to some specified alternative.

Measures of intangible components often carry the stigma of being based on subjective judgments. As a result, there may be a tendency to de-emphasize the importance of these components in the assessment of general environmental quality. At least, there has been a tendency to approach these components with considerable caution. In fact, all indices of the *quality* of environmental components, however concrete and tangible the component may be, are based upon human perception and judgment. The identification of a component as a determinant of environmental quality, and the determination of appropriate *standards* of quality for that component, rest upon human (subjective) judgments.

It is vital, then, that this perceptual-judgmental basis of environmental quality assessments be formally recognized and systematically approached. A major objective of this chapter is to review the criteria appropriate for the development of methods for systematically assessing environmental quality; in particular, methods for achieving Perceived Environmental Quality Indices (PEQIs).

WHAT IS AN INDEX

An *index* is the culmination of a measurement process that consists of several stages. First, there must be some, at least general, conceptualization of the properties or characteristics to which the index refers, some notion of what is being measured. For example, *air quality* has largely been conceived of in terms of *purity,* the absence of certain target pollutants (Library of Congress, 1973). This conceptualization has important implications for the procedures that will be used to measure the quality of air and, in turn, will have important implications for the index that is ultimately produced by this system. In particular, many elements (potentially even pollutants) of air may not be measured and, thus, can have no (direct) influence on the air quality index. The basic conceptualization of the properties or property to be measured, whether formally recognized and presented as a theory or model or held less formally, has important implications for the resulting index. The underlying conceptual bases of an index are an integral part of the measurement system and should be made as explicit as possible.

Once the conceptual basis of a measurement system has been established, operations for producing observable *indicants* of the relevant properties (or their effects) must be devised. For example, having determined that the concentrations of sulfur dioxide, carbon monoxide, etc., are the relevant characteristics for determining air quality, some method for observing the concentrations of these elements must be developed. In this instance, many aspects of the needed operations (methods for determining the concentration of sulfur dioxide, for example) could be approached rather directly. However, concentrations of the designated elements in ambient air are by no means stable over time, and a question arises as to how to represent this variability. For sulfur dioxide, the solution was to use three separate time bases (3 hr., 24 hr., and annual mean). Two important implications of adopting this particular set of operations for obtaining observable indicants are: First, the conceptualization of what is being measured (air quality) must be modified somewhat; concentration of pollutants is elaborated to mean concentrations over various time periods; second, the final index will be different from what it would have been had some other time basis been established. The operations for obtaining observable indicators, then, are also an important component of the overall measurement process. They should not be selected arbitrarily or haphazardly, and should be clearly stated and specified as they affect the interpretation of the reported index.

The final stage of the measurement process is to derive a numerical *scale value* or *index*, based upon the observed indicators. Continuing with the example of air quality measurements, after observing the concentrations of carbon monoxide, sulfur dioxide, suspended particles, nitrogen dioxide, and photochemical oxidants,· these indicators must somehow be individually (or collectively) quantified and (possibly) transformed to yield some appropriate *index* of the property being measured. The air quality index developed by MITRE corporation (Thomas, 1972) requires that a numerical value be derived for each indicator, as for example

$$I_c = \sqrt{\left(\frac{C_c 8}{S_c 8}\right)^2 + \delta\left(\frac{C_c 1}{S_c 1}\right)^2}$$

where I_c is the numerical indicator for carbon monoxide, $C_c 8$ is the maximum observed eight-hour concentration of carbon monoxide, $S_c 8$ is the 8-hour secondary standard value (i.e., 9 ppm or 10,000 mg/m^3) consistent with the unit of measure of $C_c 8$, $C_c 1$ is the maximum observed 1-hour concentration of carbon monoxide, $S_c 1$ is the 1-hour secondary standard value (i.e., 35 ppm or 40,000 mg/m^3) consistent with the unit of measure of $C_c 1$, and δ is 1 if $C_c 1 \geq S_c 1$ and is 0 otherwise.

No doubt there are alternative procedures, perhaps equally defensible, that would produce entirely different indicator values (the procedure used in the Oak Ridge Index being one example). The point is that the observations of indicators must be translated into a quantitative form and the particular procedure adopted for accomplishing that objective will have important implications for the final index that is calculated.

Quantification of the separate indicators (where more than one are involved) is followed by some procedure for translating those numbers into a single index. The MITRE procedure for combining the individual indicator values to produce the MITRE Air Quality Index (MAQI), for example, is

$$\text{MAQI} = \sqrt{I_c^2 + I_s^2 + I_p^2 + I_n^2 + I_o^2}$$

where I_c is the indicator for carbon monoxide, I_s is the indicator for sulfur dioxide, I_p is the indicator for total suspended particulates, I_n is the indicator for nitrogen dioxide, and I_o is the indicator for photochemical oxidants.

Again, other combination techniques may be equally reasonable. The particular procedures adopted for translating observed indicator values into a final index have important implications for the interpretation of the index. There may also be implications for the conceptualization of what is being measured (air quality, for example). The computation procedure used to derive the index may weight and combine indicator values in a way that was not necessarily a part of the original conceptualization (for example, all indicants are made equally important determinants of quality).

As schematically outlined in Figure 1, any index is the culmination of a total measurement system involving several interrelated processes. Decisions made and procedures adopted at any point in the process have important implications for the meaning or interpretation that should be assigned to the index. An index may nominally be a measure of air quality, for example, but it is important to understand that it is an index of air quality *as air quality is defined by the entire measurement system*. Thus, environmental indices must be developed with great care, at all stages of the measurement system that produces them. While there is no way to ensure that optimum procedures will be adopted at each stage, at least the procedures that are adopted should be made explicit so that the index can be properly interpreted and evaluated.

EVALUATING MEASUREMENT SYSTEMS

Measurement systems are traditionally evaluated in terms of the criteria of *reliability, validity,* and *utility*. This is true whether the system measures intelligence, or components of the environment such as

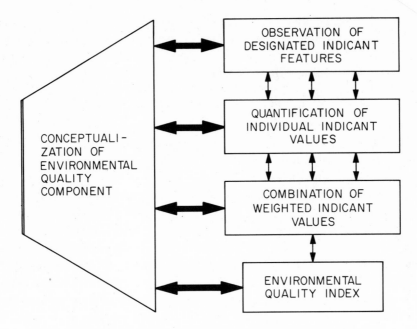

FIG. 1. Schematic of environmental quality measurement system.

temperature, air quality, or aesthetic quality. While these basic criteria are quite generally agreed upon, there is considerable variability in the specific methods for determining whether a given system meets these criteria. It is rarely, if ever, possible to conclusively show that any system "passes" on all criteria. Rather, the attempt is to determine whether the system achieves some reasonable, acceptable levels of reliability, validity, and utility.

Reliability

· The essence of the reliability criterion is *repeatability* of results; does the system yield the "same" index on repeated measurements of the "same" property. The usual approach to evaluating the reliability of a measurement is to repeatedly make measurements under what are assumed to be essentially identical conditions. To the extent that the resulting indices are the same, the measurement system is reliable.

There are some important qualifications that must be added to the above characterization of reliability. The first has to do with the *sensitivity* of the measurement system: that is, its ability to reflect (measure) differences when there are, in fact, differences. Clearly, a measurement system that produces the same index, regardless of changes in the properties being measured, would meet the criterion of reliability quite nicely. On the other hand, a highly sensitive measuring system may never produce the same index twice. Thus, a reliable measuring system is one that achieves an acceptable compromise between sensitivity and repeatability of indices.

A related qualification that may be particularly important in the area of environmental quality indices is that it may not be possible to repeat measurements under "the same conditions," if same is taken to mean identical. This is probably always true where measurements of the dynamic, constantly changing environment are concerned. Reliability, therefore, is achieved to the extent that repeated measurements under conditions that are reasonably similar, at least with respect to what are assumed to be the most relevant characteristics, yield similar (within reasonable bounds) indices.

There are a number of statistical procedures for determining the reliability of measurements. Unfortunately, few of them ensure that reasonable sensitivity criteria are also met, or that the measurements have been made under sufficiently similar conditions.

Wherever possible, environmental quality indices should be supported by estimates of their reliability and sensitivity. The standard error of measurement or the average percent error might, for example, be reported with the index.

By combining appropriate statistical procedures with rigorous and thoughtful experimental technique, a meaningful evaluation of the reliability of a measurement system can be achieved. The reliability criterion is critical since a measuring system that does not yield consistent and dependable indices will be of little value.

Validity

The textbook definition of the validity criterion is: "Does the system measure what it purports to measure?" A system for measuring air quality ought to produce indices that reflect changes or differences in the quality of air. The validity criterion is a particularly difficult one against which to evaluate measurements because it requires a comparison between what is actually being measured and the conceptualization of what is intended to be measured. Such a comparison, then, involves some consideration of the underlying conceptual bases of the index.[1]

While a measurement system may yield sensitive and reliable (consistent) indices, this provides no assurance that the index is actually related to the property that it purports to measure. The ability to evaluate a measurement system with regard to validity is limited by the degree to which the measured property is "understood"; that is, by the extent of theoretical sophistication represented. Clearly, if we have no idea of what it is we wish to measure, one index will do as well as another. This problem can be overcome by insisting that the measurement system provide a clear and explicit statement of the conceptualization upon which it is based, in effect allowing the validity of the system to be assessed in terms of how well the index it produces relates to its own stated conceptualization of what it attempts to measure (construct validity).

One approach to assessing validity is to determine the extent to which an index relates to other indicators of (nominally) the same property (concurrent validity). When there are two quantitative indices available, both purporting to be measures of the same property, the indices should correspond and the degree of their correspondence can be determined rather precisely. If the degree of correspondence is high, *both* systems may be attributed with a relatively high degree of validity. An example of how this approach applies in the area of EQIs is offered by the several indices of air quality: Extreme Value Index, Oak Ridge Air Quality Index (ORAQI), and MAQI. The three measures of air quality generally show good agreement, lending support to the validity of all three air quality measures.[2]

The cross-validation procedure described above requires that more than one index of an environmental component be available. Another

---

[1] For a more detailed discussion of validity presented in the context of psychological measurement problems, see Cronbach and Meehl (1955). Guilford and Fruchter (1973) provide a brief and readable introduction to statistical methods for validity.

[2] The essential similarity of the derivation of these indices (all three are based on measured concentrations of the same five pollutants) tends to detract from the value of their demonstrated correspondence. Some other, independently derived, index (e.g., an observer-based index of perceived air quality) would certainly be preferred as a basis for testing the validity of either of the three air quality indices.

approach to testing validity is to apply the measuring system in a number of contexts in which the general outcome can be predicted on the basis of other knowledge. For example, if it is generally agreed that the quality of air in "Purity, Colorado" is higher than that in "Smogville, California," a valid air quality measuring system should produce appropriately different indices for these two sites. Of course, this approach will necessarily provide only gross indications of validity. However, if a large number of applications produce indices that generally conform to "reasonable expectations," confidence in the validity of the index will increase.

The validity criterion is particularly critical for measurements of environmental quality. Once some environmental component comes to be represented by an EQI, there will be a strong tendency to base environmental decisions and policy, at least in part, on that quantitative index. If the index is not valid, if it leaves out some important or critical aspects of the environment, or misinterprets or incorrectly weights the importance of various aspects, environmental policies based on that index may have an unintended, possibly dangerous, impact on environmental quality. The validity of an EQI must never be assumed; it must be verified repeatedly in each situation in which the index is applied.

Utility

This criterion is less often recognized than reliability and validity, but it may be a particularly important concern for environmental quality measuring systems. The essence of this criterion is that a measurement system should produce an index that is *useful*; and EQIs should help to predict, direct, and evaluate environmental policies, decisions, and management actions.

The utility of a measuring system must be gauged, in part, by the expense and trouble involved in applying it. If an index is very difficult and expensive to obtain, it will generally be of less utility than one that is easier and less expensive. An index that costs more (in dollars, time, etc.) than the information it provides is worth cannot have much utility.

There are no simple or direct methods for determining the utility of a measurement system. Only repeated applications of the index over a period of time and in a variety of contexts will indicate its usefulness. If an EQI successfully predicts, directs, and evaluates decisions and actions, and/or tends to be related consistently to other important environmental variables and conditions, the measurement may be attributed with high utility.

SPECIAL CONSIDERATIONS FOR PEQIs

Measurement of the perceived quality of the environment, or of its components, represents a special approach to the more general problem of environmental assessment. The indices, PEQIs, that result are explicitly based upon the experiences (perceptions) and judgments of human observers. PEQIs, if developed rigorously, can provide precise standards of *quality* where more direct (physical) measures of an environmental component are available (e.g., air quality). Further, PEQIs may help indicate needed revision and extension in physical environmental assessment systems. Where no direct measures of an environmental component are yet available, PEQIs may serve as a basis for the development of appropriate direct measures. For many important environmental components (e.g., aesthetic experiences, stress, noise), PEQIs may provide the sole means of assessment.

A PEQI, like any other index, is the end product of a total measurement system. Thus, all the criteria that are appropriate for evaluating other measurement systems (e.g., reliability, validity, utility) also apply to measures of the perceived quality of the environment. Because PEQIs are based on the perceptions of human observers, a number of additional, special considerations arise.

To obtain a PEQI for some environmental component, that component must be presented to one or more human observers. The observers must perceive the component (or its effects) and somehow indicate their perceptions of the designated (relevant) properties. Any system for obtaining PEQIs, then, must define and/or select some component of the environment and devise some means of representing the relevant properties of that component to an appropriate set of human observers. Observers must be instructed to direct their attention to some relevant properties or dimensions of the environmental component and, based on their perception, to report a judgment of the "quality" of the designated properties. The final PEQI must be calculated in some fashion from the overt judgments offered by the human observers.

All of the stages indicated above must be represented in any perceptual measurement system. Each stage will have its own, potentially important effects on the PEQI that is ultimately produced by a system. Interpretation and evaluation of a PEQI must be concerned with the procedures employed at each of these stages and with their possible effects on the index.

Modes of Environmental Representation

Often the most preferred mode of representing the environment is to directly present the relevant component to observers. Direct representations may be made in a natural setting, as when the water in a river is observed from its banks. One of the principal advantages of this mode of representation is that opportunities for bias or error to intervene between the environment and the environment-as-presented are minimized. Also, there is less danger that important elements or properties of the environmental component will be inadvertently omitted from the representation.

There are also some important disadvantages of direct representations. A major problem is the difficulty of controlling extraneous factors that may affect observers' perceptions and/or judgments. For example, observers may be influenced by coincidental climatic conditions, unique but unrelated characteristics of the surrounding landscape, or any of a variety of other factors that may be irrelevant to the property or properties that are being assessed. Direct representation in the "natural" setting is generally the most expensive mode of presenting environmental components. Unless time and money are essentially unlimited, the expense of the representation procedure will be made up by other parts of the measurement system. For example, if observers are to be transported to the site of the relevant environmental components, fewer observers will be sampled.

For measures of some environmental components, it may be possible to take direct samples away from their natural setting. If, for example, the intent were to assess the quality of water along a taste dimension, there would be no need to take observers to the source of the water. A sample (in a bottle, for example) could be taken to the observers. This procedure has many of the advantages of direct natural representations, but allows for more control of extraneous factors.

However, there are a limited number of environmental components that can be sampled in this fashion. For many components (e.g., scenery, wildlife, noise) such a direct sampling procedure would be very difficult or impossible to implement.

Less direct representations are probably used most often. These may vary widely and generally depend upon the environmental components that are being represented. Photographs, color slides, sketches, or some other graphic representation may be used where various landscape properties or other *visually* perceived properties of the environment are being assessed (e.g., Daniel, Wheeler, Boster, & Best, 1973; Zube et al., 1974). Similarly, tape recordings might be used to represent "noise" pollution. Very often, verbal descriptions or even simple verbal labels ("rate the quality of *air* in your town," e.g., Saarinen & Cooke [1971]) are used as stand-ins for the environment. Because these are indirect samples of the environmental components that are being assessed, the opportunity for misrepresentation is great (Arthur, Daniel, & Boster, 1976). If the representation is biased or otherwise in error, the index based upon that representation will not accurately reflect the actual environmental properties that are of interest.

The specific measures that must be taken to ensure accurate, unbiased representations by indirect methods will differ depending upon the environmental properties being assessed and upon the particular mode of indirect representation employed. There are, however, some general considerations that may apply to any indirect representation system.

Because observers' judgments will be based upon their perceptions of the represented environment (rather than the environment itself), the quality of the representation is critical. Sharpness and color of photographs, detail of sketches, and clarity of prose in verbal descriptions may be important determinants of PEQIs based on these representations. Further, characteristics peculiar to one mode of representation may interact with relevant or irrelevant properties of the represented environment to affect observers' perceptions. Two-dimensional photographic representations may emphasize pattern and color, while reducing the effects of scale. Verbal descriptions may misrepresent many aspects of the environment and may arbitrarily emphasize or entirely overlook other properties.

Selecting the mode of representation is one of the first and most important steps in obtaining a PEQI. Some effort must always be made to confirm that the represented environment truly "represents" the relevant properties and characteristics of the environment that is to be assessed. Without this assurance, the PEQI may apply only to the representation, and not the intended properties of the environment.

Selecting Observers

To obtain a PEQI one must have a perceiver. Because different observers may perceive (and/or judge) the environment somewhat differently, PEQIs based on one set of observers may not correspond exactly to PEQIs provided by other observers. An important concern is which set of perceivers is most appropriate for a particular PEQI.

Some environmental quality concerns are very "local" in nature and, thus, the identification of relevant observer groups is relatively easy. For example, if the taste of water in a municipality were of concern, it would seem reasonable that the people who must drink the water should be the observer group to be sampled. Similarly, if the noise pollution level in a neighborhood or the quality of the recreation opportunity afforded by a neighborhood park is to be assessed, the "neighborhood" would appear to define the relevant observer group. In general, a very likely candidate for the appropriate observer group is the people who "consume" (in some sense) the environmental components (or their effects) that are in question.[3]

An alternative to basing PEQIs on the consumer group is to select the "provider" group. When the taxes paid by an individual on the east coast are allocated to the development of a national recreation area on the west coast, shouldn't the paying individual's (provider's) perceptions of the quality of recreation opportunity provided by his dollars be considered? This, of course, is a very difficult issue to deal with, but a question arises whenever general public funds are used to provide localized environmental necessities and amenities. Perhaps an even more difficult question arises when alterations of privately held property

---

[3] A hazard that must be considered in using "local" samples is created by the (usually admirable) adaptability of the human organism; water that initially tastes bad and air that smells obnoxious may, in time, be unnoticed by the observer who must consume these environmental commodities regularly.

(viewed as an improvement by the owner) have important impacts on the environment that must be shared by others.

A PEQI based on one group's judgment may indicate high levels of quality, while another group's judgments would suggest extreme degradation. On the other hand, in many instances there may be considerable agreement on the assessment of a particular environmental component (Daniel & Boster, 1976; Zube, 1974).

Sometimes the most important or most appropriate observer group will be apparent and their judgments generally comparable. On other occasions there may be several or many distinguishable groups to consider, each offering different judgments. In any event, identification of the observer group (or groups) on which a PEQI is based may be essential to the correct interpretation and application of that PEQI.

Perceptual–Judgmental Perspective

Related to the selection of an observer group is the specification of some perspective or context for making the required perceptual judgments. There are several important aspects to this problem. First, the observers must be directed to the relevant properties or *dimensions* of the represented environment; for example, the *taste* of water, the *smell* of the air, the *beauty* of the landscape, or the *enjoyment* provided by recreation opportunities. Second, some comparative *standard* must be provided or suggested; the observers must be told to judge the represented environment relative to some other presented or imagined ("the best you have ever experienced") environment. Finally, the represented environment must be presented, and the observer's judgment solicited, in some *context*. Individual observers may be approached privately and their judgments offered anonymously, or their personal judgment may be solicited in a public setting. Any or all of these factors can be expected to influence observers' judgments and thus PEQIs based on those judgments.

The selection of the relevant dimension to be assessed is not generally too great a problem—it is often defined, to some extent, by the circumstances that motivated the measurement effort. However, unambiguous specification of the relevant dimension to the observers may prove more difficult. For example, if the objective is to assess perceived air quality, observers must know whether they are to judge the (visual) clarity of the air, the smell, how it "feels" when it is breathed, or a combination of some or all of these properties. There may be even more ambiguity when the objective is the measure of landscape "beauty," the "unpleasantness" of noise, or the general "stress" levels perceived by the observer. Clearly, it is important that the dimensions attended to by the observer are the same as those (nominally) selected for assessment.

All perceptual judgments are relative. If a judgment is to be interpreted at all, it must be interpreted with regard to some standard. Sometimes the standard for comparison can be provided in the form of an alternative to the environmental component being assessed. For example, in forced-choice or paired-comparison procedures, two environmental representations may be presented and the observer required to judge one against the other. The value of one component may be measured by comparison to the other. Similarly, whenever a number of environmental displays are presented to the same observers, all of them may be assessed relative to one (or several) of the displays that have been judged. The standard for comparison will be less clear when observers are required to provide their own, as when they are asked to judge whether a given environmental element has achieved "optimum" levels, or is better (or worse) than the "best they have experienced." A PEQI is a measure of the quality of some environment (or component thereof) relative to some other (perhaps unspecified) alternative. Proper interpretation of the PEQI will depend upon having some knowledge of the standard against which it is being measured.

Human perceptual judgments are never offered in a vacuum— there must be some context in which the judged stimulus is presented and the overt judgment offered. Perhaps the most powerful (and notorious) of the contextual effects on human judgments and perceptions are produced by the presence of other humans. The environmental impact hearing, for example, is one context in which environmental quality judgments may be solicited. In this context individual perceptual judgments may be affected by any one or several of a large number of social factors. Whom does the observer nominally represent? What other groups are represented? What judgments or pronouncements have been made previously? How prestigious are the advocates of the apparent positions on the environmental problem being considered? Judgments offered under these and more subtly influential social conditions can hardly be taken as direct, accurate reflections of an individual's perception of environmental quality.

There are many other contextual factors that may influence or bias observers' perceptual judgments. The individual, the agency, or the organization nominally soliciting the judgments may be an important factor. An environmental quality survey sent out by the local chamber of commerce may yield PEQIs different from the same survey distributed by the "Advocates for a Better Environment." The observer's impression of how his reactions will be used may determine, to some extent, the judgments that he is willing to offer.

Beyond these judgmental influences, contextual factors may even affect the way in which the observer perceives the represented environment. The features of an environmental display that will attract the observer's attention, and his interpretation of the noted features, may be influenced by the apparent origin of the display. A landscape billed as a "reclaimed strip mine" may be looked at differently from one that is labeled "wilderness meadow." The observer's perspective may affect his perception and/or his judgments and, in turn, may affect the PEQI that is derived.

CURRENT STATUS OF PEQI METHODS

A number of methods have been developed for obtaining PEQIs. Each of these methods has dealt in one way or another with the basic components of perceptual measurement reviewed above. Some have been developed more formally than others, with explicit recognition and testing of the procedures adopted at each stage of the measurement process. Others have been much less formally developed—often adopting procedures rather arbitrarily, and, sometimes apparently not recognizing that the specific procedure chosen is but one of several alternatives. Many systems provide no specific tests or rationale for the procedures adopted.

Direct modes of representation have been possible in some instances, but PEQIs must, for the most part, rely upon some indirect representation of the environment. Photographs have attained considerable popularity recently, but many systems must still depend upon verbal representations of one form or another. In a few instances, specific efforts have been made to empirically verify the "representativeness" of the environmental representations employed. More often, the individual investigator's judgment has been relied upon.

Observer group selection is accomplished in a variety of ways. Usually some subset of the general public is chosen, but occasionally specific professional or "special interest" groups are identified, and in a few cases systematic comparisons among groups have been carried out. The orientation or "perspective" provided for observers and the context in which judgments are made may be the greatest source of variance among PEQI techniques. Many different types of judgment have been solicited in a great variety of circumstances.

No single method has yet emerged as the most favored among investigators. This may arise from the fact that no one method is optimal' or even applicable in all perceived environmental quality measurement problems. Nonetheless, some standardization of procedures would certainly be of great benefit to the future development of PEQIs. Where standardization is not possible, at least an effort could be made to specify more precisely all of the relevant procedures, from conceptualization to index, that have produced a given PEQI.

PEQI AND ENVIRONMENTAL POLICY

The environment-as-perceived may often be a more important determinant of human actions and responses than the environment described in terms of its physical properties. Humans' perception of the quality of their environment must always be an important concern for any environmental policies or actions. Perceptions and judgments have been and will continue to be an integral part of all environmental management decisions—sometimes these judgments are made by "experts," sometimes by political constituents, sometimes by consumers, and other times by providers. Whoever makes the judgment, a judgment is always made. One of the principal tasks for PEQIs is to systematize this human judgment element of environmental management and add to the dependability and precision of the perceptual judgments and of their effects on environmental policy.

PEQIs can serve in a number of important environmental policy roles. First, they can provide an accurate appraisal of the present state of the environment and can gauge precisely what impacts specific actions have had on the perceived quality of the environment. In that respect, PEQIs may serve a critical feedback function.

By observing the relationship between PEQIs and physical features of the environment, it is possible to determine which physical features are responsible for observed changes in perceived environmental quality. This step is crucial in developing effective predictive models to guide decisions on future policies and actions. Also, it will enable the selection of actions and plans that achieve specific environmental quality objectives.

If perceived quality of various environmental components can be assessed with some precision, it may then be possible to begin to *evaluate* these components relative to others. Determining how much a given environmental component is *worth* (in the trade-off sense) cannot be approached until some method for assessing the component is available. Well-founded PEQIs (reliable, valid, and useful) can serve all of these important environmental management functions.

Perceived Quality of Scenic and Recreational Environments

Some Methodological Issues

ROBERT O. BRUSH

Widespread concern has been expressed over the inadequacy of purely objective, physical measures of environmental quality. To enhance the habitability of our planet we need to consider cultural as well as physical and biological components of the complex environment that influence the lives of individuals and communities (Thomas, 1972). In man's relation to the biosphere, we must deal with a "real" world that does not have the same objective reality for all observers; we must deal with a subjectively perceived environment (UNESCO, 1973). An individual's view of the world, influenced as it is by his own perception and learning, differs from the view held by scientific experts, yet the concept of the world-as-perceived has considerable value in humanizing the quantitative, objective approach to managing our environment (Lowenthal, 1961). Those responsible for formulating policies, and any expert group, should become aware of their own perceptual and conceptual bias by comparing it with the views of those whose lives are affected by the policies (UNESCO, 1973). Moreover, observer-based

ROBERT O. BRUSH • USDA Forest Service, University of Massachusetts, Amherst, Massachusetts 01002.

evaluations of environmental quality should be considered at the outset along with physical measures so that we do not develop imperfect standards that abstract only the physical, purely objective components of environmental quality (Craik & McKechnie, 1974).

Milbrath and Sahr (1975) maintain that any measure of quality is inherently subjective, that there are no objective measures of environmental quality. Quality is in the eye of the beholder. An environmental condition is of high quality for an individual as long as he feels that it is, no matter what objective measures may indicate to the contrary. A given environmental condition may be judged subjectively to be at different levels of quality at different times by the same person. Therefore, Milbrath and Sahr contend that quality is not definable as a fixed attribute of physical things. Measurements should be made not of the descriptions of physical phenomena, but of the perceived quality itself. They further assert that it is now possible to study subjective perceptions of environmental quality in an objective way. A person's evaluations can be scaled and compared across environmental factors for an individual and for groups of individuals.

If we acknowledge the desirability of having perceived indicators of environmental quality, how then are we to develop the monitoring devices to measure observer response to the environment? This chapter will discuss several methodological issues and the evidence from recent research regarding the use of observers as an instrument to measure the quality of scenic and recreational environments. It will focus on observer-based ratings of scenic and recreational environments in which natural features predominate—mountains, trees, and lakes—the wide outdoors. Evidence that urban scenes are not judged by the same standards as natural scenes will be considered later. Scenic quality and the quality of outdoor recreation environments are closely related. Scenic quality was strongly associated with overall site ratings by visitors seeking recreation in two national forests in Michigan (Lucas, 1970). The importance of visual aesthetic quality has been shown to be an important factor in describing differences between physical environments (Calvin, Dearinger, & Curtin, 1972). An additional study of 76 hikers in two wilderness areas of the Northeast indicated that aesthetic experience was rated highest of the five attitudes tested, superceding emotional, physical, educational, and social experience (Shafer & Mietz, 1970). Lucas (1964) maintained that recreational resources should be defined and evaluated as they are perceived by the public using them, not by arbitrary measurements of the physical resources on recreation sites. This observer-based approach is needed, he felt, because of the personal and subjective nature of recreational and scenic resource use.

Five methodological issues involved in using observers as instruments for measuring the quality of scenic and recreational environments will be discussed in light of the evidence in recent literature.

PREFERENTIAL JUDGMENTS VERSUS COMPARATIVE APPRAISALS

One objection to subjective measures is the wide variance in responses when individuals are asked to express their personal opinion of an aspect of their environment. In light of this objection, K. D. Fines (1968) asked subjects to rate landscapes according to their scenic beauty rather than personal preference, hoping thereby to appeal to a universal standard of landscape quality.

In this discussion a distinction is made between two types of observer-based assessment. One type, called a preferential judgment, elicits an individual's like or dislike for a specific environment. The wide range of personal biases, tastes, and inclinations reflected in preferential judgments is likely to result in wide variation in responses, hardly a firm basis for establishing standards of perceived environmental quality. The other type of assessment, called a comparative appraisal, forces the observer to adopt a certain framework for making judgments, a context that compels him to consider the expected appraisal of a larger group of persons. If an observer were forced to adopt a certain psychological set, his assessment would reflect the values that he ascribes to a larger group. The variation in responses of several individuals would be less than the variation in preferential judgments of the same individuals. Therefore, this latter assessment—the comparative appraisal—may be more useful in public decision-making.

To illustrate this distinction, consider that a given individual may express very different responses regarding the same environment, depending on how the question was asked. If several village residents were asked whether they liked or disliked a familiar village scene, the range of responses might vary considerably more than if they were asked how most village residents would evaluate the scene. In the second case, the community-wide context for making the assessment might produce a greater degree of consensus regarding scenic quality, and a more stable basis for setting standards of scenic quality, than preferential judgments of like or dislike.

Greater consensus should result when observers refer to a common standard rather than their personal biases. Furthermore, the variance in indices based on comparative appraisals should be smaller than the variance in the more subjective preferential judgments. Experts or professionals who presumably have training and experience in dealing with the standards for evaluation would be expected to show greater agreement with the comparative appraisals of the general public than with preferential judgments. Indices of perceived environmental quality that were based on comparative appraisals should conform to the more widely agreed-upon standard of environmental quality. Moreover, professionals and experts most familiar with relevant standards could be relied upon to assess a given aspect of the environment in a manner that reflected the greatest degree of consensus with the general public (Craik & McKechnie, 1974).

Only one study was found that compares preferential judgments of scenes with comparative appraisals (Zube et al., 1974). From a set of semantic differential scales applied by 307 subjects to eight nonurban landscapes, one preference scale (like–dislike) and two scales eliciting comparative appraisals (beautiful–ugly and high scenic value–low scenic value) were examined. Correlations between the three scales taken two at a time equaled or exceeded .80, indicating that there may be little differentiation between preferential judgments and comparative appraisals. However, in the course of completing the semantic differential tests the investigators felt that the subjects may not have been strongly induced to report their personal preference. In another part of the same study, 123 subjects were asked when passing through nine nonurban sites to state their preference for using the sites for outdoor recreation, for residence, or for traveling through. They were also asked to evaluate the scenic quality of the nine sites. Correlations between the scenic evaluations and preference scores for the nine settings were lower, between .58 and .62. In this case, the distinction between preferential judgments and comparative appraisals is more apparent. The subjects may have been more inclined to express preferential judgments when present at the site than when viewing photographs (Zube et al., 1974).

Shafer's scenic preference model (Shafer, Hamilton, & Schmidt, 1969; Shafer & Mietz, 1970) seems to represent comparative appraisals rather than preferential judgments, even though observers had been asked to rank photographs according to their own preference. The rankings of 100 photographs by campers in the Adirondacks and by campers in the Highlands of Scotland (Shafer & Tooby, 1973) produced similar rankings and preference scores. The correlation coefficient for the scores of Americans and Scots across 100 scenes was .91. All 100 of the photographs, representative of wildlands in the United States, had been taken by professional photographers who framed the best shot according to conventional standards of artistic composition. Therefore, in ranking the photographs, the subjects were not choosing among random scenes from the everyday environment, but among environmental displays that had been preselected according to prevailing standards of scenic composition. In terms of this methodological issue, the low between-group variance would indicate that Shafer's model is one of scenic evaluation rather than scenic preference.

A technique for evaluating forest scenes reported by Daniel and Boster (1976) produced valid results for homogeneous groups regardless of changes in the slides sampled from the same landscape and regardless of changes in individuals sampled from the same populations. However, evaluations from group to group varied considerably—range managers rated the scenic quality very differently from foresters, and landscape architects seemed to use different criteria from all other groups. This suggests that the technique provides a reliable and consistent estimate of preferential judgments rather than comparative appraisals. The individuals within each group seemed to use the same standard of scenic quality, but the standard varies with each group.

Perhaps the nature of the scene accounts for the various scenic standards. The slides of the forest landscapes used by Daniel and Boster differed from those of Fines (1968), Shafer et al. (1969), and Zube et al. (1974), for example, in that the view did not extend beyond the close middleground and the sites were relatively level and moderately wooded. The forest scenes were photographed from locations and orientations that were taken at random. Because the slides were not deliberately composed to enframe the landscape elements representative of the site, they were as likely to enframe unattractive views as they were to enframe attractive views. If the slides did not appear to the observers as strikingly beautiful, well-composed scenes, then the observers may not have been appraising the slides according to any universal standard of scenic beauty. The observers may have been basing their judgments instead on personal or professional criteria. The range manager, for example, may have been influenced by the amount of grass that cattle might graze on, and the forester by the timber quality of the trees.

DEGREE OF CONSENSUS IN EVALUATIVE APPRAISALS

There is ample evidence of a high degree of consensus among individuals in making evaluative appraisals of scenic quality. A series of studies cited above indicates close agreement concerning the scenic beauty of natural landscapes among campers in mountainous terrain in this country and abroad (Shafer et al., 1969; Shafer & Mietz, 1970; Shafer & Tooby, 1973). In another set of studies it appears that judges from a homogeneous population are able to consistently differentiate everyday environments on the basis of their attractiveness. The scenes were in rural and suburban areas near Philadelphia. However, the judges agreed more in rating simply the attractiveness of a setting than they did in rating the suitability of the same setting for residential use or auto touring (Coughlin & Goldstein, 1970; Rabinowitz & Coughlin, 1970).

Several experiments reported by Zube et al. (1974) attest to a high degree of consensus in evaluating nonurban landscapes. Over 300 subjects applied 18 semantic scales to eight nonurban scenes. The subjects comprised 13 subgroups of diverse professional and demographic characteristics. Correlation among the 13 subgroups in the use of the semantic scales was high; 85% of the correlation coefficients were above .83. All the correlation coefficients below .83 involved only the subgroup of inner-city residents, suggesting that inner-city residents may have had different perceptions of nonurban landscapes.

In a related experiment, the observers showed a high level of agreement in ranking photographs of nonurban scenes on a 7-point scale. All subgroups, inner-city residents included, generally ranked each photograph in the same relative position on the 7-point scale. However, the small sample of inner-city residents differed from the suburban and rural residents by assigning lower absolute values to nonurban scenes. This supports the contention of Milbrath and Sahr

(1975) that environmental quality ratings may have two components: the relative importance of the dimension being scaled and the absolute value assigned.

In the same study a high level of agreement was found with regard to positive and negative effects of landscape features on scenic quality. These features included shrubs, signs, lakes, electric powerlines, ridges, and suburban developments, to mention a few. Again, the most obvious exception to the findings stemmed from the subgroup of inner-city residents. This subgroup accounted for 29% of the extreme responses to landscape features—the inner-city subjects valued natural elements less positively and man-made elements more positively than their rural and suburban counterparts.

The number of urban and man-made elements in a natural scene influences the degree of consensus on scenic quality. Kaplan, Kaplan, and Wendt (1972) reported that a sample of urban, suburban, and rural residents preferred natural landscapes over urban scenes. Zube et al. (1974) found that the least variance (highest agreement) in scenic evaluations between observer subgroups occurred with scenes that were predominantly natural. The greatest between-group variance occurred with scenes that contained predominantly urban elements—houses, stores, and automobiles.

Agreement between Experts and Nonexperts

Fines (1968) observed a marked difference in the rating of scenic landscapes by nonexperts and those with training or experience in landscape design. Although there was little difference in the relative ranking of landscape scenes, those persons with training and experience in design expressed a much greater range of values from least attractive to most attractive. In a study conducted by Zube (1974), an occupational bias was reflected in scenic evaluations of natural landscapes. Professionals in environmental design rated natural landscapes more highly than did lay control groups. Furthermore, nonexperts and non-professionals in environmental fields tended to be more favorably disposed than environmental-design professionals to the impact of towns or regional scenic quality. Design professionals would appear to be more sensitive to differences in natural scenic quality than nonexperts.

Graduate landscape architect students differed strongly from undergraduate psychology students in showing a stronger preference for scenes of building complexes and scenes of natural elements (Kaplan, 1973). The differences may not have been so great if the subjects had been asked to make an evaluative appraisal rather than a preferential judgment. Yet the experiment does show that professional bias influences preferential judgments.

In another study, landscape architects evaluated six forest sites in Arizona less favorably than any of the other groups tested, including foresters, forest economists, range managers, and students (Daniel & Boster, 1976). The landscape architects appeared to have stricter criteria for scenic evaluation. The views were photographed within stands of trees, with varying degrees of openness in the foreground and middleground, and in some cases included evidence of recent tree harvesting.

A cross-cultural comparison of two New York counties, an urban county outside of Buffalo and a rural county in the Adirondacks, showed that county leaders estimated scenic beauty to be of lower importance than did lay citizens (Milbrath & Sahr, 1975). A comprehensive questionnaire for estimating perceived environmental quality required participants to rank various environmental elements such as clean air, freedom to move, good educational opportunities, and abundance of consumer goods. A pilot test of the research instrument using citizens and community leaders in the two counties showed that leaders assigned lesser importance to four elements: beauty of the home, access to unspoiled nature, a pleasing landscape, and clean air. The underestimation by leaders was found in both the urban and the rural counties.

In rating the recreational environment, strong differences between managers and persons seeking recreation have already been noted. At the Manistee and Huron National Forest campgrounds in Michigan, the managers did not rate the quality of resources and facilities in the same way as visitors (Lucas, 1970). In the Boundary Waters Canoe Area, canoeists were more demanding of unspoiled natural environments than managers, yet ironically the canoeists were more inclined than managers to favor facilities and services that enhanced their comfort and convenience, and were less aware of human influences such as past forest fires, motors, seaplanes, logging, and mechanized portages (Peterson, 1974b).

At an intensively used public campground in the state of Washington, significant differences existed in the environmental perception of users and managers. In a highly developed campground in Washington, campers perceived the natural environment much more favorably than did the managers. Campers found conditions such as noise, litter, and the activities of other campers to be less of a problem than did managers. Moreover, the managers' perceptions of campers' views appeared to be a reflection of the managers' own attitudes about the quality of the camping experience (Clark, Hendee, & Campbell, 1971).

Physical Correlates of Scenic Quality

There are at present no physical indices of scenic or recreational quality equivalent to air and water quality standards against which to compare the perceived indices. Several studies do suggest that certain patterns or combinations of certain physical landscape elements correlate highly the appraisals of certain types of observers. Landforms, water, agricultural features, and natural vegetation produced positive effects on scenic evaluations of nonurban landscapes, whereas the effect of man-made artifacts depended upon the context in which they appeared (Zube et al., 1974). In predicting scenic value of wildland landscapes for campers in mountainous terrain, the presence of water in moderate proportions, patterns of forest and grassland, and the framing of foreground elements had a positive effect on scenic quality (Brush & Shafer, 1975). A study of housewives' reactions to landscape features near Philadelphia indicated that preferred patterns in natural landscapes are not wild, but man-influenced or parklike, without evidence of trash or other forms of visual pollution (Rabinowitz & Coughlin, 1970).

In the case of recreational environments, Peterson and Neumann (1969), in studying preference for beaches near Chicago, identified two groups of beach users: one that preferred a relatively empty beach with trees nearby, and another group that preferred a crowded beach with buildings in the background. Yet each group described their preferred beach being larger, cleaner, and having smoother sand. No explanation was apparent.

Another study of recreation environments found that the large numbers of people and urban development had a negative effect on the scenic evaluations of the majority of persons sampled (Carls, 1973). The sample included 270 campers at Illinois recreation areas, and 75 persons sampled from urban, suburban, and rural locations in equal proportions. Since the differences in scenic evaluations between the groups is not discussed, the findings are questionable.

Craik (1972a) found a weak but congruent relationship between descriptive dimensions and aesthetic evaluations of 50 scenes. Positively related to scenic quality were the degree that the line of sight is directed along a prescribed pathway, the extent of view greater than three miles, a wide sweeping view, and the presence of any kind of clouds. Negatively related to scenic quality was the sense of enclosure that blocks the line of sight directly ahead of the observer.

The studies cited above indicate that there seems to be physical correlates of scenic quality that apply to specific groups of people in specific environments.

Peterson (1974a) described a promising attempt to define the quality of recreational experience in terms of the user, namely as the degree of congruency between his aspirations and his perceived reality of the experience. Aspiration is defined as the desired degree of presence of a given environmental condition. Total satisfaction results when there is perfect agreement between aspiration for a given condition and the user's perception of the condition. The conditions to be measured would be those ordinary physical and social characteristics of the recreational setting which actual and potential users identify as having some effect on their recreational experience.

In developing the model, data for persons seeking a wilderness experience in the Boundary Waters Canoe Area were analyzed. Peterson measured their aspirations and perceptions regarding such conditions as long portages, sonic booms, mature virgin forests, and having to wash and bathe in cold water. The results illustrate the potential usefulness of the model to provide an overall summary rating of a recreation experience, and to identify specific conditions that determine user satisfaction or motivation.

Extra-Environmental Correlates

Observer-based appraisals of scenic quality may be influenced by the psychological set by which the observer is directed to perceive a scene in a given frame of reference. When observers were asked to attend to abstract compositional elements in a scene such as shapes, lines, and textures, the rated pleasantness of the actual scene was not affected. Yet, when asked to evaluate the human influence or to imagine how a scene might be made more pleasant, observers tended to rate the actual scene as less pleasant (Leff et al., 1974). The stimuli were everyday scenes around Burlington, Vermont. Apparently, by directing the observer's attention to human influence in the landscape or to imagine changes in the everyday landscape, the present state of the landscape is made to seem less pleasant.

Background variables such as sex, age, and familiarity with the native landscape affected personal preference for scenes from Delaware and Alaska (Sonnenfeld, 1966), and suggested that universal agreement on landscape preference was not likely. However, had comparative appraisals been elicited rather than preferential judgments, the background variables of sex, age, and familiarity may not have been influential.

Exposure to certain landscapes in childhood, similar to Sonnenfeld's familiarity with native landscapes, accounted for most of the variance in scenic value in several experiments with nonurban landscapes reported by Zube et al. (1974). Other variables such as educational status, occupation, age, and preferred leisure setting were noted. However, the amount of variance accounted for by background variables was less than 49% in each experiment.

CONCLUSIONS

There are very few studies which ask recreational visitors to evaluate their environments. Evidence in the recent literature suggests that recreational quality standards may be difficult to determine. Because of the many activities and styles of outdoor recreation and the personal and subjective nature of leisure activities, it may not be possible to establish standards of perceived quality that prove valid for large segments of the population.

With respect to scenic quality of nonurban landscapes there seems to be some basis for distinguishing between preferential judgments reflecting personal tastes and predispositions, and comparative appraisals based upon a widely held standard. Generally, where there is agreement on high scenic quality (a comparative appraisal), there is also evidence of strong preference for the scene. The reverse may not always hold true where scenic quality is low. Nevertheless, indices of scenic and recreational quality based upon comparative appraisals will probably represent broader public support.

There is evidence of a high degree of consensus as to the quality of nonurban landscapes although there may be citizens with limited experience in rural and nonurban settings who do not value highly the pastoral landscape.

There is considerable agreement between nonexperts and environmental designers as to what constitutes scenic quality in rural and wildland environments, but nonexperts tend to be more tolerant than design professionals of man-made influences, particularly those that are familiar to them, or that contribute to their own comfort and convenience. Yet, managers of recreation facilities, professionals, and elected officials do not always agree with nonexperts when appraising environmental quality.

The ratings of observers are influenced to some extent by their backgrounds and prior experience. According to preliminary studies, background variables account for more than half of the variation in scenic evaluation. The psychological set or context in which observers are directed to make their appraisals can have appreciable influence over their ratings.

There is evidence that certain physical landscape materials and features are associated with high scenic quality in nonurban environments. However, the relative proportions and context in which a given feature occurs may influence scenic evaluations. Too much water surface or too many trees may lead to monotony. Thus, there may not be physical elements that always contribute to favorable scenic evaluations, but there may be combinations and configurations of the elements that will tend to elicit favorable evaluations of scenic quality.

4

Perceived Quality of Scenic and Recreational Environments
Research Needs and Priorities

GEORGE L. PETERSON

The problem addressed in this chapter is concerned with research needs and priorities for Perceived Environmental Quality Indices for scenic and recreational environments. The overriding notion is that of measuring environmental performance relative to human purposes, so that the relative quality of alternative environments can be described and compared. The Perceived Environmental Quality Index (PEQI) differs from the Environmental Quality Index (EQI) in that it is concerned with perceptions of the environment and of environmental quality as opposed to scientific physical measurements and formal calculations of environmental performance and quality. Perhaps it is advisable to define these concepts more carefully before proceeding.

THE ENVIRONMENTAL QUALITY INDEX (EQI)

The notion of the EQI seems to have emerged as a numerical score or vector of scores that assesses the level of performance of a specific

DR. GEORGE L. PETERSON • The Technological Institute, Northwestern University, Evanston, Illinois 60201.

aspect of a given environment relative to predefined criteria—e.g., the air quality in Wilmette, Illinois, at a specified time. The criteria are generally based on human purposes or points of view, and it is generally taken for granted that the definition of "quality" is with regard to human welfare. The criteria seem usually to be defined on technical grounds as normative or prescriptive concepts of desirable environment. Emphasis appears to be on scores that can be achieved by formula or standard methodology, in convenient and simple ways, for use in environmental management and/or public information (NAS-NAE, 1975).

THE PERCEIVED ENVIRONMENTAL QUALITY INDEX (PEQI)

The PEQI notion seems still to be in a state of construction. However, it is generally agreed that concern is with how *people* perceive the environment and how they respond to it in terms of environmental preferences and choices. The purpose would seem to be to construct numerical scores or vectors of scores that measure environmental performance as seen by people, relative to their subjective criteria. It is reasonable to conceptualize the notion in at least two rather different ways. First, it can be thought of as a preferential index that measures how attractive a given environment is in an aesthetic way (i.e., pleasurable sensation) to a given person or group of people. Second, it can be defined as a judgmentally derived EQI; that is, an index of environmental quality, relative to normative or prescriptive criteria, that has been measured by means of human perceptions and/or judgments. The two kinds of PEQI would serve rather different purposes. Perhaps it is meaningful to identify still another type of PEQI: an index estimated judgmentally by person A of the attractiveness of a given environment to person B.

In summary, the first type of PEQI is an index of environmental attractiveness or preference. The second type is an EQI estimated judgmentally. The third type, if it is indeed a separate "type," is the first type estimated by judgmental methods instead of more directly through measurement of preference responses.

THE NEED FOR DEFINITIONAL AND THEORETICAL SUPERSTRUCTURE

If PEQIs are to be developed meaningfully and rigorously, the most pressing need is for more structure in the question. The structure appears to be deficient in at least four areas: framework of purposes and applications; definition of what the PEQI is; theory of the processes and phenomena which the PEQI is intended to describe or represent; and standardization and formalization of methodology for measuring and deriving the PEQI.

This chapter does not pretend to provide final answers to the need for problem structure in the question. However, there are some basic concepts that are frequently overlooked or confused in discussions of PEQIs, and it is useful to delineate these.

MEASUREMENT

The EQI and PEQI are intended to be *measurements* of environmental quality. Strictly speaking, measurement is the assignment of real numbers to states of a variable such that relationships among the numbers describe relationships among magnitudes of the states of the variable. It is not necessary to utilize all aspects of the relationships among the numbers, however, in order to have meaningful measurement. There are four "levels" of measurement that utilize more or less of the numerical relationship: nominal, ordinal, interval, and ratio (Stevens, 1962).

Nominal Measurement

Nominal measurement uses numbers as names only to identify different states of the variable. The thing being measured is identity. An example is the use of numbers to identify different players on a football team.

Ordinal Measurement

Ordinal measurement takes advantage of the direction of differences in magnitudes of numbers to represent directions of differences in magnitude among variable states. An example is the geologist's hardness scale for classifying minerals in rank order according to hardness categories.

Interval Measurement

Interval measurement adds the concept of magnitude of difference to the ordinal scale. An example is the Fahrenheit temperature scale. The difference between 90°F and 70°F is the same as the difference between 40°F and 20°F, but ratios among temperatures are not meaningful, because the zero point is arbitrary.

Ratio Measurement

Ratio measurement adds an absolute zero origin to the interval scale so that ratios among magnitudes are meaningful. In physics, calculations using the natural gas law, which involve relationships among temperature, volume, and pressure of a gas, require temperature to be measured in degrees Rankin or Kelvin, because these scales have an absolute zero origin; that is, they are ratio scales, and the calculations are ratio calculations.

Should the scale for the PEQI be ordinal, interval, or ratio? It depends on how it is to be used and the technical and definitional problems that are involved in the measurement process.

The measurement problems involved in coming up with a PEQI include the following: definition of the thing being measured; definition of the unit and scale of measurement; invention of standardized methods and instruments for measurement; analysis of the human-related consequences of changes in magnitude; and agreement on standards or thresholds as a frame of reference.

Thus, if the PEQI is to be regarded as a measurement, then it is necessary first to define rigorously what is meant by environmental quality. It must be defined in operational terms; that is, in a way that allows changes and differences in magnitude to be observed so that numbers can be assigned via the measurement method. On the one hand, Ben Franklin's kite experiment might be regarded as a "measurement" of the presence of electricity, but kites and keys are a far cry from voltmeters and ammeters.

Even with rigorous definition of environmental quality in observable terms, measurements will be relatively useless unless they are taken in standard units. A standard unit or scale of measurement must be defined and agreed upon, or it will be difficult if not impossible to compare situations. Along with the need for a standard unit of measurement is the need for standard methods of known reliability and demonstrated validity. Because the notion of a PEQI involves psychological phenomena and perhaps psychological methods of measurement, this need for standard units and standard methods is a challenge indeed.

The next step is to explore human-related consequences of changes in the PEQI score (or scores, if it is multidimensional). For any such indicator it is useful to be able to define standards or thresholds of adequacy. These thresholds should be defined with regard to acceptable levels of human-related consequences of the magnitude of the PEQI.

QUALITY VERSUS QUANTITY

It seems reasonable at this point to question whether "quality" is a "thing" that can be measured. In the sense that it is being used here, quality means "character with respect to excellence," and excellence is apparently defined in terms of desirability or preference from the subjective point of view. The phenomenon that determines the magnitude of environmental quality in any given situation is thus a human response, the act of interpreting or reacting to the environment in terms of pleasure or displeasure. Is it proper, then, to regard this concept of quality as a property of the environment, as a property of the person reacting to the environment, or as a phenomenon or process of interaction between man and environment?

A model used by Charles Morris (1956) seems useful. He differentiates among "object value, conceived value, and operational value." The object value of a thing is the value it would have, that is, the preference of pleasure it would elicit, if the person reacting to it were in possession of perfect knowledge of all its attributes and consequences. Conceived value is what is believed to be the desirability of the thing given the person's actual perceptions and conceptions of it and its consequences. Operative value is the degree of desirability the thing has as manifest by the actual choices the person makes.

Is the PEQI to be regarded as a measurement of object value, conceived value, or operative value? Related to conceived value is the notion of value relative to hypothetical criteria. This might be called abstract hypothetical value.

If the PEQI is concerned with describing human preferential response to the environment, then it is dealing with operative values. If such value or quality is defined in terms of emotional sensations, it is an individual phenomenon and must be dealt with on an individual basis.

An alternative way to approach the PEQI is to measure perceived magnitudes of environmental attributes to which environmental preference is sensitive. In this case it is not quality that is being measured, it is the perceived condition of the environment.

PREFERENCE, WELFARE, AND POLITICS

From the individual point of view, the PEQI might be: a measurement of preferential response; a measurement of perceived environmental attributes and conditions; or a prescription or judgment of what "ought" to be the preferential response if the person were perfectly informed and had perceived correctly. If the PEQI is concerned with environmental quality from the societal point of view, either it is a judgment relative to prescriptive or normative and hypothetical criteria or it is a measurement of societal preferential response, that is, interpretation of the environment in terms of social policy. In the latter case it is a *political* response to the environment and is probably not measureable. Indeed, there is a legitimate question about whether the political process of social choice, which is a process of competitive and cooperative bargaining, can be defined in a way that allows it to be measured (de Neufville & Stafford, 1971). It is in a constant state of flux and redefinition. There is certainly no normative "solution" to it, except as one adopts an ideological point of view. In short, it is a process by which individual preferences compete for influence in social choice, and, as with the game of chess, it can be measured only by its outcomes. It is possible to measure preferences of individuals and of groups of agreeing individuals, but how are the individuals to be combined to produce a social point of view? A simple average assumes that all individuals are weighted equally, but that is not a valid assumption. The political process assigns weights to individuals implicitly by the choices it makes. These weights are difficult, if not impossible, to expose.

In defining and constructing a PEQI, the issues that are political should be identified and separated from those that are technical. If it is a matter of known or knowable fact, then it is a technical matter and is subject to measurement and analysis. If it is a question that can be resolved only on ideological or value judgment grounds, then it is a political matter that should be resolved politically. When dealing with political matters in abstract and hypothetical ways, this should be made clear, and the limitations of the results exposed.

MORALITY VERSUS AESTHETICS

Santayana (1896) distinguishes between moral value and aesthetic value. Something that is of value for "moral" reasons is valued because it serves desirable ends. It is useful. Its consequences are the reasons for its value; it is not an end in itself. Something that is of value for aesthetic reasons is an end in itself. It is the object of desire, and its value does not derive from usefulness. With regard to the PEQI, it can be asked whether concern is for the aesthetic quality of the environment or for its usefulness. That is, does the PEQI measure environmental pleasure or potential pleasure that is an end in itself, or does it measure quality in terms of desirable human-related consequences of the condition of the environment? Conceivably, contact with different environmental conditions might bring about changes in the person's health or skill, for example. If these changes are desirable, then the environmental contact is desirable, and it can be said that there is quality stemming from the environment. If the individual perceives "quality" in the environment, is he responding to feelings of pleasure stimulated by the environment, or is he responding to judgments about desirable consequences and/or useful attributes of the environment? Is the object to measure the pleasure stimulated by the environment or to assess environmental utility?

INDICES OR EXPLANATIONS?

If attention is focused on developing a numerical index that indicates some aspect of perceived environmental quality, the potentially most useful product of the effort may be missed. It depends, of course, on the purpose for constructing the index. If all that is wanted is an indicator of environmental performance, then the numerical index may be perfectly adequate. However, if the purpose is to diagnose environmental shortcomings and develop policy interventions aimed at improving environmental performance, then the index does no more than point to a problem. It tells nothing about the nature of the problem and does not offer guidance on how to solve it. For purposes of environmental management, it is at least as important to understand the process by which the environment achieves its level of performance as it is to assess the level of performance. For example, if a given scenic environment is performing more poorly this year than it did last year, this is useful to know, and the index would show it. But why is it performing more poorly? What attribute or attributes of the environment have changed over the year, and what processes have caused the change? Indeed, there is a question here that needs answering: Is environmental quality something that we measure directly (by measuring preferences, judgments, etc.) or is it something that is calculated through a formal understanding of the processes by which attributes of the environment stimulate pleasure, attract preference, or generate desirable human-related consequences? The latter is to be desired, if it is possible, because in the understanding of the process by which quality is generated lies the solution to the environmental management problem. The manager needs to know not only the level of performance, but also the reasons why the performance is at a stated level. In any case, an index calculated through an understanding of the quality-related man-environment process is going to be a more valid and defensible indicator than the one that is measured directly.

MULTIDIMENSIONALITY

In addition to its lack of explanatory power, a single numerical index may simply be "unnatural." For example, if the human concern for environmental quality is a matter of "health," then the health-related EQI is intended to be an indicator of impact of the condition of the environment on health. But what is health? Is it a state of good or comfortable feelings, is it being able to perform and function in specified ways, or is it defined in terms of physiological state-of-being, as indicated by the magnitudes of various physiological parameters, for example, temperature or blood pressure? If it is defined in terms of specified magnitudes for various physiological parameters, then the state-of-being called health must be regarded as multidimensional. But, it can be argued that the various parameters of body condition are of concern *because* they impinge upon one's ability to perform and they affect how one feels. The parameters should be identified relative to the goals of performance or feelings by discovering the body conditions to which these goals are sensitive and exposing the process by which sensitivity occurs. This process, if it can be explicitly described, then becomes a *rational* way to calculate a numerical index of health from the multidimensional indicators of physical condition. Likewise, the process by which the state of the body is sensitive to the multidimensional attributes of the environment can be used as a step in calculating a health-related index in terms of the condition of the environment.

AN APPEAL FOR THEORETICAL RIGOR

The preceding discussion of underlying concepts is not complete, and it no doubt contains numerous vagaries and misconceptions. Nevertheless, it is intended to indicate a direction in which research on EQIs and, especially, PEQIs needs to go. The need is for scholarly discipline and theoretical rigor in defining and sorting out concepts, clarifying assumptions, developing theoretical structure, and conceptually testing internal validity of the concepts thus derived. Those of us who have been engaged in PEQI-related research have been heavy on words and empirical methods and light on theory and discipline. In part this is a product of the nature of the problem. In part the lack of theory and discipline is attributable to the immature state-of-the-art. But it is also in part sustained by scientific irresponsibility. There is too much ad hoc research motivated by whimsical curiosity. There is too much collecting of answers in search of a question. There is too much kite-flying on stormy nights with not enough disciplined reasoning about the nature of electricity. Do we want to rush out and measure environmental quality in unstandard and noncommensurate terms, or do we want to develop first a rigorous theoretical understanding of what we mean by quality and the processes by which it is generated?

A rigorous theoretical framework for the PEQI problem will require far more research than is feasible for review in this chapter, but some simple models will be presented here to help clarify and illustrate the points that have been made in the preceding discussion. The models will also help to articulate specific questions about PEQIs.

AN IMPACT-ORIENTED MODEL OF THE EQI

As mentioned earlier, the EQI concept seems to be based on evaluation of the environment relative to normative or prescriptive criteria of human welfare, as opposed to feelings of pleasure elicited by environmental contact. The prior discussion on "multidimensionality" suggests an impact-oriented EQI model that may be useful in constructing a PEQI model (Peterson, Schofer, & Gemmell, 1974a). Let the condition of the environment be characterized as a vector of measured environmental parameters:

$$E = e_1$$
$$e_2$$
$$.$$
$$.$$
$$.$$
$$e_j$$
$$.$$
$$.$$
$$.$$
$$e_m$$

The magnitude e_j is the quantity of attribute j measured in the environment in question.

Now let the condition of the environment be an influence on human activities and states-of-being that are regarded as important. Assume that these human variables can be identified and measured quantitatively as the vector H:

$$H = h_1$$
$$h_2$$
$$\cdot$$
$$\cdot$$
$$\cdot$$
$$h_k$$
$$\cdot$$
$$\cdot$$
$$\cdot$$
$$h_p$$

The magnitude h_k is the quantity or level of the kth human variable.

Nevertheless, these human variables simply describe a state of being. They say nothing about value or importance. For example, h_1 might be a health variable while h_2 is concerned with the level of visual pleasure created by the scenic view. Which is more important, health or scenic pleasure? When such questions are asked, the problem has moved from matters of fact to matters of value (in the individual case) and matters of politics (in the societal case).

Assume that there is a set of goals or needs. These might be personal or social, real or hypothetical. Let the rewards to these goals or needs be describable as a vector R:

$$R = r_1$$
$$r_2$$
$$\cdot$$
$$\cdot$$
$$\cdot$$
$$r_g$$
$$\cdot$$
$$\cdot$$
$$\cdot$$
$$r_q$$

Whether or not these rewards are commensurate, substitutable, and additive is a question that must be addressed, but the question will not be answered here. If they are, they can simply be added up to get a score or index of value. If they are not, then the rewards must either be taken as a vector or they must be weighted and combined in some rational way.

This model that is suggested as a starting point assumes that e_j intervenes via some process in the human variables to influence the magnitude of h_k. The magnitude of h_k is in turn interpreted via a reward process in terms of the goals, thus influencing the magnitude of r_g. This is illustrated in Figure 1.

If this is a good model (which has not been adequately tested), it clearly defines a number of important questions:

1. What are the environmental attributes of concern, and how are they to be defined and measured?
2. What are the human activity and state-of-being variables of concern and how are they to be defined and measured?
3. What are the needs and goals?
4. What is the process by which the condition of the environment influences human activities and states-of-being?
5. What is the process by which rewards are generated by the human activities and states-of-being?
6. What is the process or method by which the multidimensional rewards can be combined into an EQI?

BACKWARD-SEEKING SPECIFICATION OF A REFERENCE ENVIRONMENT

If the model in Figure 1 could be completely specified, it might be used "in reverse" to specify a reference or ideal environment. Presumably the overriding objective is to maximize the elements of R. Given suitable mathematical conditions in the formulation of the model, the equations might be solved for E^*, the optimal environmental configuration. Alternatively, if minimum acceptable levels of reward can be set for each goal or need, this information might be used to specify the minimum acceptable environment. The point is, that if environmental

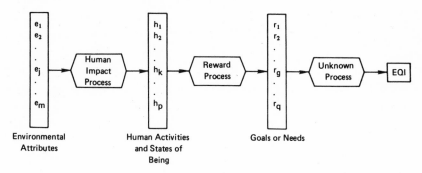

FIG. 1. An impact-oriented EQI model.

standards of excellence or thresholds of adequacy are to be established, they ought to be arrived at deductively via the kind of reasoning illustrated by the backward-seeking application of the impact model. The environmental standards are set because of the human conditions and/or rewards they imply.

AN ENVIRONMENTAL DEPARTURE MODEL

If an optimal environment relative to the purposes in question can be specified as the vector E_0, which contains the elements $e_{01}, e_{02} \ldots,$ $e_{0j} \ldots, e_{0m}$, this vector can be used as the basis for an environmental departure model for the EQI. Let the optimal environment, E_0, be a vector in an m-dimensional space. The measured environment to be evaluated is also a vector, E, in the same m-dimensional space. The two environments can then be compared as a vector of "environmental departures," A, with elements $a_1, a_2 \ldots, a_j \ldots, a_m$, where $a_j = e_j - e_{0j}$. The environmental departures are of concern because they intervene in human activities and states-of-being, causing these to generate less reward to the goals and needs than might otherwise occur. At any stage of the process, the consequences could be described by some kind of index, or the environmental departures themselves might be displayed. The latter is useful to managers because it shows what in the environment needs to be changed.

Human departures might be displayed as the difference between h_k, as determined by the actual environment, and h_{0k}, as would be determined by the ideal environment. Finally, the reward losses might be displayed individually, or they might be combined into an index in some unknown way. The environmental departures model is shown in Figure 2.

The notion of environmental departure can be used in another way. If E_0 is the vector of existing environmental conditions, and E is the vector of what those conditions would be under a given intervention policy, comparison of the two environments produces environmental departures. Given an explicit model of the human-related consequences of those departures, they can be translated into differences in the human variables, differences in rewards, or perhaps even an incremental index of environmental quality. For example, E_0 might be the environment at some future date, say 20 years hence, that would be likely if state or regional government did not intervene to regionalize local waste-water management systems. E might be the environment that would occur if planned regionalization were to take place. The EQI is produced in this case as the result of a comparative appraisal among alternative future

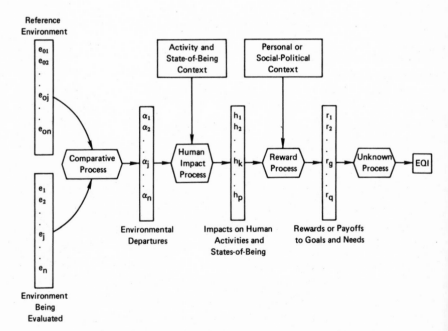

FIG. 2. An environmental departure EQI model.

environments. However, if it is a question of future environments, the E's must be predicted rather than simply measured.

Also illustrated in Figure 2 are some interaction variables that must be taken into account. The human impact process will be modified by the activity or purpose context in which the environment is being evaluated, and this will determine which environmental and human variables are of interest. If the evaluation is being done from a personal point of view, the reward process will be modified by the individual's personal characteristics. If the point of view is societal, the reward process will be modified by the social and political context. From the individual point of view, the reward process becomes a preference or utility function. From the social point of view, it is a social welfare function. For reasons already discussed, EQIs based on the social welfare function must be purely hypothetical. The prerogative is political, not technical.

A UTILITARIAN PEQI MODEL

The concept of environmental departure can be used to construct a PEQI model. Let PE be a vector of perceived environmental attributes describing what a given individual perceives to be the composition of the environment. This vector has elements $pe_1, pe_2 \ldots, pe_j \ldots, pe_m$. The quantity pe_j is the amount of attribute j perceived to be in the environment. Now define PE_0 as the vector describing the desired environment. PE_0 is a vector of aspirations or desires, and PE is a vector of perceptions. It can be argued that satisfaction with the environment, or environmental pleasure, is a function of the level of agreement between these two vectors (Peterson, 1974a). Measurement of PE and PE_0 would allow calculation of environmental departures. These environmental departures might then be combined via something akin to the model in Figure 2 or by direct theoretical or empirical construction of a utility or welfare function, written directly in terms of the departures. This PEQI model is illustrated in Figure 3. It is referred to as "utilitarian" because it is based on the assumption that the desired environment, PE_0, derives from a cognitive model of the consequences or "usefulnesses" of environmental conditions.

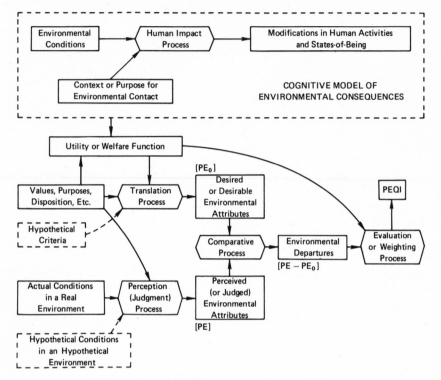

FIG. 3. Hypothetical framework for the PEQI.

SOURCES OF VARIATION IN THE PEQI

Consideration of these models suggests that there may be several sources of variation in the PEQI. It is not simply determined by the environment. These sources include: variation in the environment; variation in the perception of the environment; variation in the values, purposes, or goals that compose the context for environmental contact; and variation in the personal characteristics—including personality, culture, and life-style—of the individual.

These factors underscore the complexity of the PEQI problem and further emphasize the need to define the concepts rigorously and understand the processes that are involved.

For example, in a recent study of perceptions and motivations of users and managers in the Boundary Waters Canoe Area, it was found that summer canoeists on the average had an exaggerated perception of the wilderness character of the environment relative to how the more experienced and presumably more knowledgeable (and, hence, more correct?) managers saw it (Peterson, 1974b). Clearly, the users and managers were perceiving the environment differently. Because the canoeists were seeking wilderness, it would seem reasonable that they would judge the recreational performance of the environment to be better than the managers judged it. On the contrary, the users were more critical of recreational performance of the environment than the managers were. It must be concluded that the two groups were not only perceiving the content of the environment differently, they were also using quite different criteria to evaluate its performance or "quality."

In a study of children's preferences for playground equipment, Peterson et al. (1974c) found that adult designers and park authority officials were relatively poor judges of what eight-year-old children find attractive. For some kinds of devices, for example, sliding equipment, there were no significant differences between boys and girls, blacks and whites, or suburban and central-city residents. However, for other kinds of equipment (climbing devices) there were important sex and ethnic differences.

Studies of the preferences of high-school-age students for outdoor recreation activities and environments have shown that sex and ethnicity interact strongly to modify the process by which preferences are generated (Peterson, 1975). Degree of urbanization of the environment was the variable for which the differences were most apparent. These and similar studies indicate the complexity of the environmental preference problem in recreation. The sources of variation must be clearly identified and controlled for in the construction of PEQIs.

APPLICATION OF THE IMPACT-ORIENTED EQI MODEL: AN ILLUSTRATIVE EXAMPLE

A version of the impact-oriented EQI model described previously was used recently to develop judgmental PEQIs for alternative future environments in the Chicago region. The problem was to evaluate alternative regional waste-water management systems in a planning study conducted by the Chicago District of the Corps of Engineers (Peterson et al., 1974a,b; Schofer et al., 1974). The task was essentially to construct EQIs for the future environments that were contingent upon the various alternative regional waste-water plans. The evaluation budget was not sufficient to allow in-depth technological assessment, so it was decided to predict and evaluate the future environments judgmentally.

The task was defined as one of estimating sensitivities of environmental variables to attributes of the alternative waste-water systems, and then estimating sensitivities of sociohuman variables to the environmental parameters. A panel of experts was used to develop the initial lists of variables and then to estimate sensitivity coefficients. In order to compensate for the absence of standard measurement units and methods, the sensitivity coefficients were defined as dimensionless "elasticities," or relative sensitivities, and simple rating scales with numerical categories were used to extract quantitative judgments. More sophisticated techniques are available that might have been used to estimate the coefficients, and, more fundamentally, to extract judgmental estimates of the functional forms for the sensitivity relationships (Rappaport & Summers, 1973). No attempt was made to identify separate needs or goals in the vector R. Rather, the impacts were simply described as relative changes in the environmental and social variables.

For experimental purposes, importance "weights" were obtained for the social variables, again using rating scales, from three different groups—the experts, a group of chamber-of-commerce types from the region, and a group of professional planners from the region. These weights were then used illustratively and experimentally to construct PEQIs for the future environments.

Also for experimental purposes, the sensitivity coefficients for the relationships between the social and environmental variables were estimated twice by the expert panel and again by an independent panel of graduate students in a city-planning course. The average coefficients from each group were astonishingly similar, and analysis of variance demonstrated emphatically that the judgments were not random. The average reliability of the estimated sensitivity coefficients was estimated at 97% for the experts, and 91% between the two independent panels, although for some hard-to-define social variables the reliability was considerably lower.

Although the results of this study were by no means conclusive, they demonstrate strongly that information is contained in the judgmentally estimated numbers. In addition to the statistical criteria which clearly showed nonrandomness in the numbers, the resulting judgmental PEQIs were conceptually meaningful; that is, they seemed to make sense.

APPLICATION OF THE PEQI ENVIRONMENTAL DEPARTURE MODEL

The notion of perceived environmental departures was used recently to develop a technique for constructing PEQIs to describe perceived quality of the wilderness environment (Peterson, 1974a). A comprehensive and detailed list of environmental variables was constructed from hypotheses about motivations of wilderness recreationists. The lists were constructed of concrete, real, and "manageable" attributes in the environment, as opposed to abstract concepts and unrealities. Subjects were asked to express their environmental aspirations in terms of how desirable it is to encounter each of the items in the list while in the wilderness. They were also asked to express their environmental perceptions in terms of how likely it is to encounter each of the items in a given wilderness (the Boundary Waters Canoe Area).

A theoretical model was developed, based on assumptions about the utility function, and on the hypothesis that perceived environmental quality is a function of the degree of agreement between perception and aspiration. The results were enlightening, in that they allowed overall indices of perceived environmental quality to be calculated and specific explanation of which environmental attributes were adding to environmental quality and which were detracting from it.

THE PEQI IS THE ANSWER TO WHAT QUESTIONS?

The preceding discussion has addressed the understanding of what a PEQI is and the conceptual problems that are encountered when trying to construct one. Concerning scenic and recreational environments, what are the practical questions to which the PEQI is an answer?

Recreational and scenic environments are of concern because they are resources, the quality and quantity of which impinge upon human activities for which they are used. These activities are extremely complex and varied. In order to keep the discussion manageable and within the limited range of the author's competence, focus will be limited to recreational activity that is dependent upon "natural" outdoor environments that are wild or quasi-wild and/or spectacular. Interest in "scenic environments" will be limited to the recreational aspects of scenery. It will be considered only to the extent that it is a recreation-relevant environmental attribute.

In order to avoid excessive generality or abstraction, the discussion will focus on three examples: recreation in the Boundary Waters Canoe Area of northern Minnesota; assessment of the recreational potential of undeveloped rivers in Michigan; and satisfaction of latent demand in metropolitan areas for back-country-type recreational environments. This last example looms as one of major importance.

THE NEED FOR A FUNCTIONAL DEFINITION OF RECREATION

No attempt will be made here to define recreation. The literature is full of definitions, most of which seem to be based upon the assumption that recreation is a "thing" that has common meaning to all people. In fact, there are probably as many different meanings of "recreation" as there are people. People do things that we call recreation for a wide variety of reasons, and this is not adequately reflected in the traditional definitions. What is needed is a functional or explanatory definition in terms of why people engage in activities that are called recreational. Explanation of the functional roles of the environment in recreation will greatly enhance the ability to construct meaningful PEQIs. Those functional roles will depend on the reasons why people are contacting and interacting with the environment. One person might visit Yellowstone Park out of curiosity—an honest desire to experience environmental novelty. Another person might go to Yellowstone because of a perception that status (identity?) will be enhanced by having been there. Still another person may be looking for a way to use leisure time by "doing something" with his family, and going to Yellowstone is "something to do."

Is recreation engaged in purely because of pleasure-directed motives? To what extent do "recreative" or constructive needs guide personal choices? What, indeed, are the productive benefits to the person and society, of recreation? To what extent or at what point does recreation begin to divert time and resources away from productive channels, thus becoming a nonproductive, hedonistic consumption of pleasure for pleasure's sake?

An important research need is to find out what motivates different people to engage in various types of recreation. The personal and societal consequences of recreation, and the functional roles played by various environmental attributes in the activities, motives, and consequences also need to be understood. This is a necessary first step in the construction of PEQIs for assessing the recreational quality of the environment. Until this hurdle has been successfully negotiated, the PEQI as well as the EQI will remain a questionable empirical construct, at least as far as recreation is concerned. There is a lot of stuff in the literature about motives, but it is very disjointed. There is very little in the literature about consequences, let alone benefits. What little has been done is limited largely to economic estimation of a dollar contribution to the GNP resulting from a user day of recreation, or a consumer's surplus estimate of the utility the market has gained over and above the utility of the dollars it has had to pay for the activity. Until quality can be defined in terms of more meaningful criteria, it will have to be based on the ability of a place to attract users, in purely empirical terms.

PEQI-RELATED QUESTIONS FOR THE BWCA

Turning now to the practical problems involved in a specific example, what are the PEQI-related questions that arise in the management of the Boundary Waters Canoe Area (BWCA)? The problems faced include the following (Sierra Club, 1970; Rupp, 1970; Lime, 1970; Gilbert et al., 1972):

Management of Conflicting User Groups

This includes conflicts between local and nonlocal users, between mechanized and nonmechanized travel modes, and between recreational and nonrecreational use. For example, this last conflict involves recreational users, scientists who would use the area as an ecological laboratory, mining interests, timber-harvesting interests, forest management interests, and recreational-development interests, to name only a few. The problem is to decide the uses for which the environment of the area is best suited or to which it can be adapted most efficiently, within the framework of national and local policy. The problem also includes the question of whether to exclude certain types of use or to segregate them spacially or temporally. Some of the questions may be resolved legislatively as a matter of policy at the federal level because of the way the BWCA has been established, but many problems must be resolved at the discretion of local managers.

Evaluation of the Consequences of Proposed Interventions

The recently approved management plan for the BWCA had to be accompanied by an environmental impact statement (Superior National Forest, 1974). This statement clearly demonstrates that there is a need for better understanding of the impact of proposed changes in the environment on the quality of that environment from various points of view.

Evaluation of the Impact of External Activities on the Quality of the Internal Environment

Two major activities outside of the BWCA currently threaten to bring about changes in the internal BWCA environment. Forces are in motion toward the development of copper and nickel mining and refining near the BWCA. Certain internal environmental changes are predictable, even though the activity itself may remain outside the area. What effect will alternative plausible kinds and levels of change have on the quality of the environment for different purposes? Another example is the dumping of treated (and occasionally untreated) liquid wastes from the town of Ely, Minnesota, into a drainage system that subsequently flows through the BWCA. What is the effect on the recreational quality of the environment of changes in the water character? It has been demonstrated that clear water is one of the most subjectively important environmental attributes for BWCA canoeists (Peterson, 1974a).

Management of the Impact on the Environment of Recreational Use

One of the most environmentally threatening influences in the BWCA is the recreational use itself. In 1973 the average intensity of use during the season for the million-acre tract was about one visitor-day per acre. However, most of the use is confined to the water areas which compose 18% of the whole. This increases the average use rate to about five visitor-days per acre of water. But most of the use occurs on only a few of the lakes, and the result is that those lakes and their surrounding shores are subject to extremely intense use. The result is ecological deterioration that is not readily reversible, and social interference of the users with each other. What are the environmental-quality implications of the impacts of recreation? What are the ecological and social carrying capacities of the various lakes; for example, what levels of use of various types are ecologically and socially acceptable if the environmental quality is to be preserved at "adequate" levels?

Design and Location of Developed Facilities

Campers are encouraged (and, in fact, required in some areas) to camp only in designated places which have been identified and developed as campsites. Certain facilities are provided, such as latrines, primitive fireplaces, and cleared and smoothed tent sites. Various criteria are used by the Forest Service to decide how many campsites to place on a given lake and where to put them. However, from the users' point of view, we need methods for evaluating the environmental quality at existing campsites and at alternative locations for new campsites.

Management of Travel Behavior

As previously mentioned, some areas of the BWCA are much more attractive than others (in the sense that they "attract" more visitors). This is largely due to accessibility factors, but other things may be involved. Is it possible to assess differences in environmental quality, from the recreationist's point of view, of various locations in the area, independent of accessibility effects? If so, it would assist in predicting and controlling travel behavior, and this must be done if localized overuse is to be avoided.

Management of Forest Ecology

The typical recreationist's concept of a desirable recreational forest is one that is virgin and mature. However, perpetual encouragement of virgin and mature forests is not ecologically wise. It has detrimental effects on the forest itself, as well as on the wildlife that inhabits it. Suggested strategies for restoring more healthy conditions include managed timber harvesting and prescribed burning. But what is the impact of such actions on the recreational quality of the environment from the recreationist's point of view? If the impacts are substantially negative, do the ecological benefits justify the recreational costs? Can the recreationist be educated or diverted so as to reduce the detrimental consequences that he would otherwise perceive?

Management of Specific Environmental Characteristics

Typical wilderness visitors, at least those most common in the BWCA, are attracted to the pristine natural conditions *and* many of the comforts of home. For example, they want to experience wildlife, catch large fish, camp in virgin forests, see crystal-clear water, and travel in seldom-visited areas, while avoiding mosquitoes and black flies and enjoying the comforts of picnic tables and well-cleared campsites. What specific environmental attributes are responsible for user satisfaction and dissatisfaction? What type of use is attracted by which attributes? Will the preservation or modification of certain attributes selectively attract certain kinds of users, thus setting in motion invasion and succession processes? Can environmental attributes be selectively managed (without unacceptably altering the ecology of the area) so as to enhance the satisfaction of users and encourage desirable uses?

Imposition of Regulations and/or User Fees

Certain kinds of regulations have been imposed in order to protect the area. These include a ban on bottles and cans, restrictions of camping on certain lakes to one night only, and prohibition of mechanized travel in certain areas and limitation of allowed horsepower in others. Other regulations have been considered, such as regulation of entry rates at access points, advance reservation at campsites, and charging of user fees. What are the effects of such actions on quality of the environment and quality of the experience?

Selection of Demand

Although it is apparently not yet an overt policy, it may soon become necessary to discourage certain types of users from going to the BWCA. Some users that are potentially incompatible with the principal purposes of the wilderness preserve (such as snowmobilers and motorboaters) may be just as well served elsewhere in nonwilderness areas. How can we compare the environmental quality of wilderness and nonwilderness opportunities from various points of view? For which uses is the BWCA best suited by virtue of the environmental attributes that it possesses? Which uses should be permitted and which discouraged? Obviously, there is more to this question than assessment of environmental quality from special points of view, but the environmental evaluation is an important aspect of the problem.

The Possibility of Mining within the BWCA

The mineral deposits that have caused interest to develop in copper and nickel extraction near the BWCA have also raised questions about mining within the area. The Duluth Gabbro Complex, which is of principal interest, extends through a major portion of the BWCA. As pressures increase for production of copper and nickel, it will be increasingly difficult to maintain the sanctity of the wilderness. "It would appear that, only where some genuinely greater value is significantly affected, should carefully controlled mineral development be prevented" (Lehman, 1974). Wilderness has not traditionally been preserved on the grounds of demonstrated value in terms recognized by accountants and economists. Its actual values are unknown and not demonstrable, except in behavioral terms of people voting in favor of wilderness use of a given area instead of using it for something else. More commonly, however, wilderness has been preserved because of aggressive actions by key individuals or groups in the absence of effective opposition. In coming times of mineral shortage, when the benefits of mineral development can be clearly demonstrated, what are the benefits of wilderness preservation that should be weighed in the balance? It is likely that those benefits to present and future generations will not be explicitly articulated, because they are not understood.

THE PEQI IN WILD RIVER RESEARCH

Similar questions are being raised about undeveloped rivers in Michigan in a recently initiated study by the North Central Forest Experiment Station (Lime, 1975). Among other things, there is a need to evaluate the potential of a given river for various types of recreational use. Specifically, what is the environmental quality from the point of view of individuals such as canoeists, motorboaters, salmon fishermen, trout fishermen, and developers of residential areas and public facilities? For what uses is a river or a section of a river best suited? Which sections are worth preserving in a wild state, which can and should be returned to a wild state, and which are more suitably used in other ways?

The study is specifically aimed at exploring motivations and needs in the context of wild-river recreation, developing instruments for evaluating recreational potential and environmental quality, and developing methods for classifying rivers in terms of their environmental quality-related attributes. This last goal implies the ability to describe differences among rivers and between specific rivers and idealized environments.

URBAN "WILDERNESS" RECREATION

One of the most significant national recreation problems is that of latent demand in urban areas for recreational opportunities to satisfy the motives that attract some of the people to such places as national parks, wild areas, and forested lands. There are major segments of the urban population that do not have access to these traditional opportunities. For some, access is limited by economic and time factors. The less affluent members of society simply cannot afford the investments of time, transportation, equipment, and skill development that are required for participation in these recreational pursuits. Also, for cultural reasons, the interests tend not to develop, perhaps due in part to a history of nonparticipation. However, for the more affluent members of society who are not culturally constrained against participation, outdoor recreation in wild areas appears to be of major importance. With the advent of the energy crisis and the current recession, the number of people constrained against participation is likely to increase substantially. For example, residents of the Chicago area must travel hundreds of miles into Michigan, Wisconsin, or Minnesota in order to experience clear-water lakes and streams in wild settings. Also, demand for recreation and development will continue to erode the existing supply of opportunities.

But within the Chicago Metropolitan area there are numerous rivers, lakes, and streams. The Cook County Forest Preserves offer extensive areas of relatively wild land interwoven in the city itself. The city fronts on Lake Michigan, which has become an important sport fishery. Within reasonably short distances, there are many relatively wild shorelines and streams; the streams are badly polluted, however, and are thus not very attractive for outdoor recreation where water quality is important. What are the costs and benefits of cleaning up these streams? If these streams were cleaned up and managed as quasi-wild rivers within the urban area, to what extent would this satisfy latent demand? What, if any, portion of the people who now travel to remote areas would find suitable substitutes in these upgraded streams? In general, what are the environmental departures of the urban and near-urban resources from the idealized environmental profiles for various recreational activities? Can any of these departures be reduced at reasonable cost so as to make the urban resources suitable as substitutes for remote opportunities? Stated in another way, for what recreational motives, needs, and demands can urban and near-urban resources be made suitable at reasonable cost? The answer to these questions requires the ability to assess the recreation-specific quality and potential quality of the urban resources. Also, a lot more needs to be known about the reasons why people do and do not participate in various kinds of recreation.

As an addicted canoeist, I would say that if a river in the Chicago area could be rehabilitated to a state of clear water, quasi-wild (and clean) shorelines, and off-stream, semiprivate campsites, there would be a great surge in local canoeing activity. However, this is a surmise that would require verification through research.

SOCIAL CARRYING CAPACITY: AN EXAMPLE OF A SPECIAL PURPOSE PEQI

The concept of "carrying capacity" has become important in the wilderness recreation literature, and it is being used rather intuitively by managers in real situations to judge and control environmental quality. Carrying capacity is regarded ás having at least two principal dimensions: ecological and social. Ecological carrying capacity has to do with the ability of the natural and physical environment to withstand the effects of recreational use without irreversible damage of an unacceptable degree. Thus, it requires a definition of the use-sensitive characteristics of the environment and the expression of these characteristics in terms of an acceptable level of recreational use. It is thus a kind of EQI.

Social carrying capacity is concerned with the recreationist's perception of the quality of the "environment" with regard to the presence and behavior of other recreationists. In simplistic terms, the level of exposure to other, nonaffiliated people can be regarded as an environmental characteristic, albeit a characteristic of the social environment. Researchers and managers alike refer to it simply as "crowding." The notion is that the degree of satisfaction with a wilderness recreation experience is sensitive to the level of "crowding" experienced. The concept of social carrying capacity proposes that there is a threshold, beyond which "crowding" becomes unacceptable.

In the BWCA, managers have been able to deal pragmatically with ecological carrying capacity. It has been reduced to a question of how many campsites to develop on each lake, and this is decided in terms such as impact on water quality and suitable physical locations. From time to time decisions are made to close permanently or temporarily campsites that have begun to show too much physical deterioration.

However, the social carrying capacity concept has not been operationalized, even in pragmatic terms. It remains an intuitive, nonoperational concept that is considered by management implicitly rather than explicitly.

What are the problems in operationalizing "Social Carrying Capacity" into a PEQI? Perhaps the first step is to define "crowding." This is a catchall word that is probably not meaningful. A group of 10 canoeists traveling together does not consider itself to be crowded. But as soon as an unaffiliated party of two in a single canoe is encountered on a remote lake, feelings of dissatisfaction begin to develop. Why? Alternative hypotheses are possible:

1. *Competition for limited resources.* If there is one good campsite on the lake and the party of two gets there first, the large group will have to accept an inferior campsite or move on to another lake, which may mean a difficult portage in a state of extreme weariness.

2. *Subconscious feelings of territoriality or ownership of the area.* The group may have worked very hard to get there, and may have developed proprietary feelings.

3. *Neurotic hostility toward people.* Individuals in the group may simply have problems relating to people they do not know, and may feel personally threatened by the presence of strangers. Perhaps one of the motives that has attracted them to the wilderness is a psychological need to withdraw from demanding social contacts, to simplify their social interaction. Perhaps the individual has a fragile identity and wants a reprieve, if only temporary, from situations in which he has to undergo threatening evaluation by new people.

4. *Suspicion and disdain for others.* It is not uncommon for the wilderness traveler to view himself as a special kind of person, with greater sensitivity for and appreciation of the wilderness and wilderness activity. Strangers are unknowns. They are foreigners, in a sense, who are unevaluated and are prone to be judged as infidels or clods who do not belong there. It's a "there goes the neighborhood" kind of attitude. The wilderness traveler does not want to associate in the wilderness with people who are less sensitive and appreciative than himself.

5. *The desire to feel unique.* It is not unusual to go into the wilderness in order to seek identity. Wilderness has appeal to some because it is remote and difficult to attain. To go there is

to achieve something, to become identified as a certain kind of person. The presence of others there depreciates the uniqueness of the accomplishment. The mystique is shattered, especially if the other group roars by in a motor canoe.

6. *An honest desire to be alone and to experience nature in the absence of strangers.* The desire for privacy is not uncommon, and it is possible that many people go to the wilderness in an honest effort to achieve a special kind of privacy.

7. *Honest concern for depletion or degradation of resources.* This is related to competition for resources, but is a little different. The presence of a lot of people at a remote lake-trout lake suggests that the lake is or may become fished out. When you are alone and the fishing is bad, it is because of the moon, or because of the water temperature, for example. If the lake is crowded, it tends to be interpreted as an indication that the fish are spooked or depleted. Indeed, if it is a clear, high mountain lake or a small, clear steelhead stream, the presence of a few people will spook the fish, and there is no use trying.

In spite of the obvious psychological naïveté that is demonstrated by these hypotheses, they demonstrate that the construction of an index of social carrying capacity or social quality of the environment is not simply a matter of measuring the probability of encounter. There is a good deal of basic social and psychological research needed.

SUMMARY AND CONCLUSION

An effort to identify research needs and priorities for scenic and recreational PEQIs is bound to be incomplete because of the complexity of the problem and the immature state-of-the-art. It is hoped that the issues that have been raised here will be helpful in stimulating more rigorous thought about the problem of quantitative analysis and evaluation of the perceived environment.

In summary the principal arguments include the following.

1. The PEQI concept needs more rigorous definition. What is a PEQI, what is it for, and how is it to be constructed?

2. Problems of measurement with respect to the PEQI need to be

more carefully examined. What is the level of measurement that is desired? How can the PEQI be defined operationally? Can standard units and methods of measurement be developed? Is it meaningful to try to agree upon thresholds or standards of adequacy by considering the human consequences of PEQI variation?

3. What is meant by "quality"? Is environmental pleasure to be measured, or environmental utility? Is quality something that can or should be observed directly, or must it be calculated via explanation of man–environment phenomena? Do we measure quality or do we measure environmental conditions and decide quality by means of value judgments?

4. There seems to be some confusion with regard to separation of technical and political matters. On an individual basis values can be measured directly, but there is no valid formula for combining individual values into social values. Apparently social values must be dealt with hypothetically.

5. Should PEQI research aim at direct estimation of numerical indicators of environmental performance, or should the goal be explanation of the processes by which environmental conditions generate pleasure or utility? An index that is based on theoretical exposure of the value-generating processes will be more powerful and defensible than a direct survey-based empirical index. The explanation will also allow diagnosis of specific causes of poor performance, whereas the simple index does no more than point out that a problem exists.

6. PEQIs probably should be developed in a multidimensional or vector framework, rather than as simple scalars. Environmental quality, especially perceived environmental quality, is likely to involve complex trade-offs and substitutions among multidimensional environmental attributes.

7. The PEQI concept should be developed in terms of a model or framework that gives structure to the questions. Preferably the models would be based on theoretical explanation of quality-related man–environment phenomena.

8. There needs to be an inventory of specific real-world problems that would be served by PEQIs. There is a danger here of developing a tool that may not be well suited to the hand of the carpenter or the job he needs to get done.

9. Also needed is an inventory of the propositions and theories of man–environment interaction that relate to the PEQI problem. The literature is widely dispersed and rather disjointed.

10. At the risk of being redundant, perhaps the most urgent priority is for scholarly theoretical rigor behind any empirical or practical constructs that are attempted.

In order to illustrate and underscore these and other problems, some plausible, albeit tenuous, models have been suggested. In the specific context of outdoor recreation, some examples of applications and needs have been offered. It can be concluded that before PEQIs can go beyond ad hoc survey-based empirical measures for recreation, there needs to be a lot of basic work on what recreation is—that is, why people do it and what its consequences are. Recreational benefits and motives are poorly understood. How, then, can we define environmental quality relative to recreational use of the environment? Apparently it can be done only in terms of the environment's competitive ability to attract "user days," or in terms of preference polls and attitude surveys. These may be useful, but fall far short of satisfying the need.

In conclusion, the PEQI concept seems to have emerged in response to real needs, at least with respect to scenic and recreational environments. But progress is likely to be slow unless we succeed in pinning down more explicitly what we are talking about.

Discussion Summary

KENNETH H. CRAIK AND ERVIN H. ZUBE

The conceptual analysis of perceived quality in scenic and recreational environments arising in the prepared papers and workshop discussions was summarized in the introduction to this section. The development and application of indices for these constructs was the primary topic of workshop discussions and will be reviewed in order of the salient steps in that process.

MEASURING ENVIRONMENTAL QUALITY

Implicit in the construct of environmental quality is some sort of scaling which communicates the sense of qualitative variability among environments. The definition of such a scale or scaling procedure presents an interesting and challenging set of problems and possibilities related to measurement. One approach might be the identification of qualitative thresholds for making ordinal comparisons of environments, such that comparisons are found to be "greater than" or "less than" the threshold. The perceived threshold for specific environments suggested by Peterson would be the congruence between people's aspirations and perceptions based on independent measures of both factors. The comparative quality of the environment is then a measurement of the departure from this congruent state of aspiration and perception.

DR. KENNETH H. CRAIK • Institute of Personality Assessment and Research, University of California, Berkeley, California 94720.   DR. ERVIN H. ZUBE • Institute for Man and Environment, University of Massachusetts, Amherst, Massachusetts 01002.

GAUGING RELIABILITY AND VALIDITY OF PEQI ASSESSMENTS

Regardless of the measurement system or process used, it must, as Daniel indicates, stand the tests of reliability and validity. The measure must in fact show differences when they exist and must produce the same answers when measurements are repeated on the same environments or attributes. And further, the system must in fact measure that which it is intended to measure. This question of validity would appear to be of particular importance in the measurement of recreational settings: that is, in specifying the differences between the social and physical milieus.

APPLICATION AND UTILITY OF SCENIC AND RECREATIONAL PEQI SYSTEMS

Daniel also postulates a third evaluative criterion for a PEQI measurement system, and that is utility. In other words, the PEQI should "help to predict, direct, and evaluate environmental policies, decisions, and management actions."

Assuming the development of reliable, valid, and utilitarian measurement systems and related PEQIs for scenic and recreational environments, what are the potential areas of application? Workshop participants enthusiastically identified several, including the evaluation of alternative sites for large-scale projects, regional monitoring, impact assessment, and postconstruction evaluations. A cautionary note was also expressed, however, about the possible premature use of PEQIs by individuals and agencies before the reliability and validity of indices have been fully established. There was a general feeling of a ready, waiting, and eager constituency for scenic and recreational PEQIs.

The potential use of scenic PEQIs for the evaluation of alternative sites and for impact assessment encompasses a broad array of public and private development activities, including the location of transportation and utility corridors, the location of visitor service facilities in national parks and forests, the selection of suburban and new-town development sites, and the identification of areas for conservation and open-space programs.

Regional monitoring activities were discussed as having particular value for land-use planning programs. Gauging perceived changes in scenic quality and in the quality of recreation environments could be especially useful in monitoring the overall quality of the public landscape. The idea of the public landscape in this context refers to that portion of the landscape which is accessible to everyone. Accessibility may be either visual or physical, but either way the landscape potentially impinges, to a greater or lesser degree, on all who move through and look at it or who use it physically.

Monitoring of a full range of perceived qualities (e.g., scenic, recreational, residential, air, water) was viewed as providing a basis for comparisons between several river valleys to assess relative quality. The comparison could be on the basis of individual indices or on the basis of a cross-environment PEQI obtained by weighting and summing across all indices. The value of such an activity would, in part, be as a means of communication about the general state of environmental well-being to the residents of the two valleys. The procedure could also be followed longitudinally in a single valley as a means of informing residents of perceived changes and trends in the quality of their environment over time. The value of such monitoring activities and the cross-environment PEQI would not be so much as a predictor but rather as a descriptor.

Monitoring may also be important in the management of critical areas (that is, in maintaining a qualitative overview of areas of special aesthetic, cultural, and scientific value such as scenic agricultural valleys, historic towns, and wetlands). The concept of critical areas, and the goal of identifying, preserving, or protecting them is, in a number of variations, a part of 18 state planning programs (Council on Environmental Quality, 1972). The National Coastal Zone Management Act of 1972, relating to 30 states and territories, also calls for the identification, preservation, and protection of critical areas. Once a monitoring process of the environment is initiated, however, the observer must be maintained as a measuring instrument so that a basis is provided for assessing whether recorded changes are occurring in the environment or in the perceiver. Changes in the "real" physical world can be assessed by monitoring appropriate attributes of the physical environment. Changes in cultural values relative to the "perceived" physical world can only be assessed through study of the perceiver. As stated in the discussion, such a dual approach to the monitoring activity provides the basis for a dynamic rather than static model of quality (see Chapter 14).

Scenic PEQI systems would also be of value in the initial identification of critical areas by affording a means of making comparative appraisals of places nominated for inclusion in a critical areas system. Regional water and related land resource programs under the jurisdiction of the U.S. Water Resources Council also require the comparative evaluation of alternative sites for water-related projects and of alternative strategies for satisfying water-resource-related goals and objectives. Specific components of these comparative appraisals include scenic and recreational values of environments.

The predictive nature of environmental impact statements was also cited as an illustration of the potential value of monitoring data. Such data might document variations in perceived quality in relationship to specific environmental changes brought about by various development projects. Longitudinal data of this kind would provide a useful base for making predictions of the consequences of similar projects undertaken elsewhere in the future.

The PEQI concept was also discussed as a potentially useful and important means of incorporating public values into the planning process. For example, given a set of alternative sites for a visitor center in a national park or a campground in a national forest, place-centered appraisals could provide information about the relative scenic quality of those sites so that a broader understanding of the alternatives could be achieved by the interested public. If, however, there were serious disagreement about the basic idea of a visitor center or campground, person-centered assessments could be useful for identifying intergroup differences.

The potential for application of PEQIs in postconstruction evaluation which was suggested is indicated by the magnitude of public support for recreation development. Some $107 million, for example, were estimated to have been expended in 1973 and $137 million in 1974 as federal aid to state and local governments and indirect federal activity for the purchase, development, and operation of city recreation and park facilities. In addition, $298 million in 1973 and $321 million in 1974 were estimated to have been expended on noncity general recreation (Council on Environmental Quality, 1973, p. 469). Essentially all these funds were expended without a systematic evaluation of the perceived quality of the environments resulting therefrom.

RESEARCH ISSUES AND NEEDS

Following is a listing of research issues and needs identified by workshop participants in the concluding portion of the round table discussion. They span a range of concerns from the general—relating to the concept of PEQI—to the specific—relating to applications for scenic and recreation environments. They both summarize and expand on the conclusions and recommendations contained in the three papers.

1. There is a need for a general research planning model which places PEQI development into a broader context and which places individual research issues and needs into a priority listing. That was the overriding objective of the workshops and is the focus of this publication.
2. What is the construct validity of PEQIs? What does scenic quality and recreation quality mean? What are the aspects and constituent elements of scenic quality and recreation quality? What does the validity of the constructs require regarding empirical relationships to other variables?
3. How do people conceptualize the landscape? Are there general environmental concepts (e.g., wilderness, urban, rural, farm, park) which might serve as a basis for a perceptual landscape taxonomy? What do the words which are used to define or describe landscapes stand for; what is it that they communicate to people?
4. Are there indirect behavioral indicators of perceived environmental quality? Are there secondary sources of information (e.g., based on user or observational data) which indicate successful environments? What is the relationship of behavioral and perceptual data, and what are the constraints which are operating on behavior, such as accessibility?
5. There is a need for the development and adoption of standard definitions and procedures among researchers and for agencies.

The state-of-the-art is such that the design of standard instruments with acceptable levels of reliability and validity appears to be possible. The requirements for standard instruments need to be specified for given purposes such as critical area, scenic river or campsite identification, or landscape monitoring.

6. What is the effect of the instructional set given to the observer? For example, do the instructions to express a preferential judgment and a comparative appraisal produce significantly different results?

7. What is the difference between individual and group (consensual) judgments? What is the effect of group dynamics on judgments about environments, and what is the stability of these judgments over time as compared with individual judgments? This issue addresses the problem of how data for PEQIs might be collected within the context of continuing planning programs. This also raises the question of what effects varying contexts have upon observer judgments. Does the context of a scientific-research setting produce outcomes which differ from those obtained in a planning or environmental decision-making setting?

8. What are the interaction effects between displays and observers? What is the effect of varying displays and holding observers constant and of varying observers and holding displays constant?

9. Work is required on the replication of findings so that the question of reliability is more rigorously and consistently addressed. Both longitudinal and cross-sectional studies are required for both observers and places. What are the social system antecedents of shifts that occur in PEQI?

10. Is there a valid and viable distinction between comparative appraisals and preferential judgments? Is there a valid conceptual basis for a general place-centered appraisal and a specific person-centered assessment?

11. What is the relationship between PEQIs and physical environmental measures or components? What are the components of the physical environment that relate to the perception of satisfactory or unsatisfactory scenic and recreation environments, and that have utility for prescribing management strategies and practices?

12. There is a need for the kind of literature survey that leads to the development of research propositions and hypotheses concerning how people respond to the environment—what are the important observer characteristics which would help to explain individual and group responses (see item 7), interaction effects (see item 8), and behavioral characteristics (see item 4)?

13. What is the relative importance of nonvisual perceptual modes to perceived environmental quality (hearing, smell, touch, taste), and how might multimodal PEQIs be developed?

14. What are the possible correlations and consequences of PEQIs in terms of social–psychological variables (i.e., mental well-being, social pathology)? Does a high quality environment influence interpersonal relationships and individuals' perceptions of other persons? For example, do they see others as more friendly and dignified in beautiful settings than in ugly settings? What is the relationship with other intangible cultural and historical values such as tradition and equity?

15. What are the management needs that can be assisted by the development of PEQIs, and what form should findings take to be useful to managers? How can data be organized and presented so as to be both interesting and useful to resource managers?

16. There is a need for selected demonstrated projects which address the technical measurement problems, the logistical research issues, and the communication of information to users. The only way in which many of the identified issues and needs can effectively be dealt with is to work them out in a "real-world" setting.

III
Residential and Institutional Environments

The Constructs of Perceived Quality in Residential and Institutional Environments

The primary focus of this workshop was directed toward the residential environment. In part, this emphasis derived from the relatively smaller body of research literature on institutional environments, but also in part indubitably reflected the predominant interests of workshop participants. Although institutional environments represent a more varied and complex class of settings than residential environments, the general points and issues treated at the workshop probably apply to them as well.

In his review of research on residential environments, Marans (Chapter 7) dealt in detail with the array of residential attributes that appear to be salient to inhabitants, as revealed in studies of residential satisfaction, preferences, and other pertinent behaviors and activity patterns. The delineation of a comprehensive, standard inventory of residential attributes has not been the principal goal of past research. Thus, although useful suggestions are available, research directed explicitly to this end is a prerequisite to PEQI operational systems that would incorporate the views of the general public at this step in the process. The alternative approach would require PEQI developers to make these selections and judgments. Then, of course, demonstration of the content validity would be necessary in subsequent applications.

The distinction introduced in the first workshop between place-centered appraisals (which are environment-focused and use observers to appraise environmental qualities) and person-centered assessments (which are observer-focused and intended to assess environmental satisfactions and preferences) was found useful in the context of residential environments. For example, the criteria for construct validation was more demanding in the case of the former than the latter. In both cases, the following requirements pertain: (a) reliable and sensitive measurement; (b) changes in PEQIs due to historical and societal factors (e.g., media, fashion) which are sufficiently moderate in pace to afford a reasonable "use-period" for applications in policy and practice. In addition, environment-focused place-centered appraisals face additional validational hurdles, including: (c) systematic correlates of PEQIs with physical and social environmental variables; (d) general consensus on place-centered appraisals among subgroups of the general public (including environmental experts).

Environmental indices are typically related to the attainment of goals, such as human welfare, resource availability, or ecological integrity (NAS-NAE, 1975). Although housing research of prior decades was often directed to public health consequences, recent research appears to conceptualize residential satisfaction as a direct measure of human welfare, distinct from whatever public health or other consequences residential quality might produce. However, investigations which employ levels of perceived residential quality as an independent variable offer an important research direction. The construct of perceived residential quality itself could be broadened to entail certain consequences regarding public health, personal adjustment, and other nonexperiential outcomes, but that possibility did not emerge in the present discussions.

Perceived residential quality appears to be conceptualized by experts and laypersons as a multidimensional construct. In addition, the scale of environments warrants consideration in the conceptual analysis. A taxonomy, perhaps even a hierarchy, of spaces can be envisioned which ranges from residential interiors to dwelling units, microneighborhoods, macroneighborhoods, counties, and regions. The prospect of PEQIs for each of these residential domains raises the issue of composite residential PEQIs, and in light of the prospect of scenic, recreational, and atmospheric PEQIs, points to the possibility of some sort of cross-environment PEQI, which in turn might be indexed conjointly with physical EQIs into a master Environmental Quality Index. The risibility threshold displayed in considering this ordinal scale of composite indices varied among participants, but was rather low for the most part. However, the matter appeared to be more readily handled for the development of person-centered PEQIs than for place-centered PEQIs.

With person-centered PEQIs, a comprehensive survey of personal assessments regarding the individual's own environmental domains can be readily envisioned and was illustrated by the reports of one workshop· member (Milbrath & Sahr, 1975). For the place-centered PEQI, a cross-environment index would require conceptualization of a region of study and a sampling of its various environmental domains, combined with adequate monitoring operations for each.

The Housing and Community Development Act of 1974 indicates a specific application of person-centered PEQIs in its authorization for assessments "to determine the housing design, the housing structure, and the housing related facilities, and amenities most effective or appropriate to meet the needs of groups with special housing needs, including the elderly, the handicapped, the displaced, single individuals, broken families and large households" (Section 507). PEQIs employed in this context would be for purposes of postconstruction evaluation and as a means of providing feedback for the future.design of improved housing. The Appleyard-Carp study (1974) of the impact of the Bay Area Rapid Transit System on residential areas provides an example of the potential use of PEQIs in obtaining base line data for preparing more informed environmental impact statements and for assessing large-scale impacts on residential environments.

In the chapters that follow, Bechtel reviews alternative procedures available for developing residential and institutional PEQIs and examines sources of possible resistance to the adoption of PEQIs and other forms of policy and program evaluation; Marans surveys empirical research on the constituent elements in peoples' conception of residential quality and offers a conceptual model of factors influencing the perception of environmental quality; and Ladd turns to the pragmatic issues of whether and how research findings on perceived residential and institutional quality will be used in policy formation and practice, and addresses research requirements for bridging the gaps between environmental decision-makers and researchers and between environmental decision-makers and their user-clients.

6

The Perception of Environmental Quality

Some New Wineskins for Old Wine

ROBERT B. BECHTEL

Since the beginning of the environmental movement, an emphasis has been placed on the perception of a new entity: environmental quality. Prior to this movement, perception and perceptual studies focused on elements general to all environments, such as depth, color, texture, mobility, and other universal features. The new emphasis seeks to focus on specific aspects of the environment that are related to man's welfare. If these specific aspects are rated high, we say the environmental quality is, therefore, high; if rated low, then the environmental quality is low. Unfortunately there is far from unanimous agreement on whether many specific aspects of the environment are related to man's welfare and even some conceptual confusion as to how it is related. Nevertheless, the task is to penetrate these confusions and ambiguities and to determine if perceptions of environmental quality can be measured effectively enough to be of use in policy matters concerning environmental quality.

Before considering whether perceptions of environmental quality can meet the criteria for policy decisions, some discrepancies in the audiences who view the problem need to be examined. Previous studies have been done within the framework of different disciplines and with widely varying audiences in mind. The rubric of the Man in the Biosphere program of UNESCO is no exception. Many who think of

DR. ROBERT B. BECHTEL • Environmental Research Development Foundation, Kansas City, Missouri 64113.

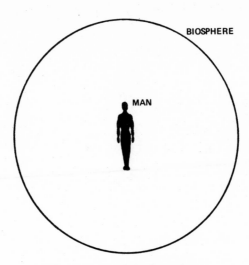

FIG. 1. Man and the biosphere.

the Man in the Biosphere program conjure up a relationship of man in the biosphere that might be represented by Figure 1. In this image the collective "man" is represented by a single individual within a sphere (the biosphere) which contains all possible influences on him. Let us say all these possible influences can be represented by stimuli that appear on the inside of this sphere so that perception of any of these stimuli can be achieved by the individual merely orienting himself to any of these stimuli. It is a simple one-to-one relationship of the individual to the environmental stimulus or stimuli.

This view of man in the biosphere may seem oversimplified, yet, when one listens to many papers on this subject, one gets the distinct impression that the perception of any event is based on this image. When questions are raised about perception of air pollution or water purity, one can sometimes almost visualize this simple diagram in the mind of the person who raises the question. But, of course, things are never this simple. The social scientist, for example, would see a second sphere surrounding the individual which acts as a semipermeable membrane in filtering stimuli to and from the physical environment of the biosphere. This second sphere could be represented as in Figure 2.

The social sphere represents all those social elements that influence perception selectively, such as culture, beliefs, attitudes, membership in groups, stage in life cycle, race, sex, and possibly even language. The intention is to convey, by the interposition of this sphere between the individual and the biosphere, the reality that no stimulus from the biosphere as a physical entity can reach the individual without being filtered through the social sphere. The social sphere is the lens that shapes and makes clear or clouds all views of the biosphere. No perception of the biosphere is possible unless the social sphere permits or defines it in some way. Some might even say that there are subtle interactions between both spheres that are independent of the individual. Still another way to express these ideas is to point out that the notion of the single individual perceiving any event in the biosphere is entirely erroneous. Any individual is never alone in his perceptions. They are shared by groups of which he is a member, and he is never separated from this group influence.

One might think that this construct is complicated enough with its interacting spheres influencing perception, but the environmental psychologists would have us go one step further. Figure 3 shows a rectangle interposed between the social sphere and the biosphere. The rectangle represents the built environment.

The purpose of interposing the built environment between man and the biosphere is to illustrate that man does not usually perceive the biosphere directly. He does not breathe nature's air or live in a forest. His daily contacts with the environment are indoor air and walls, floor, and ceiling, and his perceptions of these are far different from a natural

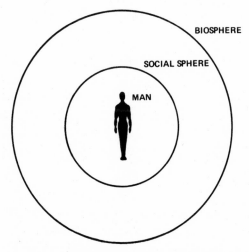

FIG. 2. Man, the biosphere, and the social sphere.

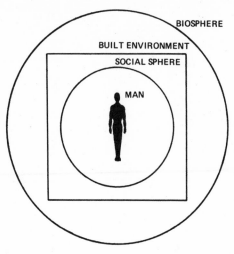

FIG. 3. Man, the biosphere, the social sphere, and the built environment.

biosphere. In short, man has interposed his own created rectangle between himself and nature so that his contacts with nature are almost always indirect and filtered by the built environment. Furthermore, this built environment is perceived only through the lens of the social sphere so that there are two semipermeable membranes which have a great influence on any perceptions of environmental quality. Not only do they act as filters to perceptions of the natural environment, but they can also be perceived as total environmental references themselves. Thus, we can speak of the quality of the natural environment, the quality of the built environment, and the quality of the social environment. While all three of these environments exist separately and independently, they also have overlapping and mutually dependent aspects. Therefore, it is helpful to keep in mind these distinctions when discussing criteria appropriate for the development of standard Perception of Environmental Quality Indices (PEQIs). Some may blandly refer to a "biosphere," some may refer only to the built environment, some only the social, or some may cover any combination of all three.

THE DREAM OF THE STANDARD PEQI

Implicit in the focus of this book is the notion that there can be such a thing as a standard Perception of Environmental Quality Index.

This seems to imply that there are such things as standard physical environmental indices that can be measured and tied to human well-being in some fashion. Does this mean there would be perceptual indices of such things as temperature, light, or humidity? Certainly there seem to be popular notions to this effect and many textbooks have been written defining the limits of temperature environments and other physical environmental aspects (e.g., Poulton, 1970; Jennings & Murphy, 1966; Folk, 1969).

The problem with this view is that it is oversimplified. Rohles (1967) has pointed out that temperature standards depend on what activity one is taking part in, how one is dressed, and many other factors. Yet even some accepted standards change, such as room temperature. The consensus of comfortable room temperature has risen several degrees in the past 25 years. Helson (1964) has pointed out that *no* perception remains static, that our perceptual organs are constantly adapting to environmental stimuli. Thus, if there is to be anything like a *standard* perception of environmental quality, it must be highly qualified by surrounding physical conditions and behavioral adaptations. While Rohles (1967) refers to this kind of research as a "can of worms," this does not mean that some ranges of perceptual quality cannot be defined. For example, such factors as the effects of altitude (Folk, 1969), diurnal rhythms, and other physiological aspects have been studied in detail. Furthermore, for specific environmental qualities there is a great deal of literature as opposed to general environmental quality where there is very little. Thus, the dream of a standard PEQI for general environmental conditions may have to be postponed for the time being while specific PEQIs are being further developed.

HOUSING RESEARCH

Research into the quality of the residential environment has taken many forms. Sanoff (1970) investigated the connotative meaning of house forms by using the semantic differential. He discovered that there are differing dispositions towards house forms even among very homogeneous groups. This does not bode well for those hoping for standard PEQIs on house forms.

The use of the semantic differential as a measure of environmental perception is widespread. Osgood, Suci, and Tannenbaum wrote the original text in 1957, and one has only to review the proceedings of the conferences of the Environmental Design Research Association to realize that its use has been prodigious (Bechtel, 1975). However, in using such an instrument one is measuring what is called *connotative* rather than *denotative* meaning. Allport (1955) makes this careful distinction. Connotative meaning is the quality of associations with an object. It is not quality that one can point to, such as color, hardness, or other denotative aspects. It is adjectival qualities, such as good–bad, strong–weak, and active–inactive. In fact, if one takes these three pairs of words, they express exactly what the semantic differential has been found to measure, and these three factors have emerged in cross-cultural research (Snider & Osgood, 1969). Throughout the world, the semantic differential has become to many people a kind of universal measure of environmental quality. Lowenthal (1972a) of the American Geographical Society and his associates have performed a tour de force in making environmental assessments of the quality of four United States cities. Kasmar (1970) felt there needed to be a list including specific and more denotative environmental qualities and tested 64 categories to measure perceived environmental quality. These categories included the ones shown in Table I.

Another approach to measuring environmental quality was taken by Shelly (1969), who measured total environments according to their human satisfaction potential. In some cases a questionnaire was used, in others behavioral observation. After carefully measuring the environmental qualities that were associated with human satisfaction, Shelly arrived at a bimodal classification of satisfaction sites in the environment. One type was the drive-reducing sites. These were places where people went to lower drive states—places to rest and relax and generally lower their bodily-need state. Homes were largely seen as drive-reducing sites. A contrast were the drive-arousal sites, places where people went to have their drives *increased* and then satisfied. Such places were supermarkets, movies, some night clubs, restaurants, and other stimulating environments. Thus, Shelly saw a close relationship between drive states and selection of specific sites. The drive-arousal environments were noisier, more colorful, and only slightly more active than the drive-reducing environments. One advantage of Shelly's work is that it has been done cross-culturally and seems to be substantiated in environments outside the United States.

TABLE I. A Lexicon of Environmental Descriptors

Adequate size–inadequate size	Good ventilation–poor ventilation
Appealing–unappealing	Huge–tiny
Attractive–unattractive	Impressive–unimpressive
Beautiful–ugly	Inviting–repelling
Bright–dull	Modern–old-fashioned
Bright colors–muted colors	Multiple purpose–single purpose
Cheerful–gloomy	Neat–messy
Clean–dirty	New–old
Colorful–drab	Orderly–chaotic
Comfortable–uncomfortable	Organized–disorganized
Comfortable temperature–uncomfortable temperature	Ornate–plain
Complex–simple	Pleasant–unpleasant
Contemporary–traditional	Pleasant odor–unpleasant odor
Convenient–inconvenient	Private–public
Diffuse lighting–direct lighting	Quiet–noisy
Distinctive–ordinary	Roomy–cramped
Drafty–stuffy	Soft lighting–harsh lighting
Efficient–inefficient	Sparkling–dingy
Elegant–unadorned	Stylish–unstylish
Empty–full	Tasteful–tasteless
Expensive–cheap	Tidy–untidy
Fashionable–unfashionable	Uncluttered–cluttered
Flashy colors–subdued colors	Uncrowded–crowded
Free space–restricted space	Unusual–usual
Fresh odor–stale odor	Useful–useless
Functional–nonfunctional	Warm–cool
Gay–dreary	Well balanced–poorly balanced
Good acoustics–poor acoustics	Well kept–run-down
Good colors–bad colors	Well organized–poorly organized
Good lighting–poor lighting	Well planned–poorly planned
Good lines–bad lines	Well scaled–poorly scaled
Good temperature–bad temperature	Wide–narrow

Cantril's self-anchoring scale is an instrument that has had various uses throughout the world (Cantril, 1965). Its advantage over other instruments is that it provides some measure of degree of quality. A disadvantage is that it has been used in such a general sense. Researchers have typically used it to rate the quality of a nation. Bechtel (1975) used the self-anchoring scale to measure the quality of a public housing environment and discovered that environment was considered by the residents to have deteriorated in the last five years.

The self-anchoring scale uses a simple 10-rung ladder chart which is scored as indicated in Figure 4. Once the respondent indicates the

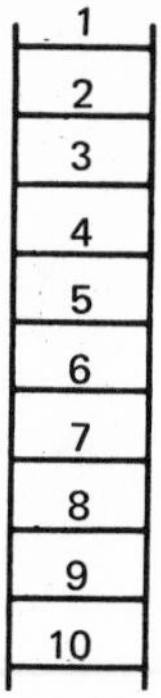

FIG. 4. Self-anchoring scale.

three rungs of the ladder, he is asked to list his hopes and aspirations, fears and worries about the particular environment. These statements are then coded according to a standardized system (Cantril, 1965). In the case of public housing, it was discovered that the physical appearance of the project was the chief concern expressed by the respondents.

A set of observational scales has been in use by Roger Barker and his associates for over 25 years. These scales include action patterns, behavior mechanisms, autonomy, welfare, and penetration levels.

Action pattern scales include: aesthetics, business, education, government, nutrition, personal appearance, physical health, professionalism, recreation, religion, and social contact. Each scale has four subscales on participation, supply, evaluation, and learning. Basically, the scales are rated on the amount of man-hours spent doing each action pattern.

Behavior mechanisms include: affective behavior, gross motor activity, manipulation, talking, and thinking. Each scale has three subscales on participation, tempo, and intensity. These scales also are largely rated on the number of man-hours.

Richness is a concept derived from combining the greatest amount of contact with the largest variety of kinds of people, the greatest variety of behavior, and the maximum responsibility. Settings that are high in richness have an index that combines all three of these factors. This scale is a rough measure of quality of life, but it has an almost total emphasis on *social* quality.

Autonomy is the ability to decide one's own fate on four subscales that measure performance, entrance, finance, and policy decisions.

Welfare is a scale measuring whether any setting is created for the benefit of any particular group such as children, the elderly, or enlisted men.

Penetration levels are really measures of responsibility levels for the people present in any setting. The highest level is a one-man-show type of setting where the events would not take place without that person. The lowest level occurs when the person has no influence on the setting whatsoever, very much like the sidewalk superintendents watching a construction project.

Barker's scales were used extensively to measure environmental qualities of communities. For example, *Qualities of Community Life* (Barker & Schoggin, 1973) details the environmental qualities of an English and an American town over a period of 10 years. Barker's scales have also been used in a questionnaire format (Bechtel & Ledbetter, 1975).

The previous examples of instruments used to measure various aspects of the environmental qualities of housing are by no means exhaustive. They are illustrative of the kinds of instruments in use today for measuring environmental qualities, and they fail or succeed according to the intended uses of their authors. The semantic differential, the most widely used instrument, has not been used to measure degrees of quality. It could conceivably be used for this purpose if it were first standardized on a large population measuring representative environmental aspects. Shelly's questionnaires are also universal in their potential application and could be used for any of the three environments: social, built, or biosphere. Cantril's scale could also be adapted for universal use. Barker's scales have already been applied to a wide diversity of environments, but they refer more to the social and built environment than to the natural or biosphere. Kasmer's lexicon refers directly to the built environment and would need adaptation for use in the social or biosphere realms.

HOUSING PRESENTATIONS

How one presents the environmental qualities to be measured by any of these instruments is critical. Sanoff (1970) used models and pictures. Cantril relied on the respondent's memory of the real environment. Barker (1968) observed behavior in the natural environment and used informants.

But research in the natural environment may not always be possible, and there is concern for finding ways to present stimuli of the environment for evaluation. Seaton and Collins (1972) have done as careful a job as any and find that color slides seem to evoke results similar to the natural environment. They carefully compared responses to slides, photographs, models, and the natural environment. It was a classical type of experiment. However, their concern was with how to present architectural designs, not how to evaluate every environmental quality and, as such, their method is a model to be followed for other environmental aspects. Their target was the design of the built environment. Their assumption was that the social sphere was held constant since their subjects were relatively homogeneous. Other aspects of the biosphere were not measured.

As Seaton and Collins' article states, the factors which affect judgments are *what* is being judged, *who* is doing the judging, and *what kinds* of judgments are being required. Two other factors are the way the stimuli are *presented* and the *conditions* of presentation. Seaton really only tried to measure the way stimuli were presented and attempted to control for the other factors.

As has been pointed out elsewhere (Bechtel, 1975), *what* is being presented can be confused by the subject. Any complex stimulus can be confused because the subject may be responding to only a part of the stimulus and not to the whole as the researcher intends. Usually a query must be made of the subject as to what aspect of the stimulus he is responding to, some part or the whole. Another confusion involves the connotative or denotative modes discussed earlier. Unless specifically instructed, respondents may confuse the two.

The kinds of judges making the evaluations is also critical. In Osgood's first text (Osgood et al., 1957), an example was given of how artists' responses to a work of art were far different from laymen's. In the same manner, architects, engineers, or experts of any kind will have responses to stimuli in the realm of their expertise that are characterized by a greater number of responses and a greater differentiation of responses. The experts will be more specific and more verbal.

What kinds of judgments to obtain is the subject of long debates among statisticians, psychometricians, and behavioral scientists. For example, scales of 10 units are often recommended for analytic purposes. Yet a recent methodological study comparing the results of principal components factor analysis on the same data when different scale units were used (ranging from two to nine intervals) found that the magnitude of the effect for number of scale intervals was not large and the pattern · of rotated factor loadings was not appreciably affected (Martin, Fruchter, & Mathis, 1974). The optimal number of scale intervals probably depends more upon the investigator's purposes than upon analytic requirements.

Much is said among psychologists about whether scales should be nominal, ordinal, or fixed. Nominal scales are devised merely by assigning numbers without quantitative value. Ordinal scales are employed when items are ranked but space between the ranks is indeterminate. Fixed ratio scales have precise intervals between numbers that are equal quantities, like the degrees on a thermometer. In measuring human beings, there is some consensus that Binder's (1964) conclusion is still correct, that the best that can be obtained is ordinal scaling, or ranking. Thus, although we can measure temperature precisely with a thermometer, we cannot measure a human's response to temperature with the same degree of precision. The most that we can hope for is to determine whether one temperature is hotter or colder than another.

How the stimuli are presented is another critical factor. One caveat must always accompany any simulation in the laboratory: It must have ecological *validity*. Seaton was careful about this when comparing his slides to the real building. Rohles (1967) only discovered his laboratory error in measuring critical minimal temperature exposure for manual work by direct observations of behavior in the field. In short, every fact determined by laboratory or simulation must be found to exist in the same fashion and to evoke the same response in the real world.

Conditions of presentation are also a critical factor. Seaton and Collins mentioned that their tent used to house drawings for presentation had to be able to withstand the rains of British Columbia, but they do not say that their conclusions may be valid for only sunny days, *or* for both sunny and rainy days.

Thus, there are five major factors influencing any presentation of stimuli to subjects: the nature of the stimulus, the characteristics of the judges, the kinds of judgments to be made, the medium of presentation, and the conditions of presentation. Much more environmentally oriented research needs to be done in these five areas before rules can be drawn for the development and use of the PEQI. In addition, even when all these problems have been solved, there is still the final requirement of ecological validity.

An equally critical requirement of *discriminant* validity has been aptly demonstrated by Danford and Willems (1975). Their research shows that the measuring instrument needs to be able to discriminate between stimuli. This was dramatically illustrated by showing that the semantic differential technique did not discriminate between the presentation of buildings and presentation of only verbal stimuli. Thus, if the method cannot discriminate among stimuli it is of questionable utility.

INSTITUTIONAL RESEARCH

In some ways the assessment of environmental qualities of institutional environments has progressed further than in any other area. Jackson's development of the Characteristics of the Treatment Environment (CTE) has been followed by Moos's Ward Atmosphere Scale (WAS) and then by scales for correctional and various community environments. Jackson's approach was to build his scale around the observable aspects of the mental hospital operation. Moos followed some of the same types of questions but emphasized the feeling and mood components of the environment. He includes involvement, support, spontaneity, autonomy, practical orientation, personal problem orientation, anger and aggression, order and organization, program clarity, and staff control as subscales. His work is described in detail in *Evaluating Treatment Environments* (1974).

Care has been taken on these kinds of scales to establish both reliability and validity. They are the latest instruments available for these specialized kinds of environments and environmental qualities. But these measures concentrate more on the social environment. They do not ask how warm the buildings are, or whether there is a noticeable odor, or how the design of the buildings makes one feel. Thus, if one were to try to assess those aspects of the environment, one would need to construct a new scale.

Bechtel (1972a) and Bechtel and Ledbetter (1975) have adapted the behavior setting methodology to measuring institutional settings such as public housing and military bases. This follows Barker and Gump's (1964) assessment of schools. The behavior setting survey is particularly adept at characterizing the environment as a whole. Barker and Gump (1964) were able to characterize large schools as *over-*

manned compared to small schools which were *undermanned*. The public housing environment was diagnosed as a *dependent environment* (Bechtel, 1972a) and military bases in Alaska were characterized as *temporary environments*. It became apparent through these studies that the built environment was subordinate to the social or managerial aspects of the environment. If the physical environment did not suit managerial goals, it was changed. Only secondarily did the physical environment influence the management, and that was largely to perpetuate and make permanent what management intended. This is not happy news for the environmental psychologists who feel that the built environment dictates human behavior, but it places into proper perspective the dominance of the social over the physical aspects of the built environment.

The same limitations discussed in the section on housing measures also apply to the institutional. Most of the institutional measures, however, have high ecological validity, since they were developed in the field. The simulation of these institutional environments is still rare in the research field.

POLICY ISSUES

The Bearers of Not-So-Glad Tidings

Since the days when oriental tyrants slew the messengers of bad news, people have been reluctant to bear unhappy facts to those in high office. It is a part of our culture (and perhaps all cultures) to isolate people in authority from unfavorable information. Shirer (1960) documented this process for the Hitler regime. Stotland and Kobler (1965) documented how this process destroyed a mental hospital. Examples abound in our own government. Is there need to mention the Vietnam War, or Watergate? Or even the assessment of oil reserves by Hubbert (1974)?

Social scientists are all too aware of the long line of expensive research commissioned by the government only to be quietly ignored as was the Kerner Report or to be contemptuously disdained as was the study on pornography. Hadley Cantril (1967) lamented how his report on the support of Castro by the Cuban people went unread. If only it had been read by someone in authority, he felt, the Bay of Pigs would never have happened. How then, in the face of this kind of resistance, can measurements that assess environmental quality be used to influence public policy? The scientist who attempts to face this question has one comforting assurance. Our civilization has advanced to the point where at least he will not be slain on the spot.

But perhaps this is an unfair hyperbole since the problem does not exist in government only. In many ways the scientists have been just as guilty that their research has not been used. The average social scientist is affiliated with a university, and this has meant that he is under pressure to publish in his field. The publications in psychology alone amount to over one million pieces of literature per year. The flood is so great that the task of translating this material into practical knowledge is formidable. Reizenstein (1975) reports a recent poll of architects, 80% of whom regard social science research as unusable in their practice.

In the fifth EDRA conference proceedings, Volume 2, edited by C. P. Wolf, there are numerous examples of the use of 14 methods for the measurement of social impact. Presumably, these studies have had varying degrees of effect on whether dams were built and housing projects modified, and whether environmental impact statements considered social impact properly. For examples of use of this kind of research the reader is referred to this volume. The reader is warned, however, that even though social impact statements are required by law, the legal and administrative history has been "ambiguous and ambivalent." In short, the view is that although there is a vast amount of information available in the social sciences, its use in such practical areas as perception of the environment is still under development.

Evaluation: A Professional Dilemma

There are probably many instances in which PEQI measures of some sort were included in environmental impact statements. I know of one example in which I participated personally, but the effect of that part of the statement is impossible to assess. There is virtually no feedback from the governmental agencies or officials who read the statement except to build or not to build the project. And, if one is inclined to try to find out about one's efforts, conducting follow-up evaluations of environmental projects can involve professionals in a conflict-of-interest situation. For example, should the architect evaluate his own buildings? Some prominent firms are doing just that so that they can learn from past mistakes. Yet, Lou Gelwicks, an architect, feels that this places the person doing the evaluation in a conflict-of-interest position. Why should the person who does research for the architect to develop his design also be placed in the position of evaluating the success of the design? Should not evaluation be done by an outside organization that does not have an interest in its own prior suggestions or is in some way beholden to the architect? Gelwicks has formed a new corporation for his evaluators so that they can keep a separate identity and avoid conflict of interest. Not all professionals are so concerned. Ferebee (1971) reports on the indifference of many architects to evaluation. Yet how can environmental impact statements ever have any credibility unless they are validated by research following construction? So far, environmental impact statements are largely one more exercise a builder must go through to get his project approved. Whether that exercise is ever going to be more meaningful than a perfunctory genuflection can only be shown by systematic postconstruction evaluation.

How Do We Perceive the Physical Environment?

The discussion so far has dealt with instruments and studies in residential and institutional environments that have focused on the social and built environments. Some of the instruments, such as Cantril's self-anchoring scale, could be adapted for measuring one-dimensional or general qualities such as perceived level of water or air pollution. The self-anchoring scale would provide a past-time context for the present perceived level and a future expectation.

The number of categories that would be relevant for any index could best be derived by use of the semantic differential. Before using the content code of the self-anchoring scale, it would be best to establish content categories by a preliminary factoring of semantic responses. These categories could then be included in a self-anchoring verbal-response coding scheme. The factoring with the semantic differential would provide the best aggregate of words for any index and would also show the most important groups of words within factors.

Suppose, however, one were to try to develop a perceived scale of air pollution or air quality or try to develop an index of perceived water pollution? What is there to do beyond the relative scale provided by Cantril? Actually, the scaling of human perceptions has a long history. Torgerson (1958) and Coombs (1964) provide relatively recent summaries of measurement and scaling techniques in psychology. Measurements of various senses, such as hearing, have been very well standardized (American Standards Association, 1960). Standardization requires a relationship between some independent physical measurement such as a decibel and responsive behavior such as ability to hear. The unit of hearing that relates to decibels is a phon. A phon is defined as .0002 microbars of a decibel of a free progressive wave of frequency 1000 cycles per second presented to listeners facing the source, and judged by the listeners to be equally loud. There is even a scale of noisiness developed by Kryter (1959) which is a perfect model for use in establishing levels of noise pollution.

A problem that remains tricky in scaling, however, is the attempt to scale the just noticeable difference. This is the smallest unit a human can notice on a sensory dimension. For example, if temperature increases, can the human detect a one-degree increase, or does it take two degrees? This is the old classical problem of Weber's law. This law states that the size of an *increment* in stimulation that is just noticeable is a constant proportion of the standard stimulus, $\Delta S/S = K$.

But if measurement should be in the extremes, the predictions are poor. It only seems to work in the central portion of sensitivity. Stevens (1962) attempted to get around these measurement problems by asking observers to judge the size of a stimulus by comparing it to some other standard, well-recognized stimulus. He indicates that this works well for *prothetic* continua where one has to judge quantities but not so well for qualities such as pitch. Stevens has plotted these magnitude estimations for loudness, brightness, lightness, smell, taste, temperature, vibration, heaviness, electric shock, and others.

It is even possible to combine measures of smell, taste, hearing, and other dimensions and to combine these into geometric models. Thus, it would be theoretically possible to construct a multidimensional model of Perceived Environmental Quality with ranges of perception, judged ranges of pleasantness and unpleasantness, comfort and discomfort. The tools are there, the techniques are there, only the work remains to be done. Of course, the psychophysicists who have developed these scaling techniques have had no reason to consider either the mediating effects of the social environment or the contrasting influence of the built environment. Scales developed for environmental quality would have to take these two factors systematically into account.

One illustration of how much work needs to be done before arriv-. ing at a PEQI is provided by Wall (1973). He did a small study of public response to air pollution. He chose three towns in England because of their contrast in exposure to air pollution. One was publicly called the filthiest spot in England, the second was relatively free of air pollution, and the other occupied a sort of midway position. His results are worth noting. The abridgements and interpretations are my own responsibility.

> Subjects believe air pollution could be judged by sight.
>> Subjects were aware of legislation as it affected their areas.
>> Publicity, combined with the legislation, tended to make residents regard the problem as overcome.
>> All residents were uniform in their ideas of how to control pollution, and differing strategies in their areas had apparently no effect on these ideas.
>> If one wants to understand how pollution control decisions are made, house-to-house surveys is not a good method.

The study suggests some important points. First, despite knowledge of invisible gases such as carbon dioxide and carbon monoxide, subjects still believed they could judge pollution by "seeing" it.

This finding suggests a possibly dangerous basis for policy. A recent CBS documentary on television revealed that water plant experts were responding to "taste and smell" criteria for how their water should appear. Residents complained if the water did not taste or smell correctly, and these complaints influenced the officials' behavior in the purifying process. They tried to control for smell and taste. The purpose of the documentary was to point out that the water contained possibly dangerous carcinogens which could be neither smelled nor tasted.

Suppose someone were to develop a successful PEQI for air, and it turned out that clear air with high visibility and good smell were the chief criteria. Does that mean that there would be political or bureaucratic pressure. to give the people what they can see and smell to the neglect of the invisible and odorless pollutants? It would seem a far better policy to trust to scientific measurements and carefully controlled epidemiological studies to determine acceptable levels of any kind of pollution.

In any case, the Wall study and others (Tognacci et al., 1972) suggest that decisions are made by powerful groups, not by public opinion, so far at least, in environmental matters, and that professionals have a vested interest in things as they are with an unwillingness to change them (Sewell, 1971; Layton, 1971) so that decisions which are likely to be made may have a high probability that PEQIs could be used to justify less stringent levels of control.

Thus, it is with a strong note of caution that I would urge anyone to develop standardized Perceived Environmental Quality Indices, for there is every reason to believe that because of the peculiar properties of human perception, these will be far less stringent than physically based instruments, and thus may add to the inertia against upgrading the environment. There is too much chance that, by trusting to our own senses, a good publicity campaign and a few laws passed could quickly convince us our problems were over.

Perceived Quality of Residential Environments
Some Methodological Issues

ROBERT W. MARANS

Environmental planners and designers have given more attention to the residential environment than to any of the systems that interact to make up the metropolitan area. This attention is understandable. The residential environment is viewed as the place where an individual can relate himself socially and functionally to the complex world around him. It is considered to be richly diverse, both physically and socially, and constantly changing in terms of an aging landscape and a mobile population. And by design and redesign, it offers planners the opportunity to improve the quality of the physical surroundings and, in a very direct way, the livability of metropolitan area residents.

Contemporary planners and designers have often suggested that improving the quality of the residential environment can profoundly affect the quality of people's lives. These thoughts stem from the work of Ebenezer Howard, whose models for garden cities were established with the belief that a better and spiritually more enriched life would be available for community residents. In recent years, empirical data have demonstrated that the residential environment may not be as germane to the quality-of-life experience as Howard and his followers believed. In fact, when compared to other aspects of life such as health, friendship, work, marriage, and financial well-being, the way individuals feel about

DR. ROBERT W. MARANS • Institute for Social Research, and College of Architecture and Urban Planning, The University of Michigan, Ann Arbor, Michigan 48104.

their communities, their neighborhoods, and their housing is relatively unimportant to the overall quality-of-life experience (Andrews & Withey, 1974; Zehner, 1974; Campbell, Converse, & Rogers, 1976). Nevertheless, the components of the residential environment are perhaps subject to more public design than any of the other situations individuals find themselves in.

It could be argued that the residential environment will become more important to the quality-of-life experience for people in metropolitan areas in the future. The possibility of additional energy shortages, and our questionable ability to provide highly improved public transportation for everyone, present us with the prospect of becoming an increasingly homebound society. It is also conceivable that a slowdown in our rate of economic growth will limit opportunities for employment and the concomitant frequent shifts in place of residence. Under such conditions, the quality of residential environments will receive increasing attention, as will the procedures for monitoring both the attributes which contribute to that quality and the public's perceptions of them.

This chapter concentrates on a set of methodological issues relating to the perception of residential environmental quality. Before doing so, however, a body of research that deals with people's responses to residential environments is reviewed. This review is intended to be illustrative rather than comprehensive and sets the stage for the discussion of methodological issues which follows. In the final part of the chapter, a conceptual model is presented for organizing research on the perception of residential quality. Components of this model are central to many of the issues raised in the preceding sections.

PAST RESEARCH

Much of the recent research on residential environments has focused on the analysis of satisfactions, preferences, and actual behavioral patterns that occur within these environments. Although this research is often directed towards other ends, taken as a whole, it provides insights into the meaning of residential quality to different groups of people and demonstrates the types of methods which have been used in the investigations.

Research on Satisfaction

On the basis of an increasing number of studies of individual communities and neighborhoods, it is becoming quite clear that a vast majority of residents are either moderately or totally satisfied with the place in which they live. What is less clear from the studies is the specific set of features or attributes of those communities and neighborhoods which lead people to respond favorably and, conversely, which attributes produce negative responses among the remainder of residents. Gans (1967) in his classic study of a new suburban community, found most residents extremely happy and well adjusted after their moves, contrary to the belief of many planners. The high level of satisfaction was attributed to the desire of residents to change their former lifestyles; the new environment afforded them the opportunity to do so. The low density of development and the segregated land use contributed to their increased sense of privacy and satisfaction with their nuclear family situations. Among those who were dissatisfied, this pattern of development fostered a sense of isolation.

In a series of studies of low- and moderate-income housing developments aimed at producing user criteria for environmental design, Sanoff (1973) and his associates found that the chief reason for positive evaluations was neighborhood solidarity, the perceived similarity of value orientations among neighbors. Although other researchers reported similar findings (Caplow & Forman, 1955; Lansing & Hendricks, 1967; Keller, 1968; Lansing, Marans, & Zehner, 1970), many have found physical attributes of the environment associated with both residential satisfaction and dissatisfaction. These attributes include the level of upkeep of buildings and grounds, the amount of private outdoor space, and noise factors.

Research has also been conducted on people's assessments of specific types of residential settings. Studies of the elderly have indicated that they are more likely to be satisfied when they are concentrated in high-density developments which afford them opportunities for socializing, than in situations where they are socially isolated (Rosow, 1967; Michelson, 1970). Other studies have shown that people in public housing often express lower levels of satisfaction with their neighborhood arrangements than do occupants of nearby slums (Hollingshead & Rogler, 1963; Yancy, 1972). Dissatisfaction with public housing is generally associated with a lack of privacy, lack of communal facilities, management problems, and poor architectural layout (Saile, Boradah, & Williams, 1972; Cooper, 1972; Newman, 1972). Yet a carefully documented study of a public housing project and a slum neighborhood in Baltimore has demonstrated greater community and personal satisfaction in the former (Wilner, Walkeley, Pinkerton, & Tayback, 1962). In both cases, the quality of housing was not considered poor. Indeed, studies have shown that people in poor quality housing frequently express high levels of environmental satisfaction (Fried & Gleicher, 1961; Andrews & Phillips, 1970; Campbell et al., 1976). While the physical attributes of many of these residential settings often facilitate desired patterns of behavior (or at least do not impede them) and indirectly influence environmental satisfaction, the perception of the sociocultural makeup as being supportive is critical to environmental well-being.

Research conducted in planned residential environments shows that high levels of resident satisfaction are associated with the overall concept of a planned community and the provision of a range of community facilities, even when these facilities are not used by residents (Werthman, Mandel, & Dienstfray, 1965; Zehner, 1972; Weiss, Burby, Kaiser, Donnelly, & Zehner, 1973). Facilities considered desirable include community buildings, playgrounds, swimming pools, golf courses, and tennis courts.

The type of dwelling and proximity to neighboring structures are aspects of the individual house most strongly related to community satisfaction. Lansing and Hendricks (1967) and Michelson (1969) found that people living in single-family houses on large lots evaluate their neighborhood environments more positively than do people living in other types of residential structures, including single-family houses on small lots. Indeed, data from a recent national survey show that satisfaction with one's dwelling is strongly related to assessments of community and neighborhood (Campbell et al., 1976). Similar characteristics have been reported as sources of satisfaction and dissatisfaction in studies of public housing projects. In the ill-fated Pruitt-Igoe development, the physical space and amenities of the dwelling, including separate rooms for family members and hot water, were attributes liked most by occupants (Yancy, 1972, p. 130), while Cooper (1971) reports that small kitchens, lack of dining space, and lack of space for hobbies are the main sources of dissatisfaction for public housing residents in San Francisco.

The research on satisfactions and dissatisfactions demonstrates the array of attributes and situations which contribute to perceptions of residential quality. Similarly, a body of research aimed at understanding what people look for when choosing a place of residence and other preference studies provide additional clues as to what is valued in the residential environment.

Research on Preferences

Over the years, strong preference for single-family housing has been empirically demonstrated (Foote, Abu-Lughod, Foley, & Winnick, 1970; Lansing, 1966; Michelson, 1969; Hinshaw & Allott, 1972). People cite the desire for home ownership and indoor and outdoor private space as the most important reasons for their preferences. Yet it is clearly recognized that the respondent's life-style and life cycle strongly influence preferred type of housing (Michelson, 1970).

Similar social characteristics as well as physical attributes have been found to influence preferences for living in communities of different sizes. Dillman (1973), in an extensive review of such studies, suggests that community-size preference is an indirect expression of a desire for certain community attributes and a desire for an improved quality of life. He reports that preferences for rural living are associated with low crime, clean air and water, and a better environment in which to bring up children, while people who prefer city life point to the recreational and cultural opportunities, better schools, and the possibility of contact with a wide variety of people. Quality-of-life factors for those people opting for medium-sized communities were institutional services (e.g., medical care and police protection) and orientations toward community social life (community pride and friendliness of neighbors) (Dillman & Dobash, 1972).

Attributes associated with preferences for rural and medium-sized communities in many instances are similar to those valued by people in thinking about an ideal community or preferred neighborhood in which to live. Lamanna's study (1964) in Greensboro, North Carolina, found that, next to having good roads and sidewalks, status factors (the right kind of people and "a town we can look up to") ranked highest in importance among residents. Adult respondents in another North

Carolina study (Wilson, 1962) described their ideal neighborhood as spacious, beautiful, good for children, exclusive, countrylike, and close to nature, while Peterson (1967), in attempting to identify preferences for the visual appearance of neighborhoods, found physical quality and "harmony with nature" to be the most significant dimensions of choice. Even studies of adolescents and college students reveal strong preferences in the same direction. Ladd's exercise with black youth from low-income backgrounds indicates that the vast majority—56 out of 60—wanted a suburban house with a large yard, open space, and lots of land around it (1972, p. 111). Similarly, Hinshaw and Allott (1972) show that college students, irrespective of ethnic background and income level, express strong preference for single-family neighborhoods which are safe and near good schools, transit stops, friendly neighbors, and parks.

As a way of identifying attributes of residential quality, most of the above researchers have either asked people directly about their hypothetical choices for residential environments or have had them respond to real stimuli or simulations of real stimuli. However, Wilson (1962), in his effort to determine factors influencing residential preference, used a trade-off game, an approach designed to identify attributes of environmental quality which people are willing to forgo in favor of having other attributes. Most of his respondents valued paved streets much more than having big shade trees in their yards (1962, p. 396). Using similar techniques, other researchers have shown that air quality ranks higher than access to schools (Robinson, Baer, Banjeree, & Flachsbart, 1975, p. 95), access to shopping centers is more important than access to freeway ramps (Peterson & Worrall, 1970), and housing unit privacy is valued over quality of building materials (Borkin & Clipson, 1975). Still other researchers have shown that while a vast majority of prospective home buyers would like an open view from their front yards, only half of them would be willing to pay $2,000 to have it (Knight & Menchik, 1974).

In situations where an array of attributes is known to be important to residential satisfaction or preference, the use of trade-off games can determine the relative quantities of each attribute necessary to achieve high levels of perceived quality. Another way of determining the trade-offs that people make among environmental attributes is to observe their behavior, that is, their actual choices of residential environments and their activities within them.

Research on Behavior

A number of studies have considered people's assessments of residential environments as determinants of moving behavior. Research has been reported on the reasons people have moved from one dwelling to another (Butler, Chapin, Hemmens, Kaiser, Stegman, & Weiss, 1969; Lansing, Mueller, & Barth, 1964; Foote et al., 1960; Wolf & Lebeaux, 1969) and on factors associated with the desire to move (Rossi, 1955; Kasl & Harburg, 1972; Newman, 1974). In both types of studies, sources of dissatisfaction with the previous (or present) residential environment have been reported. These often include lack of adequate space within the dwelling, neighborhood considerations, and the high costs of housing. Taken together, dissatisfaction with characteristics of the dwelling is more important in the desire to move than dissatisfaction with attributes of the neighborhood (Newman, 1974). However, studies have shown that for the elderly, neighborhood attributes are at least as important as the dwelling itself in the decision to move (Carp, 1969; Hamovitch & Peterson, 1969).

Additionally, in high stress neighborhoods, the desire to move is strongly influenced by neighborhood assessments, including perceptions of its safety and traffic (Kasl & Harburg, 1972; Appleyard & Lintell, 1972). Neighborhood and community attributes are also more dominant than housing considerations in the decision to move to new towns. The appeal of places like Reston lies in their proximity to nature, recreational opportunities, and other community facilities, whereas for nearby traditional suburban communities, a good buy on housing, good schools, and proximity to work are factors attracting community residents (Zehner, 1972).

In addition to residential mobility, there exists an extensive body of literature on the behaviors of people within their residential environments. Studies have focused on neighboring (Festinger, Schacter, & Back, 1950; Gans, 1962; Fried & Gleicher, 1961; Suttles, 1968; Michelson, 1970), on recreation and play (Lansing et al., 1970; Gold, 1972; Marans & Mandell, 1972), on crime (Newman, 1972), or have dealt with an entire spectrum of household activities (Chapin & Hightower, 1965; Michelson & Reed, 1975). Many of these studies have considered relationships between the specific places where behaviors take place and people's level of satisfaction with the activity.

Still others have investigated relationships between activity patterns and overall environmental satisfaction. The extent to which behavior in residential environments is viewed as a satisfactory experience can influence the quality of life of an individual. Additional explorations along these lines will no doubt contribute to our understanding of the components of residential quality.

Methods of Inquiry

The above studies have demonstrated that a variety of methods have been used in an attempt to learn about the quality of residential environments. Many of the studies have produced comparable findings, thereby building a knowledge base for researchers and planners alike. Nevertheless, contradictory results have appeared in studies operating on the same conceptual basis. These variations may be a function of the respective methods of inquiry used. For the most part, interviewing techniques or mail questionnaires have been an integral part of the research. But even within the context of interviewing, different approaches can be taken. As Craik (1970) has noted, interview situations can differ both in the way researchers decide to ask their questions and in the format by which they receive responses.

We have seen that several researchers have used photographs or drawings as a stimulus for information on people's thoughts about the residential environment. Others have devised games which enable people to think about their preferences and the trade-offs they are willing to make in selecting among various environmental attributes. Still others have made use of techniques derived from market research such as conjoint analysis and paired comparisons, while scale models of residential and other environments have been built for the explicit purpose of eliciting subjective responses from people.

Additional interviewing techniques have been employed on the site using tape recorders to record perceptions. Much of this work stems from the efforts of Lynch (1960) and his colleagues (Lynch & Rivkin, 1959). These same researchers and others (Ladd, 1972; Orleans, 1967) have had their subjects draw maps which were then used to describe environments and identify key attributes within them.

With respect to behavioral responses, approaches other than asking residents about their activity patterns have been used. Observation of behavior within residential settings is the most obvious technique (Barker & Schoggin, 1973). Yet, time budgets have been incorporated in the survey process as a way of determining activity patterns both inside and outside the residential setting (Michelson & Reed, 1975). There is little question that the use of a combination of techniques offers great potential for increasing our understanding of man–environment interactions. Whether this combination of techniques is applicable to measuring the perceived quality of residential environments remains to be determined.

SOME METHODOLOGICAL ISSUES

As a result of our overview of past studies on people's perceptions of residential environments, a number of methodological issues emerge which warrant special attention. Before discussing these issues, however, two comments of a definitional nature are appropriate.

Definitional Issues

First, there is some question as to what constitutes the residential environment. For most of us trained in the environmental design professions, the residential environment consists of a hierarchy of social and physical units. At one level, there is the individual dwelling and the land associated with it. We have already seen that a person's assessment of his dwelling and its attributes are central to his environmental well-being and thoughts of changing place of residence. At another level, there is the spatial community within which an individual's dwelling is located and in which the full range of daily activities takes place. This is also the level where an array of services and experiences influencing his quality of life are provided. This macrolevel of the residential environment is represented by the city and region, although quite often it is an area without political or clearly definable boundaries. Between the larger community and the individual dwelling is the neighborhood— that part of the metropolitan area with which residents identify and which has received considerable attention from the environmental design professions over the years. The history and use of the neighborhood unit in planning are well documented and need not be dealt with here

(Perry, 1929; Stein, 1957; Pearson, 1962). For the most part, it has been conceived as a building block in creating larger communities and has been defined by particular physical boundaries and a specific number of people.

Research on people's responses to neighborhoods, however, has ignored these imposed definitions of what constitutes a neighborhood unit. The work of Gans (1962) and others (Lee, 1968; Lansing et al., 1970) suggests that Clarence Perry's traditional neighborhood has less meaning for residents than the microneighborhood, often represented by a small grouping of houses, or one or two blocks. Utilizing clusters of houses selected for sampling economies, several surveys have been made on people's responses to the microneighborhood, defined by the four to six houses facing one another on a city street (Lansing et al., 1970; Mandell & Marans, 1972; Zehner & Chapin, 1974). While this unit of analysis has established credibility among researchers and represents an area to which residents can direct their responses, it is not clear whether it is entirely appropriate for environmental planners and designers. Nor is it clear whether it is the most meaningful neighborhood for all groups in the population. Indeed, studies by Lee (1968), Ladd (1970), Keller (1968), and Stea (1969) have tried to identify social and physical factors which constitute "neighborhood" for various groups of people. Similarly, in a study that the Institute for Social Research is now conducting in the Detroit metropolitan area, a sample of residents living in a variety of geographic settings was asked to indicate which of several descriptive definitions of neighborhood was most meaningful to them. Preliminary data reveal some surprising findings. Of the 1200 people interviewed, no more than 20% and no fewer than 8% responded in any single category. Whereas 8% of our respondents said the microneighborhood of five or six dwelling units best described their neighborhood, about 20% indicated that either the immediate block, a two-to-five block area, or a square mile was the most meaningful neighborhood for them. The specific ways in which particular subgroups of the population living in different settings respond have yet to be determined. Yet it is apparent that a common definition of neighborhood—based on physical boundaries—is inappropriate to all residents. Nevertheless, for purposes of this chapter and environmental planning, it is convenient to discuss the residential environment as constituting a hierarchy of living units.

A second comment of a definitional nature concerns itself with the meaning people attach to the term "quality of the residential environment." The review of past research has indicated that in thinking about quality, people consider much more than the aesthetic or physical attributes of their residence. Dimensions of the residential environment to which people respond positively or negatively include many sociocultural as well as physical attributes. Certainly, residential quality takes into account the appearance of the area including its landscape and the form of the built environment. But it also includes people's perceptions of such things as composition of neighborhoods, the relative safety of the areas, and the friendliness of neighbors. The challenge remains for the environmental planner and researcher to determine the complete bundle of attributes that constitute high-quality residential environments.

Methodological Issues

Now that operational guildelines have been established as to what constitutes the residential environment and what its qualitative dimensions are, we can turn to some of the methodological issues raised by the preceding review. These issues are addressed by discussing a number of questions that are being asked by researchers and environmental planners who deal with perceptions of residential environments.[1]

What are the appropriate types of responses that should be measured in understanding the quality of residential environments? We have seen that most of the past studies on residential environments have focused on three types of responses—preferences, assessments, and behaviors. Preferences for and assessments of residential environments are directly related to perceived quality. An expression of preference implicitly provides an indication of what is liked and disliked (or at least liked to a lesser degree) while such likes and dislikes are made explicit with assessments or expressions of satisfaction. Although both types of responses continue to be studied and are appropriate under different circumstances, there is considerable controversy over which one represents a more viable and valid measure of residential quality.

The use of preferential expressions of residential choice requires

---

[1] The set of questions being examined is neither representative nor exhaustive but addresses some of the key issues raised under the workshop guidelines. At the same time, the tentativeness of the discussion following each question reflects as much the author's limited perspective as it does the current state of knowledge.

the researcher to cast in a hypothetical mold a resident who may like his living situation and has no plans to move. In many instances, these residents may be recent movers or home buyers. In either case, the validity of expressions of preference from residents who are not contemplating alternatives should be questioned. But in situations where a group of prospective movers is the subject under investigation, preferential responses may be an appropriate means of identifying salient dimensions of residential quality.

Similarly, there is some question about the validity of measures of environmental assessment or satisfaction with one's place of residence. This concern is related to the problem of dissonance reduction—the tendency for an individual to avoid conflict between past actions and the resulting current attitudes. It has been argued that people often refuse to recognize or admit their dissatisfaction with a past decision such as the selection of their present place of residence. This refusal to recognize or admit dissatisfaction may occur at the conscious or subconscious levels. In a similar vein, it has been suggested that some people have a tendency to respond in ways which are socially desirable or positive. Indeed, studies of the perceived quality of life and its residential components indicate that measures of satisfaction lean strongly toward the positive: only a very limited minority of people confess to any general lack of happiness or dissatisfaction with any domains of life (Marans & Rodgers, 1975; Campbell et al., 1976). To what degree then are these positive measures gilded, if, indeed, they are at all?

Using data from a national survey, Campbell, Converse, and Rodgers have shown that response tendencies among certain groups of people produce an upgrading of reported satisfaction. But these biases, for the most part, are not very large. Moreover, the biases tend to apply more to general assessments than to assessments of specific attributes (Campbell et al., 1976, chap. 4). These findings suggest that while there is some justification in questioning the validity of responses dealing with overall assessment (that is, satisfaction with housing and satisfaction with neighborhood), response bias tends to diminish considerably in assessments of specific attributes of these environments. The latter type of assessment is perhaps more germane to issues of environmental quality for residents who do not contemplate moving.

Although preferential and assessment responses to specific environmental attributes have a direct bearing on residential quality, behavioral responses to residential settings can either directly influence these perceptual responses or be influenced by them. In the first instance, the quantity and quality of behavioral activities such as neighboring, participating in community organizations, and the play of children can determine how residents assess the places in which they live. At the same time, these assessments together with assessments of physical and other social attributes can influence residential activity patterns or another type of behavior—a desired or actual move to another residential setting (Newman, 1974).

Whose responses should be tapped? In the measurement of physical environmental quality indices, there is little question as to who is best qualified to make the measurements. Despite the fact that there are competing indices for air and water quality, competent and highly trained technicians are equipped to measure, with a high degree of reliability, the amount of sulfur dioxide in the atmosphere or the chlorophyl count in water. Most of us are content to let the "experts" determine when the level of contaminants in the air and water become physically dangerous. We are equally content to let these experts maintain accurate and regular measurements of the physical attributes of these elements. We may be less compliant in having "experts" establish levels of quality that do not take into account our perceptions of ambient air and drinking water. We may become downright hostile if our feelings are ignored when a different set of "experts" establishes levels of quality for environments we live in and use on a day-to-day basis.

The question of whose perceptual responses should be tapped in assessing the quality of residential environments is highly debatable. On one hand, it could be argued that environmental planners and designers, by virtue of their training, experience, and relative objectivity, are capable of judging the goodness or badness of residential areas with respect to their visual quality. Similarly, by knowing which attributes (trees, grass, low crime rates) and conveniences (parks, shopping, nearby off-street parking) are salient for different groups of people, planners are well equipped to judge the physical quality of their environments.

On the other hand, the judgments of environmental planners and designers, and those of area residents are not always congruent, as we shall see shortly. Likewise, the fit between perceptions of environmental quality and hard physical or objective measures is often far from perfect (Jacoby, 1972; Mandell & Marans, 1972; Marans, Newman, Wellman, & Kruse, 1976). Recognition of these differences suggests that plans and programs related to improving environmental quality should be made on the basis of several factors including what people say about the environment. When that environment is residential, the perceptions of people who live there are essential. Earlier, we discussed two types of perceptual responses—preferences and assessments. Assessments, or expressions of satisfaction with one's neighborhood and housing, were considered appropriate measures of residential quality for people who were not contemplating a change in residence. Preferences imply choice, and the expressed choices of prospective consumers can also indicate salient dimensions of residential quality.

In addition to the professional planners and designers on one hand and residents and prospective movers on the other, a third group of judges of residential quality could be considered. This group would represent the community at large and would be made up of a sample of citizens who would make quality assessments of each residential area within the total community environment.[2] This approach has been used as part of a research program in Marin County, California, where a sample of residents was asked to judge the region and a number of its subareas in terms of how they liked them and how they compared them with other regions and subareas (Craik & McKechnie, 1974). In addition to identifying areas perceived by residents as being high and low in environmental quality, these judges identified physical attributes of the areas which differentiated them. Another important purpose of the research was to distinguish between the observer's preferential judgments and their comparative appraisals with the expectation that the latter would display greater agreement in what constitutes environmental quality. This important distinction has methodological implications for judging residential quality by people who live within a single residential area. Before addressing the issue of preferential judgments and comparative appraisals, I would like to discuss the question of agreement between resident and "expert" assessments.

To what extent is there agreement between residents and "experts" in their assessment of the quality of residential environments? Historically, planners and environmental designers have assumed that their background and training have adequately prepared them to judge the goodness or badness of residential neighborhoods. Little, if any, attention was paid to the feelings of the neighborhood's residents in

---

[2] The concept of representative judgments of the quality of nonresidential urban environments and natural environments has been operationalized in the past. See, for example, Sonnenfeld, (1966); Winkel, Malek, and Theil (1969); and Craik, (1972b).

making these judgments. Although increasing numbers of residential planners had begun to question their own fallibility, particularly in light of the disastrous social consequences of urban renewal and public housing (Gans, 1962; Fried & Gleicher, 1961; Hartman, 1964; Ittelson, Proshansky, Rivlin, & Winkel, 1974, p. 270), systematic attempts had not been made until recently to compare planners' assessments of residential environments with those of the residents. Three empirical studies that make these comparisons suggest that while there is some agreement among the two groups in assessing certain attributes of the environment, there is apparent disagreement on what constitutes residential quality between residents on the one hand and environmental planners on the other.

Using data from a probability sample survey of the adult population living in private dwellings throughout the Detroit region, Lansing and Marans (1969) found only partial agreement between planners and residents in what constitutes a high-quality. residential environment. For planners who judged neighborhoods on the basis of physical characteristics, the degree of openness, degree of pleasantness, and degree of interest were associated with neighborhood quality. The only rating that was related to rating of overall satisfaction by the residents was the degree of pleasantness.

Using similar techniques, findings were reported for studies of residential environments in Greensboro, North Carolina (Kaiser, Weiss, Burby, & Donnelly, 1970), and Sydney, Australia (Troy, 1971). Kaiser and his associates showed that neither the quality of public services as perceived by planners nor their judgments of overall neighborhood quality were related to the satisfaction of residents with their neighborhoods. Moreover, the planners' assessments of the upkeep and amenity level showed only weak relationships to resident satisfaction. In the Sydney study, which used town-planning students as surrogates for professional planners to assess dimensions of quality in neighborhoods evaluated by residents, only partial agreement was found as to what constitutes a cónvenient residential environment. Although there was a significant degree of agreement between the two measures in evaluations of convenience to shopping, public transport and places of entertainment, there was no agreement on the evaluation of convenience to churches and to schools. In addition, when student and resident assessments of individual attributes of the residential environment were compared, low correlations were found. The lack of agreement between residents' and students' assessments was most obvious in judgments of the area's aesthetics, in assessing whether it was safe for children to play, and in determining whether the environment was good compared with other areas of similar socioeconomic character throughout the region (Troy, 1971, p. 98).

These studies have indicated the fallibility of environmental planners and designers in judging residential quality and, concomitantly, in making decisions which take these judgments into account. Indeed, the growing body of research on people's responses to residential environments has sensitized planners to the many conditions which are deemed important to quality living. Yet the very nature of environmental planners and designers as an elitist group of "experts" and their lack of any emotional involvement in the residential environments they judge suggest that total agreement between their assessments and those of the residents can never be achieved.

Is there a distinction between preferential judgments and comparative appraisals of residential environments? It has been suggested that one obstacle to using perceived environmental quality indices is the pervasive individual and group variations among observers: Observer-based assessments reflect only personal tastes, inclinations, and biases, and are merely expressions of subjective likes and dislikes (Craik & McKechnie, 1974). This subjectivity suggests that the reliability and generality required of environmental quality indices may not be achieved. Craik and McKechnie have persuasively argued that despite individual differences in backgrounds and personal tastes, greater agreement among observers can be displayed with comparative appraisals than with preferential judgments. In making comparative appraisals, observers could judge the relative quality of an environment against some explicit or implicit standard of comparison while their preferential judgments would express personal likes or dislikes in the specific environment.[3] If a panel of observers were to examine 20 suburban communities, for example, the members might differ widely in their personal preferences or level of satisfaction with each. If, however, they were asked to appraise the communities comparatively against the standard of "an excellent suburban development," they might well display greater agreement.

---

[3] The preferential judgment as used by Craik and McKechnie is analogous to what I have referred to as environmental assessments or expressions of satisfaction and dissatisfaction. It should not be confused with the preferential choice response discussed earlier.

In the Marin County study mentioned earlier, Craik and McKechnie were able to empirically demonstrate greater consensus among observers in their comparative appraisals of environmental quality than in their preferential judgments. It should be remembered, however, that the observers represented a subject pool of Marin County residents who were part of an experiment and who were not being asked to assess the quality of the particular residential area in which they lived. Whether or not a group of observers would differ from each other in their preferential judgments (assessments) and comparative appraisals of their own residential areas remains to be tested.

The interesting question raised by the Craik-McKechnie distinction centers on the external standard of comparison against which comparative judgments of residential quality are made. Even if an observer were provided with an example of "an excellent suburban development" and asked to make comparative appraisals of other residential environments against that standard, it is possible that the judgments would implicitly reflect the observer's own unique bundle of standards. These standards might include the kinds of residential environments the observer experienced in the past, including the one liked the most, his perceptions of the kinds of environments friends and family live in, and his image of the "typical American neighborhood" for the "typical American family." A group of observers with a highly diverse set of past experiences and other standards of comparison might, in fact, evaluate a residential area using the comparative appraisal approach with as much variety as would appear in their preferential judgments and assessments of the area.

Recent research at the Institute for Social Research concerning residents' assessments of the quality of their own neighborhood and housing environments has shown that standards of comparisons used by respondents act in the formulation of satisfaction levels (Campbell et al., 1976, chap. 6). Using data from a national survey, Campbell, Converse, and Rodgers suggest that the level of satisfaction with one's neighborhood or housing derives from some greater or lesser gap between an estimate of an actual situation and one to which the individual aspires. Moreover, an individual's aspirations with respect to housing and neighborhood are a function of his standards of comparison, including the most liked past residential experience and his judgment of the quality of the residential area in which most of his family, his friends, and the typical American family live.

The placement of referents by individuals relative to their own situations varies considerably. It is also possible that individual interpretations of the quality of an imposed referent would vary, whether it were the excellent suburban development or other residential areas in the region. It seems appropriate then that further testing of the distinction between preferential judgments and comparative appraisals be made with special attention given to the nature and meaning of the standard of comparison being imposed. At the same time, the question of greater or lesser consensus should be addressed in comparative appraisals of residential quality by people from the same residential area. Moreover, the two approaches (comparative appraisals and preferential judgments) should be tried in residential settings containing a variety of population mixes.

To what extent is there consensus among different population subgroups in appraising residential environmental quality? It was suggested earlier that preferential judgments or assessments of environmental quality display an array of subgroup differences reflecting individual situations, tastes, inclinations, and dispositions. Furthermore, these differences might be muted or eliminated if comparative appraisals were used in assessing quality (Craik & McKechnie, 1974). Indeed, Craik and McKechnie have carefully demonstrated that substantially more background and dispositional factors relate to preferential judgments of quality than to comparative appraisals. Groups associated with liking the Marin County region were married, non-Jewish, and Republican, while there were no relationships between marital status, religion, or political affiliation in the comparative appraisals. Whether or not the comparative appraisal approach would yield different responses based on background characteristics of people who assess their own residential areas remains to be determined.

Differences between subgroups in assessing environmental quality have been found in several studies dealing with the residential environment. Lamanna (1964) identified major subgroup differences when asking his sample of adult residents to consider attributes important in making a town an ideal place to live. Black respondents gave greater importance to physical than to social values, while for white respondents, sociability factors were relatively more important. Differences in the value placed on specific attributes were also found between men and women, people on both sides of 40, and low- and high-status occupational groups.

In other studies of attitudes toward specific neighborhood and community attributes and services, differences between population subgroups have been displayed (Zehner, 1972; Andrews & Phillips, 1970; Schuman & Gruenberg, 1972; Norcross, 1973; Zehner & Chapin, 1974). In many instances, subgroup differences tended to be small. Among racial groups, however, major differences in levels and determinants of satisfaction were identified. In their report on a study of black and white residents in 15 American cities. Schuman and Greenberg (1972, p. 376) found major differences in attitudes towards city services among the two groups, depending on the racial mix of their residential area. Zehner and Chapin (1974, p. 114) also found racial differences in the assessment of a Washington neighborhood, with black residents rating the neighborhood lower than white residents. An analysis of recently collected national data revealed several subgroup differences, in addition to race, in people's assessments of their communities and neighborhood environments (Marans & Rodgers, 1975). Not all the findings were as anticipated, however. People with reported annual family incomes below $5,000 are, if anything, more likely than those with higher incomes to express complete satisfaction with their communities. A similar pattern was found for those with low educational attainment, in which case over half of all respondents said they are completely satisfied with their place of residence. The inverse relationship beween education and satisfaction in part reflects differences in age, since older respondents tend to have less education than younger respondents. Indeed, the relationship between age and community satisfaction is nearly monotonic.

Life cycle groups also differ in their expressions of satisfaction: Married persons with older children or without children are the most satisfied with their places of residence. When several background characteristics are considered simultaneously in relation to community and neighborhood satisfaction, life cycle is, in fact, the most important predictor, followed by race. However, additional multivariate analysis of the data showed that the relationship between background characteristics and community satisfaction is mediated by the influence of background characteristics on assessments of specific community attributes; that is to say, subgroup differences are greater when specific features of the residential environment are being judged than in global measures of environmental satisfaction.

In several of the above-mentioned studies, the sample of people whose perceptions were being tapped represented populations in large geographic areas (the entire nation) or living under special situations (residents of large cities or new communities). In other studies, the sample represented populations of specific communities and neighborhoods. To determine the full extent to which subgroups of a population assess the quality of the same residential environments differently, additional studies of the latter type are required.

What relationships exist between observer-based appraisals and physical environmental quality indices? It has been argued on several occasions that the difficulties in dealing with the myriad of urban problems are compounded by the inadequate information base upon which decisions on the allocation of resources are made. The productivity of city services or impacts of proposed public and private projects are generally measured in economic or physical terms; frequently such measures miss the mark. Although most economic or physical objective data are accurate, their shortcoming lies in the fact that people do not respond to them as they are objectively measured. People respond to their *perceptions* of the situation which the physical data are intended to describe, and often their perceptions do not agree with the picture given by the official statistics. For example, Jacoby's study (1972) of perceptions of air quality in the Detroit region showed a lack of congruence between the perceptions of area residents and actual physical objective measures of air quality. Similarly, a recent study of lakeside residents in northern Michigan found only partial agreement between actual water quality measures and perceptions of water cleanliness (Marans et al., 1976). Decisions affecting the environment should certainly take into account physical objective measures. But they should also take into consideration the probable behavior of people in response to the proposed decisions: such behaviors are a function of people's values and assesments of their current situations.

Available data show that where relationships exist between physical objective measures of the residential environment and people's assessments of them, these relationships are not always strong. As one example, a physical attribute of the residential environment associated with residential quality is the extent of crowding (Schorr, 1963). Density of development, either in terms of people per room, dwelling units per acre, or people or dwellings per square mile, has been used as an objective physical measure of crowding. In a study of perceptions of neighborhood quality using national survey data, Marans and Mandell

(1972) found that an objective density measure (number of households per acre) was significantly but far from perfectly related to subjective measures of crowding: For both the interviewers' assessment of how built up the neighborhood was, and the respondents' perception of neighborhood crowding, the product–moment correlations with actual density were identical ($r = .47$). When the objective measure of density and background variables were considered in relation to neighborhood satisfaction, 20.6% of the total variance was explained. However, when the respondents' perceptions of crowding were substituted for objective density, the proportion of variance accounted for increased to 34%, indicating that the subjective appraisal was measuring things other than density per se.

Similarly, housing condition as measured by the degree of delapidation and age has often been used as an index of residential quality (Kain & Quigley, 1970). Yet several studies have indicated that less advantaged socioeconomic groups are subjectively more satisfied with their dwellings than objective housing condition indicators would suggest (Rossi, 1955; Gans, 1962; Hollingshead & Rogler, 1963; Campbell et al., 1976).

Other researchers have looked at the proximity of neighborhood and community facilities as an indicator of residential quality and found little or no relationship to satisfaction with place of residence (Lansing et al., 1970; Troy, 1971; Zehner & Chapin, 1974). Still others have shown that proximity to selected community facilities does not reflect the way people evaluate these facilities (Burby, 1974; Marans et al., 1976).

We do not know the extent to which there is agreement between other physical residential environmental quality indices and people's responses to the situation the indices are measuring. Current work at the Institute for Social Research is aimed at gauging the congruence between perceptions of neighborhood residents and actual conditions around them. In addition to a number of physical conditions, other objective indices associated with residential quality are being considered, including crime statistics, pupil–teacher ratios, and ethnic composition of neighborhoods. We continue to operate under the premise that the perceived quality of the residential environment is a function of social as well as physical attributes, and that the extent to which these attributes can be objectively measured and understood in relation to people's perceptions will result in more informed decision-making.

A CONCEPTUAL MODEL FOR UNDERSTANDING RESIDENTIAL ENVIRONMENTAL QUALITY

On another occasion, a conceptual model was presented within which people's responses to residential environments could be explored (Marans & Rodgers, 1975). It seems appropriate that this model be reviewed here. Although it is intended to aid in an understanding of residential satisfaction and, ultimately, determinants of residential mobility, the components of the model are central to many of the methodological issues which have already been discussed.

The basic purpose of the model is to suggest the ways in which the objective attributes of the residential environment, both physical and sociocultural, are linked to subjective experiences of people in that environment. Various subjective experiences are included in the model; these differ in the directness of their assumed association with the objective attributes. One type of experience (that of perception) is presented as being directly linked to the objective environment, although it may be influenced by other factors as well. Other subjective experiences—in particular, assessments and satisfactions—are indicated in the model as being only indirectly linked to objective environmental attributes. Furthermore, additional factors, such as personal characteristics, are shown to influence the subjective experience. Therefore, their relationships to objective attributes are expected to be weak. To ignore the indirectness of the relationship between objective attributes and satisfaction would be to risk misinterpretation and falsely conclude that objective attributes of people's residential environments are almost irrelevant to their experience in those environments. It is the intent of the model to make explicit the linkage between objective attributes and subjective responses including perception, assessments, and satisfaction measures.

These linkages are displayed in Figure 1 for different levels of the residential environment. Satisfaction with any level as expressed by an individual is dependent upon his evaluation or assessments to several attributes of that environment. The attributes which are most relevant to satisfaction can, of course, be determined empirically. For example, for a residential subdivision, the relevant attributes might be the population composition, the number of trees, the amount of open space available for private use, the value of homes, the responsiveness of government

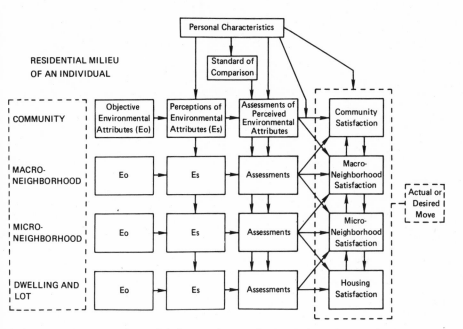

FIG. 1. A conceptual model for understanding residential environmental quality.

to complaints, the kinds and degrees of citizen involvement in local government, and the upkeep of the area.

A person's assessment of a particular attribute of his environment is considered dependent upon two things: his perception of it, and the standards against which he judges it. As I indicated earlier, the concept of a standard of comparison is a complex one. Its components may include expectation levels (i.e., what a person expects from his residential areas prior to his moving in), aspiration levels (i.e., what a person thinks could be true of the residential area in which he now lives or the environment in which he hopes to live), equity levels (i.e., what a person thinks should be true of his residential area, given the amount he has invested in his monthly payments, including taxes), and reference group levels (i.e., what a person believes to be true of the places where others live—others with whom he identifies—families, friends, and those with similar occupations, incomes, etc.).

A person's perception of a particular attribute is shown as

dependent on but distinct from the objective environmental attribute. The way a person perceives the environment is not necessarily equivalent to the environment as it actually is; the possibility of bias or inaccuracy of perception is recognized and, as indicated, has been demonstrated by previous research.

I noted earlier that the objective environment may contain more than physical attributes. It may be defined in sociocultural, organizational, or fiscal terms as well. Certainly, measures of attributes or objective environmental attributes may be unreliable. In particular, as we attempt to match objective conditions with subjective experiences, we are often forced to develop new techniques for measuring objective indices so that these can be directly linked to individual respondents in a survey. (Parenthetically, the development of new measurement techniques for objective environmental indices presents a formidable challenge for the environmental design profession and for others concerned with evaluating residential environments.)

A final element worthy of consideration is a set of variables labeled "person characteristics." This general term is meant to include all characteristics, tastes, experiences, and dispositions of an individual living in a residential environment that can influence his perceptions and assessments. The model suggests that biases and inaccuracies in perceptions may be systematically related to person characteristics. For instance, people of different ages, races, and incomes may have diverse perceptions of security or the recreational facilities offered in the same community. Or people may be characterized by a particular response style, e.g., a tendency to report what is thought to be socially desirable—planned communities are great!

Personal characteristics can also influence an individual's standard of comparison. In addition to socioeconomic characteristics such as age, race, and income, background characteristics such as the kinds of environments a person has experienced and his perceptions of the currently available alternative residences may determine the standards against which residential situations are evaluated.

In sum, the figure shows the basic elements by which we suggest that subjective experiences—namely, perceptions and assessments of residential quality—are linked to objective environmental attributes. Implicit in the model is the notion that satisfaction with one's place of residence is related to the assessments and perceptions of *many* attributes of the residential environment. At the moment, we do not know whether these assessments and perceptions are additive or interactive; nor do we have a complete picture of the way the different levels of the residential environment interact with one another. For example, one's feelings about one's dwelling are strongly related to one's feelings about one's neighborhood. But we do not know if a person's evaluation of the attributes of the area immediately around his dwelling (his microneighborhood) will influence his feelings about attributes of the larger development or community in which he lives. Such relationships can be determined in studies which consider quality assessments at different levels of the residential environment.

In summary, this chapter has attempted to do several things. First, it has sampled from among a wide range of empirical studies bearing on the perceived quality of residential environments. In doing so, it has looked at studies of environmental assessment, preferences, and behaviors, and the methods of inquiry used in these investigations. Several methodological issues were then considered. These dealt with the types of responses appropriate to understanding residential environmental quality, the question of whose responses should be tapped, the extent of agreement in assessments between "experts" and nonexperts and between different population subgroups, and the extent of agreement between subjective appraisals and objective measures of quality. Another issue focuses on the distinction between preferential judgments and comparative appraisals. Finally, a conceptual model for organizing research on the quality of residential environments was presented.

8

Perceived Quality of Residential and Institutional Environments

Research Needs and Priorities

FLORENCE C. LADD

For several decades researchers have attempted to identify features which contribute to the success or failure of residential environments, that is, housing and neighborhoods. The community studies of the Chicago-trained sociologists, research on housing attributes associated with residential mobility (Rossi, 1955), and examinations of the effects of housing on health and performance (Wilner & Walkeley, 1963) were in the vanguard of studies leading toward an understanding of some fundamental aspects of the quality of residential environments. Studies of the environmental features of institutions, including Osmond's (1957) work in psychiatric hospitals, Sommer's (1969) research in college settings, and Goffman's (1962) analysis of total institutions, and the hospital research of Ittelson, Proshansky, and Rivlin (1970) have identified some responses to institutional environments. Research on institutional settings, however, has not kept pace with the studies of residential envi-

DR. FLORENCE C. LADD • Department of City and Regional Planning, Graduate School of Design, Harvard University, Cambridge, Massachusetts 02138.

ronments; the latter are considerably more numerous and more varied, providing a substantial basis for further research on perceived qualities of housing and neighborhoods. This chapter, therefore, focuses primarily on residential environments. The variety of types and functions of institutional environments and their users make it difficult to generate a meaningful list of research needs in the area of perceived quality which would be applicable to most institutional settings. Where it seems appropriate, however, a research agenda developed here which refers to the perceived quality of residential environments might be extended to institutional environments.

USES OF RESEARCH ON PERCEIVED ENVIRONMENTAL QUALITY

It seems advisable to begin with some caveats based upon consideration of the numerous factors involved in the assessment of the quality of residential environments and changing events which, in turn, change the indicators of residential quality and evaluation of those indicators. First of all, a rather complex system of indices is required to accommodate the perceiver and environmental factors which are part of the PEQI equation. With regard to residential environments, the following sets of factors are listed merely to suggest the range and type of categories this discussion takes into account:

Perceiver Groups	Environmental Factors
Residents	Region
Developers	Urban–suburban–rural
Mortgage bankers	Neighborhood configuration and
Real estate board	type
members	House type
Politicians	Age of housing and neighborhood
Planners	
Architects	
Urban designers	

Associated Factors
_____

Social:
    Density/crowding
    Privacy
    Security
    Human dimension of delivery of services
    Identification with other residents
Physical:
    Location
    Location in relation to services
    Spatial configuration of home and
       neighborhood
    Physical amenities
    Safety
    Aesthetics
    Open Space
    Ventilation
    Air quality
    Noise level
    Vegetation

These lists suggest the complexity and interdependency of attributes associated with residential environments as well as the groups that determine where residences are located, what they look like, and, to some extent, how they are used. To complicate matters and matrices further, changes in the sociocultural context, in economic events, media-influenced styles, and the moment in history may change the salience and evaluation of environmental qualities. To arrive at a meaningful assessment of the interaction of the myriad of factors which influence perceived residential quality, well-coordinated, large-scale, long-range research must be undertaken with all the guidance, guidelines, and visionary planning the relevant federal agencies can muster—in addition to their financial support. The caveat refers to the point that there is little evidence of the federal capability to make a long-range commitment to social research on housing and neighborhoods.

This point leads to questions about the legislation which is stimulating research on environmental quality and the federal intentions with regard to the research results being generated. The focus on housing and neighborhood quality stems from the National Environmental Policy

Act. Many issues which have been subsumed under the rubric of quality of residential environments are contained in existing housing codes and zoning regulations. The true vintage of these issues is recognized by Bechtel (Chapter 6), who detects an old wine in new wineskins. While the PEQI concept is new, the constructs underlying PEQI are not at all new with regard to housing. The establishment of criteria and the specification of indicators of at least a minimal level of housing quality has been a central aspect of housing codes since the turn of the century in the United States (Martin, 1971). What lends a new flavor to the PEQI blend is the emphasis on aspects of the environment related to human welfare, as Bechtel points out, and the acknowledgment of the importance of the perceptions and evaluations reported by residents themselves. We must hope that the new emphasis is an expression of a new commitment—that environmental quality indices which pertain to housing and neighborhoods will not be handled as unevenly as the enactment and enforcement of housing codes.

Will the new emphasis make a difference in the applicability of the research? How will research results be used and how can researchers maximize the accessibility (and readability) of their findings? Those questions bear directly upon the selection of problems for study and the scale of the research. Bechtel (Chapter 6) reminds us that vast numbers of federally sponsored research projects have yielded results that have not been used by their federal sponsors. He reminds us, too, that scientists themselves have been responsible for the lack of application of results. We have been more concerned with communicating with our colleagues than with our federal sponsors and policy-makers. Furthermore, researchers have been reluctant to take the risk of advocating a position or making the recommendations that their data support. (In the field of residential environments, Gans and Rainwater are among the few notable exceptions.) Unwilling to highlight results which have applied implications and make recommendations, the researcher handicaps the policy-maker who has neither the time nor the expertise to examine the qualifications surrounding the findings, read other relevant literature, and then derive an interpretation which bears on the problem which he or she confronts. The area of perceived environmental quality offers researchers an opportunity to develop research strategies and forms of reporting results which can be of great value to policy-makers and others.

RESEARCH AGENDA

In this research agenda, the highest priority is placed on the quality of the housing and neighborhood environments of the poor, the working class, and the lower middle class in urban, suburban, and rural areas in the United States as the residents themselves perceive them, and as others who influence the residential options of these populations perceive the same residential environments. The rationale for focusing on the residential environments of these socioeconomic groups is that the quality of their dwellings and neighborhoods, by their standards and the standards of others, probably need to be upgraded. The line of research suggested here goes beyond the question of identifying indices of perceived quality of residential environments of the underclass; it is addressed to the applied question of how to improve the quality of relatively impoverished housing and neighborhoods. This approach requires that we consider how residents perceive the quality of their environments, their levels of satisfaction with their environments, the range of residential environments to which they have been exposed, and their expectations and aspirations with regard to residential environments.

Initially, large sample surveys should be made of perceptions of residential quality held by poor, working-class, and lower-middle-class male and female respondents who vary with regard to race, ethnicity, stage in the life cycle, and residential history. There should be considerable variety in their residential environments with an adequate representation of urban, suburban, and rural settings and regional contexts as well. Studies should be longitudinally designed, focusing on panels of environments and respondents who would respond periodically to researchers' inquiries so as to reveal changes in perceptions of salient environmental attributes and responses to physical and social change.

Using a panel of environments selected for study, research on individuals in roles which influence the residential choices and environmental quality of poor and low-income families and individuals should be conducted. Included in this group would be planners, policy-makers, managers of housing authorities, mortgage bankers, maintenance workers, developers, and architects. Comparisons of their responses with the responses of residents is of critical importance. The discrepancies are likely to reveal differences in priorities and sources of conflict which may be negotiable. Marans (Chapter 7) draws our attention to studies in which the judgments of environmental planners and designers have been compared with those of residents. For example, in their study of neighborhoods in the Detroit area, Lansing and Marans (1969) found only partial agreement between planners and residents with regard to what constitutes a high-quality residential environment. Identification of differences between signs of quality used by residents and other professional environmental groups as well as differences which exist among professional groups—for example, between planners and developers or between planners and managers of housing developments—may serve as a basis for formulating strategies for improving the quality of residential environments where assistance is needed most. What is likely to be the extent of agreement between residents and professional environmental groups or between two professional environmental groups when a residential environment of poor quality is under study? What action can one take when the discrepancy between group responses is considerable? When the residents assign a higher value to the quality of their environments than the experts? What elements and increments of change would be required to raise the quality of a residential environment to a level that is acceptable to both lay and professional groups?

A major objective of this research approach is to determine differential perceptions of the quality of residential environments on the part of several groups and to discover ways of improving these environments and their perceived quality. Other purposes of the research would be to determine which environmental attributes are most salient for the respondents; how they evaluate those attributes; and how they would like to have the highly salient, negatively evaluated elements upgraded. In short, we should determine the nature of their priorities for change in the residential environments in question.

The techniques for eliciting environmental perceptions are predominantly verbal. Observational data should be gathered along with verbal reports of perceptions. When the observed behaviors of residents are compared with their reported perceptions we gain a better understanding of those perceptions.

Emphasis has been placed on residents' perceptions of their own environments. To gain a broader understanding of the selection of indicators of quality and the extent to which familiarity with environments influences perceptions, it would be desirable to have the same groups—residents and "experts"—judge a variety of residential areas. This might be accomplished through the presentation of photographs or slides of selected novel settings. Using an experimental research design, it would be possible to expose a subsample of resident respondents to the novel settings, which they would evaluate, and then to ascertain the extent to which their standards are influenced by the exposure in comparison to residents who are not asked to evaluate the other settings.

It should be made explicit that, although previous research has emphasized the quality of the exterior of home environments, it is extremely important to assess the perceived quality of interiors which are likely to have greater significance for the quality of life and well-being of residents.

Hierarchies of qualitative indicators should be established for groups on a normative basis. Trade-offs that residents are willing to make and the dollar value that they associate with environmental attributes should be established.

These are only a few suggestions within the framework of one approach to the study of the perceived quality of residential environments. Construed more broadly, the agenda would include basic research items which would expand our understanding of the process of environmental perception. Such an agenda would include theoretical and methodological issues. This agenda, however, is addressed only to immediate residential inequities.

REPORTING FINDINGS

In the interest of making research results more readily available, it is suggested that more visual material be used in reports. The studies of Scheflen (1971), Perin (1972), and Craik and his associates have demonstrated how the use of videotapes, photography, and film enhance the clarity of environmental studies. While verbal descriptions of signs of environmental quality are generally clear, there are many attributes which would be more widely understood if they were illustrated. Studies which make use of visual presentations of environmental settings and their elements increase the likelihood that the respondents, researchers, and audience for the research share a similar set of referents. In reporting findings, it would be particularly useful to include with the research report an illustrated manual on indices of quality in residential environments to show examples of features the respondents selected as indicative of environmental quality along with the evaluation and level of priority they assign to those features. To be sure, the presentation of data in this form would be of limited value. A considerable portion of environmental attributes (perhaps the most important ones) associated with quality are neither physical nor visible, and therefore would be impossible to illustrate. Still, a collection of this type would show the evaluations of environmental features along with the social characteristics of groups of respondents.

A catalogue of illustrated environmental elements, with the level of salience and evaluation indicated by residents and other groups of respondents, would be a useful contribution. Provisions could be made for new entries. It might be cross-indexed to show where one might find related environmental examples and their salience and evaluation. An illustrated cross-reference file of perceived indices of residential quality might also be developed which would show level of salience and evaluation by groups and also how environments of different types and in different contexts are evaluated.

The value of an information system on perceived indices of residential quality and its effectiveness would depend on whether and how it is used. This brings us to the question of educating the public, professionals, and others working in the area of housing and neighborhood quality to understand and make better use of the research and resources being developed in the interest of improving substandard residential environments.

It is interesting to observe that the environmental education movement has as its focus the conservation and restoration of the natural environment. The attention of the public has not been drawn to the quality of residential environments. We are not reminded that homes and neighborhoods are also environmental resources which, in some sectors of our cities and rural areas, need to be upgraded in order to move more families and individuals toward the goal of a "decent home and a suitable living environment" as pledged by the 81st Congress in the National Housing Act of 1949. There are no television and radio appeals for improving the quality of residential life in the still-blighted areas of cities in the United States and in the pockets of inadequate housing in rural areas. There are no powerful interest groups urging the improvement of residential quality in "blighted" areas.

Improved collaboration between the Department of Housing and Urban Development and the National Environmental Policy Act is needed. Their collaboration could result in the expansion of environmental education programs, for example, when then might include education for selection and use of residential environments. The development of research on the relationship between housing codes, housing authorities, and zoning regulations, on the one hand, and the quality of residential environments, on the other, may lay bare some problems which have prevented the effective enforcement of housing codes. Research, for example, which deals with the relationship between the enforcement of housing codes in an area and the perceived quality of residential environments in that area may indicate the level of effectiveness of codes and suggest revisions in procedures for code enforcement. The results of research on environmental quality are more likely to be used if such connections are made between findings and their application.

To be sure, it is important to pursue the basic research questions which relate to the assessment of indicators of perceived quality of residential and institutional environments. Yet, we must not be preoccupied with the search for understanding perceived environmental quality while there continue to be major economic, social, and psychological problems confronting a sizeable segment of the population in the U.S. which are not unrelated to their residential and institutional environments. There is a place for action research in the area of the environmental quality of housing, neighborhoods and institutions.

Discussion Summary

KENNETH H. CRAIK AND ERVIN H. ZUBE

The conceptual analysis of perceived residential and institutional quality yielded by the workshop discussions was reviewed in the introduction to this section. The other primary concern of the discussions was the goal of devising indices of these constructs that would be scientifically defensible and practically useful. The main topics can be surveyed in light of the procedural sequence entailed in the development and application of PEQIs for residential and institutional environments.

OPERATIONAL DEFINITIONS AND MEASUREMENTS OF PERCEIVED RESIDENTIAL QUALITY INDICATORS

In their contributions, Bechtel (Chapter 6) and Marans (Chapter 7) reviewed the various response formats pertinent to the development of standard survey instruments for perceived residential quality. An extensive battery of techniques is available, including ratings of satisfaction and preference, semantic differential scales and other environmental descriptors, and self-anchoring scales. Ladd (Chapter 8) underscored the special appropriateness of visual–pictorial and three-dimensional materials in the conduct and reporting of research. In addition, observational methods for studying overt behaviors in residential contexts were

DR. KENNETH H. CRAIK • Institute of Personality Assessment and Research, University of California, Berkeley, California 94720.   DR. ERVIN H. ZUBE • Institute for Man and Environment, University of Massachusetts, Amherst, Massachusetts 01002.

nominated for consideration, including behavior setting surveys and activity logs. The latter approach diverges from the emphasis of PEQIs upon experiential–perceptual qualities and would appear to constitute a movement toward indirect indicators, which must be linked conceptually to perceived environmental quality.

Marans's review seemed to favor the use of satisfaction ratings of specific attributes of the residential environment, at least with on-site users not contemplating a move. The primarily descriptive techniques (i.e., checklist, Q-sort decks, environmental descriptors) would require subsequent evaluative weightings reflecting validly the construct of perceived residential quality.

WEIGHTING SCHEMES FOR DERIVING INDICES FROM INDICATORS

If an array of residential attributes is appraised for a place or sample of places, then some method of weighting each indicator is required to compute an index. In the refinement of water pollution indices, for example, the attributes are selected and the weighting of them is conducted by experts, presumably expressing scientific–medical judgment. In devising indices of perceived residential quality, the general public can be readily engaged in the selection of constituent elements and in devising the weighting scheme for them. For place-centered appraisals, Marans points to the use of trade-off games and related procedures, whose results can offer a guide for the weighting process. For person-centered assessments, Milbrath and Sahr (1975) have asked participants concurrently to appraise the quality of residential features and to gauge their relative importance. Thus, the weighting can be handled in an idiographic manner in generating and assessing residential person-centered assessments.

Note that if, instead of considering residential well-being a primary component of human welfare, PEQIs were conceptualized in terms of their consequences for, say, personal adjustment or public health, then the weighting scheme could be established through statistical analyses that identify the perceived residential qualities most predictive of the goal state or criterion.

STANDARD OPERATIONS FOR APPRAISING
PERCEIVED RESIDENTIAL QUALITY

The factors implicated in issues regarding the appraisal system for residential PEQIs include several parameters often noted and heeded in basic research on environmental perception (i.e., observer characteristics, media of presentation, response formats). Discussion also emphasized the importance of instructional sets and the social context of the PEQI assessments.

The extent of influence of observer differences upon residential PEQI appraisals represents, of course, an important facet of the construct validity of place-centered PEQIs. In practical appraisal operations, knowledge of the specific relationships would be important for understanding and properly interpreting results.

The ways in which residential environments are presented to observer panels in PEQI assessments can vary with the purposes at hand. In regional monitoring and in postconstruction evaluations, the actual residential settings can be presented in some manner to observational teams. In fact, most residential research on environmental quality reports the appraisals of user-inhabitants of their own residential settings. Unlike scenic research, rarely do participants in residential research assess several environments, or indeed any beyond their own abode. Thus, comparisons between PEQIs based upon touring panels and upon on-site resident samples are needed. The use of simulations of residential environments is inescapable in some contexts of application (e.g., environmental impact assessments at the preconstruction state). In other instances, simulation—often photo-slides—is employed in research requiring observer appraisals of multiple residential environments. In all cases, evaluation of the psychological effectiveness of the simulation techniques in evoking responses comparable to those elicited by the actual environments is essential, but thus far, simulation techniques have been employed largely in the absence of validational evidence.

The nature of the response formats speaks to the issue of the domain of residential attributes considered salient by user-inhabitants and encompassed in the construct of perceived residential quality. Instructions and the psychological sets they evoke in observers have received little systematic attention, although recent research (Leff et al.,

1974) has demonstrated their important role generally in environmental perception. Instructions which call for comparative appraisals versus preferential judgments presumably evoke or tune distinctive psychological sets, and thus illustrate the bearing of psychological sets on PEQIs. The use of standard environments as marker or reference points for PEQI panels also relates to the role of psychological sets. The social context of the appraisals (e.g., an architectural jury, a citizens' committee empaneled by a court, a controversial and heated public hearing) received considerable discussion. The paucity of research on many of these factors affecting observer assessments was noted.

EVALUATING THE RELIABILITY AND VALIDITY OF APPRAISAL SYSTEMS FOR PERCEIVED RESIDENTIAL QUALITY

Evidence on the reliability or potential reliability of a PEQI appraisal system appears to be scarce, or inaccessible. Since, in most research, participants have reported upon satisfactions regarding their own environment, we lack the straightforward indices of reliability and sensitivity of measurement that would be provided by touring panels appraising an array of environments. Studies of appraisals for multiple environments have tended to employ simulated presentations whose generality to actual environments is largely undetermined, or have entailed preference judgments regarding hypothetical rather than real-life choices. Finally, investigators who may have gathered pertinent data have tended not to analyze the findings psychometrically (i.e., from the point of view of standard psychological measurement criteria).

Research reports bearing upon construct validity of PEQIs have tended to highlight obtained differences between individual and groups in their perceptions of residential quality. Marans notes a generally substantial level of agreement and consensus, within the context of pervasive and theoretically interesting variation. An appropriate analytic standpoint for gauging the dimension of "degree of agreement-variation" among observer groups has not yet been adequately formulated for use in appraising this facet of PEQI construct validity. For example, research findings have tended to be analyzed by tests for statistically significant differences but have not been accompanied by indices of the percentage of variance the differences account for. Specifically, the pragmatic implications of differing levels of intergroup variation in PEQIs warrant systematic analysis and research. Unlike the case of reliability and sensitivity of measurement, the topic of construct validity finds quite a few studies that address issues germane to PEQI development but whose mode of analysis and interpretation miss the mark of being truly pertinent and informative.

Validity findings on systematic correlates between PEQIs and physical correlates are fragmentary but appear to demonstrate some orderly and positive relationships. Especially in the case of place-centered PEQIs, this kind of systematic correlation is important to their utility, for some leverage on the physical environmental side is needed to provide guidance and criteria for environmental policy, planning, design, and management. Of course, the correlates need not be isomorphic in content and referent (e.g., adequacy of dwelling lot size may be more highly correlated with landscaping variables than square footage) nor be redundant measures (i.e., perfectly correlated). In the case of person-centered PEQIs, if their correlates are entirely on the side of social, personality, and other psychological factors, they would be of much reduced relevance to environmental policy and management, although perhaps pertinent to educators and counselors. Even so, content validity of measures of environmental well-being requires demonstrated adequacy, and calls for systematic tests of their acceptance by environmental experts and the general public as reasonably covering the domain of environmental well-being.

The issue of the possible stability of the construct of perceived residential quality across societies and cultures and over time in a given society seems surrounded with a wealth of folklore but is scandalously bare of scientific findings. The folklore generated considerable concern among workshop participants over the variability of standards of quality, especially in the face of mass media influences, and raises an issue about the "use-period" of PEQI monitoring results and the extent to which their temporal stability makes them pragmatically valuable. Certainly, until evidence comes in on this issue, continuous scrutiny of the PEQI system, with updating, would be essential to its credibility, effectiveness, and functional value.

EVALUATING THE UTILITY OF RESIDENTIAL PEQI MONITORING SYSTEMS

A recurrent theme of the workshop discussions was the concern, voiced also by Ladd (Chapter 8), that judgments of the general public be included in each step of the PEQI operational system: in analyzing the construct of perceived residential quality, identifying the construct salient elements, weighting the construct indicators for a composite index, and constituting panels for appraisal purposes. Implicitly and explicitly, these requirements were underscored as essential to the credibility of PEQI appraisal of residential and institutional environments.

A second theme stressed the need for a sophisticated psychometric perspective upon the entire process of PEQI development and use. There appeared to be general consensus that no innovations in measurement were required for developing and evaluating a residential PEQI appraisal system, and that any obstacles encountered in the path to that goal were likely instead to be either substantive (e.g., the criteria for construct validity might not be met in the real world of people and places) or sociopolitical (e.g., that even a valid PEQI system might be avoided or misused by decision-makers, or shunned by the general public).

The discussion often took an anticipatory direction, speculating on the likely fate of any effort to develop a residential PEQI appraisal system. A negative orientation foresaw: (1) substantive difficulties in demonstrating adequate intergroup consensus and environmental correlates to support the construct validity of place-centered PEQIs; (2) premature use of incomplete PEQIs leading to rigidification and the neglect of critical attributes of perceived residential quality; (3) a misuse of PEQIs (e.g., to permit slighting of "nonperceptual" structural or other "nonperceptual" elements of environmental quality); (4) a hostile reception and rejection of PEQIs by the public officials and environmental professionals threatened by the prospect of program evaluations; (5) a misunderstanding of PEQIs (because researchers and monitoring personnel fail to communicate their concepts and findings effectively to officials and the general public); (6) an insensitive use of PEQIs, thwarting intuitive design and planning and hindering innovation; and (7) manipulation of PEQIs by the mass media and susceptibility of PEQI to fads and other short-run fluctuations.

A positive orientation envisioned PEQIs as an aid to rational policy formation and implementation, permitting systematic appraisal of perceived residential quality and assessment of sense of residential well-being, gauging the extent of social equity attained in their distribution, contributing to the development of environmental impact statements, and affording standard methods for conducting postconstruction evaluations and program evaluations. In these roles, a PEQI appraisal system would provide a means for policy and practice to respond constructively to legislative and administrative mandates, already "on the books" for inputs from and communication with the general public, for greater attention to noneconomic factors, and for agency accountability via program evaluation and feedback.

RESEARCH ISSUES AND NEEDS

Discussion of research issues and the nomination of needed lines of inquiry formed the concluding portion of the round table discussion. A full listing of nominated projects is provided below. The order of proposed undertakings has been rearranged to form a more coherent sequence.

1. To formulate a theory of the way people experience environmental quality and models of the processes entailed in environmental evaluations (e.g., depicting how people decide that certain features of the environment work or are satisfactory, and that others do not or are not).
2. To analyze the concept of residential and institutional satisfaction, especially its dynamic properties and relation to psychological needs.
3. To compare the properties of residential and institutional PEQIs with those of economic indices and social indicators.
4. To develop a taxonomy of perceived residential environments, incorporating: (a) types of residential settings (e.g., town houses, high-rise apartments, 1930s developments); (b) classifications of perceived environmental attributes (versus structural members and other "hidden" aspects); and (c) levels of scale (i.e., from interiors to dwelling units, microneighborhoods,

macroneighborhoods through counties and regions) and to devise comparable taxonomies for institutional environments.

5. To identify background factors that influence perception of environmental quality (e.g., age, life cycle, environmental experience, socioeconomic status), and to differentiate among notions of perceived environmental quality held by significant user-constituencies.

6. To identify and conceptualize the basic environmental components and features that constitute perceived residential and institutional quality, on the basis of pertinent empirical research involving the general population and significant subgroups.

7. To construct standardized instruments for comparative studies of perceived residential quality and perceived institutional quality, with special emphasis upon pictorial and other non-verbal as well as verbal procedures and with the goal of flexible instruments that can be adapted to differing kinds of project evaluations.

8. To design substantive social science research on environmental problems and issues so that PEQIs and related measures emerge as by-products.

9. To search for correlations between perceived environmental quality and physical environmental attributes and conditions.

10. To investigate longitudinally the roles of familiarity, use, and adaptation upon environmental satisfaction and upon appraisals of perceived environmental quality.

11. To study the influence of social and institutional factors (e.g., personal control vs. managerial control) upon perceived residential and institutional quality.

12. To examine the relationship between anticipated experiences of environments and actual experiences, and the extent of congruence between predicted PEQIs (at preconstruction or preoccupancy stage) and obtained PEQIs (at postconstruction or occupancy stage).

13. To conduct sociopsychological research on the professional use of PEQI feedback information in architectural and planning firms and agencies at the project level; and on the use of PEQIs in social indicator monitoring programs at the regional planning level.

14. To organize clearinghouse and translation services for making PEQI information comprehensible and usable by environmental professionals and for facilitating the incorporation of PEQI information and feedback into the ongoing planning and design process.
15. To explore ways of gathering and presenting PEQI information (possibly in conjunction with preconstruction simulations) that would serve as a means of broadening public consideration and acceptance of innovative designs and creative enhancements of environmental quality.
16. To study how individual designers and planners intuitively and informally appraise residential and institutional quality and gauge the relative success of constructed projects.
17. To investigate the influences of social institutions (e.g., mass media, commercial advertising, education) upon environmental aspirations and taste and upon the appraisal of perceived environmental quality by laypersons and experts.
18. To conduct cross-national studies encompassing a wide range of cultural and environmental settings, focusing upon differing perceptions of environmental quality and on differing societal mechanisms for obtaining and using observer-based appraisals.

IV
Air, Water, and Sonic Environments

The Constructs of Perceived Air, Water, and Sonic Quality

The constructs of perceived air quality, water quality, and sonic quality entertained by workshop participants appeared to differ from or entail significant expansions of the constructs that have guided most prior research on the perception of air, water, and noise pollution. In the case of research on air and water, the environmental perception studies have been formulated in the context of already available physical indices of pollution, which are based upon public health and economic impact considerations. Yet Barker (Chapter 10) and Coughlin (Chapter 11) point out that the constructs of perceived air quality and water quality embody a reference to amenity values which are distinct from the goals of public health and economic efficiency. Similarly, Weinstein (Chapter 12) notes a distinction between the perceived qualities of the sonic environment and the almost universal emphasis in current research upon annoying conditions of noisiness.

Thus, an important distinction emerged regarding the focus of research: First, research on the development of indices might deal with the *perception of amenity attributes* of air, water, and sonic environments, and second, research on observer indices might focus upon the *perception of pollutants,* as defined by current physical pollution indices. Previous research has dealt almost entirely with the perception of air quality and water pollution and with annoyance reactions, rather than perceptual–cognitive appraisals, concerning facets of the sonic environment.

In the case of air and water, research exploring laypersons' conceptions of air and water quality has been designed and interpreted within the framework of physical pollution indices based upon public health and economic impacts, as judged by scientific–medical opinion. Thus, the construction of survey instruments and the interpretation of findings have tended to highlight discrepancies between laypersons' definitions of air and water quality (primarily visual qualities) and scientific–technical definitions of pollution. In contrast, research directed to laypersons' constructs of air, water, and sonic amenities, paralleling studies of residential satisfaction and preference, are almost entirely lacking.

The main tradition of research on noise perception is removed from the goal of perceived indices of sonic quality in two ways: First, research has been concerned with *emotional reactions* to the sonic environment (i.e., annoyance reactions) rather than *perceptual–cognitive appraisals,* and, second, as in the case of air and water, studies have dealt with negative emotional reactions to distressing attributes of the sonic environment rather than with enjoyable experiences of its potential positive qualities.

In all three environmental domains, the distinction between perception of amenities and perception of pollutants appears meaningful. Further, the need for greater attention to the neglected task of conceptualizing the amenity attributes for air quality, water quality, and sonic quality was evident. Decisions on the salient elements constituting these quality constructs should involve the general public, and thus research on conceptions of favorable climates and "beautiful days," on the positive features of streams, rivers, lakes, and oceanfronts, and on pleasing natural and man-made sounds warrants a high priority.

Previous research on the perception of air, water, and sonic quality has also combined strictly perceptual–cognitive reports on environmental attributes (e.g., presence–absence judgments, saliency ratings) with additional response modes, including emotional (e.g., annoyance, concern) and resource-use activities. Thus, three response levels can be envisioned for each environmental domain.

The perceptual–cognitive response, which is central to the PEQI construct, is often referred to as "awareness" or "sensory perception" in these research literatures. Obviously, the annoyance and concern reactions are presumed to be directed to, or are responsive to, negative attributes (e.g., noise, pollution). Perceptual–cognitive appraisals and concern about air and water pollution; annoyance reactions to noise; and uses of varyingly polluted water bodies constitute the bulk of studies on observer responses to atmospheric and resource quality. Neglect of research on perceptual–cognitive indices of air, water, and sonic amenities is striking.

Since the perception of air and water pollution entails criteria established by scientific–medical judgment, the role of either personal preferences or generally understood standards of excellence seems slight. These perceptual–cognitive reports could be said to be descriptive and predictive of prescribed criterion conditions; rather than being simply judgments of the presence or absence of valued attributes, they call for accuracy of detection of physical properties.

In our preliminary search for contributions on atmospheric environments, we soon learned that expertise spanning the three domains of air, water, and sound was rare indeed, or at least rarely claimed. Thus our division of effort among policy application, methodology, and research priorities had to give way. Fortunately, we succeeded in recruiting colleagues with sufficiently broad scope to take on all three tasks for a given environmental domain: Barker on perception of air quality, Coughlin on perception of water quality, and Weinstein on perception of noise. The arrangement proved to be most effective and afforded comparative analysis in the workshop discussions that provoked some insights into relative emphases and oversights regarding concepts, methods, and policy perspectives within each environmental domain.

Planning for Environmental Indices

Observer Appraisals of Air Quality

MARY L. BARKER

Air pollution is defined by technical experts in terms of "nonequilibrium" with respect to specific physical, biological, and chemical parameters. Most air quality indices in the United States rely on two classes of federal ambient air quality standards: primary standards which are designed to protect human health, and more stringent secondary standards which are intended to protect materials, vegetation, and amenities. However, there are many air pollutants for which there are no federal standards as yet and none of the many air quality indices have gained widespread support (National Academy of Sciences-National Academy of Engineering, 1975, p. 23).

Air quality management involves a great deal of uncertainty. Air pollution has a complex origin, and there is a long causal chain between measured characteristics of pollutants and their effects. A number of specific problems can be identified:

1. Uncertainty regarding measured levels of pollution. Methods and instruments are available to measure particulate matter, sulfur dioxide, carbon monoxide, oxides of nitrogen, and oxidants. However, (a) only particulates and sulfur dioxide are

DR. MARY L. BARKER • Department of Geography, Simon Fraser University, Burnaby 2, British Columbia, Canada.

monitored routinely in many places; (b) the number of monitoring sites is often inadequate; (c) stations are not always located
to provide representative data.

2. The degree of risk to human health, materials, and vegetation
from various pollutants and synergistic combinations is unclear.

3. Very little is known about the effects of air pollutants on
amenity values.

4. There are no established guidelines for acceptable levels of risk.

5. Pressure from organized interest groups (e.g., polluters) can be
considerable.

Given the existing situation, there is an obvious need to develop a
mutual understanding among groups of experts, and between decision-
makers and the public. One means of accomplishing this task may be to
develop·Perceived Air Quality Indices in order to clarify policy goals, to
gauge the effectiveness of specific air quality management programs,
and to facilitate an exchange of information between the public and the
decision-makers. Before taking such a step, it is necessary to evaluate
what is known about observer appraisals of air quality, what policy
issues are involved, and what the research priorities are.

OBSERVER APPRAISALS OF AIR QUALITY

Four critical areas can be identified from a review of preliminary
work conducted on the perception of air pollution. These are: the degree
of consensus among individuals and community groups in assessing air
quality; the extent of agreement between expert and lay appraisals of
air quality; the relationships between observed appraisals and physical
measures of air pollution; and observers' characteristics in relation to
air quality appraisals. Each of these will be discussed in terms of the
existing state of knowledge and the implications for the possible
development of perceived air quality indices.

Individual and Community Assessments of Air Quality

There appear to be wide variations in levels of awareness of and
concern for air pollution. Such variations include not only those between

individuals, but also variations in degree of community awareness and concern in different cities. Factors which contribute to these reported differences include: nature of the pollution hazard—types, amounts, frequency, and sources of pollutants; characteristics of individuals and communities; variations in questionnaire design; and time lag between opinion surveys. Differences in questionnaire design and the scarcity of comparative studies involving a number of cities make direct comparisons between survey results impossible. However, a number of insights can be gained regarding level of awareness, knowledge, and concern about air pollution.

Level of awareness has been tapped by various means, ranging from asking people to identify any disadvantages of living in their community, to posing a direct question, "Is air pollution a problem in this neighborhood?" Most surveys indicate a broad range of opinion within the particular community or city in question. Even in areas experiencing low levels of pollution, a substantial minority feels that an air pollution problem exists. A clear example is provided by the results of a collaborative research effort in which one questionnaire was used in three cities in the United Kingdom (I.G.U. Air Pollution Study Group for the U.K., 1972).

In 1971, questionnaire surveys were carried out in Sheffield, Edinburgh, and Exeter. In each city, a random stratified sample was used, based on local air pollution levels. A large majority of the people interviewed in Sheffield and Exeter denied the existence of an air pollution problem. In Edinburgh, 53% of the respondents identified an air pollution problem (see Table I). These responses are particularly interesting in light of current pollution levels, and the history of pollution control attempts in the three cities. Overall, Sheffield and Edinburgh have similar values of mean winter smoke concentrations

TABLE I. Awareness of Air Pollution in Three U.K. Cities[a]

City	Is air pollution a problem in this area? %				Sample size	Average winter smoke concentrations, 1966–69 ($\mu g/m^3$)
	Yes	No	Doubtful	Don't know		
Sheffield	25	65	7	3	120	120
Edinburgh	53	47	—	—	360	120
Exeter	22	72	3	3	120	40

[a] I.G.U. Air Pollution Study Group for the U.K. (1972).

(120 $\mu g/m^3$, 1966–1969), while much lower values are experienced in Exeter (40 $\mu g/m^3$).

Sheffield has experienced dramatic improvements in smoke levels in recent years as a result of the adoption of smoke abatement measures by the local government. However, air pollution still reaches high levels in some areas. The city government launched a determined publicity campaign aimed at bolstering the "clean air now" image of Sheffield. There has been much less improvement in Edinburgh, where no publicity campaign was used. Although both cities experience similar levels of smoke concentration, many Sheffield residents have accepted the publicity campaign slogan of "the cleanest industrial city in Europe" (Wall, 1972, p. 8). Air pollution is no longer regarded as a serious problem by many people there.

The conclusions to be drawn from these collaborative studies are twofold: Wide differences in awareness exist in a single community, and recognition of a local air pollution problem is only partly influenced by direct sensory perception. Indirect experience, such as information provided by mass media or publicity campaigns, plays an important, if not dominant, role.

A number of studies suggest that people have particular aspects of air pollution in mind when asked to express their awareness and level of concern. A sizable proportion define air pollution in terms of particular effects and suspected causes (Schusky, 1966; Crowe, 1967). This impression was substantiated when Crowe's definitional types were applied in the three U.K. cities. Crowe set up four categories to group the various definitions offered by people: "causal"—those naming a source (e.g., industry, cars); "effectual"—those noting results (e.g., dirty windows, irritation of the eyes); "specific"—those mentioning particular pollutants without discussing cause or effect (e.g., smoke); and "combinatorial"—involving a group of the other categories (e.g., dust from the factory dirties the windows and washing).

Almost half the respondents in Sheffield, Edinburgh, and Exeter defined air pollution in terms of combinations of causes, effects, or specifics (see Table II). To many, air pollution meant damage to household objects caused by visible pollutants from various industrial sources. When asked directly about household effects, more than 62% of the Exeter group, and over 35% of the Sheffield group mentioned possible damage to health. These results support those obtained by Crowe, who found that most people did not define air pollution in terms of a health

TABLE II. Definitions of Air Pollution in Three U.K. Cities[a]

City	Definitions %					
	Causal	Effectual	Specific	Combinational	Don't know/ other	Sample size
Sheffield	12.5	9.2	29.2	45.8	3.3	120
Edinburgh	8.6	26.9	12.2	41.4	10.9	360
Exeter	20.0	2.5	28.3	40.0	9.2	120

[a] I.G.U. Air Pollution Study Group for the U.K. (1972).

hazard until asked specifically if it was harmful to health. An overwhelming majority then said yes. He suggests that the more tangible and observable features (e.g., smoke, dirt) may be masking a more abstract, but real, concern regarding the possible effects of air pollution (Crowe, 1967, p. 155).

It is interesting to note that while many people in Sheffield recognized some adverse effects of air pollution, they tended to deny that it affected them financially. People who recognized the existence of a local pollution problem somehow were able to deny that they themselves were adversely affected (Wall, 1973, p. 242). This appears very similar to the situation where people recognize that smoking is bad for health, but continue to smoke because "it isn't going to happen to me."

The degree of concern about local air pollution is influenced by a number of factors, including direct sensory perception, information from other sources such as the news media, and salience of the problem. Residents of a polluted district may be well aware that the problem exists but feel that other local problems are more important. Miller (1972) found that community leaders in the eastern United States assigned a low priority to air pollution in relation to other problems. Given a list of 12 problems, only 5% (out of a sample of 400) said that they had most interest in air pollution. Most leaders assigned much higher priorities to race relations, unemployment and poverty, housing and urban renewal, public education, and crime. When asked to identify which problem they were currently working hardest on, less than 1% said air pollution.

People who are not community leaders may appear unconcerned or apathetic because there are no well-defined channels for taking effective individual action (Rankin, 1969). In such cases, frustration may result in people denying that the problem exists, transferring concern to other areas where direct participation is possible, or assuming that someone (usually the government) is taking care of it.

Level of concern is often measured by asking people to rank air pollution in relation to other community problems, or to rank it along a 5-point scale ranging from "very serious" to "not at all serious." Both methods have produced impressions of varying degrees of concern in different cities, at different times (see Table III). In 1969, a Gallup Poll survey in the United States revealed that 36% of those surveyed considered air pollution to be most important among a list of seven environmental problems (McEvoy, 1972, p. 226).

In 1959 and 1962, respectively, approximately 45% of the respondents in Buffalo said that air pollution was "very serious" or

TABLE III. Salience of Air Pollution Problem

Year	Place	Description of problem .	Percentage of respondents	Problems ranked before air pollution
1959	Buffalo	"very serious and serious"	44	1. Unemployment 2. Juvenile delinquency 3. Car accidents 4. Alcoholism
1962	Buffalo	"very serious and serious"	46	1. Unemployment 2. Juvenile delinquency 3. Communicable diseases
1963	St. Louis	"very and somewhat serious"	38	1. Juvenile delinquency 2. Unemployment 3. Lack of recreational areas and programs
1967	Toronto	"very or moderately unsatisfactory"	88	None
1969	U.S. (National Survey)	"most important"	36	None
1970	Tucson	"very and somewhat serious"	66	1. Littering
1971	Edinburgh (U.K.)	"very and somewhat serious"	27	1. Traffic 2. Vandalism 3. Unemployment 4. Sewage disposal 5. Drugs and alcoholism
1971	Ljubljana (Yugoslavia)	"most serious"	44	None

"serious." It ranked fourth or fifth behind such problems as unemployment and juvenile delinquency (De Groot, Loring, Rihm, Samuels & Winkelstein, 1966, p. 245). A study in St. Louis in 1963 revealed similar trends. Eighty-eight percent of the respondents in a Toronto survey conducted in 1967 rated levels of air pollution as "very" or "moderately unsatisfactory." (Auliciems & Burton, 1971, p. 71). No other problems were ranked as being more important. As Buffalo and Toronto experience somewhat similar levels of pollution, the upsurge in concern is probably the result of increased media attention to air pollution and environmental problems in general. This may also account for the 66% "very" or "somewhat serious" responses in Tucson, where only littering was ranked higher than air pollution as a local problem (Saarinen & Cooke, 1971, p. 265).

The Tucson study bears out the need for caution in interpreting such measures of concern. Whereas 66% of the respondents said that air pollution was serious to some degree, only 13% felt that air pollution was a disadvantage when asked an open-ended question, "What are some of the things that you don't like about living in this area, things that you think are disadvantages?" Nineteen percent felt that there were none, and no problem emerged as a major disadvantage. Of all the measures of observer assessments of air quality (including awareness, knowledge, concern), special care should be given to interpreting levels of concern. Without careful attention, it is possible either to underestimate concern because other problems are seen to be easier to do something about, or to overestimate concern by leading the respondent with loaded questions. (Saarinen's study, which examined a variety of local environmental problems using different types of questions, points the way to improvements in questionnaire design.)

Expert and Lay Appraisals of Air Quality

The importance of air pollution levels represents a high degree of uncertainty, not so much in terms of its causes or physical properties, but in terms of the significance of measured properties. The extent of risk to health and community well-being is not always well defined. Air pollution is chronic and insidious rather than sudden and visibly dramatic. Only a limited range of pollutants and their effects is visible, and it is difficult to establish air pollution as the specific or unique cause of damage in many cases. Given the complexity of the problem, differences can be anticipated between expert and lay appraisals of air quality, and perceived means of coping with air pollution. These discrepancies are partly determined by the decision context, people's experience with the environment in question, their view of their role, and their ability to cope with uncertainty.

A scientist or technician defines air pollution in terms of particulates and gaseous contaminants which may pose a health hazard or inflict other damage if they persist above threshold concentrations over a certain period of time. These are the criteria used to establish ambient air quality standards. People living in a polluted community are more likely to define air pollution in terms of tangible characteristics (e.g., smoke, haze, bad odors) and observable effects (e.g., dirty laundry, tarnished paint).

The training of scientific personnel tends to be oriented toward a probabilistic view of the world which is not matched by the layman, who may be less at ease with uncertainty in the face of imperfect knowledge. Air quality standards are based on some notion of the probability of deleterious effects occurring when concentrations of contaminants exceed specified threshold levels. The expert uses scientific observations providing data on the production of pollutants and ambient air quality at fixed sites to assess the distribution and seriousness of pollution in a particular community. In a highly mobile society, the personal hazard is changing continually as people move between home, work, and recreational activities, or change their place of residence. The local residents may be aware of and concerned about dustfall and bad odors, but totally unaware of the presence of toxic gases if they lie outside olfactory threshold levels (e.g., carbon monoxide, low concentrations of sulfur dioxide). People may deal with the uncertainty surrounding causes and possible effects of pollution by denying or denigrating the problem (e.g., we don't have it here, it's worse over there). Alternatively, they may admit the existence of pollution, but deny that it affects them personally (Wall, 1973, p. 242).

There are no known studies that have compared awareness and concern about air pollution among experts and residents of a particular community in the United States. However, there is indirect evidence of differences in surveys which have compared community awareness and concern to measured physical pollutants. While recognizing substantial differences between expert and lay appraisals of air quality, it is important not to overlook possible variations among the experts themselves.

While investigating differences in attitudes between public health officials and engineers concerned with water resource management in British Columbia, Sewell (1971) found that the two groups varied in their relative concern for regional problems. The engineers ranked environmental quality problems (air, water, and land pollution) fourth behind social problems (poverty, unemployment, education); urban growth and transportation; and drugs, alcoholism, and crime. Public health officials ranked environmental quality problems above all others. The professions were investigated in two independent surveys in 1967 and 1969. One factor contributing to the different priorities may have been that the public health officials were interviewed in 1969, when the media were paying growing attention to environmental problems.

There were no significant differences in definition or concern about air pollution among five specialist groups in Toronto (Barker, 1973, p. 363). Five student groups were interviewed in a study investigating the ability of potential environmental decision-makers to deal with complex environmental information. Five groups were selected as a sample of the professions and disciplines concerned with air quality evaluation and management: law, medicine, engineering, economics, and geography. Seventy percent of the students defined air pollution in terms of the impact of natural and man-made materials on some part of the environment (either adverse effects upon the environment or quality of life in general, specific effects on the physical and psychological well-being of people, or a range of impacts on the biosphere, health, buildings, and esthetic values). The remaining 30% defined air pollution as any unnatural (i.e. human) addition of impurities into the atmosphere, without identifying any consequences. The lack of variation between the specialist groups was surprising. It might be expected that physicians, for example, would place a heavy emphasis on health impacts, and yet these accounted for only 40% of the medical student responses.

The specialists did not differ in their concern for air pollution as a problem in metropolitan Toronto. Sixty-seven percent ranked air pollution first or second in relation to housing, water pollution, transportation, noise, and inadequate recreation space. Despite agreement on definitions and concern, the five groups held very different views on their potential role in air quality management, and varied in their ability to handle environmental information in a complex and flexible fashion. These results suggest that while specialists hold a common definition of and concern for air pollution, differences in perceived role and information-handling ability will have a major impact on decision-making (including the setting of goals, examination of impacts, analysis of alternative means of adjustment, and selection of management strategy).

Observer Appraisals and Physical Indices of Air Pollution

Public opinion surveys carried out in a number of cities over the last 10 years indicate a positive relationship between awareness of and concern about air pollution, and some physical measures of air quality. Precise comparison of results is impossible because of: different types of pollutants in the various locations; different methods of pollution monitoring and presentation of data; different averaging times of pollution counts; and variations in questionnaire and sampling techniques. However, in general, an increasing proportion of the populations sampled express dissatisfaction or concern about air pollution as concentrations of particulate matter increase. The relationship between observer-based appraisals and gaseous pollutants (e.g., sulfur dioxide, oxides of nitrogen, and hydrocarbons) is more obscure. A number of specific studies are reviewed here, as examples of the ranges of techniques and results.

In 1964, people living in the Greater St. Louis area were asked whether they believed that air pollution was present, and whether they regarded it as a nuisance (U.S. Department of Health, Education and Welfare, 1965). The responses were compared to local pollution levels, measured as suspended particle concentrations and a soiling index. Thirty percent of the sampled population were aware of air pollution in areas where the annual geometric mean value of suspended particles was 80 $\mu g/m^3$, 50% in areas with 120 $\mu g/m^3$, and 75% in areas with 160 $\mu g/m^3$. The proportion of people who considered air pollution to be a nuisance rose from 10% in areas experiencing 80 $\mu g/m^3$ to 40% at 200 $\mu g/m^3$ (annual geometric mean). No concern was expressed at levels less than 50 $\mu g/m^3$. (See Figures 1 and 2.)

De Groot et al. (1966) used two independent samples taken in 1959 and 1962 to determine public opinion about air quality in Buffalo, New York. The proportion of people who considered air pollution as a

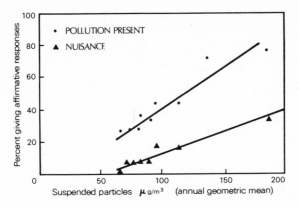

FIG. 1. Relationship between suspended particulate matter and public opinion in St. Louis metropolitan area.

serious community problem was used as a measure of concern. This was compared to a total score of air pollution derived for areas surrounding nine monitoring stations recording suspended particles, sulfation levels, and dustfall. (A single score was possible for each area because the three pollutants were similarly distributed.) The frequency of "serious" responses increased as air quality deteriorated, although the relationship does not appear to be linear. In addition, there was a positive relationship between frequency of days with acute levels of dustfall and suspended particles, and public opinion.

In Nashville, Tennessee, public opinion data were compared with aerometric data from 123 sampling stations (Smith, Schueneman, & Zeidberg, 1964). Low, medium, and high pollution scores were derived from seasonal and annual geometric mean values of dustfall and sulfation levels at each station. The opinion survey included questions concerning the nuisance aspects of air pollution (whether the exterior of the house got too dirty, whether cars got dirty too quickly, and whether too much dust collected on porches and windowsills). Another question, measuring "bother" by air pollution, was embedded in a series of questions relating to health. In response to a direct question, 23% of the respondents said they were bothered in some way by air pollution. There was a positive relationship between particle concentrations and "nuisance" responses. A weak positive relationship existed between pollution level and concern about air pollution as a health problem that

Awareness and Concern		Measured Physical Effects
(St. Louis opinion survey. U.S. Dept. of Health, Education, and Welfare, 1965)		(U.S. Dept. of Health, Education, and Welfare, 1969)
40% Air pollution as "nuisance"	200	
75% Aware 33% "Nuisance"	160	Visibility reduction to 5 miles (Persistent concentrations, not annual geometric mean)
50% Aware 20% "Nuisance"	120	With SO_2 concentrations $>120\ \mu g/m^3$, children likely to experience increased incidence of respiratory disease. With SO_2 concentration $>30\ \mu g/cm^2$ per month, increased deathrate for persons over 50 likely.
30% Aware 10% "Nuisance"	80	Adverse health effects noted. Adverse effects on materials.
Not a "nuisance"	40	
	0	

$\mu g/m^3$ Particulate matter
(annual geometric mean)

FIG. 2. Damage thresholds for particulate matter, and public opinion in St. Louis metropolitan area. Source: U.S. Dept. of Health, Education, and Welfare (1965, 1969).

needed attention. Opinions were influenced by the frequency of days of unusually high pollution.

In a study of Birmingham, Alabama, Stalker and Robinson (1967) found that public attitudes toward air pollution were significantly related to both the annual and winter geometric mean levels of dustfall ($r = .80$, and $r = .82$, respectively; $p < .001$). It appears that as dustfall reached and exceeded 40 tons/square mile/month, 50% of the population considered air pollution to be a general nuisance. At 30 tons/square mile/month, 33% considered air pollution a nuisance. Variations caused by dustfall alone explained 49% (spring) and 68% (spring) of the association between all air pollutants measured, and public opinion.

There was a weaker association between levels of particulate matter and public opinion. Fifty percent thought that air pollution was a general nuisance when mean annual or summer suspended particles reached 230 $\mu g/m^3$, and one-third said that they were adversely affected at 150 $\mu g/m^3$. Public opinion was unrelated to measured gaseous pollutants (i.e., aldehydes, oxides of nitrogen, and sulfur dioxide). However, it should be noted that aldehyde and sulfur dioxide concentrations were very low in most areas.

Jacoby (1972) notes that increased exposure to dustfall, sulfur dioxide, and particulate matter leads to increased concern about air pollution in Detroit ($r = .40$, $r = .32$, $r = .34$, respectively; $p < .001$). Mean monthly figures for dustfall (tons/square mile/month), suspended particles ($\mu g/m^3$), and sulfate index (μg SO_3/100 square cm/day) were used to derive a two-year average at 24 stations. Respondents were assigned air pollution levels for each index on the basis of distance from a given station. The three measures were highly correlated and proved to be largely substitutable as predictors of concern (see Figure 3 for dustfall-concern relationship). Jacoby found concern to be highly localized and not community-wide. People were likely to be concerned if they lived with high levels of pollution. (This positive relationship persisted after controlling for degree of development, length of residence, ownership, income, race, social position, and housing quality.)

The results from these and similar studies suggest that the strongest physical stimuli influencing community awareness of air pollution are particulates (e.g., smoke), soiling of buildings and household objects by dustfall, and visibility reduced by haze. Perception of gaseous pollutants such as sulfur dioxide, oxides of nitrogen, and oxidants depends mainly on sense of smell rather than on visible cues. Although the evidence collected so far suggests a reasonable agreement between

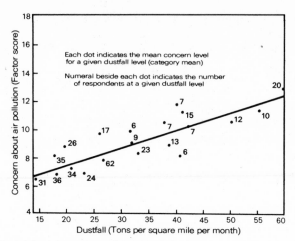

FIG. 3. Relationship between dustfall and concern about air pollution in Detroit. Source: Jacoby (1972). Printed with permission of the Department of Geography, University of Michigan.

observer-based appraisals and physical measures of air pollution, a number of doubts remain unresolved. These concern the accuracy of public assessments of the incidence of gaseous pollutants and the seasonal distribution of pollutants.

The extent of public awareness of gaseous contaminants is a critical issue in assuring the value of perceived environmental quality indices. Some toxic gases are odorless (e.g., carbon monoxide) and cannot be detected by any of our primary senses until symptoms of physiological damage appear (e.g., dizziness, fainting). Others may persist in very low and imperceptible concentrations, but still cause serious physiological and material damage over a long exposure period. Olfactory threshold levels for gaseous pollutants are difficult to determine because of possible synergistic or antagonistic combinations, variability in individuals' perceptions, and the health of the perceiver. However, there are indications of people's inability to perceive toxic gases in the concentrations that generally exist in many cities.

In one study, Toronto residents were unable to perceive differences between degrees of continuously monitored gaseous contaminants (Barnes, 1968). A comparison of olfactory thresholds, lowest observed values of physiological effect, and existing concentrations of major contaminants in Toronto suggests that gases can be perceived only rarely by the primary senses (see Table IV). In this case, direct sensory perception of air pollution must be related to the visual and olfactory stimuli of less hazardous elements rather than to potentially toxic gaseous pollutants. The findings of the earlier study in Buffalo tend to support this conclusion. Important inconsistencies appeared in the relationship between sulfation level (apparently little different from Toronto) and community perception. Similar findings have emerged from studies of observer-based appraisals of water quality. In an investigation of recreationists' perception of water quality in lakes around Toronto, more than 70% of the respondents defined polluted water in terms of appearance, odor, or taste (Barker, 1971, p. 40).

More evidence of the gap between physiological perception of air pollution and people's awareness is found in Barnes's study of Toronto residents. Respondents were asked to indicate which of six specific effects of air pollution applied to them personally. The list consisted of ill effects from particulate matter; dust; odor; discoloration of buildings, laundry, etc.; respiratory irritation; irritation of eyes; and poor visibility or haze. The 56% who said they were affected by particulate matter is a credible finding, as is the 21% affected by poor visibility. However, it

TABLE IV. Gaseous Concentrations in Central Toronto, Threshold and Physiological Effect Levels (ppm)[a]

			Concentrations per hour				
	Olfactory		Mean			Number of	
	threshold	Physiological			Maximum	hours in	Exceeding
Pollutant	level	effect level	Worst month	Year	in year	years	ppm
SO$_2$	.5	.3	.13	.07	.88	37	>.4[b]
			.07	.05	.50	3	>.4[c]
			.17	.10	1.15	112	>.4[d]
NO$_2$	.1	.3	.05	.04	.22	2	>.2
CO	—	2.7	4.15	3.04	15.00	2648	>4.0
Oxidants	.2	.3	.03	.02	.13	0	>.15
	(in smog)	(in smog)					
Hydrocarbons	Various	?	4.14	2.10	15.00	4	>10.0

[a] Auliciems and Burton (1971).
[b] Average of 5 stations.
[c] Least polluted stations.
[d] Most polluted stations.

TABLE V. Seasonal Awareness of Pollution and Concentrations in Toronto[a]

	Spring	Summer	Fall	Winter
SO_2 deposition mean ppm/month (20 stations)	18.8	7.9	15.7	24.7
Hydrocarbons mean ppm/month	3.3	1.0	0.7	1.7
Dustfall mean tons/sq. mile/month	31.4	24.2	22.8	23.8

	Percentage of respondents who observed no seasonality	Percentages of respondents who judged pollution worst according to season			
Toronto	24.5	16.5	31.0	17.0	11.0
Neighborhood	40.5	11.0	25.0	14.0	9.5

[a] Auliciems and Burton (1971).

was surprising to note that 30% reported experiencing respiratory irritation, and a further 30% mentioned eye irritations. Toronto is not subject to photochemical smog and it is highly unlikely that toxic gases have often reached concentrations sufficient to induce respiratory or eye irritation.

When asked if air pollution is worse in any particular season, Toronto residents indicated that summer was the most polluted, despite physical evidence to the contrary (see Table V). Sulfur dioxide reaches maximum levels in winter, while aromatic hydrocarbons and particulate matter peak in spring. (Concentrations of nitrogen dioxide and oxidants do not appear to be seasonal.) The lack of agreement between observer-based appraisals and measured pollution suggests that awareness may be more related to the seasonal behavior of people than to actual pollution levels (Auliciems & Burton, 1971, p. 78).

Given the Toronto findings, it would be worthwhile to reexamine the data from previous studies which cite agreement between awareness and the character and seasonal distribution of pollution. It may be that apparent or positive relationships between observer appraisals and sulfur dioxide are the result of the coincidence of particulate and sulfation levels in a particular city. Alternatively, sulfur dioxide has reached sufficient concentrations to be detectable by the local population. In general, all the studies indicate high levels of public awareness, but point to the conclusion that awareness may be the result of factors in addition to or other than direct experience.

Variations in Air Quality Appraisals as Related to Observer Characteristics

Observer appraisals of air quality have been examined in relation to: socioeconomic characteristics (including age, sex, education, occupation, income, and length of residence); personality variables; complaint rates; and neighborhood characteristics (e.g., housing quality). In only one area, Buffalo, has physiological impairment been compared to observer appraisals.

A unique feature of the Buffalo survey was the availability of medical test results, for some of the respondents in the 1962 sample (De Groot et al., 1966, p. 246). Because of the small sample and wide variations in factors (e.g., age, height) influencing pulmonary function, a measure of breathing capacity was used to indicate level of impairment caused by such diseases as bronchitis and emphysema. The investigators found that more people with severe respiratory impairment said that air pollution was "serious" compared to the other respondents. As bronchitis and emphysema tend to occur more frequently among the elderly, this group is probably more aware and concerned about air pollution than the rest of the population.

In general, studies investigating awareness of and concern about air pollution in relation to socioeconomic characteristics have yielded inconclusive results. Income, education, and occupation have been positively related to concern in some investigations (Smith et al., 1964; Medalia & Finker, 1965) but not in others (De Groot et al., 1966). The discrepancies are due largely to differences in settings, populations, sample designs, and questionnaire techniques.

In Detroit, Jacoby (1972, p. 252) found that concern was not limited to a particular social class, income, age, or racial group, and he dismissed the stereotypes of middle-class whites expressing greater concern. However, higher socioeconomic groups assigned a higher priority to air and water pollution in relation to other urban issues. Lower socioeconomic respondents placed higher priorities on noise and neighborhood appearance. (There were no significant differences between races in ranking priorities.) In an earlier study in St. Louis, Schusky (1966) noted that white suburbanites were more concerned with air pollution than black inner-city residents, who were bothered by poor housing and a rundown neighborhood. Although there are conflicting results regarding the relationship between race and concern, there is evidence that people at low socioeconomic levels, living in the more polluted urban core, are concerned about air pollution but assign higher priorities to more obvious and pressing problems.

In Nashville, Tennessee, groups of high socioeconomic status who tended to live in the relatively cleaner suburbs expressed low concern for air pollution as a community problem (Smith et al., 1964). At high levels of pollution, respondents with high socioeconomic status were more concerned, while at medium and low pollution levels, respondents with lower socioeconomic status showed greater concern. The study brought out the relationship between socioeconomic level and distance from the urban core as it affects trends in concern for air pollution. Jacoby (1972) makes the point that the deteriorating social and physical environment of a neighborhood will contribute to concern for air pollution. In his Detroit survey, low-quality housing was related to concern for air, water, and noise pollution.

In the United Kingdom, one conclusion drawn from the collaborative studies in Edinburgh, Sheffield, and Exeter, was that age, socioeconomic status, and neighborhood interact (Kirkby, 1972, p. 27). Areas with the highest pollution levels were those in which respondents had the lowest mean incomes and social status. Increasing age and low socioeconomic status combined to produce more passive behavior. The most concerned group were middle-class people less than 40 years old and middle-aged skilled workers. Kirkby summarizes overall trends in the three cities by describing two response stereotypes: the first, active concern among skilled workers and middle-class men less than 65 years old, living outside the most polluted areas; and the second, a resigned, passive response from female pensioners living on a fixed income in areas with the highest pollution levels.

In general, the results of a number of studies suggest that an apparent lack of awareness and concern among poor people living in the most heavily polluted areas may be masking other factors. These vary from greater concern about other urban problems to resignation in the face of uncertainty, the inaction of local officials, or fear of higher taxes if action is taken. Of course, some people will not be aware or concerned, particularly in the less heavily polluted areas. Thus, there is a definite need to extend beyond simple estimates of concern and preferences for certain kinds of action, to include a range of individual and community characteristics that influences the choices made and action taken or not taken.

Personality factors may contribute to variations in individual assessments and response to air pollution. This area has received very little attention, but existing studies have focused upon personal theories and beliefs about how events are caused (attribution of causality) and degree of personal control over one's life (Swan, 1970; Kirkby, 1972). It has been hypothesized that people who believe that air pollution is an inescapable act of God or fate will take few measures to protect themselves. On the other hand, people who believe that they are in control of their own destiny may be more likely to take more effective measures to protect themselves. They may recognize the possibility of changing the situation through their own actions, or by pressuring others to take action. No significant relationships have been found between either attribution of causality or external–internal locus of control and responses to air pollution. Both Swan and Kirkby concluded that deficiencies in the psychological tests and sample sizes used prevented a rigorous testing of these notions.

Measures of exposure to pollution appear to be better predictors of concern about air pollution than do complaint rates. In Detroit, there was a very weak relationship between expressed concern in a particular area and local complaint rates ($r = 0.12$, $p < .05$; Jacoby, 1972, p. 179). However, there were stronger relationships between complaint rate and dustfall levels ($r = 0.40$, $p < .001$), and between dustfall and concern ($r = 0.40$, $p < .001$).

Samuels (1971) found some agreement between complaints and level of pollution on Staten Island. Polluted areas had a complaint rate of 20 per 1000 population, while cleaner areas had a much lower rate of 2 per thousand. Although a large proportion of the respondents said they felt concerned about air pollution, the Interstate Sanitary Commission received only 374 complaints from the 61,731 households on the island in 1966. Reasons for the lack of complaints emerged from Samuels's survey. Forty-one percent felt that others had already complained, making their own action superfluous, and a further 20% felt that it was useless because the government would not do anything.

In Sheffield, England, 20% of the respondents said that they would complain and get action from a third party when asked what they would do if air pollution got particularly bad (Wall, 1972, p. 15). However, the number of complaints received by local public health officials fell far below this potential. Either the people who said that they would complain do not feel that the problem is that bad, or they have a similar reaction to the Staten Island respondents. However, there is a problem in specifying the nature of the relationship between observer appraisals and complaints, because complaint records are usually available for neighborhoods or communities rather than specific households.

An Overview of Observer Appraisals

Measured variations in awareness of and concern about air pollution are based upon the nature of the pollution hazard, extent of personal exposure, and the characteristics of individuals and communities. There is evidence to suggest that: differences in daily or seasonal activity patterns of residents lead to significant variations in awareness, as people are exposed to different types and concentrations of pollutants; and awareness is influenced by indirect stimuli such as publicity given to the issue of air pollution, as well as direct sensory perception.

Some degree of consensus exists between observer appraisals and physical measures of air pollution. An increasing proportion of the population is bothered by air pollution as concentrations of particulate matter increase. The dominant physical stimuli are visible pollutants (e.g., smoke), reduction of visibility by haze, soiling from dustfall, and offensive odors. In general, people are unaware of gaseous pollutants unless they are present in very high concentrations, when physical discomfort (e.g., irritation of eyes and nose) can be experienced. There are some discrepancies between the seasonal distribution of pollutants and awareness, which may be explained in terms of variations in activity patterns among community residents.

Differences between lay and expert appraisals can be anticipated because of variations in the decision context, experience, perceived role, and ability to cope with a highly complex and uncertain situation. For example, scientific assessments of community hazard will differ from degree of personal hazard as people move between home, work, and recreational pursuits.

Substantial variations in survey methods have led to conflicting evidence regarding relationships between observer characteristics and environmental appraisals. (This is particularly true in the case of socioeconomic indices.) Social status and personal health appear to play important roles in awareness and concern about air pollution. Several studies indicate that air pollution has low salience, either because there are few channels for expressing dissatisfaction, or because people assign higher priorities to solving other urban problems.

POLICY AND PROCEDURAL ISSUES

Given the complexity and uncertainty associated with air pollution, and the limitations of physical indices of air quality, observer appraisals could be used in preparing environmental impact statements, evaluating ongoing programs and projects, and communicating trends in air quality to decision-makers and the public. However, criteria, standard measures, and means of implementation have to be established before such observer appraisals can play an explicit role in air quality management programs.

Criteria for Developing Standard Perceived Air Quality Indices

To a large extent, decision-makers rely upon complaint records as an index of community concern about air pollution. Complaints may be useful in locating specific sources emitting pollutants, but they are inappropriate as guides to community appraisals of an overall problem. There must be some concern for complaints to be received, but intense concern may exist which bears little relation to the number, kind, or cause of complaints.

Secondary standards for ambient air quality, prescribed by the federal government, are intended to protect amenity as well as to limit damage to vegetation and materials. Despite this explicit goal, no means have been established for identifying or measuring the impact of air pollutants upon amenity or esthetic values. Levels of perceived pollution and nuisance thresholds could well form the basis of observer indices of air quality. Assessments would include checklists and scales for use in identifying the presence and intensity of perceptible pollution (e.g., haze, smoke, odors). Perceived impact and estimates of the significance of damage effects (i.e., in terms of psychic and monetary costs) could be treated in a similar fashion.

Stalker and Robinson (1967) have suggested that ambient air quality standards should be set on the basis of perceived nuisance. For example, pollution could be limited to the extent that less than one-third of the population would complain. This would correspond to an annual geometric mean value of 160 $\mu g/m^3$ for particulate matter in St. Louis (U.S. Department of Health, Education and Welfare, 1965). One of the dangers of this approach is that the thresholds for dustfall and suspended particles selected in such a manner could incorporate acceptance of or resignation to polluted conditions on the part of the population affected. Also, perceived nuisance thresholds may exceed levels at which imperceptible damage occurs. For example, adverse health effects have been identified at concentrations of suspended particles as low as 80 $\mu g/m^3$ (annual geometric mean), particularly when in association with sulfur dioxide (see Figure 2). On the other hand, Samuels (1971, p. 31) notes that more stringent ambient air quality standards have been adopted as a result of the contributions to public hearings held as a requirement of the amended Clean Air Act of 1967.

The question of whether resigned acceptance or higher expectations are being incorporated into ambient air quality standards also has to be faced when developing indices from observer appraisals. Measures of salience and the priority attached to dealing with air pollution should be used in conjunction with observer appraisals. If perceived air quality indices are to be used as criteria for selecting physically based indices and standards, then nuisance thresholds and thresholds of physical damage will have to be compared very carefully. In cases where perceived nuisance exceeds physical damage thresholds, observer indices of air quality should be taken into very serious consideration. Where the damaging pollutants are imperceptible gaseous contaminants, scientific assessments must play a dominant role.

Discrepancies between physical and perceived seasonal distributions of pollution have been explained in terms of seasonal variations in activity patterns. People tend to be more mobile in summer and notice haze and smoke, even though measured levels of pollution may be greater at other times of the year. If this phenomenon is widespread, it will be essential to develop person-centered as well as place-centered indices of air quality. Person-centered assessments would comprise an individual's comparative judgments of home, workplace, transportation, and recreational environments. From these judgments, a series of indices could be derived to describe the perceived quality of that particular set of atmospheric environments. Differences in "environmental well-being" among various social groups could be better inferred from such measures rather than from place-oriented assessments of air quality because of differences in access and mobility.

Given a decision to develop person- and place-centered assessments of perceived pollution levels and nuisance, sets of observers and methods of presenting information must be chosen. An overriding question is who should be the observers? On what bases should they be selected, and by whom? One approach would be to give community residents a voice by encouraging participation by a broad cross-section of local interests, including major polluters, those affected by air pollution, and environmental action groups. Some may feel that representatives of local pollution sources should be excluded on the grounds that this group is better able to present its case within the existing political framework. Exclusion of such groups would tend to give the observer panels an adversary role. In addition, this particular criterion fails to recognize less obvious but significant sources of pollution, including private trans-portation.

To avoid some of these problems, person-centered assessments by residents could be accompanied by place-centered assessments by user-panels (e.g., workers in an industrial plant, housewives in a residential area) and site visits by observers representing a broad cross-section of community interests. If perceived air quality indices are to be incor-porated within the management process, it would be useful for site-visit panels to have access to expert opinion and scientific data on monitored pollutants, as well as local user assessments. This would provide one means of improving information exchange, and could contribute to the process of making trade-offs between perceived and measured pollution at the local level.

Using Perceived Air Quality Indices in Policy Formation and Decision-Making

Observer-based indices of air quality have not been used in the formulation and implementation of air management programs, which have relied upon physical indices of pollution and assessments of risk from various forms of damage. Public input has been limited to hearings held as part of the process of establishing regional ambient air quality standards. Given the restricted forum for public opinion, perceived air quality indices have a number of potential applications, including:

1. Identification of the potential impact of an additional source of specific types and amounts of pollution in the preparation of an environmental impact statement. Some indication of likely impact upon amenity values could be gained by monitoring perceived pollution and nuisance from existing sources, and relating these to the proposed addition.
2. Assessment of the extent to which changes in air quality (e.g., a reduction in particulate emissions) are reflected in changes in perceived nuisance. In this way observer-based indices could serve as one measure of the success or failure of an air pollution control program.
3. Communication of trends in air quality to decision-makers and community residents in a language that all can understand.

Clearly, it is important to take into account public concern about air pollution in any management program, and to provide information which will not only increase awareness but offer some guidelines for individual adjustment and action. In order for information programs to be effective, it is essential to understand how people behave in response to information about day-to-day fluctuations in air quality, and to warnings about air pollution episodes.

Existing information and warning systems, using physically based indices, are probably ineffective because they use scientific terminology and fail to provide guidelines for appropriate individual action. An index based upon coefficient of haze is reported each day through the mass media in Detroit. The M.U.R.C. Index (Measure of Undesirable Respirable Contaminants) is claimed to create public interest but it may have the opposite effect (Jacoby, 1972, p. 250). The measure assumes a positive relationship between community perception and the index value, and it is based upon the false premise that air pollution is a city-wide rather than a neighborhood problem.

Little consideration was given to the kinds of information useful to the public, or to public response when the Air Management Branch (Ontario Department of Energy and Resources Management) established an air quality index in Ontario in 1970. The index was intended as a management tool and it specified thresholds which served as cues for government action. (Such actions range from initial warnings of intermediate readings to major polluters to ordering shutdowns.) As a second stage; a decision was taken to inform the public of action being taken, and index readings (representing sulfur dioxide and particulate levels) were released through the mass media. Changes in public attitude towards air pollution were not anticipated, and if changes were to occur, no provision was made for public response to be articulated within the decision-making process. The index was designed solely as a means of informing the public of government action to reduce air pollution levels in the major centers of Ontario.

In 1971, a study was initiated to examine the impact of the index in four Ontario cities: Toronto, Windsor, Ottawa, and Sudbury. Telephone interviews were administered in a pretest, posttest design. Three sets of interviews were conducted at monthly intervals prior to the introduction of the index in Windsor and Sudbury. This phase was followed by a second series of interviews after the index had been in operation for some time. London (Ontario) and Ottawa were used as control cities to take account of possible changes in public awareness and concern resulting from factors other than the index. There was no significant increase or decrease in concern about air pollution in the four cities. The index had generated neither undue alarm nor false complacency. It has been readily accepted and continues to function as an informational and management tool. It may well be that no attitude change will occur until the index includes information about personal adjustments and outlets for individual action.

For people to make adjustments to daily fluctuations in air quality (e.g., by adopting insulating techniques or by altering their pattern of activity), they need information about existing conditions and forecasts describing future expectations. Individuals and groups who are sensitive to air quality variations have to be provided with information which will not inhibit their range of choice. This means providing forecasts that are responsive to the needs of specific activities and groups, including recommendations as to the full range of options open in making adjustments. This imposes a number of demands on behavioral research, including the need to investigate responses to information from various sources and in different forms, and the ways in which information is used in making choices about alternative actions. As personal nuisance and sensitivity thresholds have not been defined for various community groups, perceived air quality indices could provide criteria for selecting the appropriate information.

A major issue to be faced is that of incorporating observer appraisals of air quality within an overall policy and management framework. There have been a number of instances where conscious attempts have been made to consult and incorporate the views of people affected by environmental management proposals, notably in the field of water resources. In the Delaware Estuary Comprehensive Study, Chevalier and Cartwright (1971) report that there was a concerted effort to involve the relevant public (i.e., those members who would affect and would be affected by the plans). A Water Use Advisory Committee was established to help develop a consensus among the different views of water management choice in the river basin. The Committee served as a vehicle for increasing the participation and cooperation of 16 interest groups, ranging from industrial water users to organizations wishing to improve the aesthetic and recreational amenities of the region. Flow of information was encouraged between the government agencies responsible for policy and management programs, and the interest groups concerned.

In essence, the Committee provided a means of articulating group values and preferences within the decision-making process. As a first step, each member group was asked to identify its water use and quality needs in the form of a general narrative. Each specified water quality indicators where possible. As a second step, the Committee summarized information on the specific location of present and desired future water uses, with the ranges of individual quality criteria associated with each use. These summaries were then returned for comment to the member organizations. In this way, the various goals and desires could be related within one frame of reference. On the basis of the work of the Water Use Advisory Committee, four "water use/quality objective sets" were drawn up, along with estimates of the costs and quantifiable benefits for each alternative.

The lesson to be learned from the Delaware Estuary Comprehensive Study is that user appraisals of existing and desired water use and quality can be effectively incorporated within the policy and management process. There is great potential for applying a similar approach to regional air quality management programs. Advisory committees could be set up to increase participation and cooperation among the many community interests. Air use and quality needs could be described by each group, with air quality expressed in terms of scientific and observer appraisals. Alternative objective sets could be drawn up, based upon a range of social welfare goals and specifying different thresholds of nuisance to be tolerated. In cases where perceived nuisance is low in the presence of damaging concentrations of gaseous pollutants, physical parameters should be used to establish air quality standards. Observer appraisals should play an important role in cases where perceived nuisance exceeds the threshold levels for physiological damage. Alternative management programs could then be evaluated in terms of the relative social costs and benefits of reducing scientifically assessed risk and perceived nuisance by varying amounts.

RESEARCH NEEDS

The value of perceived air quality indices in the decision-making process depends upon the reliability of observer appraisals, the construction of standard measures, and the development of means for including them within a policy and management framework. The preceding review of behavioral research in this field underlines the absence of most of these requirements. Some but not all sources of variance among observer appraisals have been identified. There are no standard, comprehensive measures of perceived air quality. Perceived environmental quality indices have not been used in any air quality management programs to date.

Large, unexplained differences in perceptions of a community air pollution problem would invalidate observer appraisals as useful tools in the decision-making process. There are quite wide variations in awareness and concern, both within and between communities. Some of the variance can be explained in terms of differences in sample and questionnaire design, and time lag between surveys. However, differences remain which can only be explained by reference to the nature of the pollution hazard and to the personal characteristics of observers. Experience of the hazard, personal health (particularly susceptibility to pulmonary diseases), and social class appear to affect responses to air pollution. One problem in specifying the nature of these relationships has been the diffuse nature of the research effort, where different measures of awareness, concern, and salience have been used with few doubts raised about their equivalence.

Cross-sectional studies which use identical sampling and questionnaire designs in communities with different kinds and levels of pollution hazard could resolve some of the apparent inconsistencies. In the one instance of collaborative research, consistent relationships between observer appraisals and social class and experience of the hazard were uncovered in a number of cities (I.G.U. Air Pollution Study Group for the U.K., 1972). A major task is to eliminate sample design and interview techniques as sources of response variation. Specifically, it would be useful to separate out awareness, concern, and salience, which have been used interchangeably in the literature, but which have different implications for observer responses and adjustment to air pollution. It is critical that the range, and nature of personal characteristics influencing observer appraisals be defined. It may well be that social class and other factors act as surrogates for different hazard experiences because of variations in mobility and activity patterns.

With a few notable exceptions (e.g., Hewings, Auliciems, Burton, Schiff, & Taylor, 1972) public attitude surveys have been one-shot case studies with no attempt to examine changes in awareness, concern, and adjustment in relation to changes in pollution hazard or in information from external sources. Longitudinal studies would provide further tests of the consistency of observer appraisals and their responsiveness to external change.

There have been no attempts to develop standard perceived air quality indices. The existing body of research has employed a wide range of criteria and questionnaire techniques for identifying and measuring observer appraisals and response to air pollution. However, we should seriously consider a shift from total dependence on questionnaire interviews to include more interactive approaches. A major effort is required to define criteria and construct scales, checklists, slide sequences, and other procedures as measures of person- and place-centered appraisals. Criteria would include awareness and nuisance thresholds for perceptible pollutants, perceived damage, and perceived significance of impacts. Means of field-recording of responses and techniques of field observation for site-visit groups appear to be the most appropriate avenues to pursue once the relevant criteria have been identified.

Behavioral research faces a major challenge if a serious attempt is made to broaden the range of choices available to groups affected by air pollution, and to incorporate their appraisals within the decision-making process. Although there is reasonable evidence of a positive relationship between some physical measures of air pollution (e.g., dustfall and particulate matter) and observer appraisals, there have been few, if any, studies of the relationship between public perceptions and air pollution indices (e.g., M.U.R.C.). Discrepancies are likely, and these suggest eventual problems in the credibility and public acceptance of physical indices, which have their own limitations. Where the indices reflect gaseous contaminants as well as particulate matter, the discrepancies will be large, unless the levels of the two groups of pollutants are coincidental, or the concentrations of detectable gases have exceeded olfactory thresholds. Variations in response to different types and concentrations of pollutants need to be investigated, particularly in light of apparently inconsistent appraisals of gaseous contaminants.

A major area for investigation lies in the response to information about air quality and management programs. A number of studies suggest that indirect stimuli, such as information from public authorities or mass media, play an important role in influencing community perceptions. In one instance, publicity campaign material has lessened concern about air pollution despite physical evidence that a problem persists (Wall, 1973). Do people vary in their reaction to information from different sources and presented in different ways? What thresholds exist in the presentation of and response to information that affect the process of choosing alternative means of adjustment? Information networks clearly play an important role in community response to air pollution, but these questions have been largely ignored in the research effort to date. Sample designs and techniques have been oriented toward studies of the individual. It would be particularly useful at this stage to reorient research and focus on group interactions.

The inclusion of behavioral research findings within a comprehensive decision framework places critical demands on the cooperation among researchers, planners, and groups within the community at large. An evaluation of apparently successful attempts at community participation (e.g., the Delaware Estuary Comprehensive Study) should offer some guidelines as to actions to be encouraged and approaches to be avoided. The ultimate test lies in establishing a regional air quality management framework in which community appraisals play a role in setting policies and standards, and where comprehensible information is exchanged among experts and community groups.

11

The Perception and Valuation of Water Quality

A Review of Research Method and Findings[1]

ROBERT E. COUGHLIN

Water pollution has been with us for a long time; men have been aware of its presence and have described it in general terms. As their knowledge of biology and chemistry advanced they applied those sciences to its measurement. Aside from limited measurements of drinking water supplies, however, it is only for the past 40 years that water quality data have been collected systematically on water bodies, and only for 15–20 years that data have been collected for a large number of locations. Limnologic measurements of water quality were virtually unknown 15 years ago.

Today if you ask a water chemist or biologist what constitutes pollution and what acts as a good measure of it, you probably will not get a simple answer, and the answers of various scientists will vary considerably. Since there is no single accepted index of water pollution, it is often hard for the nonphysical scientist to know just what is meant when pollution is being discussed. Some efforts have been made to develop a single index of water quality (Brown, McClelland, Deininger, & Tozer, 1970; O'Connor, 1972; Council on Environmental Quality,

[1] This investigation was supported in part by Contract No. 68-01-3199 between the Environmental Protection Agency and the Regional Science Research Institute.

DR. ROBERT E. COUGHLIN • Regional Science Research Institute, Philadelphia, Pennsylvania 19101.

1972), but these have been only partially successful in reducing the multidimensional character of the concept.

Now the social scientist has entered the field, perhaps realizing that water quality is too important to people (and to government policy) to be left to the physical scientist alone. Most of the effects of water quality are not registered through market mechanisms, and its effects cannot all be measured in economic losses to waterfront industries, fisheries, or homeowners. Many of the losses caused by poor water quality are quite outside the economic sphere as traditionally defined. Many do not even affect such activities as swimming, boating, or fishing. The effects also go beyond physical health. They are more in the realm of aesthetics and morality, reflecting the kind of world we want to live in, the kind of responsibility we feel as stewards of the earth.

Since these concepts are so closely bound up with man's value systems, we cannot avoid concluding that man's perception of water pollution is a central consideration in measuring water pollution. To rely solely on objective chemical measurements is not sufficient.

The perception of water quality has a reality of its own which is just as valid, and perhaps of more importance in human decision-making than the reality of the measurement of physical and chemical properties of a water body. Unfortunately, because of our desire to be "scientific," and because of the prestige of numbers (especially those preceded by dollar signs), public decision-making has tended to set aside perceived qualities and to base decisions on what can easily be quantified.

The purpose of this chapter is to discuss some of the methodological considerations in measuring people's perception of water quality, review research which has been done on this subject, and thereby provide a basis for the exploration of where research and policy should go from here.

METHODOLOGICAL ISSUES IN STUDYING THE PERCEPTION OF WATER QUALITY

As in studying the perception of any aspect of the environment, and to a lesser extent of any measurement in physical science, it must be borne in mind that we are concerned here with a relationship between an observer, on the one hand, with all his senses, at whatever level of efficiency they are operating, and affected by his past experiences and associations, and the phenomenon observed, on the other hand, with all its properties. The specific relationship is recorded through some particular measuring instrument, generally in our case some sort of questionnaire.

While this chapter is addressed to the direct relationship between observer and phenomena observed, called perception, it is well to bear in mind that in many situations people may express strong awareness of water quality even though they have not directly experienced the water body in question. Such awareness may be most important in determining the support for legislation and administration programs for pollution abatement. Whereas information received earlier from newspapers, radio, television, and other sources are of relatively less importance in direct perception, they are of primary importance in shaping awareness.

If results of perception studies are to mean anything beyond "it all depends on the individual," we must be satisfied that there is a general agreement among members of a population group on the perception of a particular environment. Correspondingly, some particular environments must be perceived differently from others; observers must be able to differentiate between environments. The ideas of agreement and differentiation are diagrammed in Figure 1.

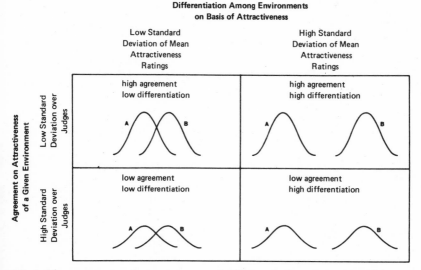

FIG. 1. The concepts of agreement and differentiation diagrammed for two sample environments, A and B.

Although it was stated previously that perception of the environment is a phenomenon in its own right separate from physical measurements of the environment, if no relationship can be demonstrated between the two, the identification of environmental perception will be of little value in changing or preserving the world we live in. If water quality is to be changed, we will have to be concerned with changing the concentrations of certain chemicals, and with other nonperceptual matters. Therefore, we must be able to show some reasonable, though perhaps rough, relationships between water quality as perceived and as measured by physical scientists.

Finally, as in all scientific endeavors, measurements should be replicable: by another researcher using the same instruments, with the same observers at another time when the physical situation is the same, and with comparable groups of observers.

What Is Perceived and by Whom

Levels of water pollution are not constant. They vary on a seasonal cycle based on general rainfall, temperature, and vegetation patterns; on a daily cycle based on light and temperatures; and are affected by random events such as the discharge of particular chemicals, or sudden showers which flush streets and parking areas of oils and dirt. Different pollutants are in evidence at different times; some can be brought under control readily by public programs, others require more heroic efforts. Therefore, the relevance for public policy of any study of pollution perception is affected by what pollution cycle it is measuring. And sometimes it is difficult to tell what situations are being described by a statement of perception, since the observer, especially if he is a resident or frequent user, has probably observed the water body under many levels of pollution.

Perception is affected very much by the use which an observer makes of a water body. Does he live near it, work near it, or visit it explicitly for recreation? The person who walks or drives by a water body can be expected to perceive it differently from a person who wades or swims in it, one who boats on it, or one who fishes in it. These uses suggest four distinct and discrete levels of water quality which probably can be recognized by most people, and have obvious connotations for public policy: water clean enough for swimming and human consumption; water clean enough to go fishing in (that is, clean enough for native fish to live in), but not clean enough to swim in or drink; water clean enough for boating only; and water so foul that even boating is not pleasant.

Specific Problems of Research Procedure

Research on environmental perception involves a number of logistical problems. In order to determine levels of agreement and differentiation, a substantial number of observers should observe the *same* places under exactly the *same* conditions. That is, they should be reacting to the same environmental stimuli. Any place out-of-doors changes slowly in aspect as the seasons change, and suddenly as weather changes. Even within a single day of constant weather conditions the impact of a scene can change dramatically as the angle of the sun changes—freshness, sharp light, and deep shadows of morning give way to a flat, washed-out look at noonday, and are replaced by the tranquility and softness of evening light. Observers only an hour apart might perceive quite different phenomena, and relative ratings with other locations could be confused.

If the research plan calls for bringing observers to the sites, the problem of the changing aspects of the day is combined with the growing weariness of the observer (somehow, sight-seeing is tiring work). The approach to each site, too, may affect the perception of the site. Strong positive or negative reactions to adjacent areas just experienced may linger to affect perceptions of a particular place.

Because of the difficulty of scheduling visits of observers in such a way as to minimize such problems, and because of the expense and complexity of such field observation, much research on environmental perception has been done not in the field, but from color photographs. Results have been quite convincing, and discrepancies between the reactions to such environmental displays and the environment itself appear to be within acceptable limits.

Water pollution, however, is so subtle visually that it probably cannot be identified well from photographs or other environmental displays. Therefore, the observers, it would seem, must do their perceiving in the field.

Two approaches appear to be possible. Either take the observers to the sites of water pollution, or find people on or near the site and determine their perceptions.

The first approach has the advantage that the observers can be the same for all sites and can be selected to be representative of any group desired, but has inherent the logistical problems alluded to above.

The second approach, of going to people already on or near the site, normally involves interviewing residents or water users. Logistical problems are greatly simplified, but the result is a different set of observers for each site studied. These sets then must be related analytically through social, economic, or personality characteristics. And there is no general agreement on the characteristics which can be counted on to explain observer-related variation in perception.

The householder, and to a lesser extent the user, reacts not only to the current water quality conditions, but to his experience and memory of water quality conditions in the past—and it is not possible to know what past conditions affect his present perceptions.

Samples of user populations are almost necessarily made up of persons favorable to the site, and tolerant of its pollution. Residents may share similar positive biases. Panels of traveling observers, however, can be constituted to be more representative of the population at large, or of any group appropriate for the research (for example, a minority group which might not normally have free access to the site).

Thus, there appears to be no simple procedural approach which meets all research objectives and is yet practical.

RESEARCH ON THE PERCEPTION AND EVALUATION OF WATER QUALITY

Introduction

Several subject areas would seem to be appropriate for study: the physical, chemical, and biological characteristics of a water body; the perceptions which are held of these characteristics; the resulting preferences and attitudes toward the water body; and the uses to which it is put. These subject areas are depicted in Figure 2.

Research on these subject areas has been scanty. In fact, we are

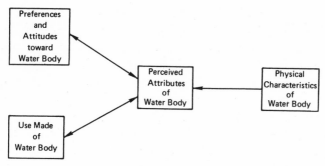

FIG. 2. Subject areas for study.

aware of only six research programs which have addressed these subject areas: that of the Regional Science Research Institute (RSRI); Mary Barker at Simon Fraser University; Robert Ditton and Thomas Goodale at the University of Wisconsin and the University of Ottawa, respectively; K. Jack Kooyoomjian and Nicholas L. Clesceri at the Rensselaer Fresh Water Institute at Lake George, New York; Elizabeth L. David at the University of Wisconsin; and Gene Willeke at Stanford University.

David's work was somewhat more limited than that of the other researchers in that she restricted herself to determining how people would characterize water pollution in general, and did not try to determine their perception of water quality at specific sites.

Both Mary Barker and the Rensselaer group studied lakes, while RSRI studied small streams. Willeke studied a large bay. Barker, Willeke, and the Rensselaer group surveyed users and households. The Regional Science Research Institute also surveyed households, but much of its work was done by taking a group of observers to visit all the sites. Barker, David, Willeke, and especially Ditton and Goodale and the Rensselaer group had large numbers of respondents. Therefore, more weight may be given to their findings than to those of RSRI, whose efforts were more of a pilot nature, in which ways of gathering and analyzing data were explored.

The work done at the Regional Science Research Institute was part of a larger effort to look into the measurement of aesthetic benefits of various configurations of natural and built-up areas that might be achieved through strong land-use controls (Coughlin & Hammer, 1973). As part of this overall work, explorations were made of agreement and differentiation, consistency over time, the use of photographs as opposed to direct field observation, and interviewing in group and individual situations. These studies indicated that individuals do appear to prefer some natural environments over others, with substantial levels of agreement and consistency in their preferences. They preferred parklike scenes to less groomed and more natural land-scapes, and responded negatively to obvious noxious human influences such as junk. Although most of the sites studied contained streams, preferences expressed for these sites did not appear to have been dominated by the streams themselves.

Therefore, to learn more about the perception of streams, two studies were undertaken which focused on how stream preferences are influenced by water quality.

In the first study, the Pollution Perception Study (Scherer & Coughlin, 1971), 12 streams were selected which were as similar as possible physically, but which varied in water quality. Twelve observers, lower-middle-class housewives for the most part, were taken to these sites over a period of two consecutive days. Each filled out a questionnaire on each site, with respect to the area within about 100 feet from the observation spot. While the respondents filled out their questionnaires, two staff researchers rated the stream on a number of attributes referring to physical characteristics and water quality. In addition, water quality samples were taken for all the streams within an hour of each stream site interview.

Subsequently, laboratory analyses were done for the 17 chemical characteristics of the water. Based on these chemical analyses, the streams were grouped roughly by level of organic load. Also, the Water Quality Index was computed for each stream. Although the range among streams was rather wide, extreme conditions are not represented. None of the streams could be described as having unusually good water quality; and there was no dramatic evidence of pollution, such as severe discoloration or major accumulations of foam or scum.

The second RSRI study, the Water Quality–Distance Study (Coughlin, Hammer, Dickert, & Sheldon, 1972), was designed to determine how the attitudes held by residents and the uses they made of nearby streams are affected by water quality and the distance from the stream. For this study a household survey was employed, and published data on water quality were used.

We will now examine the findings of these studies which relate to several basic research questions.

What Is Perceived as Pollution?

An individual's behavioral response to polluted water is based on information supplied by others or on his direct perception of the water body. A primary question, then, is, "How can you tell if the water is polluted?" Answers to this question were obtained by Mary L. Barker in a survey of beach users and lakeside cottage residents in metropolitan Toronto. The results were classified as indicated in Table I.

Willeke's study of San Francisco Bay came up with a somewhat similar characterization of water pollution (1968). Visual evidence of various sorts was cited frequently in response to an open-ended question, with reference being made to debris; garbage; dead fish, birds, and animals; oil; foam; filth; dirty, murky, scummy water; and characteristics such as discoloration, muddy, slimy.

It would be of interest to determine the extent to which visual characteristics, odors, or scientific tests are relied on to identify water pollution. Unfortunately, that is not possible from the published data on these two studies, which refer to the percentage of all responses, rather than to the percentage of all respondents. Since it is much easier to identify specific visual characteristics than specific smells or scientific tests, visual attributes turn up most frequently in the published results.

TABLE I. Criteria Used to Identify Pollution: Results from M. L. Barker
(Percent of All Responses)

Criterion	Beach users %	Cottage residents %
Appearance (algae and floating material)	55.8	47.4
Odor	14.7	11.3
Taste	0.8	1.3
Scientific tests, signs posted	4.1	15.0
Don't know, cannot tell	24.6	25.0
	100.0	100.0

Source: Barker (1971).

The characteristics of perceived water pollution were explored by. Elizabeth L. David in a more general way, without reference to any particular body of water. In a household survey of adults in Wisconsin, an open-ended question was asked: When you think of pollution in lakes or rivers, how would you describe the water? The results, given in the first row of Table II, indicate that green scum and algae, and murky, dark water are the most readily mentioned characteristics. Sewage was mentioned by only 10%, and chemicals (including DDT) and disease germs by only 3% each. A similar response pattern resulted when the respondents were handed a card with six characteristics listed and asked to pick the one thing that "would be most likely to indicate that the water was polluted" (see second row in Table II). Green scum or algae ,was the most frequent choice, suds and foam second, and murky, dark water third.

The study by Ditton and Goodale (1973) found that outdoor recreation participants have a perception of water quality which is significantly different from that of nonparticipants. Participants were more apt than nonparticipants to describe the bay as dirty. Of participants, boaters are most tolerant of bad water quality; swimmers are least tolerant.

TABLE II. What Is Perceived as Water Pollution: Results from E. L. David[a]
(Percent of all Responses)

	Algae or green scum	Murky, dark water	Suds and foam	Debris	Cans and glass	Weeds
When you think of water pollution how would you describe the water? (open-ended question)	40	35	10	20	5	10
Which of the following would most likely indicate the water was polluted?	40	20	25	10	1	3
Which three things on list would deter swimming?	80	40	30	40	70	40

[a] Compare results along rows only, not down columns.
Source: David (1971).

TABLE III. Perceived Characteristics of Eutrophic Lakes:
Results from Kooyoomjian and Clesceri of Rensselaer

	Large lakes	Small lakes
Growth of algae, plants, or scum	55%	50%
Not very clear, muddy	36	44
Buildup of shoreline growth	25	35
Strange odors	29	37
Dead fish	45	35
Strange colors	18	23
Film of gasoline or oil	8	23
No objections	9	5

Source: Kooyoomjian J. J., & Clesceri, N. L. (1974).

Perceived Pollution and Objectively Measured Pollution

Neither the Barker nor the David study makes any objective identification of water quality and, therefore, gives us no insight into the
relationship between pollution as perceived by laymen and pollution as
measured by scientific observers.[2]

In the Rensselaer study perceptions of four lakes were identified.
Two of the lakes were oligotrophic (nutrient-poor) and two were eutrophic (nutrient-rich). Each of these pairs consisted of one large and one
intermediate-sized lake.

The eutrophic lakes were perceived by large proportions of the
respondents to have several attributes characteristic of trophic state, and
of several other attributes which might relate to other problems (Table
III). These characteristics were found by far fewer observers of the
nutrient-poor lakes; no characteristic was identified by more than 12%
of the respondents, except films of gasoline or oil and dead fish, which
were mentioned by about 18 and 20%, respectively, at both lakes.

Cottage or homeowners, fishermen, and other "recreationists"
were questioned separately. "No objections" were cited by recreationists
most frequently, and by cottage owners least frequently. Recreationists,

[2] The Barker study included a field group rating of each water body, with (1) indicating high
quality and (4) indicating low quality. These ratings were not related analytically to perceptions
of water quality, however.

however, did complain more than the other groups about unclear and muddy water, strange colors, and floating objects. Fishermen complained more than the others about films and oils and dead fish on the surface. Cottage owners had more complaints than the other groups concerning strange odors, algae, and irritations to eyes or skin caused by water.

These results indicate the untrained observers have little trouble in recognizing a nutrient-rich condition. It is not possible from this study, however, to determine how perceptions would change for a given change in the degree of eutrophism, since only two conditions were defined: nutrient-rich and nutrient-poor.

If perceptions are to be related to physical conditions, then both must be represented by variables measured on cardinal scales or at least on ordinal scales. In the RSRI Pollution Perception study, water quality was measured by 17 chemical characteristics (all on cardinal scales) and rated on 10 "objective" characteristics. The chemicals for each stream were summarized in the Water Quality Index (Brown et al., 1970) and streams were also classified by organic load.

Of the perceived water attributes, "polluted" was correlated with the largest number of chemical characteristics. It was strongly correlated (.01 level of significance) with chemical oxygen demand, nitrates, and total dissolved solids (179°). It was correlated significantly but less strongly (.05 level of significance) with fecal strep, total phosphate, orthophosphate, nitrogen dioxide, chlorine, total dissolved solids (103°) water temperature, dissolved oxygen, and the Water Quality Index. Other more specific perceived water attributes, especially "transparent," "clean," and "healthy," also were correlated with a large number of chemical characteristics.

The perceived water attribute "polluted" was also found to be correlated with a number of objective ratings: strongly (.01 level) with percent mud and with a rural–urban index; and somewhat less strongly (.05 level) with discoloration and percent rocks. Several other objective characteristics were hypothesized to be related to pollution, but correlations were not found between them and pollution, or any other perceived attribute. These objective characteristics were algae, rooted aquatics, floating solids, scum, bubbles, and clarity. The lack of significant correlations with these aspects of pollution is somewhat puzzling, particularly in view of the substantially higher levels of correlation between perceived attributes and the chemical measurements which were performed with rigorous laboratory procedures. The problem may lie in the imprecision of the "objective" measurements.

Effect of Perceived Pollution on Attitudes and Preferences

It would seem from the foregoing limited studies that people are able to perceive water pollution, and that their perceptions are reasonably consistent with scientific measurements of chemical, biological, and physical properties of the water body observed. Now to be addressed is the question of whether this perception affects attitudes about the site and preferences for it in comparison to other sites.

A person's attitude toward a stream or lake is affected not only by the condition of the water, but also by the characteristics of the surrounding land. These include natural and man-made elements, with all their social connotations. Attitudes and preferences, thus, depend on a whole configuration of elements, of which water quality is only one.

The Regional Science Research Institute Pollution Perception study attempted to explore attitudes by asking the following basic preference questions, to be answered on a scale of 1 (dislike) to 5 (like). "How much do you like the area within about 100 feet which you can see from this spot?" "How much do you like the stream itself?" and "How much do you like the surrounding area?" An additional question was, "Would you like to come back here to do (certain specified activities)?"

Analysis of the responses to these questions indicated that the respondents had a high level of agreement in their attitudes toward a particular stream, and that they clearly preferred some streams to others. Attitudes towards the surrounding areas were not so clear-cut. Agreement was not as complete and differentiation among sites was not so clear. Consistently, attitudes toward the site as a whole were a mix of the two. This distinction is illustrated in Figure 3.

Correlations between the three basic preference questions and perceived attributes of the water are generally high, but tend to involve those attributes which have been seen to be least closely related to pollution. The highest correlation is with the attribute "pleasant," which was earlier found to be correlated with only one chemical measurement

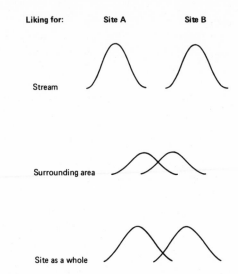

FIG. 3. Generalized findings on agreement and differentiation.

(and that correlation was apparently spurious).[3] Correlations involving the perceived attribute "polluted" were quite small. The correlation between "liking for stream" and "polluted" was among the lowest, and the correlation between "desire to come back" and "polluted" was not significant at the .05 level. Somewhat higher correlations were observed for several other attributes which might be associated with water pollution, namely: transparent, clean, inviting color, and healthy.

The low association between pollution and preference was borne out in direct correlations between responses to the chemical measures and to the basic preference questions. No significant correlations were found. Analysis of variance of streams classified by organic load provides additional evidence that, for this group of observers and streams, water pollution was not an important determinant of preference.

To summarize, the results obtained for the basic preference questions indicate that although observers may be able to discern pollution reasonably well, they may not consider it of great importance to the attractiveness of the site as a whole or even of the stream itself. Liking

[3] Rural streams which tended to receive high ratings on "pleasant" also had high measured levels of fecal coliform, probably due to wastes from grazing herds. Other chemically measured aspects of water quality generally indicated unpolluted water.

the stream does appear to be strongly related to perception of the stream water, but seems to involve characteristics such as "pleasantness," which may not be directly related to water pollution. Even though pollution does not appear to be important to these observers, they do exhibit a high level of agreement on the relative attractiveness of overall stream sites.

Effect of Perceived Pollution on Use

Beyond attitudes and preference toward a place are the uses made of it. Willeke (1968) found that a person's evaluation of the present condition of the bay is very distinctly related to whether his recreational activities have been affected. The "proportions of persons whose recreational activities have been affected by pollution is more than twice as great among persons who think the Bay is polluted as among persons who do not think the Bay is polluted or are not sure."

Barker (1971) found that people used beaches even though the water was obviously polluted. She reported a "tendency among beach users, especially those who used the same beach frequently, to deny or discount the pollution levels at the place with which they were familiar and to express the view that pollution was worse or more widespread elsewhere." However, it is not possible to deduce from her study how use was influenced by perceived pollution.

The RSRI Pollution Perception study approached the subject of use by asking to what extent the respondent would enjoy doing each of several activities at each stream site. (The respondent was asked to assume that he enjoyed each activity equally.) Many significant correlations were found for water-related activities (playing in the water, fishing) and various chemical characteristics of the water. All these correlations indicated that more pollution was associated with less desire to undertake an activity at the site. No correlations were found between chemical measurements of water quality and perceived suitability of the site for activities not related to water (i.e., relaxing, meditating; enjoying the scenery; picnicking).

Significant differences were also found between mean value of each of the water-related activities for each of the four organic load groupings of streams. Significant differences were not found between non-water-related activities for organic load groupings, except for picnicking, and there the relationship appears to be spurious.

A separate study (referred to earlier as the Water Quality–Distance study) was done by the Regional Science Research Institute to explore more fully how water quality affects a person's judgment of a stream site's suitability for given activities and his actual use of the stream site for those activities. This study was done by interviewing 312 residents who lived in various locations which were near 30 different stream sites. Chemical data on water quality, which had been collected on a monthly basis over 2–3 years, were available for each stream site. Since it is not known whether residents base their attitudes and actions on average or extreme water quality, several alternative water quality variables were prepared. Two average observations were computed for each site: the mean and median. In addition, two extreme observations were selected: the second worst month for each chemical and the July observation for the most recent year. The Water Quality Index was computed for each of these alternative sets of water quality variables.

Multiple regression equations were estimated to relate questionnaire responses on suitability for use and actual use (as dependent variables) to water quality, distance of residence from stream, number of children in household, and drainage area of watershed (as independent variables). The last variable, drainage area, has direct implications for the size and character of the stream. (It and distance between stream and residence were expressed in logarithmic form so that given increments to small areas or distances would have more effect than the same increments to large areas or large distances.)

The results of the regression analysis indicate that the higher water quality actually is: the less the stream appears to the residents to be polluted, the better opinion they have of its general attractiveness, the more suitable they consider it for nearly all activities listed, and the more they engage in those activities. The respondents' desire to live closer to the stream and their belief that their own houses and houses right next to the stream are worth more because of the stream also tend to be stronger if the stream's water is cleaner.

In most of the 18 equations concerning suitability for use and actual use, number of children is significant, and in many of them the log of distance between stream and residence is significant. Generally, at least one chemical variable is significant in each equation, with a wide variety of chemicals appearing in the various equations. The summary Water Quality Index is significant in four equations—in more equations than any single chemical. However, the Water Quality Index falls short of acting as a general indicator of water quality which provides explanation of most of the variables concerning perception and use of streams.

A second summary index of water quality was derived by taking the first principal component of each set of 16 chemical measurements. The score of each stream site on this component was then computed to serve as the index. The first principal component, one should note, involves a weighting of chemicals only on the basis of the extent to which each chemical is correlated with the others, not on the basis of which chemicals are judged to be most critical to "water quality." Therefore, it is not formed, like the Water Quality Index, by any explicit concept of water quality. Instead it is determined entirely by the set of chemical characteristics represented in the data on which the principal component analysis is done.

A substantially greater number of significant correlations occur with the first principal component than with the Water Quality Index, although some correlations with the Water Quality Index are higher than with the first component.

The probability of using a stream site falls with increase in water pollution (measured by the first principal component) for nearly all activities: wading and fishing, for which the relevance of water quality is direct; but also walking, sitting, bird watching, and picnicking, for which water pollution is relevant through its effects on aesthetics. Ice skating and ball playing do not appear to be affected by differences in water quality.

It should be noted, too, that the degree of pollution perceived by the respondents is consistent with the computed first principal component based on chemical measurements. Once again this supports earlier findings that nonexperts' perception of water pollution is consistent with many, if not all, chemical characteristics of a water body.

The relationships between measured water quality, use made of the stream, and distance of residence from stream can be summarized in a graph such as Figure 4. (Each curve relates to a different level of water quality.) This shows how the probability that a resident will use the stream bank as a place for walking varies with distance from the stream,

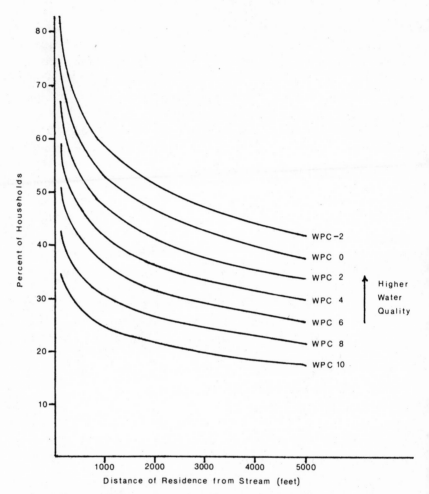

FIG. 4. Effect of water pollution and distance to residence on percent of households which use stream for taking a walk.

and with the water quality of the stream. Such a set of relationships is very useful for planning. It indicates the increased probability of use of the stream if water quality is improved.

The area under the curve for the existing water quality level can act as an index of the present total use which is made of the stream bank as a place for walking, assuming a uniform density of population. Raising the level of water quality to that of a higher curve would add an additional area under the relevant curve, and increase the use index correspondingly. The ratio between the use index with poor water quality and the index with improved water quality is a measure of the increased use which would be made of the stream site. Such analyses can provide the planner with a way to quantify some of the noneconomic benefits of water pollution abatement. To perform this task adequately, the analysis must encompass the important relevant variables and be based on sound empirical studies.

The Valuation of Water Quality Effects

The increased use which will be made of a site if water quality is improved is only one of the values which derive from water quality improvement. The valuation of water quality, and of the natural environment in general, cannot be reduced to a single dimension. A set of discernibly different types of values are involved, although there is some overlap between them. One categorization of these values is (Berry, 1975; Berry, 1976):

Recreational values—among the most prominent, though not necessarily the most important. Swimming, wading, fishing, walking, picnicking are among the activities relevant here.

Contemplative and aesthetic values—what Kenneth Craik (1961) calls ". . . that complex of memories and instincts which are awakened in the average man by the word 'beauty.'" These may be enjoyed by simply knowing that an environment exists, without even actually visiting it.

Functional values—in which the environment functions to promote human welfare, production, or consumption. For example, cleaner water may act to reduce disease, reduce economic loss downstream due to dirty water, reduce water treatment costs downstream.

Ecological values—in which plant and animal communities are felt to be valuable in themselves and therefore ought to be protected. The concern here is not for the well-being of people but for the well-being of other forms of life for their own sake.

The economist typically looks at value from a restricted viewpoint. A thing has value if someone is willing to give up something (usually money) for it. Value is stated in terms of the trade-off of money or other goods which would be made for, say, an improvement in water quality. An elaborate analytic structure has been developed in which such trade-offs are related to the individual's prespecified and alternative resulting levels of utility. Such utility values may summarize a good proportion of the types of values listed above—recreational, contemplative, functional, and ecological. However, they cannot reflect these values fully. The idea of trading off money, or anything else, to compensate for the diminution of several of these values appears to be so foreign that one could not expect this ingenious economic analysis to suffice.

Bearing in mind that it does not tell the whole story, the utility approach, nonetheless, provides a worthwhile method for estimating a major portion of the value of changing the level of perceived water quality.

In its simplest application the utility approach involves asking people about their willingness to pay (with regard to their present income levels) for a level of water quality in a particular stream or lake with certain perceptual attributes. This is essentially a two-dimensional trade-off question—exchange of money for water quality. Although many practical objectives may be raised against simply asking about people's willingness to pay (people might lie, refuse to answer, or have no idea what they would be willing to pay), exactly this kind of question has been answered before for open space with results which have stood up under scrutiny (Berry, 1974; Berry & Coughlin, 1973; Knetsch & Davis, 1966; Brown & Hammack, 1972). And now a study is under way on the willingness to pay for water-based recreation.[4] Because this method can handle only one general attribute of water quality at a time, however, a most robust method is needed.

Such a method is the so-called Cassandra method (Berry & Steiker, 1974), which has been developed and used in evaluations of open space at the Regional Science Research Institute. It is being applied to the perception of water quality in a study which has just begun.[5]

Whereas asking about willingness to pay involves only a two-dimensional trade-off (water quality and money), the Cassandra method incorporates multidimensional trade-offs. In particular, the respondent is shown a short list of scenarios concerning a stream or lake which he

[4] Study for EPA being performed by Urban Systems Research and Engineering, Inc.
[5] Contract with EPA concerning: "Economic Quantification of Aesthetic Considerations of Water Quality Benefits from Abatement of Visual Pollutants."

or she lives near or which he or she is visiting. These scenarios have varying quantities of attributes. The respondent is asked to rate each scenario on a scale of 0 to 100, with a score of 50 or more indicating approval of the scenario. Thus, it is possible to consider simultaneously the effect of several water quality attributes, including the annual cost to the individual household of maintaining various water quality levels. One of the scenarios should correspond closely to existing conditions, and the respondent would be told this. For example, a set of scenarios for a stream near the respondent's home may look like the following:

Respondent's ratings	Annual cost to respondent	Water quality attribute(s)		Amount of trash and litter along banks
1. _____	$5	a_1	b_1	Almost none
2. _____	$10	a_2	b_2	A lot
3. _____	$40	a_3	b_3	Almost none

The elements of each scenario are selected using the Gram-Schmidt orthonormalization method (Lipschutz, 1968, p. 283), such that the quantities in each column are independent (uncorrelated). Attributes like "water safe enough for swimming" and "amount of trash and litter along banks" are ordinal and are quantified by ranking them: 1, 2, 3, and so on. The purpose of using uncorrelated attributes is so that the partial correlations between scores on scenarios and attributes are unambiguous (i.e., not collinear).

The Cassandra method can be used with three or four attributes with little difficulty on the part of the respondent. With the exception of cost to the respondent, the attributes selected for analysis correspond to the major components of the perception of water quality.

Pooling of respondents by distance of their home from the stream or lake, socioeconomic background, demographic similarities, etc. allows one to regress the respondents' ratings on the (repeated sample of) attributes. The regression coefficients then identify which attributes are most important to that group of respondents. Moreover, the coefficient of each attribute divided by the coefficient of the cost attribute yields a marginal rate of substitution between attributes in terms of dollars or willingness to pay.

Empirical research using this technique for valuation of people's perception of water quality is just now getting under way. Therefore, results cannot yet be reported.

CONCLUSIONS

General relationships, based primarily on research conducted by RSRI, are summarized in Figure 5. The results of this pilot research indicate that people can perceive water pollution and that the perceived attributes reflect a good number of, if not all, commonly measured physical attributes. Preferences for a water body are related to perceived attributes of the water itself, and even more strongly to perceived attributes of the surrounding area. The judged suitability of a water

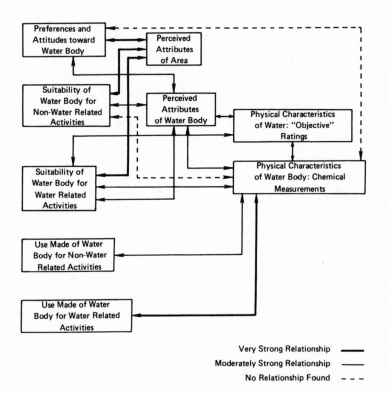

FIG. 5. General summary of relationships found in RSRI research on perception of water quality.

body for various activities, also, is related to perceived attributes of the water body and even more strongly to perceived attributes of the surrounding area.

Actual use made of water bodies is related to chemical characteristics of water pollution. Indices which summarize diverse chemical attributes of water quality are correlated with perception and use and so are useful in relating the perceived environment to the physical environment.

The relationships drawn in Figure 5 must be considered "impressionistic," since they summarize relationships between numerous specific variables, and the pattern of these individual relationships varies substantially. At any rate, all these relationships are tentative, since they are based in most cases on one study, often employing a small number of observers, and concerning only a limited variety of environmental situations. The relationships must be probed by repeated studies before we can point to a true body of agreed-on scientific findings.

Less work appears to have been done on the valuation of perceived water quality than on the perception, itself, of water quality. However, methods involving two-dimensional trade-offs and multidimensional trade-offs have been used to a limited extent and appear to be promising approaches to scaling many, if not all, of the values people assign to water quality.

Human Evaluations of Environmental Noise[1]

NEIL D. WEINSTEIN

State Route 18 comes to a sudden end in the center of New Brunswick, New Jersey. The automobiles traveling on its six lanes create huge traffic jams as they enter already congested city streets or try to cross a narrow bridge across the adjacent river. For years city leaders have hoped to extend Route 18 through New Brunswick, threading the roadway between the dormitories of Rutgers College and the Raritan River. As plans for the extension became concrete, Rutgers students began to lobby actively to keep the highway from being built.

Just two months before an environmental impact study of the project was to be completed, arrangements were made to include in the final report an assessment of the human impact of the highway. A study was quickly carried out by two psychologists (Suedfeld & Ward, 1972) to determine student reactions to the anticipated noise levels. Powerful loudspeakers placed outside a dormitory broadcast recorded highway sounds toward the building for three days. Observers in classrooms located on the first floor watched for possible changes in classroom

[1] The preparation of this chapter was supported in part by a grant from the Rutgers University Research Council. I would like to thank Gretchen Condran and Carol Weinstein for their helpful comments on an earlier version of this manuscript.

DR. NEIL D. WEINSTEIN • Department of Human Ecology and Social Science, Cook College, Rutgers University, New Brunswick, New Jersey 08903.

behavior, and students completed questionnaires giving their evaluations of the noise. Reactions to the sound were "uniformly, strongly, and sometimes violently negative" (Suedfeld & Ward, 1972, p. 70). Several times the cables to the speakers were cut, and students vowed that the equipment would be destroyed if it were ever left unguarded.

Yet, the final summary prepared by the engineering firm conducting the impact studies (New Jersey Department of Transportation, 1972) did not even mention the findings from the simulation; it referred only to published Federal Highway Administration noise standards. A different section of the impact statement referred to the "indignation, hostility and prejudicial attitude of an apparent majority of those who participated in the . . . experiment" (p. 1–97), implying that the students' evaluations should be ignored because their minds were made up before the study began. Denying even the relevance of the simulation to the impact studies, the report declared that "ideally, such testing should have been conducted on an existing campus along an already established freeway where (a) students, faculty and others would have had time to adjust to the ambient noise levels and (b) the subjects would not be fighting the threat of new construction" (p. 1–92).

This case history illustrates some of the controversies which arise in attempts to use human appraisals to assess environmental quality. Should human perceptions or physical indices be used to evaluate the environment? What groups of people should be chosen as judges of environmental quality? In what setting and in what form should their evaluations be gathered? How do the possibilities of conscious or unconscious bias affect the potential usefulness of person-based evaluations? Answers to such questions have immediate practical consequences, determining which impacts are allowed to occur and how environmental regulations are established.

There are convincing reasons why human appraisals are needed. High levels of noise have a wide range of unpleasant effects on people (Kryter, 1970; U.S. Environmental Protection Agency, 1971b, 1974b), but the only clearly documented *health* hazard is hearing loss. If environmental quality is defined solely in terms of health, then a limit of 70 decibels (chosen to protect hearing) appears to be safe, even on a long-term basis. Still, nearly half of the people who actually live with this amount of noise are highly dissatisfied (U.S. Environmental Protection Agency, 1973, p. 31).

In order to specify a noise level which people find acceptable, one clearly has to take into account behavioral effects—interference with communication, relaxation, and sleep; subtle changes in physiological state; distraction and decreased mental efficiency—which do not necessarily lead to any illness. Unfortunately, these effects are difficult to study under natural conditions and are very hard to quantify. Attempts to define environmental quality in terms of these behavioral phenomena are further complicated by the fact that a person's reactions are strongly influenced by other factors, such as the setting in which the noise occurs and the importance of the activity which is interrupted. People are far more tolerant of noise on a city street than in the privacy of their living room, and even a barely audible sound can be infuriating if it keeps someone from falling asleep. It seems that the only way to learn whether the disruptive effects of noise are within acceptable bounds is to ask the people who are actually exposed to the noise.

It is interesting to note that while noise standards based upon human evaluations will be far more restrictive than standards based upon direct health effects, the opposite is true for most types of air and water pollution. Person-based appraisals of air and water quality reflect two main factors: the presence of substances which have odors or unpleasant tastes or which produce haze, dustfall, or turbidity; and people's general impressions of the healthfulness of their surroundings gained from information in the mass media (Barker, Chapter 10; Coughlin, Chapter 11). Although human beings are very responsive to information received from the auditory system, they are not so sensitive to hazardous substances in air and water. Many toxic agents, including carbon monoxide and infectious bacteria, cannot even be detected by our senses. Since air and water pollution do not repeatedly intrude to disrupt our daily activities, in the absence of informational campaigns designed to arouse public opinion, standards for pollutants based upon individual judgments of environmental quality will generally be less restrictive than standards based upon health hazards.

The focus of this chapter is the individual's evaluation of noise within the community where he lives. It will describe scales constructed to measure these evaluations, the relationship between noise level and dissatisfaction, factors other than noise which influence annoyance, and ways these person-based noise indices might be used for predicting and assessing environmental quality.

MEASUREMENT AND INTERPRETATION

Indirect Assessments: Community Action, Complaints, Laboratory Simulations, and Site Visits

There are several different ways one might try to learn how individuals feel about the noise in their home environment. Organized community action—passage of noise ordinances, legal suits brought against major noise sources, testimony before public meetings on noise problems—is one possible indicator. These are the responses airport operators worry about and the factors which have been most responsible for stimulating noise research. Another approach is to monitor complaints made to police, newspapers, airport officials, and highway administrators. Like community protests, complaint activity can be determined inexpensively from public records. Both responses, however, represent a very small proportion of the population and are sensitive to a variety of extraneous factors. Complainants, for example, are not typical community residents. They are not necessarily any more bothered than others exposed to the same noise levels, but they generally have more confidence that their complaints will bring action because they are better educated, wealthier, and have higher status occupations (Borsky, 1973; Tracor, 1970b). Organized community action is a very unstable indicator. It is strongly influenced by community structure and leadership and by the likelihood that protest and action will pay off. Since both approaches yield poor predictions of the sentiments of an average individual within the community, investigators are practically unanimous in rejecting them as indicators of environmental quality (Borsky, 1973; McKennell, 1974; Rylander, Sörensen, & Kajland, 1972).

A third paradigm (Kryter, 1970) brings subjects to a laboratory where they are asked to judge the loudness or noisiness of separate sounds. While much has been learned in this manner about the intensity and frequency characteristics of perceived noisiness, the difficulty of extrapolating from these brief exposures to an overall judgment of the complex home environment is obvious.

A different procedure would employ a traveling panel of judges who would rate the noise in the various sites they visited. Such a panel would have the advantage of bringing the same set of attitudes to each location. Still, listening to noise while standing on a street corner is not an ideal way to decide what it is like to actually live in a neighborhood, and the visitors' assessments would probably be influenced by the sound levels which exist in their home communities, raising questions about how the participants should be selected. Panels of judges may turn out to be most useful in conjunction with more direct assessments of community opinion, where discrepancies between the residents' and visitors' evaluations might provide information about the possibility of adaptation and about particular attitudes which sensitize or desensitize people to noise.

Direct Assessments: Community Surveys

It appears that the most appropriate way to determine human evaluations of environmental noise is via direct responses to interview questions in community surveys. Most of the many noise surveys which have been conducted around the world follow a similar format, disguising themselves as general studies of community living conditions. Residents are given opportunities to mention noise spontaneously in response to questions about the things they dislike in the neighborhood or about the things which they would like to change, before any specific questions about noise are asked. The more structured and direct the question, the greater the percentage who report dissatisfaction (Jonsson, Arvidsson, Bergland, & Kajland, 1974). So long as the purpose of the interview is disguised, few people spontaneously refer to noise even in areas where a large proportion of the residents say it bothers them, in response to specific questions. Failure to mention noise in the early stages of the interview, then, does not necessarily imply that people are satisfied with this aspect of their environment. They may think the interviewer is really interested in community services or housing and may be thinking about these topics.

The specific noise questions may be phrased in terms of the noisiness of the neighborhood—"very quiet" to "very noisy" (Galloway & Jones, 1974), the acceptability of the existing noise level—"definitely satisfactory" to "definitely unsatisfactory" (Griffiths & Langdon, 1968), the frequency with which people feel annoyed by the noise—"never" to "very frequently" (McKennell & Hunt, 1966), or the degree of annoyance noise causes—"not at all annoyed" to "very much annoyed" (Rylander et al., 1972). Answers to these questions may depend upon the specific words used to label the scales (Jonsson, 1964; Jonsson, Paccagnella, & Sörensen, 1969; Tracor, 1970, p. 33). For example, *irritation* is considered a stronger term than *disturbance,* and *annoyance* is considered stronger still. In a laboratory study where several groups used differently labeled scales (Sörensen, 1970), the stronger the term, the smaller the number of people who appeared to be bothered by the aircraft and highway noises they listened to.

Evaluative Judgments versus Annoyance

How a question is phrased should depend upon the kind of response one wants to measure. All dimensions of the environment can be evaluated on scales labeled "high quality–low quality," "desirable-undesirable," or "like–dislike." These are evaluative judgments, cognitive classifications based upon commonly accepted standards, personal preferences, and, to some extent, on available alternatives. A scale ranging from "very noisy" at one end to "very quiet" at the other would represent an evaluative judgment. Most noise surveys, however, have attempted to assess "annoyance," often in relation to activities which are disturbed. In doing so they are using the individual's self-reports to indicate whether noise is causing any adverse behavioral effects or emotional distress, not whether the noise level lives up to some abstract standard of environmental quality.

Although investigators seldom attempt to explain what they mean by annoyance, it seems that annoyance in this context should be identified as a mild form of anger (cf. Borsky, 1961, p. 169, 1973, p. 4; Cason, 1930). As an emotional state it combines cognitive activity with the action tendencies and physiological changes which together compose the feeling of anger (Arnold & Gasson, 1968). This identification is supported by several strands of evidence. First, the words *irritated, aggravated,* and *angry* are often used in place of *annoyance* to indicate somewhat weaker or stronger versions of the same response (Jonsson et al., 1969; Tracor, 1970a, p. 33). Second, anger is the typical reaction to the frustration which occurs when a person is prevented from reaching a desired goal (Berkowitz, 1962; Lazarus, 1966). In the same way, annoyance usually occurs when noise interferes with conversation, relaxation, sleep, or similar activity. Finally, anger tends to be strongest when a person believes that the harm or frustration he experiences is unnecessary and could have been avoided and when the injury is interpreted as an affront to his self-worth (Lazarus, 1966, pp. 205–207). Similarly, people are particularly annoyed by noises which seem unnecessary (squealing tires, motorcycles) and which imply a disregard for their rights (neighbors playing loud music late at night).

A vicious circle may exist in which the more angry a person feels, the more difficult it is for him to attend to anything other than the sound. This, in turn, further disrupts the activity he has been engaged in. In this way, a person's attitudes toward the noise and noisemaker may determine both his annoyance and the degree to which activities like reading, relaxing, and sleeping are actually disturbed.

When annoyance is regarded as a negative emotion rather than as an aesthetic preference, it may be easier to understand why many people believe a quiet environment is more than just an amenity and why exposure to high levels of noise can be an extremely unpleasant and distressing experience. (Samples of public comments can be found in U.S. Environmental Protection Agency, 1972, pp. 338–351.) If anger is a natural response to interruption, then noise-provoked annoyance is not a passing fad arising from current values but part of our biological inheritance. The intensity of the annoyance, however, will be a function of the degree to which the individual views the noise as inevitable and unavoidable or as an unnecessary insult.

Deciding that annoyance is an emotional state alerts us to a number of potential measurement difficulties. The assessment of emotions is a notoriously difficult subject. Self-reports of emotions often correlate very little with physiological indicators of emotional arousal (Lang, Rice, & Sternbach, 1972). An accurate report requires that the person be fully aware of his inner feelings, be able to classify and describe these feelings, be able to relate his own descriptions to the categories offered by the interviewer, and be candid in his description of these feelings. People are often unaware of their own emotions, however, and anger is a particularly threatening emotion which is often repressed or distorted. People also find it difficult to describe how they feel, and they may be quite unwilling to talk about their emotions with an interviewer who appears suddenly at their front door. Negative emotions, in particular, are dissonant with the socially desirable image we wish to present in public (Phillips, 1973). Psychologists designing tests to identify people who consistently respond to questions in a socially desirable manner (Crowne & Marlowe, 1960) find that such people will not admit to feeling anger, irritation, or annoyance and deliberately include questions about these emotions in their scales. Some people tend to interpret any expression of emotion as an indication of mental illness (Lefcourt, 1966). Furthermore, different cultures vary in the interpretations they give to open expressions of emotion (Pancheri, 1975). Because of these factors, it is possible that annoyance is consistently underreported by those interviewed.

Obviously, I think it is 'useful to make a distinction between appraisals of the noisiness or perceived quality of an area, on the one hand, and assessments of annoyance on the other. These two variables are probably determined by somewhat different situational and personality factors and represent somewhat different internal responses. Although the variables usually parallel each other, they do not always agree. Some people say that an area is rather noisy and even interrupts their activities, but that they do not feel bothered by the noise (e.g., Borsky, 1961, p. 50; Jones, 1971). Others are upset by relatively faint sounds. Evaluative judgments may be somewhat easier to measure accurately, but annoyance seems to be a more severe and undesirable impact. Both approaches should be pursued until more is known about their differences and similarities.

Comparative Judgments

A different type of question, unlike those already considered, asks the individual to put aside his own personal likes and dislikes and compare his environment with some commonly understood standard of quality (Craik & McKechnie, 1974). In the present context such a comparative judgment might ask an individual how the noise in his neighborhood compares with that in most other communities. In contrast to evaluative judgments, such appraisals are expected to show greater consensus among raters and less dependence upon individual idiosyncrasies. Comparative judgments have not yet been used to rate environmental noise. One might argue, however, that the role of person-based environmental quality indicators is, precisely, to determine how individuals feel about their environment. An approach which specifically asks people to set aside their own personal judgments in making an evaluation must be influenced by community stereotypes and by conjectures about how others feel. If a person living in a very noisy area, for example, does not realize that others share his distress, the comparative judgments he gives may be consistently biased toward more neutral evaluations than judgments based upon what he himself feels.

Scale Construction

A single question is used as the index of dissatisfaction in some surveys (Grandjean, Graf, Lauber, Mejer, & Müler, 1974; Griffiths & Langdon, 1968), but often a number of questions (usually between 5 and 12) are combined to form a composite scale (Leonard & Borsky, 1974; McKennell, 1963; Tracor, 1970b). There is no agreement on which method is best. Most research on aircraft noise, however, has followed the procedure worked out by Borsky (1961) in which the respondent is asked whether noise disturbs a list of specific activities, such as reading, television watching, and sleep, and how annoying he finds each disturbance. The answers are then formed into a Guttman scale. The activities interrupted do seem to form a hierarchy as Guttman scaling requires (with television mentioned most frequently and sleep least often), but sometimes the hierarchy is not very well defined. A number of investigators have suggested that a simple summation of the annoyance responses is preferable to the more complicated Guttman procedure (McKennell, 1969; Tracor, 1970b; Grandjean et al., 1974).

Yet a third method of scale construction assigns different weights to the questions according to the relative scores obtained from factor analysis (Connor & Patterson, 1972, pp. 127–133; Tracor, 1970b). Although principal moments factor analysis does appear to be a reasonable way to determine which items most strongly tap the same general dimension, the factor rotation used in these studies does not seem appropriate. The factors obtained by rotation are largely a matter of the pool of items under consideration. Adding several questions about sleep interference, for example, will probably cause sleep disturbance to appear as a second factor. When the principal factors are rotated, the contribution of the sleep questions to the first factor (which reflects general annoyance) will be minimized. If only the first factor is then used to indicate the problems caused by noise, sleep will not be properly represented and the results obtained (Connor & Patterson, 1972, pp. 133) will be poorer than if equal weights had been assigned to all items in the pool. Experience in attitude measurement suggests that unit weights are usually preferable since unequal weights are often unstable and do not improve predictive ability significantly (Nunnally, 1967, pp. 277–279).

Scale Validation and Interpretation.   Perhaps because all the questions used in the various scales of dissatisfaction seem so eminently reasonable, there have been relatively few attempts to determine the reliability or validity of noise indices (exceptions are Jonsson et al., 1974; McKennell, 1969, 1974), or even to discuss the kinds of evidence that might be needed to establish these properties. When indices are based upon several questions, measures of internal consistency are usually reported and are sufficiently high to indicate that the items included are directed toward the same content (McKennell, 1963, p. J-9; Office of Population Censuses and Surveys, 1971, p. 80). On the other hand, since the questions employed are usually phrased identically and are asked one after the other, the apparent internal reliability may be inflated by the similarity in wording and the respondent's desire to appear consistent. Reports of test–retest stability, which would help to resolve this question, are rarely reported. One German study (Rohrmann, Schümer, Schümer-Kohrs, Guski, & Finke, 1974) noted ambiguously that the stability of its survey variables was "on the whole satisfactory," while Borsky (1972) in an unpublished study reports test–retest correlations of .75, so perhaps these fears are unwarranted. Nevertheless, more attention needs to be paid to the stability of measures used, especially since stability is the only measure of reliability which can be used with a single question index. None of the studies using such an index has ever reported test–retest data.

Having criticized relatively objective indicators of dissatisfaction like complaint frequency and organized community action, we must admit that an individual's thoughts and feelings are internal responses and cannot be measured directly. Consequently, it is impossible to propose a set of external criteria which are sufficient to determine the validity of the self-report measures generally used. Still, an index of noise disturbance would be unreasonable if it were totally unrelated to noise exposure, or to specific behaviors like decisions to move to a quieter area and advocacy of strict noise control regulations. These behaviors are influenced by far too many extraneous factors, however, to make us want to use them instead of answers to more direct questions. Bragdon (1970), for example, found that the people who were most bothered by aircraft noise were *least* willing to share in the cost of noise control; they felt strongly that since they were not responsible for the noise, they should not have to pay to have it removed.

The proper interpretation of the measurement scale eventually selected can only be established by demonstrating its links with other opinions and behaviors. It should increase in a reasonable manner with noise level and with other noise-related attitudes, but these should be regarded as establishing the meaning of the scale, not its validity.

Investigators of noise around London's Heathrow Airport (McKennell, 1963, 1974; Office of Population Censuses and Surveys, 1971) have made the most notable and systematic attempts to establish the meaning of the annoyance scale employed in their surveys. By demonstrating its relationships to a variety of other questions they have shown that a Guttman scale based upon activities disturbed does have all the properties desired of a measure of annoyance. Yet, a simpler one-question scale used in a Scandinavian survey (Rylander et al., 1972) also had these same general properties.

The goal of most noise research has been to develop a physical indicator to summarize the noise levels in a community which will predict how people rate their environment. Numerous studies have attempted to maximize the relationship between the human evaluations and the various physical measures of noise exposure considered. Since this work is primarily concerned with the size of the correlation coefficient, only relative measurements are important and little attention has been given to establishing the meaning of different points on the annoyance scales (a point also discussed by Jonsson et al., 1974). This distinction between absolute and relative measurements has immediate, practical implications. Many surveys have been analyzed in terms of the percentage of people highly annoyed at a given noise level, and discussions of possible noise standards using these findings are phrased in terms of the number of people who would be highly annoyed by the maximum level permitted (U.S. Environmental Protection Agency, 1974a). These discussions proceed without any serious effort to decide at what point a person should be classified as "highly annoyed." Does a person who indicates that he is very annoyed when noise disrupts one activity qualify for this label, or must he indicate that he is very bothered by the disruption of seven different activities? These different criteria would have a huge effect on the number of people who appear to be protected or unprotected from serious disturbance by the proposed standards.

When the index is based upon a single question—for example, a question which asks whether the individual is not annoyed at all by noise, a little annoyed, moderately annoyed, or very much annoyed—the interpretation of different scale points is relatively straightforward because the language in which the results will be interpreted is the same as the language in which the questions were asked. When a scale is based upon a half dozen different questions or more and scores can range from 0 to 45, the situation is more complex. In this case, only additional studies can determine the significance of the combined score.

The same process which established the interpretation of the 6-point Guttman scale used in the Heathrow Airport studies also gave meanings to each of the scale points. Scores of 4 or more were chosen to indicate that people were "highly annoyed" because the typical person with this score rated himself very much annoyed when asked directly, mentioned aircraft more frequently than all other problems in the neighborhood, and tended to say that his sleep was disturbed. Any cutting point, however, is necessarily arbitrary. Why should sleep rather than rest and relaxation be singled out? On what basis do we decide that a person who considers himself moderately annoyed is not adversely affected? Furthermore, the frequency with which noise is singled out as a neighborhood problem must depend on the number of other serious problems which confront a community. In spite of these questions, this dichotomization is far more defensible than it would be if such supporting data were not available.

Measurement problems have been discussed at length in this section in order to indicate the various factors which need to be considered and controlled, not to suggest that person-based indices are impractical or that the assessment of environmental quality should be limited to physical indicators. All the assessment techniques discussed, whether emphasizing evaluative judgments or annoyance, and based on one question or several, seem to provide meaningful, quantitative measures of human appraisals. On the other hand, these measurement scales are not interchangeable. The correlations between similar indices are sometimes surprisingly low. In my own work I constructed two scales of annoyance from data collected in a large community survey (Appleyard & Carp, 1973). One scale contained questions referring to activities disturbed by noise and asked how annoying each disturbance was. The other mentioned a series of different noise sources and asked how much annoyance each of these caused. The two scales showed a high degree of internal consistency, but, in spite of the similarity of phrasing, the correlation between the two was only .54. A question phrased in terms of the noisiness of a community in one study showed even less agreement (a correlation of .32) with a scale of annoyance employed at the same time (variables 2 and 19 in McKennell, 1963). Since there is at present no good reason to choose any one scale over another, research should continue with different scales, ideally with several represented in each study of environmental noise, until their relative merits become clear. However, since people are unaccustomed to evaluating their attitudes and emotional responses in terms of a prescribed set of categories, it seems likely that indices based upon several questions and referring to specific, familiar situations will prove more accurate and stable than indices based upon a single question or questions asking for global evaluations.

APPLICATIONS

Dose–Response Relationships

The scales devised to quantify human evaluations have been used in several different kinds of investigations. A number of studies of specific communities have tried to learn whether local residents were seriously bothered by noise without attempting to relate their reactions to the noise levels actually present (Bragdon, 1970; U.S. Department of Housing and Urban Development, 1967). These studies help to assess general levels of discontent, locate trouble spots, and determine the relative importance of different noise sources. For most purposes, however, accurate noise measurements are also needed. If a close correspondence can be shown between the noise level and human reactions, the physical indicator can be used to set standards which will prevent dissatisfaction, to anticipate the impact of new projects, and even to identify regions where people feel that noise is a serious problem and abatement measures are needed without ever contacting the residents directly.

Thus, the goal of most research has been to obtain a "dose-response" curve relating individual annoyance to the physical levels. The endeavor is complicated by the fact that noise is a complex stimulus which varies in frequency, intensity, impulsiveness, duration, and time of day. Investigators have gone to great lengths to find a way to combine these characteristics into a single statistic adequately representing the entire noise environment (Galloway & Bishop, 1970; Kryter, 1970; U.S. Environmental Protection Agency, 1974a). Generally, the optimal weighting is defined as the one which correlates best with the judgments of community residents (Borsky, 1961; Griffiths & Langdon, 1968). Most of the scales used are very highly intercorrelated.

No matter what complicated numerical measure of noise exposure has been finally used in the surveys, the results have been about the same. The noise level alone is a surprisingly poor predictor of individual dissatisfaction. At best, it accounts for 25% of the variance in annoyance (McKennell, 1974), though values of 10% to 15% are more common (e.g., Griffiths & Langdon, 1968; Tracor, 1970b). The great effort expended in accurately recording the noise exposure and creating reliable attitude scales suggests that relatively little of the unexplained variance represents outright measurement errors.[2] The majority appears to reflect genuine individual differences in reactions to the noise. Even in the most intense noise zones there are people who live without apparent concern or ill effects. But in areas with much lower exposures there are still individuals who find the noise levels intolerable.

The relationship between annoyance and exposure appears to be linear, but some investigators of aircraft noise (e.g., Rylander et al., 1972) have suggested that when flights are infrequent, annoyance is practically independent of noise level. The precise shape of the dose-response curve at moderate exposures has important implications for

---

[2] The unexplained variance does not appear to be due to differences between indoor noise levels and the levels measured outdoors. A study which attempted to correct for the shielding effects of different housing styles found lower correlations between annoyance and the estimated indoor intensities than between annoyance and the outdoor values (Tracor, 1970b).

policy decisions. Anthrop (1973, p. 96) quotes the public testimony of the general counsel of the Air Transport Association on this subject: "If anything has been learned from the exhaustive studies made of noise complaints, it is that no matter how much the noise level is reduced there will remain an ineradicable hard-core group of complainants. Both British and American studies indicate that this constant hard-core group of complainants constitutes about 30% of the population near airports." The speaker is apparently talking about annoyance rather than formal complaints since the latter are never this frequent, but the implications of his remarks are clear nonetheless: There is no point in formulating strict noise standards if below a certain level dissatisfaction is independent of exposure. While it does appear that individual differences are somewhat more pronounced at lower levels (Borsky, 1961), in fact, the number of people annoyed declines steadily with the noise level, and in truly quiet settings only 5% are bothered (Alexandre, 1974).[3]

When the responses of all individuals exposed to the same noise level are grouped together and the average value is plotted against the physical indicator, the correlation always increases dramatically—from .46 to .98 in one example (McKennell, 1974). Working with grouped data, however, has two serious disadvantages. First, it gives one the false impression that people experiencing the same level of noise all react the same way. Agencies setting standards on the basis of such data might underestimate how much people differ. A better method than working with a statistic like the mean or mode is to indicate the number of people falling into each category of disturbance. Using the percentage of individuals who are highly annoyed as the dependent variable is a step in this direction, but the arbitrary nature of the label "highly annoyed" must be kept in mind.

The second unwarranted conclusion encouraged by the use of grouped data is that the factors responsible for the individual differences are unimportant and can be safely ignored. This perspective is reflected in the following curious statement:

> In most cases, the average group response can also be interpreted as the average individual's response during his life period. That is to say, each

---

[3] A recent federal report (U.S. Environmental Protection Agency, 1973, p. 32) suggests that the dose–response curve tends to level off at noise levels below about 60 decibels, but data in this same document (pp. D-5 to D-8) do not appear to support this conclusion.

individual changes his attitudinal biases according to various factors and personal experiences not necessarily connected to the noise or even to the environment in general, which lead to fluctuations of each individual's attitude. The average group response does, to some extent, express the individual's response averaged over longer periods of his life (U.S. Environmental Protection Agency, 1974a, pp. D-22–D-23).

McKennell (1974) questions whether the attitudes which lead *individuals* to differ must be equally distributed among all *communities*. If significant attitudes and experiences are present to a different extent in a peaceful suburb from that in an urban center, for example, the slope, intercept, and linearity of the dose–response curve may all be different. Changing noise measures and annoyance scales tend to obscure variations in dissatisfaction from one study to the next, but McKennell's suggestion does seem to be borne out. At the same level of exposure, substantial differences in annoyance have been observed between Sweden and Italy (Jonsson et al., 1969), between small and large cities in the United States (Patterson & Connor, 1974), and among different large cities (Grandjean et al., 1974; Tracor, 1970b), though some observers believe that the similarities across settings are more striking than the differences (Alexandre, 1974; U.S. Environmental Protection Agency, 1974a).

Non-Noise Factors Influencing Annoyance

Many attempts have been made to discover the personal, social, and situational factors which produce these differences in annoyance from person to person and from place to place. Successful research in this area will make it possible to predict reactions to new noise sources and might help to identify particularly sensitive groups or settings which should receive extra protection from noise. A third aim would be to identify attitudes contributing to annoyance which might be altered by public relations campaigns.

Demographic variables—sex, age, education, income, occupational status, owning one's own home, having economic connections with the noise source—have been included in most studies and generally have insignificant correlations with annoyance (Borsky, 1961; Griffiths & Langdon, 1968; McKennell, 1963). Personality factors are undoubtedly involved to some extent, but they have received only cursory attention in the survey research. The identification of annoyance with anger, though, suggests that people who have difficulties in experiencing and expressing anger may be particularly bothered by noise. Most of the research on individual differences has focused on a number of specific attitudes which consistently show substantial correlations with measures of annoyance (Borsky, 1961; Galloway & Jones, 1974; Grandjean et al., 1974; Hazard, 1971; McKennell, 1963, 1969, 1974). Among these are: the belief that the source of noise does not serve an important function, the belief that the party responsible for the noise could reduce it but chooses not to for insufficient reasons, the number of complaints made about other aspects of the community, the belief that noise affects one's health, fear (in studies of aircraft noise), the belief that one can no longer adapt to the noise, and general attitudes toward noise. In one large survey over 200 variables were considered (Tracor, 1970b). The equation finally developed to predict annoyance contained dozens of parameters and raised the correlation with the annoyance scale from .37 to .78.

While it is often claimed that such multivariate equations "explain" annoyance, there are serious difficulties in this interpretation. Many of the variables just seem to be alternative ways of assessing annoyance. In one case (Hazard, 1968; Tracor, 1970b), a question concerning adaptability was considered for possible use in the annoyance scale but was eventually dropped. Then this same variable was inserted into the equation used to predict annoyance! It is also unclear whether many of the other attitudes identified are causes or consequences of annoyance (a point also raised by Alexandre [1974]). Does the belief that noise adversely affects one's health, for example, precede or follow exposure to intense aircraft activity? Some attempts have been made to establish causal relationships from this correlational data by using path analysis techniques (Leonard & Borsky, 1974; Tracor, 1970b), but the stringent and probably unrealistic assumptions underlying such analyses (Blalock, 1964) make them less than convincing.

If these attitudes do not predict annoyance in any meaningful sense, then they cannot be used to anticipate reactions to changes in noise levels. If they are just different ways of expressing annoyance, then they do not provide a means by which annoyance might be reduced. Only one attempt to influence annoyance in a field setting has been reported (Cederlöf, Jonsson, & Sörensen, 1967; Sörensen, 1970). In this case an intervention designed to improve attitudes toward the source of the noise was quite effective in reducing reported annoyance. A group of people living near a military airport in Sweden were given a souvenir book commemorating the 50th anniversary of the Royal Swedish Air Force and were led to believe that their neighbors all felt that the operations of the Air Force were very important. Several weeks and even several years later they reported being less bothered by the aircraft noise than a control group drawn from the same community.

Two other factors which may influence appraisals of environmental noise are prevailing public opinion and time of year. Increasing public awareness of noise pollution encourages people to question whether familiar sounds are really necessary. In Europe the sound of church bells has become a new noise abatement target (U.S. Environmental Protection Agency, 1971a). Noise complaints display a strong seasonal cycle, reaching a peak in the spring and summer months when windows are kept open (Patterson & Connor, 1974). It is possible that annoyance reactions are similarly affected.

Another pair of variables which might be important are the length of time an individual has lived in the community and whether or not he knew about the noise when he first moved there. Studies find repeatedly that long-term residents are just as bothered as those arriving more recently (Borsky, 1961; Griffiths & Langdon, 1968; Jacoby, 1972). It has been suggested (Office of Population Censuses and Surveys, 1971, p. 9) that this trend reflects a growing dissatisfaction with rising noise levels rather than a failure to adapt to a stable environment. Because community surveys are conducted at a single point in time, several variables are always confounded in their results: the length of residence, the self-selection of people migrating into and out of the area, and the steady increase in noise which has occurred in many areas, particularly around airports.

Data collected in the second Heathrow Airport study (Office of Population Censuses and Surveys, 1971, pp. 19–28) showed a fairly complicated pattern. New arrivals were the least disturbed by noise, perhaps because they chose this area as their home. For other residents different trends emerged, depending on the noise levels to which they were exposed. At the lower levels people appeared to become accustomed to the noise; their annoyance decreased with length of residence. But at the higher noise levels annoyance increased with years of exposure. Supplementing these specific results was the general observation that annoyance scores did not increase between 1961 and 1967 in spite of a great increase in air traffic. In fact, fewer people in 1967 than in 1961 reported being "more bothered by aircraft this year than in the past" or being afraid of aircraft crashing. These results suggest that some form of adaptation had occurred.

At present, no information is available about the *initial* impact of noise from new highways or airports beyond the informal observation that complaints are most frequent and vocal when projects are first opened. It seems likely that distress, annoyance, and dissatisfaction are much greater at first than they are several years later, unless the noise levels are very intense or continually increasing. (Note that a long-time community resident who has just been subjected to a new source of noise is not in the same situation as a person who has just moved into an area where the noise was already in existence.) After a few months most people probably become resigned to the noise and regard it as an unfortunate but unavoidable addition to their environment. Such a reappraisal would be adaptive in the sense of minimizing feelings of annoyance. Those who do not adjust probably try to move away. This scenario is hypothetical; the longitudinal research which would be necessary to establish the actual pattern of adjustment has not been carried out.

Our lack of understanding of adaptive processes makes it impossible to say anything concrete about the differences between short-term and long-term impacts or to interpret intelligently perceptions of the environment gathered from individuals exposed to a given situation for differing periods of time. These problems become critical when we search for the appropriate procedures for predicting and defining environmental quality.

Predicting Noise Impacts

The array of personal, cultural, and situational variables which modify feelings of annoyance should convince anyone that no single curve will accurately predict reactions to noise in all circumstances. These are not simple stimulus–response interactions. Rather than hastily endorse one particular dose–response curve because it appears to be the best available, we should try to understand the factors which change dissatisfaction from one site to the next, perhaps using different curves to predict noise impacts in different settings. For example, this approach has already been used to predict community protests (Galloway & Bishop, 1970; U.S. Environmental Protection Agency, 1974a, p. D-18). There is no reason to expect that situational factors will always operate in a simple and obvious manner. For example, a British survey (Bottom, 1971) found that people exposed to high levels of both aircraft and traffic noise were *less* bothered in general than people exposed to the same aircraft noise but less traffic noise (where the aircraft noise was more salient).

It is not yet clear how different these various dose–response curves would actually be. The range of noise sources and residential environments which have been examined so far in community surveys has been extremely limited and different measures of annoyance have made comparisons difficult. Aircraft and highway traffic are the only noises which have been carefully studied. A moderate degree of agreement has been found in studies of aircraft noise (Alexandre, 1974; U.S. Environmental Protection Agency, 1974a), but the full extent of this agreement has not been determined. Almost all research has been conducted in large cities; the one investigation which looked at smaller cities (Patterson & Connor, 1974) found very different reactions to noise.

Another limitation of the available dose–response curves is that all are based upon surveys of people exposed to long-standing noise sources. If reactions change over time, it makes a big difference when people are asked to evaluate noise conditions. Different test procedures reflect fundamentally different conceptions of a satisfactory environment. At one extreme is an environment which people can eventually learn to endure. At the other is an environment which people will regard with favor. Taking the first position, Sonnenfeld (1966) argues that we should exploit to the fullest man's ability to adapt to surroundings which are less than ideal. Dubos (1965), on the other hand, warns that people may acquiesce to repeated environmental insults only to realize one day that their surroundings have become intolerable.

If adverse reactions are greatest when the noise first appears, I believe that test procedures should emphasize the initial response, rather than waiting to see whether residents finally become resigned to the noise. I am not suggesting that initial reactions are all-important or that negative evaluations should be sufficient to veto any project. I do wish to imply, however, that dissatisfaction at the end of a few weeks or months proves that environmental quality has deteriorated, even if several years later the noise is no longer uppermost in the minds of community residents.

An appropriate reference group might be one which has had a few weeks or a month to adjust to the situation. The evaluations gathered after any shorter period of time might reflect the group's preconceptions more than the actual noise levels. The authors of the Route 18 Impact Statement were probably justified in questioning to what extent the students' responses represented their reactions to the noise or their opposition to the highway extension.

Whenever a proposed environmental change is irreversible or so different from past projects that one cannot predict its impact, a field simulation like the one carried out by Suedfeld and Ward (1972) should be considered. It might be difficult, however, to gain the cooperation of an adequate number of people for a sufficient length of time. If a simulation is attempted, participants should be stratified into those whose initial attitudes toward the project are favorable, neutral, and unfavorable. Negative reports from the first two groups at the end of the test would counteract charges of prejudice and bias. Positive reports by people originally opposed to the project would aid its acceptance by the community.

POLICY IMPLICATIONS

If reactions to noise were determined solely by the physical stimulus, the use of human evaluations in formulating noise standards and government policy would be relatively straightforward. The person-based indicator of environmental quality would be used to decide what kinds of noise bother people and how community noise should be measured. This physical measure would be calibrated in terms of the amount of dissatisfaction produced at different levels. Regulations and abatement policies would then refer to the physical indicator. The specific group of people used to calibrate the noise scale would be unimportant since reactions would depend only on the physical properties of the sound.

In reality, many factors influence reactions to noise. Evaluations may change from person to person, from community to community, and perhaps even from year to year. It is not that some groups like noise and others do not; the variations reflect different degrees of acceptance of an environmental feature that all find undesirable. When individuals or neighborhoods differ in their previous experience with noise, how much they value quiet, whether they believe the noise can be reduced, and whether they think the source of the noise performs a useful social function, not only will they express different amounts of dissatisfaction, but the extent to which the same noise levels actually disrupt their daily activities will probably be different too.

How does one use these varying responses to guide public policy? Two kinds of situations can be distinguished. One involves new noise sources. Whether or not a noise-producing environmental change is allowed to occur should depend upon the predicted impact of the noise on the people who would be directly affected, and not upon some fixed noise standard applied in all settings. Communities with residents who actively sought out quiet surroundings would be able to preserve this aspect of their environment. They would not have to accept a noise standard just because it appeared to be an economically feasible goal for the entire nation. If residents would not be annoyed by a new sound, the project would be allowed to proceed.

The situation is different if existing noise sources are already seriously disturbing a community. When a regulation is established which will force industries to undertake expensive noise control programs, the regulation has to be based upon the noise level rather than upon the evaluations of the people affected. Otherwise, an airline would be faced with a noise limit which differed from one airport to the next and which might change from year to year if public attitudes toward noise changed. If a company were very unpopular, neighborhood residents might be hypersensitive to the noise it produced and insist on noise controls so stringent the company would be put out of business. Yet, even in this class of situations, where remedial programs are required, human evaluations are still needed to decide what the noise limit should be. This level should be based upon the annoyance the noise produces, as estimated from surveys sampling a wide variety of locations and noise sources.

CONCLUSION

This chapter has examined various ways that evaluations of environmental noise can be measured, the relationship between these appraisals and physical noise levels, and procedures for predicting how people will respond to environmental changes. A fundamental question is whether negative evaluations of noise should be treated like any other opinions, or whether they represent undesirable impacts which can undermine the health and welfare of the individuals affected. Some part of a person's aversion to noise may just indicate a learned social value, a conviction that quiet (like attractive parks and good schools) is a desirable feature in a community. At least as much of a person's annoyance, however, reflects the unpleasant behavioral effects and emotional distress which are produced. Governments around the world generally agree that people deserve protection from such disturbances. These impacts are difficult to measure, so we use the reports of neighborhood residents to determine their presence and severity.

Self-reports are subjective; they cannot be verified by any external test. Consequently, there is some concern that the courts would throw out any noise statute based upon human appraisals on the grounds that it is arbitrary and capricious. Yet, when a community's response is still strongly negative after a reasonable length of time, it seems that the only defensible conclusion is that the noise does represent a substantial deterioration in environmental quality in the eyes of the residents.

If one decides that subjective reports cannot be used to formulate policy, there is a tendency to look for an objective indicator which is more or less closely related to the human evaluations. This is the strategy adopted by the U.S. Environmental Protection Agency (1974a) in a document proposing "levels of noise requisite to protect public health and welfare with an adequate margin for safety." This report explicitly abandons annoyance as an untenable, "subjective" criterion (p. 7) and instead bases its standards upon speech interference. The negative impact of noise, however, is not reducible to its interference with speech; at the limit recommended to protect speech (55 decibels) about 17% of the population would still feel highly annoyed (U.S. Environmental Protection Agency, 1974a, p. 23). If we believe that people should be able to live in surroundings that they find tolerable, person-based indicators are essential. If they are rejected and standards are based instead upon some easily measured, objective criterion, community changes will be allowed to occur which appear to satisfy all regulations but which large numbers of people will regard as a significant degradation of environmental quality.

13

Discussion Summary

KENNETH H. CRAIK AND ERVIN H. ZUBE

The conceptual analysis of perceived air quality, water quality, and sonic quality emerging from the workshop discussions was summarized in the introduction to this section. Attention otherwise focused upon the development and application of indices for these constructs. The principal topics can be reviewed in light of the critical steps entailed in the derivation and use of PEQIs for air, water, and sonic environments.

REFINING INSTRUMENTS FOR MEASURING INDICATORS OF PERCEIVED AIR, WATER, AND SONIC QUALITY

There was widespread recognition at this workshop of the need for improved and standardized survey instruments. The annoyance scales for noise are perhaps closest to attaining the level of adequate standard instruments, although room for technical improvements remains (e.g., establishing the meaning of points along the scales; dealing with social desirability and other factors affecting emotional reports). In contrast, the reporting of types and numbers of perceived amenities in the sonic environment (e.g., birdsongs, winds, bells, surf, music, fountains) has received attention only rarely (e.g., Southworth, 1969), and survey instruments await development.

DR. KENNETH H. CRAIK • Institute of Personality Assessment and Research, University of California, Berkeley, California 94720.   DR. ERVIN H. ZUBE • Institute for Man and Environment, University of Massachusetts, Amherst, Massachusetts 01002.

For improving present surveys of perceived air and water quality, the instructional sets for recording perceptions of amenities and perceptions of pollution can be more strongly clarified and differentiated. Instruments for the former await development and further conceptualization of the properties and constituent elements of perceived air and water quality (e.g., weather conditions, sunsets, rainfalls, distance visibility, cloud formations, and sky coloration for air quality, and comparable elements for water quality). For the perception of pollution, comprehensive checklists of visual, olfactory, and tactile indicators could be constructed and observers could be clearly instructed to attempt to detect pollutants. A composite PEQI for air quality might combine perceived amenities and perceived pollution. Parallel considerations would apply to the development of standard instruments for measuring indicators of perceived water amenities and water pollutants.

WEIGHTING THE OBSERVED INDICATORS TO DERIVE A COMPOSITE INDEX

The indices of noise annoyance are the only observer-based measures which serve as criterion measures and standards for the development of physical indices. In contrast, the various air and water pollution indices, for example, are physical measures derived from scientific–medical judgment regarding impacts on public health and property damage; they are not based upon observer reports.

Weinstein (Chapter 12) notes the issue of cutting points on the noise annoyance scales. In some cases, the standard setting is based upon the percentage of observers who would be highly annoyed by the maximum level permitted. This decision implies that a person moderately annoyed is not significantly affected. When the annoyance index is based upon a composite of observer indicators (e.g., sleep disturbance, conversation interference, rest and relaxation hindrances), the question of weighting the elements arises (e.g., should sleep disturbance be assigned greater weight than conversation interference?). Obviously, the rationale for these weightings cannot be separated from the decision on who should participate and be consulted in making them and, in particular, how input from the general public can be incorporated at this critical step in the construction of PEQIs.

Public participation in the weighting of indicators and the establishment of cutting points is also considered by Barker (Chapter 10) and Coughlin (Chapter 11) in their discussions of indices for perceived water and air amenities. Barker points to the procedure of the Delaware Estuary Comprehensive Study (Chevalier & Cartwright, 1971) as a possible model for community input and Coughlin notes the potential of the utility and Cassandra approaches to examining trade-offs and weightings made by experts and laypersons.

REVISING STANDARD MONITORING OPERATIONS

There was considerable concurrence across the three environmental domains of research and application that longitudinal and comparative studies of multiple communities (including cities of varying size) would be required to understand fully the functioning and validity of PEQIs for air, water, and sonic environments. For air and sonic quality, monitoring should be conducted on neighborhood units and aggregated to city-wide units. For the appraisal of perceived water quality, more variety and types of water bodies (including rivers) should be studied. In the perception of air, water, and sonic quality, investigations should include preonset studies for major environmental transformations, studies of observer (i.e., newcomer) adaptation to fixed environmental conditions, and studies of response to incremental environmental changes.

Both place-centered appraisals and person-centered assessments were envisioned. In the case of place-centered appraisals, the composition of PEQI panels offers important choice points. On-site users and residents are limited by adaptive trends, self-selection to the site, unrepresentative sampling, and lack of comparative perspective. However, for person-centered assessments, their use is, of course, essential. Weinstein (Chapter 12) notes, in addition, that annoyance measures for noise conditions are considered most valid when based upon on-site user reactions. Touring panels were considered important complements to on-site user panels in appraisals of perceived air and water pollution and would be equally important for the appraisal of perceived air, water, and sonic quality. In this regard, environmental perception and appraisal kits were discussed, and the possibility of enlisting civil servants who travel widely in cities (e.g., welfare workers, postal workers, police officers, visiting nurses) to constitute monitoring teams was explored.

APPRAISING THE RELIABILITY AND VALIDITY OF PEQIs FOR AIR, WATER, AND SONIC QUALITY

Confidence was expressed by workshop participants that reliable and sensitive observer-based indices for air, water, and sonic quality could be developed which would possess greater validity and utility than current uses of complaint records and organized community actions as factors in decision-making and policy.

The validational requirements for indices for perceived amenities differ in noteworthy ways from those for perceived pollutants.

In the case of indices for perceived air, water, and sonic amenity, development remains at such an early stage that no reliability or validational evidence is available. Both indices would require reliable measurement and theoretical understanding of the nonenvironmental factors influencing them. In addition, place-centered PEQIs require adequate levels of consensus among observers, and sufficient correlates with environmental attributes must be demonstrated.

In the case of perceived air and water pollution, the constructs themselves require further clarification. In particular, the conceptual relation of perceived pollution indices to the various physical pollution indices warrants examination. First, the physical air and water pollution indices currently undergo continual modification, and competing formulations of them coexist. Thus, the criterion for perceived pollution indices remains undefined, and will be so until standard, stable physical indices are established. Second, it is evident that certain components of air pollution (e.g., carbon monoxide) and water pollution (e.g., bacterial elements) are not detectable by human observers. Thus, the construct of perceived water and air pollution is senseless unless appropriate boundaries are placed upon the construct. Of course, this specification process may take the form of an empirical delineation, entailing research on the detectability of various physical states of air and water pollution. Third, for maximum effectiveness, observers in perceived pollution research should be carefully tuned to their task, and instructional sets that clearly differentiate perception of physical pollutants from perception of amenity should replace vague references to air quality. Fourth, perceived pollution indices must be used with systematic knowledge of the nonenvironmental factors that may influence them (e.g., mass media campaigns, adaptation levels, demographic variables, personality characteristics of observers) and in light of demonstrated levels of predictive validity. Current evidence on predictive validity shows correlations between perceived air and water pollution and appropriate physical indices that are generally positive. The validity of perceived pollution indices would probably be enhanced by recourse to use of touring panels—who would be less influenced by adaptational processes, would possess a comparative perspective, and would be task-oriented. Thus, they would be less affected by the seasonal bias found in on-site observers, which probably reflects the role of incidental versus focused observations. However, these possibilities warrant scientific scrutiny.

The reliability and content validity of·noise annoyance indices are relatively well established. Weinstein (Chapter 12) highlights the distinguishing characteristic of noise annoyance indices as measures of emotional states (i.e., a mild form of anger) and underscores the relevance of problems encountered in attaining valid assessments of emotional states (e.g., observer limitations in reporting on emotional states accurately; unwillingness to admit to negative emotions; reluctance to discuss any personal feelings with interviewers). These hurdles have not been fully scaled; indeed, they have rarely been attempted, thus far. The implication for monitoring programs is the possibility of systematic underreporting of noise annoyance conditions. Weinstein also emphasizes the need for comparative longitudinal community studies of noise annoyance, with monitoring spanning the preonset periods in noise level alterations, as a prerequisite for attaining adequate predictive validity in noise annoyance indices.

EVALUATING THE UTILITY OF PEQI OPERATIONAL SYSTEMS FOR AIR, WATER, AND SONIC QUALITY

A useful role for observer-based indices was envisioned in air quality and water quality management programs and in noise control programs. Observer-based indices can serve as criteria for identifying and setting physical indices and standards, or can constitute a basis for separate thresholds which would complement physical pollution thresholds. Place-centered appraisals employing observer-based indices can be used in establishing goals and appraising performance of pollution abatement and control agencies, as well as in conducting environmental impact assessments and communicating trends to policymakers and the general public. Person-centered assessments using observer-based indices can monitor the level and distribution of these facets of a sense of environmental well-being throughout society.

Such applications of reliable and valid observer-based indices of air, water, and sonic quality would occur in a legal and administrative context. An informal review of legislative and administrative mandates and sanctions for the use of PEQIs and related indices yielded readily cited instances at state and federal levels, for each environmental domain under discussion. The U.S. Clean Air Act of 1967 entails federal secondary standards regarding amenity value; water quality criteria at the federal as well as many state levels also encompass secondary standards regarding appearance and amenity value, while the U.S. Noise Control Act of 1972 employs language concerning health and welfare (with the latter concept including subjective reactions). In addition, the National Environmental Policy Act (NEPA) and many parallel state acts generate requirements for environmental impact statements, including assessments of impacts by projects upon recreational–scenic areas and indirectly upon air, water, and sonic amenities. The legal standing of observer-based appraisals of environmental quality appeared to be less clear-cut at this time, with some precedents established regarding scenic quality. However, federal agencies (e.g., Environmental Protection Agency) have shown reservations regarding their degree of consensus and temporal stability and the consequent possibility that courts would judge them to be arbitrary and capricious bases for public decision-making. Empirical evidence on these points, lacking at present, is thus clearly needed.

Discussion focused upon administrative practices and the need for agency staff to gain a fuller understanding of the feasibility and nature of PEQIs and the specific operations entailed in their application. Unlike the first and second workshops, procedures for monitoring operations received specific consideration, probably because of greater experience among members of this workshop with monitoring programs for physical pollution indices. For example, the development of standard environmental perception and appraisal kits was explored, as well as the possibility of enlisting civil servants as touring appraisal panels.

The cautionary notes sounded in this workshop dealt with recognition of the present early stage in index development, the neglect of amenity indices, and technical psychometric limitations of current indices (especially the potential for underestimating noise annoyance). Concerns about misuse of indices for perceived air, water, and sonic amenity and pollution were relatively muted. More emphasis was placed upon the danger of ineffectual and invalid indices, due to lack of understanding of their properties and functions by agency personnel and to their use in public information campaigns which fail to offer a full range of guidelines and interpretation.

A scientific perspective upon the application of observer-based indices in policy and management also pervaded the discussion. A theoretical model of the entire management process was deemed necessary to guide research on the administrative and programmatic impact of the use of a PEQI system, on the effectiveness and consequences of such monitoring systems, and on the role of social-system factors and various classes of participants in decision-making on index development and monitoring, as well as upon the interpretation and use of monitoring information.

RESEARCH ISSUES AND NEEDS

The final segment of the round table discussion was devoted to nomination and discussion of research issues and needs, in the form of specific projects. A full listing is provided below, grouped according to procedural sequence and related content. Brief and incomplete discussion of priority rankings appeared to identify Projects 1, 4, 5, 12, and 17 as among the more urgently needed undertakings.

1. To define terms and criteria for PEQI appraisals clearly and to foster consensual, cooperative use of them.

2. To examine the relationship between perception of pollution and perception of amenity.

3. To conceptualize and measure air, water, and sound amenities, following the pattern of current research on perceived residential and scenic quality.

4. To distinguish between awareness of environmental problems and direct perception and experience of them.

5. To investigate the reliability, validity, and utility of PEQI and related instruments.

6. To compare on-site resident-users and touring panels in the conduct of observer appraisals of environmental quality.

7. To develop and train PEQI monitoring teams (e.g., composed of public health workers, policy officers).

8. To standardize physical measures of pollution, recommend a definitive index for each environmental domain, and issue a uniform framework of levels and thresholds.

9. To correlate physical pollution measures and indices with observer appraisals and to analyze factors at play in large discrepancies.

10. To determine the perceptual synergistic effects of air, water, and sound conditions.

11. To investigate differences between attitudes and perceptions of the immediate sources of pollution and of the broader societal forces involved in them.

12. To undertake a national survey of the whole range of conditions, types, and sites, and participants entailed in the perception of environmental quality, through collaborative research efforts, including: (a) development of a comprehensive battery of standard instruments; (b) investigation of long-term and cumulative impacts; and (c) determination of variations in local mythologies of environmental quality and their role in pollution control and abatement policy.

13. To conduct studies of reactions to major environmental change, using PEQI appraisals prior to and following its onset, and to compare the relative impacts of gradual, incremental change and sudden, dramatic change.

14. To undertake demonstration studies in the application of PEQIs in predictions (e.g., environmental impact assessments) and in follow-up evaluations, and to relate anticipated to obtained impacts upon perceived environmental quality.

15. To organize comparative, longitudinal studies in systematically selected communities.

16. To disseminate information yielded by observer-based appraisals, e.g.: (a) to study the impact of attempts to inform and/or change public opinion; (b) to relate attitudes and perceptions of pollution problems and policies to attitudes toward publicized indices of physical

pollution issued by governmental agencies; and (c) to undertake analyses of propaganda and persuasion campaigns dealing with environmental quality issues.

17. To investigate social and environmental contexts affecting the perception of environmental quality, e.g.: (a) to define the role of community structure (e.g., neighborhood cohesion; power relations; employment patterns; formal and informal political–administrative systems) in the perception of and adjustment to perceived environmental pollution; and (b) to define the role of physical environmental contexts in perception and adjustment (e.g., baseline levels of perceived environmental quality; scale of analysis—local to regional).

18. To examine the impact of environmental elites, experts, and laypersons in policy and programs; e.g.: (a) to investigate the characteristic roles of elites, experts, laypersons, special interest groups, polluters, et al., in policy formulation and implementation; (b) to compare environmental cognition and perception, and analyze the extent of mutual understanding, among types of environmental experts and professionals; (c) to determine the degree of congruence between community elites and community residents in their environmental values and appraisals; and (d) to gauge the effectiveness and competency of environmental experts (e.g., professionals, technicians) and elites (e.g., key community leaders) in policy formation and implementation regarding perceived environmental quality.

19. To assess people's valuations of perceived environmental quality (e.g., in their hierarchy of values, in monetary terms).

20. To conduct case studies of pollution control and abatement programs that have notably failed or succeeded and to explore the role of environmental awareness and perceptions in accounting for their differential outcomes.

21. To identify and interpret legal and administrative sanctions and mandates for use of observer-based appraisals of environmental quality in public decision-making and to review precedents and outcomes of their introduction in court cases.

22. To determine how PEQI appraisal systems might be institutionalized (e.g., the issues of where, when, how, who, financing, licensing, personnel standards) and to examine separately the potential institutional arrangements for place-centered and person-centered PEQI operational systems.

V
Overview

Summary and Research Strategies

KENNETH H. CRAIK AND ERVIN H. ZUBE

TYPES OF OBSERVER-BASED INDICES FOR ENVIRONMENTAL QUALITY

Review of the three research workshops reveals the recurrence of themes and issues across the environmental domains, but also important matters addressed in one area and neglected in others. For example, Table I represents estimates of the current state-of-the-art for research on the major issues delineated in Chapter 1, across the principal environmental domains. This summary matrix consists of best estimates of the number of studies available, based upon recent review papers by Brush, Marans, Barker, Coughlin, and Weinstein, discussed in the three research workshops, and a final consultative review session attended by participants drawn from each of the research workshops. Table I is descriptive of the present organization of research activity.

A pervasive lack of coordination across environmental domains is evident, due in part to independently developing research traditions and to different sponsoring agencies and potential users. The overall effort to devise observer assessment systems for environmental quality will gain immensely from coordinated endeavors and a unified conceptual framework.

DR. KENNETH H. CRAIK • Institute of Personality Assessment and Research, University of California, Berkeley, California 94720.   DR. ERVIN H. ZUBE • Institute for Man and Environment, University of Massachusetts, Amherst, Massachusetts 01002.

TABLE I. Research State-of-the-Art: Estimates

Research issues	Environmental contexts					Environmental media			
	Urban environment	Natural environment (scenery)	Recreational environment	Residential environment	Institutional environment	Air	Water	Sound	Land
Distinction between comparative appraisals and preferential judgments	None	Some	None	Some	None	None	None	None	None
Consensus among individuals and groups	Little	Some	Some	Some	Little	Some	Little	Considerable	None
Agreement between experts and laypersons	Little	Considerable	Some	Some	Little	Little	None	None	None
Relationships between observer-based appraisals	Little	Considerable	Considerable	Some	Little	Some	Little	Considerable	None
Feasibility studies of developing standard PEQIs	None	Some	Some	Little	Little	None	None	Considerable	None

Comparisons of work on the various domains of perceived environmental quality also indicate differences in concepts and methods which, combined with terminological confusions, may jointly interfere with coordinated enterprise. Figure 1 represents an attempt to make these differentiations explicit and to offer distinguishing terminology.

Environmental Domains

At present, the identification of environmental domains seems necessarily arbitrary; those domains proposed in Figure 1 reflect foci of current research interest. Within each domain, the issue of scale and contexts arises: Residential quality encompasses interiors, dwelling unit, microneighborhood, macroneighborhood, county, and region; contexts for water include lakes, streams, rivers, oceanfronts. In addition, overlapping relationships can be readily envisioned, e.g., the natural and sonic environment can form a part of the residential environment; in

Environmental Domains

Observer Indices of Environmental Quality	Visual urban environment	Visual natural environment (Scenic)	Recreational environment	Residential environment	Institutional environment	Air	Water	Sound	Land	Environmental Attributes
PEQIs										
perception of amenity										amenity attributes
perception of degradation										degradation attributes
EERIs										
pleasure										pleasurable attributes
annoyance										annoyance attributes
OBPI										current physical pollution indices

FIG. 1. Potential types of observer-based indices.

some respects the recreational and residential environments are specific classes of institutional environments; the attributes of water often take their character from their natural or urban environmental contexts. Empirically, synergistic effects may be discovered in the interaction of perceived qualities of the various environmental domains.

Observer Indices of Environmental Quality

Distinctions among types of observer-based indices are especially useful, because of selective linkages in the research literature between kinds of indices and environmental domains (see Figure 1). Observer indices of scenic quality have focused upon the perception of amenities, while indices for recreational and residential environments have dealt with the perception of amenities and degradations (often in the form of bipolar rating dimensions). These indices entail primarily perceptual–cognitive operations concerning the presence or salience of qualities and in conjunction can yield Perceived Environmental Quality Indices (PEQIs). A second form of observer indices are reports upon emotional reactions to environmental domains and can be termed Environmental Emotional Reaction Indices (EERIs). The most prominent use of this type of observer index occurs in the monitoring of annoyance reactions in the environmental domain of sound, but concern ratings regarding air and water conditions may also be cited. Satisfaction ratings are frequently employed, especially in assessing recreational and residential quality, but their status as PEQIs or EERIs depends upon the instructional set: If adequacy of fit (or discrepancy) between observed and criterion conditions is stressed, the resulting index is primarily a PEQI; if pleasurable experiences is emphasized, it is more appropriately interpreted as an EERI. In most research on observed air and water quality, the main intent has been to determine the extent to which observers can detect the various physical components of current environmental quality indices based upon public health and economic consequences. Since the term *pollution* is widely employed in connection with these physical indices, their detection by human judges may be fittingly called Observer-Based Pollution Indices (OBPIs). Thus, EERIs and OBPIs are distinct from PEQIs but can supplement them in appraising environmental quality.

Environmental Attributes

The search for physical attributes which correlate with the various indices yielded by observer appraisals of environmental quality warrant distinctive terms (see Figure 1). In the case of PEQIs and ERRIs, the observer-generated indices possess intrinsic definitional status, but their systematic physical correlates would provide a functional leverage for modifying the environment to meet goals of perceived environmental quality and for establishing standards and guidelines for environmental policy, planning, design, and management. Noise standards, for example, are derived from physical attributes of sound which correlate with annoyance reactions. In the case of OBPI, the physical pollution indices hold primary definitional status in environmental policies and programs having public health and economic goals. To avoid confusion between physical correlates of PEQIs and EERIs, on the one hand, and the more generally familiar physical EQ indices based upon public health and economic considerations, the terms *amenity attributes* and *degradation attributes* and *pleasure attributes* and *annoyance attributes* are suggested. Of course, scientific research may ultimately show redundancies among certain classes of environmental attributes (e.g., degradation attributes and physical pollution indices).

A full array of PEQIs and EERIs can be envisioned for each environmental domain, although little effort has been made in some of the required directions. In many environmental domains, the OBPIs will constitute "empty cells," unless comparable pollution or related physical indices of environmental quality entail somewhat different constructs and validational requirements, which will be reviewed below.

RESEARCH* AGENDA

The overriding purpose of the research workshops was to examine the current state of the field and to derive a plan for coordinated research on the development and application of observer appraisal systems for environmental quality. The emergent research agenda can be presented in two parts. The first section will deal with issues entailed in the development of observer appraisal systems for environmental quality. The second section will focus upon the construction of theoretical process models for (1) the functioning of observer appraisals; and (2) the generation and use of PEQI operational systems in environmental policy, planning, design, and management.

The Development of Observer Appraisal Systems for Environmental Quality

The development of a system of observer indices requires a clear notion of the constructs to be measured; adequate indicators for each construct; operations for appraising specific environments; a rationale for weighting multiple indicators to yield an index; empirical demonstration of the reliability and validity of the measurement network; and evidence of its scientific and pragmatic utility. Identified issues and recommended research projects will be outlined for each component of the system. This review sets forth the full array of research operations required to attain adequate levels of measurement and is indicative of the level of research support needed for this purpose.

Conceptual Analysis

One of the most obvious cases of fragmentation in current research appears at the conceptual level. The basic constructs of perceived quality for the several environmental domains have received insufficient conceptual analysis singly and almost none as a network of constructs. As understood by experts and laypersons, what is entailed by the constructs of:

> perceived urban quality
> perceived natural quality
> perceived recreational quality
> perceived residential quality
> perceived institutional quality
> perceived air quality
> perceived water quality
> perceived sonic quality
> perceived land use quality?

The development of PEQIs requires examination of the constituent qualities of amenities and degradations for each environmental domain. The extensive research on the multidimensional facets of residential quality illustrates this strategy, although it has not been directed specifically to index development (see Marans, Chapter 7).

The development of EERIs requires examination of the appropriate emotional reactions that might be considered valid indirect indicators of environmental quality. The extensive research on the use of annoyance indices in noise research illustrates this strategy, which should be complemented by techniques for recording pleasurable emotional reactions.

The construct of OBPIs is fully established by the current physical EQ indices based upon public health and economic consequences. The physical indices serve as criteria for testing the concurrent validity of observer-based indices. Two areas of conceptual analysis warrant attention. First, some components of the criterion EQ indices are known to be nondetectable by human observers (e.g., gaseous and bacterial pollutants). Thus, reasonable construct boundaries must be established for OBPIs in the air and water domains. Secondly, it is not yet clear whether health-oriented physical indices will be established in other environmental domains (e.g., land-use indices), although discussions along those lines have appeared. However, this effort is independent of the matters presently at hand, except as it eventually yields such physical indices.

Aside from its content, every perceived environmental quality construct encompasses several general properties: that reliable, sensitive indices of them can be constructed; that cultural changes in the constructs occur at a moderate pace; and that physical correlates of construct indices can be identified. Another construct property, which evoked considerable discussion and mixed opinion, is the extent of consensus with which observers can apply the construct indices to specific environmental contexts. Of course, construct indices for the several environmental domains may vary in their location along this continuum from high consensus to low consensus. Research recommendations regarding these general properties will be outlined in the section on construct validity.

Recommendation 1. That intensive case studies be conducted in the humanistic tradition, focusing upon individuals' experiences of environmental quality at the level of personal experience and to identify salient attributes in each environmental domain.

Recommendation 2. That for each environmental domain, coordinated research projects, surveying representative samples of laypersons and appropriate experts, study the constituent elements of perceived environmental quality. Purpose: to establish comprehensive, standard inventories of appropriate indicators for each perceived environmental quality construct, as well as suitable measures of positive and negative emotional reactions for each environmental domain.

Standard Methods for Construct Indicators

Any attempt to examine and draw conclusions from the research literature is replete with difficulties resulting from the lack of standard methods. This situation offers especially severe obstacles to identifying long-term trends and comparing analyses across investigations. The results of research embodied in Recommendation 1 would provide useful guidelines for the design of standard methods for PEQIs and EERIs. The methods for PEQIs, EERIs, and OBPIs should use instructional sets that clearly and effectively orient observers to the distinctive tasks involved in each form of index. A wide array of scaling methods is available for PEQI development, including rating scales, paired comparisons, similarity judgments, magnitude estimates, rank ordering, and sorting. In addition, three-dimensional representations, pictorial and graphic displays, and verbal formats are appropriate.

Recommendation 3. That standard techniques be developed for recording perceptual–cognitive reports of the presence and salience of construct indicators and for registering emotional reactions. The methods of psychological test construction and scaling should be employed to produce succinct and readily understood procedures. Preliminary studies of the content validity of the techniques should be conducted with representative samples of laypersons and experts. Purpose: to construct a battery of standard techniques for monitoring each domain of perceived environmental quality.

Indicator Weighting for Index Derivation

If multiple indicators are employed for a perceived environmental quality construct, then a weighting scheme is necessary to yield a single index. In the development of PEQIs for each environmental domain, the weighting rationales should take into account the priorities and concerns of the general public. Similarly, in deriving EERIs, the weighting of various kinds of annoyances, irritations, concerns, etc., and of various forms of positive emotional reactions, should reflect the relative importance attached to them by the general public.

Recommendation 4. That through trade-off games, importance ratings, utility analysis, and other techniques be employed to determine the relative significance of constitutive elements of the various perceived environmental quality constructs for representative samples of the general public. Purpose: to provide guidelines for weighting schemes that would best reflect public priorities.

Standardizing PEQI Operations

A striking commonality across the three workshops took the form of agreement in identifying the critical steps in establishing monitoring operations for specific environments. For each environmental domain, the options include: selection of observers; selection of medium of presentation; and selection of instructional sets and response formats. These factors are important components of a theoretical model for the process of observational appraisal, which will be reviewed below. At this point, only those options important in devising an appraisal operation will be discussed.

Selection of the most appropriate observers will depend upon the purpose of the appraisal operation. If the intent is public communication regarding regional trends, then a representative sample from the specific area would be required; if the purpose is to gauge project impact, then a representative sampling from the surrounding local population might be most suitable. As a policy stance, there appeared to be consensus that for planned environmental interventions or modifications of any scale or form, a representative sampling of those individuals most affected should be surveyed.

The medium of presentation for the environment to be assessed presents two kinds of procedural decisions. First, there is the choice between on-site observers and touring panels. There are a priori advantages and disadvantages to be cited for each possibility, but in fact, little scientific knowledge of their relative modes of performance is available. Second, the use of simulated rather than direct presentations of the environment to be assessed is often logistically attractive and is sometimes inescapable (e.g., preconstruction assessments and impact reviews). Not enough is known about the psychological effectiveness of simulation techniques, specifically concerning the equivalence of perceived environmental quality assessments for actual and simulated presentations.

The standard response formats for recording construct indicators have been discussed previously. A remaining question is whether factors of context and instructional set can increase consensus for perceived environmental quality assessments of specific places.

Another important factor in standardizing PEQI operations is that of defining standard units and classes within each of the environmental domains. This is particularly important in enhancing the utility of PEQIs. If the purpose is to compare trends in environmental quality across a number of physical environmental domains in different regions, it is important, for example, that the variability in classes or types of housing, recreational, and institutional environments or water (i.e., pond, lake, stream, river, ocean, etc.) be recognized and identified.

Thus far, the issues in measurement have dealt with those questions arising in place-centered appraisals. In person-centered assessments, observers report upon their own individual home range and its component environments (e.g., workplace, residence, recreational sites, treatment environments, public urban places). Selection of observers would depend upon the purpose of analyzing the prevailing sense of environmental well-being, such as delineating social equity or conducting regional comparisons. Of course, the ultimate selection of pertinent environments is actually made by the observers themselves, who report upon the experience of their own personally identified and delimited environments. A procedural issue involves the lengths to which the person-centered, or idiographic, strategy is to be taken. If it were limited to requesting observers to specify and report upon their personal array of environments, then standard instruments could be employed. However, carrying the idiographic approach further, observers could be requested to identify their own constituent elements for each perceived environmental quality construct and also to weight them individually. Instead of judging the quality of residential attributes that are specified and weighted by the researcher, the observer would supply his or her own set of pertinent attributes, weigh their relative importance and employ them in recording judgments of perceived residential quality for a specific environment. Pragmatically, it is not evident that these steps would yield notably different outcomes for assessments of environmental well-being.

Recommendation 5. That for each environmental domain, studies determine the differences between perceived environmental quality appraisals rendered by touring panels and on-site users. Purpose: to determine the practical consequences of this choice for the results of observer appraisals of environmental quality.

Recommendation 6. That for each environmental domain, studies explore the maximum effectiveness of simulation techniques for achieving equivalence in PEQIs and EERIs with actual presentations. Purpose: to determine the practical consequences of this choice for the results of observer assessments of environmental quality.

Recommendation 7. That research study the effects, separately and jointly, of instructional set (i.e., comparative appraisals versus preferential judgments); social role (e.g., member of environmental jury); use of standard marker environments and touring panels in increasing interrater agreement in the use of PEQIs. Purpose: to identify ways of enhancing the generality of perceived environmental quality appraisals.

Recommendation 8. That research on the sense of environmental well-being study the impact of extending the idiographic strategy from the specification of personal environments to the identification of PEQI constructs and the use of individualized weighting schemes. Purpose: to gauge the practical importance of these options for assessing environmental well-being.

Recommendation 9. That research be conducted within each appropriate environmental domain on conceptual taxonomies and constituent physical components of classes, types, and scales of environmental settings. Purpose: to establish a means of maximizing comparability of findings across studies.

Reliability and Validity of Observers' Appraisals of Environmental Quality

Standard psychometric criteria for appraising the adequacy of measurement can be applied to PEQIs, EERIs, and in OBPIs in a straightforward fashion. For PEQIs and EERIs, two forms of test–retest reliability are appropriate. First, appraisals yielded by the standard measurement system for the same environments should

demonstrate stability over time, even though the measurement operations may entail the use of different panels of observers from one
appraisal to another. Second, average test–retest reliabilities for individual observers should be sufficiently stable to support the notion that
perceived environmental quality constructs are more than whimsical
effects of mass media influences, fashion, and other nonenvironmental
factors.[1] In addition, the measurement system should display adequate
sensitivity in differentiating between environmental settings and
conditions.

The importance of evaluating the content validity of the PEQI and
EERI survey instruments has been considered previously, especially for
place-centered appraisals of perceived environmental quality. In addition, adequate content validity of assessments of environmental well-
being may require an idiographic approach to the content of survey
instruments. From one point of view, the validity of a weighted index is
gauged by its correlation with a single overall rating of PEQ. From
another point of view, a weighted index based upon independently
identified constituent elements and a weighting system offers a possibly
distinctive but potentially more valuable form of information. The single
overall rating suffers from the disadvantage of not revealing changes
over time in constituent elements of PEQI. In either case, analysis of
discrepancies between the two kinds of measures is itself a worthwhile
topic for research.

Concurrent and predictive validity of the indices requires examination of their correlates with physical environmental attributes. The
constructs of perceived environmental quality and of environmental
emotional reactions embody the notion of systematic links to the
physical environment. Moreover, the practical value possessed by
observer appraisal systems of environmental quality would be muted if
they did not afford guidelines and criteria for environmental policy,
planning, design, and management. And in the case of OBPIs, adequate
correlations with current physical pollution indices carry most of their
validational weight.

The search for amenity and degradation attributes and pleasure
and annoyance attributes is tied to the PEQIs and EERIs in each envi-

---

[1] Analysis of the extent of interobserver agreement over diverse samples, the temporal stability of
the indices, and the effectiveness and comparability of environmental simulations can be
approached in an integrated manner via generalizability theory (Cronbach, Gleser, Nanda &
Rajaratnam, 1972).

ronmental domain and explores the full range of environmental dimensions and characteristics that may correlate with the indices. Multiple regression of environmental characteristics against PEQIs and EERIs will serve to identify the most effective combinations of environmental attributes for decision-making purposes. In seeking to discover indicators for OBPIs, the search is tied to the current physical pollution indices and covers the full range of observer responses that may function to detect the presence and strength of physical pollutants.

The degree of consensus demonstrated among observers in appraising perceived environmental quality has important conceptual and pragmatic implications. If consensus is high, then the generality of the perceived environmental quality constructs is enhanced. If consensus is low, then a taxonomy of observers based upon agreement in the use of PEQIs and EERIs must be developed, the various environmental attributes must be established for each PEQI and EERI subgroup, and observer characteristics for predicting membership in the PEQI and EERI subgroups must be discovered. With low-consensus PEQI and EERIs, this strategy would amount to the development of differentiated systems of environmental attributes, guidelines, and standards. This endeavor might warrant an examination of possible group variation, not only in the use of PEQIs, but in constructs and constituent elements of perceived environmental quality and in weighting schemas. In some environmental domains, the major subgroup distinction may consist of laypersons and environmental experts. If parallel sets of lay and expert PEQI and EERI systems emerge, the result would have to be accommodated by our conceptual understanding of perceived environmental quality and in applications of the PEQI operational systems. Of course, it is possible that as individual observers in standardized PEQI, EERI, and OBPI assessment and monitoring systems, experts may display substantial agreement with laypersons, while at the same time differing in their preferred constructs, constituent elements, and weighting schemas for perceived environmental quality. Indeed, experts may differ depending upon whether they are responding personally or in their professional–technical roles.

In the case of OBPIs, significant variations among observers may reflect differences in their accuracy of detecting the presence and strength of physical pollution conditions. Identification of observer characteristics that predict variations in accurate performance may offer selection criteria for establishing OBPI panels. Before closing this section on reliability and validity, it must be noted that the credibility—or face validity—of appraisal systems for perceived environmental quality requires the involvement of the general public in its development and operation.

Recommendation 10. That for observer appraisals in each environmental domain, tests be conducted on the test–retest reliability and sensitivity of monitoring systems and on the temporal stability of specific observer appraisals. Purpose: to demonstrate adequate levels of reliability for PEQI appraisals.

Recommendation 11. Once standard appraisal systems are established for PEQIs and EERIs, that systematic search be conducted for amenity and degradation attributes and for pleasure and annoyance attributes within each environmental domain. Purpose: to identify physical environmental attributes to serve as guidelines and standards.

Recommendation 12. That the most effective OBPI for the various environmental domains be sought through systematic exploration of those observer responses that may detect or correlate with the presence and varying strengths of physical pollution indices. Purpose: to identify response modes that will afford maximally valid OBPIs.

Recommendation 13. Once standard operational systems are established for PEQIs and EERIs, that studies of consensus and variation in perceived environmental quality appraisals be undertaken and, to the extent that systematic variations are noteworthy, that they be accommodated within scientific and applied uses of the operational system. Purpose: to demonstrate the generality of PEQIs, and, where appropriate, to delineate the properties of their variability.

Recommendation 14. That individual differences in the accuracy of OBPIs be studied, and, if found, that the search for possible selection criteria for membership on OBPI panels be undertaken. Purpose: to explore the utility of selection criteria for OBPI panels.

Recommendation 15. That the general public, in the form of representative samples and advisory committees, participate at critical stages in the development and operation of PEQ appraisal systems for each environmental domain, including: (a) conceptual analysis; (b) survey instrument construction; (c) selection of weighting schemes; (d) monitoring panels; and (e) application and interpretation. Purpose: to enhance the credibility, public acceptance, and effectiveness of PEQI operational systems.

Multidisciplinary Collaboration

Effective action upon the foregoing recommendations for the development of environmental quality observer appraisal systems will demand the mobilization of a broad array of expertise from the environmental and social science disciplines. Table II suggests some of the more pertinent disciplines for each of the fourteen recommended endeavors. The listing is not inclusive but serves to illustrate the scope and complexity of the challenge. Obviously, the intent is not to advocate an overly compartmentalized undertaking; indeed, just the opposite kind of cross-disciplinary organization and coherence is a prerequisite for worthwhile accomplishment.

Conceptual Model of the Observer Appraisal Process

Examination of workshop discussions and recent review papers gives evidence of considerable commonality in the general conceptual

TABLE II. Pertinent Disciplines for Recommendations on the Development of Environmental Quality Observer Appraisal Systems

Recommendation	Pertinent disciplines
1	Behavioral geography; environmental psychology; survey research
2	Scaling; psychometrics; survey research
3	Environmental planning; resource economics
4	Behavioral geography; environmental psychology
5	Environmental design; behavioral geography; environmental psychology
6	Environmental psychology
7	Behavioral geography; environmental psychology; survey research
8	Environmental science; environmental planning; architecture; landscape architecture
9	Scaling; psychometrics; survey research
10	Environmental science; environmental planning; architecture; landscape architecture; behavioral geography; environmental psychology
11	Environmental science; behavioral geography; environmental psychology
12	Environmental science; environmental management and administration; behavioral geography; environmental psychology
13	Environmental science; personality assessment and selection
14	Environmental science; environmental management and administration; behavioral geography; environmental psychology

schema of processes and components entertained regarding an observer's rendering of a PEQI. Figure 2 represents an attempt to depict this shared conceptual model, based in part upon schemas proposed by Peterson (Chapter 4), Marans (Chapter 7), and Coughlin (Chapter 11).

Social system properties and functions serve as independent variables for (1) influencing the kinds of prevailing environmental settings that might be available for appraisal (via institutions and regulations for formal and informal environmental policy, planning, design, and management); (2) affecting and fostering observer characteristics pertinent to observational appraisal of environments (via child-rearing practices, education, training, mass media programs, public information campaigns); and (3) shaping the context in which observer appraisals of perceived environmental quality are rendered (e.g., its social atmosphere—conflicting, persuasive, coercive, etc.; its settings—public hearings, PEQ appraisals and monitoring panels, etc.; its procedures—instructional sets, individual versus group judgments, etc.).

The perception of environmental qualities (IVA) is envisioned as a function of environmental characteristics (IIIA) and observer charac-

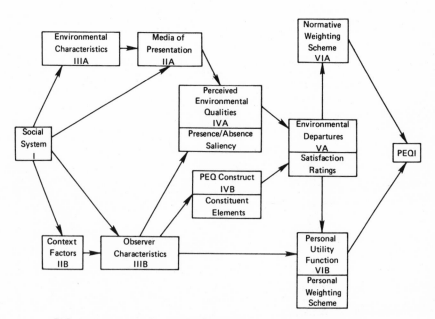

FIG. 2. Conceptual model of the observer appraisal process.

teristics (IIIB), of course, but the role of each is mediated, respectively, by the media of presentation (IIA) and context factors (IIB).

Environmental characteristics (IIIA) encompass the entire taxonomy of objective physical dimensions. Only those environmental characteristics displaying correlates with PEQIs and EERIs function as environmental attributes (i.e., amenity and degradation attributes; pleasure and annoyance attributes); many reliably measured physical environmental characteristics may be functionally irrelevant to perceived environmental quality.

A great deal more knowledge is needed to identify observer characteristics (IIIB) which affect perceived environmental quality appraisals. At present, there appears to be a greater consensus on which characteristics should be studied than on which ones actually influence the rendering of PEQIs. The list of variables warranting investigation across all environmental domains includes, in addition to personal PEQ constructs (IVB) and personal utility functions (VIB): age, sex, physical health, socioeconomic status (i.e., occupation, education, income), life cycle stage, environmental training, social role, type of early environmental experience, personal values, religious affiliation, political orientation, notions of social equity, environmental aspirations and expectations, leisure activity patterns, environmental belief systems, environmental attitudes and dispositions, response styles, and various other personality variables.

The role of environmental characteristics is mediated by the ways in which they are presented to the observer. Salient factors in selecting the media of presentation (IIA) have already been noted: (1) the option of touring panels versus on-site users (entailing the role of comparative perspectives, familiarity, and adaptation) and (2) the choice between direct field presentations and an array of simulation techniques (e.g., sketches, photos, films, videotapes, scale models). Similarly, the major context factors (IIB) have already been discussed, which can activate or selectively tune certain observer dispositions and abilities.

In the kind of operational system for place-centered appraisals that has been the principal consideration of this report, observers record their degree of satisfaction with perceived environmental qualities on survey instruments (VA), and then a normative weighting system (VIA) is applied to yield PEQIs in the form of comparative appraisals. However, if instead, observers make global judgments of perceived environmental quality, or if an idiographic strategy is employed that includes use of their personal constituent elements and weighting schemes, then components IVB, VA, and VIB, entailing individual PEQ constructs, environmental departures, and personal utility functions come into play to yield PEQIs in the form of preferential judgments.

Note that the entire model can be scrutinized at critical stages of the psychological process, through behavioral reports of (1) presence/ absence and saliency ratings (IVA); (2) constituent elements of personal PEQ constructs (IVB); (3) satisfaction ratings (VA); (4) analysis of personal weighting schemes (via trade-off games, policy extraction techniques, etc.) (IVB), and (5) reported PEQIs. Furthermore, the linkages between components represent psychological processes of perception, cognition, and judgment, which can also be studied through empirical behavioral analyses.

The conceptual model presented in Figure 2 is not dissimilar to traditional models in psychological and geographical research, but its application to environmental perception displays several distinctive features. First, its longitudinal emphasis entails a time scale which is much more extended than that of typical laboratory studies of perception. Second, distinctive properties of the stimuli employed in environmental perception studies include multidimensionality and a wide range of physical scales, from rooms to regions. Third, the magnitude of the stimuli typically employed often requires simulated presentations. And fourth, compared to laboratory research, the issues studied frequently appear to be directly relevant to the well-being of research participants and thereby modify the traditional role of the participant in psychological research. For example, research findings in environmental perception frequently relate to public policy issues.

The range of research issues that warrant investigation for the purpose of delineating the processes and functioning of this model is extensive, and the domain for research recommendations is open-ended. The following set of recommendations constitutes a ·sampler of scientific probes at critical points throughout the conceptual schema and is illustrative rather than exhaustive of significant lines of inquiry generated by the model.

Recommendation 1. Studies of the antecedents of PEQ constructs and personal utility functions and their operations (e.g., how the PEQ construct interacts with specific perceived environmental qualities to yield satisfaction ratings; how the personal utility function is deployed in specific appraisal settings to yield person-centered PEQIs).

Recommendation 2. Studies of the effects of observer variables and context variables upon perceived environmental qualities and satisfaction ratings (with each set of variables held constant in the analysis of the other).

Recommendation 3. Studies of the effects of environmental variables and media variables upon perceived environmental qualities and satisfaction ratings (with each set of variables held constant in the analysis of the other).

Recommendation 4. Studies of the influence of familiarity upon environmental preference and studies of the process of perceptual adaptation to environmental conditions and trends (e.g., degradation).

Recommendation 5. Studies of the influences of social system variables (e.g., child-rearing; education) upon those observer characteristics which can be shown to play a significant role in the perception of environmental quality.

Recommendation 6. Studies of the influences of social system variables (e.g., legal, administrative, professional factors) upon the nature of context factors and typical settings for obtaining observer appraisals of environmental quality (including comparative studies of communities as well as cross-national investigations).

Recommendation 7. Studies of the influence of social system variables (e.g., professional practice, scientific knowledge, communications technology) upon the kinds of media of presentation used in observer appraisals of environmental quality (including comparative studies of communities as well as cross-national investigations).

Recommendation 8. Studies of the influence of social system variables (e.g., intellectual traditions, political movements, cultural belief systems) upon the selection of the environmental characteristics and settings that are subjected to observer appraisals (e.g., analysis of the processes that result in certain environmental contexts and attributes becoming identified as environmental problems and as significant environmental impacts).

Conceptual Model for Application of PEQI Operational Systems

The previous section of this chapter illustrated that workshop participants were not content with a theoretical model of individual observer processes, but instead sought to take account of social system influences upon those processes. The aspiration for a broad scientific perspective was also evident in discussions of the PEQI operational system. The advantages of a conceptual model to guide research on the development and use of observer appraisal systems for environmental quality were reiterated with conviction and persuasiveness. In part, of course, this conceptual model is reflexive, placing the activities, purposes, and impact of the research workshop series itself under scientific scrutiny.

The conceptual model for the development and use of PEQI operational systems was less explicit and well articulated than that for the individual observer appraisal process, but Figure 3 captures some of the major components and relationships. Social system properties and conditions (I) are viewed as factors in generating the needs for environmental quality policies and programs (II) (e.g., arising via technology, population, complexity of social structure, etc.). Through the actions of governmental bodies, the need for PEQI operational systems (III) is expressed via legislative and administrative mandates and sanctions. Administrative and scientific institutions (IV) serve the function of reviewing feasibility and suggesting guidelines and research priorities. Subsequent development will probably require some form of institutionalized research coordination (V) which would promote and supervise demonstration projects (VI), conduct program evaluations (VII), and engage in other necessary research and development activities.

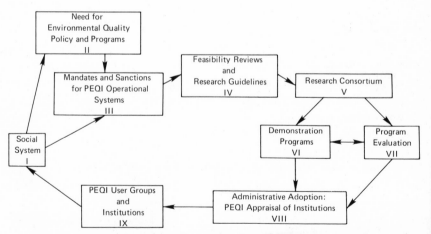

FIG. 3. Conceptual model for the application of PEQI operational systems.

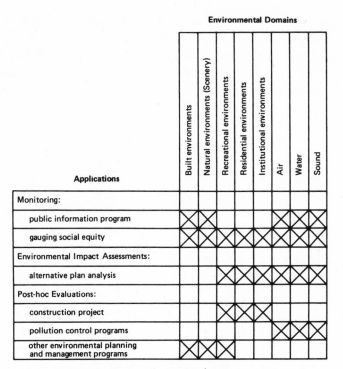

FIG. 4. Potential contexts for PEQI demonstration projects.

A wide array of candidates for selection as 'demonstration projects can be envisioned. Figure 4 depicts the most likely and appropriate contexts for application of PEQI operational systems.

The criteria for evaluating the effectiveness of PEQI operational systems and methods for gauging their impact upon the performance of agencies, firms, and other institutions (Fig. 3, VII) received concerned but fragmentary discussion. They are topics that deserve fuller analysis and review. Similarly, the implications of administrative adoption of PEQI operational systems (VIII) received less attention than they warrant, discussion being limited primarily to the training of appraisal panels and teams. Discussion of the relationship of PEQI appraisal operations to user groups and institutions (IX) focused upon the form and content of communications in public information programs and residential postconstruction evaluations and upon the interpretations and subsequent actions of those who receive such information. Clearly, other relationships must be studied as well. For example, the degree of centralization between PEQI operational institutions and user institutions will likely vary with environmental domain, being highly centralized for air, water, and sound; moderately centralized for urban and scenic domains; and decentralized for residential, recreational, and institutional domains. The impact of the PEQI operational systems upon the policies, practices and performances of user groups and institutions (IX) would constitute an influence upon and modification of the social system. The linkages among components of this conceptual model represent such social processes as collaboration, negotiation, supervision, consultation, etc., which can be analyzed through the methods of sociology, public administration, and related disciplines.

The present report on the PEQI research workshops can be viewed as an emergent from stage IV of the process depicted in Figure 3, following upon a similar review of the status of environmental indices more generally, issued by the Environmental Studies Board of the National Academy of Sciences-National Academy of Engineering (NAS-NAE, 1975). The deliberations of the research workshop series highlighted several additional worthwhile steps that are embodied in the following recommendations.

Recommendation 1. That a complete inventory be assembled of legislative and administrative mandates and sanctions for the use of observer appraisals of environmental quality at the federal and state levels, across environmental domains, plus an interpretive summary of pertinent legal precedents and decisions.

Recommendation 2. That coordination of research on the development and application of observer appraisal systems for environmental quality be undertaken through a nationwide consortium that would promote collaborative efforts, including demonstration projects, at multiple centers and enlist the participation of scientists, practitioners, policymakers, and agency staff.

Recommendation 3. That cross-national research on societal influences upon perceived environmental quality appraisals be organized in conjunction with the U.S. Directorate for Project 13: Perception of Environmental Quality, UNESCO Man and the Biosphere (MAB) program. In particular, that the possibility of joint U.S.-Canada endeavors be explored for selected contexts, such as the MAB projects on coastal zone ecology and on urban ecosystems.

Recommendation 4. That research programs be undertaken in an orderly and meaningful sequence, clarifying and resolving issues at each step, and thereby reducing the cumulative sense of uncertainty and indefiniteness that currently surrounds the overall network of factors affecting perceived environmental quality appraisals.

Recommendation 5. That attention be given to devising institutional mechanisms for safeguarding against misuse of PEQIs in demonstration projects. Such mechanisms might include review panels and contractual agreements among participating scientists and organizations specifying responsibilities for the proper treatment and communication of PEQIs and related findings.

Recommendation 6. That advance discussion and planning proceed on the formulation of detailed criteria and the development of procedures for gauging the effectiveness, utility, and impacts of PEQI operational systems, including mechanisms for documenting beneficial influences and detrimental consequences of their implementation.

Recommendation 7. That advance planning and studies be conducted on the use of PEQIs in public information programs and other feedback contexts, including consideration of modes of presentation, interpretative procedures, and guidelines on their meaning and uses.

Recommendation 8. That PEQIs be employed in substantive scientific research (e.g., the function of the level of PEQI as an independent variable in affecting migration, community morale, mood states, etc.).

CONCLUSIONS

The contributed papers and workshop discussions served their purposes most effectively in clarifying issues in the development and understanding of Perceived Environmental Quality Indices. It is hoped that the resulting conceptual frameworks, stocktakings of methods and empirical findings, and recommendations will prove useful in the programmatic planning of individual researchers and of supporting agencies. If the editors were permitted a few concluding impressions and generalizations, they would deal with the issues of feasibility and immediately useful next steps. We were left with the sense that no psychological measurement barriers stand in the way of developing PEQIs, but the enterprise will entail a substantial program of skillful and sophisticated collaborative research. The diversity of background characterizing workshop participants is representative of the heterogeneity of the "PEQI guild" of scientists, policy-makers, and practitioners, while the discussions themselves amply demonstrated the noteworthy communalities in their concerns and pursuits. An institutional mechanism is urgently needed to serve the conceptual and methodological clearinghouse function which the workshops began to provide. Finally, it is evident that current research on the perception of environmental quality and experience with policy applications of indices in other contexts have reached a maximum value in alerting investigators and decision-makers to the likely issues entailed in the development and use of PEQIs. Further advances seem to require that the next step be the conduct of serious, cautious, self-critical, and carefully analyzed demonstration projects in which PEQIs are constructed, used, and evaluated in the real-world context of environmental policy, management, and practice.

References and Bibliography

Alexandre, A. Decision criteria based on spatio-temporal comparisons of surveys on air-craft noise. In U.S. Environmental Protection Agency (1974b), pp. 619–626.

Allport, F. *The theories of perception and the concept of structure*. New York: Wiley and Sons, 1955.

American Standards Association. *American standard acoustical terminology*. New York: American Standards Association, 1960.

Anderson, T. W., Zube, E. H. (Ed.), & MacConnell, W. P. *Predicting scenic resource values, studies in landscape perception* Amherst: Institute for Man and Environment, University of Massachusetts, 1976.

Andrews, F. Social indicators of perceived life quality. Paper presented at the VIIIth World Congress of the International Sociological Association, Toronto, August 1974.

Andrews, F., & Phillips, G. The squatters of Lima: Who they are and what they want. *Journal of Developing Areas,* January 1970, *4,* 211–224.

Andrews, F., & Withey, S. Assessing the quality of life as people perceive it. Paper presented at the Annual Meeting of the American Sociological Association, Montreal, Canada, 1974.

Anthrop, D. F. *Noise pollution*. Lexington, Massachusetts: D. C. Heath, 1973.

Appleyard, D., & Carp, F. The BART residential impact study: A longitudinal empirical study of environmental impact. In W. F. E. Preiser (Ed.), *Environmental design research* (Vol. 2). Stroudsburg, Pennsylvania: Dowden, Hutchinson and Ross, 1973, pp. 296–306.

Appleyard, D., & Carp, F. The BART residential impact study: An empirical study of environmental impact. In T. G. Dickert & K. R. Domeny (Eds.), *Environmental impact assessment: Gudelines and commentary*. Berkeley: University Extension, University of California, 1974, pp. 73–88.

Appleyard, D., & Craik, K. H. The Berkeley environmental simulation project: Its use in environmental impact assessment. In T. G. Dickert & K. R. Domeny (Eds.), *Environmental impact assessment: Guidelines and commentary* Berkeley: University Extension, University of California, 1974, pp. 121–126.

Appleyard, D., & Lintell, M. The environmental quality of city streets: The residents' viewpoint. *Journal of the American Institute of Planners,* March 1972, *38,* 84–101.

Arnold, M. B., & Gasson, J. A. Feelings and emotions as dynamic factors in personality integration. In M. B. Arnold (Ed.), *The nature of emotion*. Baltimore: Penguin Books, 1968, pp. 203–221.

289

Arthur, L. M., Daniel, T. C., & Boster, R. S. *Scenic beauty assessment: A literature review.* U.S.D.A. Forest Service, 1976, in press.

Auliciems, A., & Burton, I. Perception and awareness of air pollution in Toronto. University of Toronto Department of Geography Working Paper No. 13, Toronto, 1970.

Auliciems, A., & Burton, I. Air pollution in Toronto. In W. R. D. Sewell & I. Burton (Eds.), *Perceptions and attitudes in resources management.* Ottawa: Information Canada, 1971, pp. 71–80.

Barker, M. L. Beach pollution in the Toronto region. In W. R. D. Sewell & I. Burton (Eds.), *Perceptions and attitudes in resources management.* Ottawa: Information Canada, 1971, pp. 37–47.

Barker, M. L. Information and complexity: The conceptualization of air pollution by specialist groups. *Environment and Behavior, 1974, 6,* 346–377.

Barker, R. *Ecological psychology.* Stanford, California: Stanford University Press, 1968.

Barker, R., & Gump, P. *Big school, small school.* Stanford, California: Stanford University Press, 1964.

Barker, R., & Schoggin, P. *Qualities of community life.* San Francisco: Jossey-Bass, 1973.

Barnes, P. A. Community awareness and concern with air quality in Toronto: A pilot study. Unpublished B. A. thesis, University of Toronto, 1968.

Bechtel, R. B. Dependency: An unintended result of public housing policies. Greater Kansas City Mental Health Foundation/ERDF, 1972. (a)

Bechtel, R. B. The public housing environment: A few surprises. In W. J. Mitchell (Ed.), *Environmental design: Research and practice.* Los Angeles: University of California, 1972, pp. 13-1-1 to 13-1-9. (b)

Bechtel, R. B. The semantic differential and other paper and pencil tests: A caution against yielding too early to temptation. In W. Michelson (Ed.), *Behavioral research methods in environmental design.* Stroudsburg, Pennsylvania: Dowden, Hutchinson and Ross, 1975.

Bechtel, R. B., & Ledbetter, C. B. The temporary environment. Final report of the Cold Regions Habitability Project. Hanover, New Hampshire: Cold Regions Research and Engineering Laboratories, 1975.

Berkowitz, L. *Aggression.* New York: McGraw-Hill, 1962.

Berry, D. Open space values: A household survey of two Philadelphia parks. RSRI Discussion Paper Series, No. 76, October 1974.

Berry, D. The image of urban open space. Northwestern Anthropological Association, meetings, 1975.

Berry, D. Preservation of open space and the concept of value. *American Journal of Economics and Sociology,* 1976, in press.

Berry, D., & Coughlin, R. E. Economic implications of preserving ecologically valuable land in Medford, New Jersey. RSRI Report, 1973.

Berry, D., & Steiker, G. Landscape, image and design: A survey of open space planners. RSRI Discussion Paper Series, No. 77, December 1974.

Binder, A. Statistical theory. *Annual Review of Psychology,* 1964 *15,* 277–310.

Blalock, H. M. *Causal inference in nonexperimental research.* Chapel Hill: University of North Carolina Press, 1964.

Borkin, H., & Clipson, C. Determination of housing preferences. Ann Arbor: Architectural Research Laboratory, The University of Michigan, 1975.

Borsky, P. N. Community aspects of aircraft noise. Washington, D.C.: National Advisory Committee for Aeronautics, 1952.

Borksy, P. N. Community reactions to air force noise—Part II—Data on community studies and their interpretation [WADD Technical Report 60-689 (II)]. Dayton, Ohio: Wright-Patterson Air Force Base, 1961. (NTIS No. AD 267 057).

Borsky, P. N. Special analysis of community annoyance with aircraft noise reported by residents in the vicinity of John F. Kennedy airport. Washington, D.C.: National Aeronautics and Space Administration, unpublished report, 1972.

Borsky, P. N. A new field-laboratory methodology for assessing human response to noise. (NASA CR-221). Washington, D.C.: National Aeronautics and Space Administration, 1973.

Bottom, C. G. A social survey into annoyance caused by the interaction of aircraft noise and traffic noise. *Journal of Sound and Vibration,* 1971,*19*,473–476.

Bragdon, C. R. *Noise pollution: The unquiet crisis.* Philadelphia: University of Pennsylvania Press, 1970.

Brown, G., & Hammack, J. A preliminary investigation of the economics of migratory wildfowl. In J. Krutilla (Ed.), *Natural environments.* Baltimore: Johns Hopkins, 1972, pp. 171–204.

Brown, R. M., McClelland, N. J., Deininger, R. A., & Tozer, R. G. A water quality index—Do we dare?. National Symposium on Data and Instrumentation for Water Quality Management. University of Wisconsin, Madison, July 1970.

Brush, R. O., & Shafer, E. L., Jr. Application of a landscape preference model to land management. In E. H. Zube, R. O. Brush, & J. Gy. Fabos (Eds.), *Landscape assessment: Values, perceptions and resources.* Stroudsburg, Pennsylvania: Dowden, Hutchinson and Ross, 1975.

Bruvold, W. H., Ongerth, H. J., & Dillehay, R. C. Consumer assessment of mineral taste in domestic water. *Journal of the American Water Works Association,* 1969, *61,* 575–580.

Burby, R. Recreation and leisure in new communities. Center for Urban and Regional Studies, University of North Carolina, Chapel Hill, unpublished report, 1974.

Butler, E., Chapin, F. S. Hemmens, G., Kaiser, E., Stegman, M., & Weiss, S. Moving behavior and residential choice: A national survey. Washington, D.C.: Highway Research Board, 1969.

Calvin, J. S., Dearinger, J. A., & Curtin, M. E. An attempt at assessing preferences for natural landscapes. *Environment and Behavior,* 1972, *4*(4),447–470.

Campbell, A., Converse, P., & Rodgers, W. *The quality of American life.* New York: Russell Sage Foundation, 1976.

Cantril, H. *The pattern of human concerns.* New Brunswick, New Jersey: Rutgers University Press, 1965.

Cantril, H. *The human dimension: Experiences in policy research.* New Brunswick, New Jersey: Rutgers University Press, 1967.

Caplow, T., & Forman, R. Neighborhood integration in a homogeneous community. *American Sociological Review,* 1955, *15,* 357–366.

Carls, E. G. The effects of people and man-induced conditions on preferences for outdoor recreation landscapes. *Journal of Leisure Research,* 1973, *6*(2),113–124.

Carp, F. M. Housing a minority group elderly. *The Gerontologist,* 1969, *9,* 20–24.

Carp, F. M., Appleyard, D., Shokrkon, H., Zawadski, R. T. Residential quality prior to the opening of BART. BART Impact Studies, BART-II, Part II, Volume III. Berkeley: Institute of Urban and Regional Development, University of California, 1973.

Carp, F. M., Zawadski, R. T., & Shokrkon, H. Dimensions of urban residential quality. Berkeley: Institute of Urban and Regional Planning, University of California, 1974.

Cason, H. Common annoyances: A psychological study of every-day aversions and irritation. *Psychological Monographs,* 1930, *40*(2), Whole No. 182.

Cederlöf, R., Jonsson, E., & Sörensen, S. On the influence of attitudes to the source on annoyance reactions to noise—a field experiment. *Nordisk Hygienisk Tidskrift,* 1967, *48,* 46–59.

Chapin, F. S., & Hightower, H. Household activity patterns and land use. *Journal of the American Institute of Planners,* August 1965 *31,* 222–231.

Chevalier, M., & Cartwright, T. J. Public involvement in planning: The Delaware River case. In W. R. D. Sewell & I. Burton (Eds.), *Perceptions and attitudes in resources management.* Ottawa: Information Canada, 1971.

Clark, K. *Landscape into art.* Boston: Beacon, 1961.

Clark, R., Hendee, J. C., & Campbell, F. L. Values, behavior and conflict in modern camping culture. *Journal of Leisure Research,* 1971, *3*(3), 143–159.

Connor, W. K., & Patterson, H. P. Community reaction to aircraft noise around smaller city airports (NASA CR-2104). Washington, D.C.: National Aeronautics and Space Administration, 1972.

Coombs, C. *A theory of data.* New York: Wiley and Sons, 1964.

Cooper, C. St. Frances Square: Attitudes of its residents. *American Institute of Architects Journal,* December 1971, *56,* 22–25.

Cooper, C. Resident dissatisfaction in multi-family housing. In W. M. Smith (Ed.), *Behavior, design and policy aspects of human habitats.* Green Bay: University of Wisconsin—Green Bay Press, 1972, pp. 119–145.

Cooper, C. C. *Eastern hill village.* New York: Free Press, 1975.

Costantini, E., & Hanf, K. Environmental concern and Lake Tahoe: A study of elite perceptions, backgrounds and attitudes. *Environment and Behavior,* 1972, *4,* 209–242.

Coughlin, R. E., & Goldstein, K. A. The extent of agreement among observers on environmental attractiveness. RSRI Discussion Paper Series, No. 37. Philadelphia: Regional Science Research Institute, 1970.

Coughlin, R. E., & Hammer, T. R. Stream quality preservation through planned urban development, EPA-R5-73-019. Washington, D.C.: U.S. Government Printing Office, 1973.

Coughlin, R. E., Hammer, T. R., Dickert, T. G., & Sheldon, S. Perception and use of streams in suburban areas: Effects of water quality and of distance from residence to stream. RSRI Discussion Paper Series, No. 53. Philadelphia: Regional Science Research Institute, March 1972.

Council on Environmental Quality. Environmental quality: Third annual report. Washington, D.C.: U.S. Government Printing Office, 1972.

Council on Environmental Quality. Environmental quality: Fourth annual report. Washington, D.C.: U.S. Government Printing Office, 1973.

Craik, K. H. Environmental psychology. In K. H. Craik, B. Kleinmuntz, R. Rossow, R. Rosenthal, J. Cheyne, & R. Walters (Eds.), New directions in psychology (Vol. 4). New York: Holt, Rinehart & Winston, 1970, pp. 1–122.

Craik, K. H. The assessment of places. In P. McReynolds (Ed.), Advances in psychological assessment (Vol. 2). Palo Alto, California: Science and Behavior Books, 1971, pp. 40–62.

Craik, K. H. Appraising the objectivity of landscape dimensions. In J. V. Krutilla (Ed.), Natural environments: Studies in theoretical and applied analysis. Baltimore: Johns Hopkins University Press, 1972, pp. 292–346. (a)

Craik, K. H. Psychological factors in landscape appraisal. Environment and Behavior, 1972, 4, 255–266. (b)

Craik, K. H. Environmental psychology. In P. H. Mussen & M. R. Rosenzweig (Eds.), Annual review of psychology (Vol. 24). Palo Alto, California: Annual Reviews, 1973, pp. 402–422.

Craik, K. H., & McKechnie, G. E. Perception of environmental quality: Preferential judgments versus comparative appraisals. Berkeley: University of California, unpublished report, August 1974.

Cronbach, L. J., & Meehl, P. E. Construct validity in psychological tests. Psychological Bulletin, 1955, 52, 281–302.

Cronbach, L. J., Gleser, G. C., Nanda, H., & Rajaratnam, N. The dependability of behavioral measurements: Theory of generalizability for scores and profiles. New York: Wiley and Sons, 1972.

Crowe, M. J. Towards a 'definitional' model of public perceptions of air pollution. Journal of Air Pollution Control Association, March 1968, 18, 154–157.

Crowne, D. P., & Marlowe, D. A new scale of social desirability independent of psychopathology. Journal of Consulting Psychology, 1960, 24, 349–354.

Danford, S., & Willems, E. Subjective responses to architectural displays: A question of validity. Environment and Behavior, 1975, 7(4), 486–516.

Daniel, T. C., & Boster, R. S. Measuring scenic beauty: The scenic beauty estimation method. USDA Forest Service Rocky Mountain Forest and Range Experiment Station Research Paper, 1976, in press.

Daniel, T. C., Wheeler, L., Boster, R. S., & Best, P. Quantitative evaluation of landscape: An application of signal detection analysis to forest management alternatives. Man–Environment Systems, 1973, 3(5), 330–344.

David, E. L. Public perceptions of water quality. Water Resources Research, 1971, 7, 453–457.

Davis, G., & Roizen, R., 1970, Architectural determinants of student satisfaction in college residence halls. In J. Archea and C. Eastman (Eds.), EDRA Two: Proceedings of the 2nd Annual Environmental Design Research Association Conference. Pittsburgh: Carnegie-Mellon University, 1970, pp. 28–44.

Dearinger, J. A. Aesthetic and recreational potential of small naturalistic streams near urban areas. Research Report No. 13. Lexington: University of Kentucky Water Resources Research Institute, 1968.

De Groot, I., Loring, W., Rihm, A., Samuels, S. W., & Winkelstein, W. People and air pollution: A study of attitudes in Buffalo, N.Y. *Journal of Air Pollution Control Association,* 1966, *16*(5), 245–247.

de Neufville, R., & Stafford, J. H. Evaluation of a public system: Welfare maximization. In *Systems analysis for engineers and managers.* New York: McGraw-Hill, 1971, pp. 226–256.

Department of the Army. Evaluation of impacts arising from alternatives for managing wastewater in the Chicago–South End Lake Michigan Area. Corps of Engineers, Chicago District, 1973.

Dickert, T. G., & Domeny, K. R. (Eds.). *Environmental impact assessment: Guidelines and commentary.* Berkeley: University Extension, University of California, 1974.

Dillman, D. A. Population distribution policy and people's attitudes: Current knowledge and needed research. Urban Land Institute, unpublished paper, 1973.

Dillman, D. A., & Dobash, R. *Preferences for community living and the indications for population redistribution,* Bulletin 764. Pullman, Washington: Washington Agricultural Experiment Station, 1972.

Ditton, R. B., & Goodale, T. L. Water quality perception and the recreational users of Green Bay, Lake Michigan. *Water Resources,* June 1973, *9,* 569–579.

Dubos, R. *Man adapting.* New Haven: Yale University Press, 1965.

Ertel, M. The Connecticut River system: A workshop on research needs and priorities. Institute for Man and Environment and Water Resources Research Center, University of Massachusetts, Amherst, 1975.

Fabos, J. Gy. An analysis of environmental quality ranking systems. Recreation Symposium Proceedings, Northeastern Forest Experiment Station, U.S., Forest Service, Upper Darby, Pennsylvania, 1971, pp. 40–55.

Ferebee, A. Design for human behavior. *Design and Environment,* Winter 1971, 23.

Festinger, L., Schachter, S., & Back, K. *Social pressures in informal groups.* New York: Harper & Row, 1950.

Fines, K. D. Landscape evaluation—a research project in East Sussex. *Regional Studies (U.K.),* 1968, *2,* 40–55.

Folk, G. *Introduction to environmental physiology.* Philadelphia: Lea and Febiger, 1969.

Foote, N., Abu-Lughod, J., Foley, M., & Winnick, L. *Housing choices and housing constraits.* New York: McGraw-Hill, 1970.

Fox, I. K., & Wible, L. F. Information generation and communication quality objectives. *Natural Resources Journal,* 1973, *13,* 134–149.

Fried, M., & Gleicher, P. Some sources of residential satisfaction in an urban slum. *Journal of the American Institute of Planners,* November 1961, *27,* 305–315.

Galloway, W. J., & Bishop, D. E. Noise exposure forecasts: Evolution evaluation, and land use interpretations (FAA-NO-70-9). Washington, D.C.: Federal Aviation Administration, 1970. (NTIS No. AD711 131).

Galloway, W. J., & Jones G. Motor vehicle noise: Identification and analysis of situations contributing to annoyance. In U.S. Environmental Protection Agency (1974b), pp. 785–803.

Galloway, W. J., Clark, W. E., & Kerrick, J. S. Highway noise: Measurement, simulation and mixed reactions. National Cooperative Highway Research Program Report No. 78. Washington, D.C.: National Academy of Sciences-National Academy of Engineering, 1969.

Gans, H. J. *The urban villagers: Group and class in the life of Italian Americans.* New York: Free Press, 1962.

Gans, H. J. *The Levittowners.* New York: Pantheon Books, 1967.

Gerst, M. M., & Moos, R. H. The social ecology of university student residences. *Journal of Educational Psychology,* 1972, *63*(6), 513–525.

Gilbert, C. G., Peterson, G. L., & Lime, D. W. Toward a model of travel behavior in the boundary waters canoe area. *Environment and Behavior,* 1972, *4*(2), 131–157.

Goffman, E. *Asylums.* Chicago: Aldine, 1962.

Gold, S. Nonuse of neighborhood parks. *Journal of the American Institute of Planners,* November 1972, *38,* 369–378.

Goodey, B. Perception of the environment: An introduction to the literature. Centre for Urban and Regional Studies, University of Birmingham, Birmingham, England, 1971.

Grandjean, E., Graf, P., Lauber, A., Mejer, H. P., & Müller, R. A survey of aircraft noise in Switzerland. In U.S. Environmental Protection Agency (1974b), pp. 645–659.

Griffiths, I. D., & Langdon, F. J. Subjective response to road traffic noise. *Journal of Sound and Vibration,* 1968, *8,* 16–32.

Guilford, J. P., & Fruchter, B. *Fundamental statistics in psychology and education.* New York: McGraw-Hill, 1973.

Gutman, R., & Westergaard, B. Building evaluation, user satisfaction, and design. In J. Lang, C. Burnette, W. Moleski, & D. Vachon (Eds.), *Designing for human behavior: Architecture and the behavioral sciences.* Stroudsburg, Pennsylvania: Dowden, Hutchinson and Ross, 1974, pp. 320–330.

Hamovitch, M., & Peterson, J. Housing needs and satisfactions of the elderly. *The Gerontologist,* 1969, *9,* 30–32.

Hartman, C. The housing of relocated families. *Journal of the American Institute of Planners,* November 1964, *30,* 266–286.

Hazard, W. R. Community reactions to aircraft noise. *Proceedings of the Conference on Progress of NASA Research Relating to Noise Alleviation of Large Subsonic Aircraft* (NASA SP-189), (National Aeronautics and Space Administration, Ed.). Washington, D.C.: National Aeronautics and Space Administration, 1968, pp. 661–671. (NTIS No. N69-11542).

Hazard, W. R. Predictions of noise disturbance near large airports. *Journal of Sound and Vibration,* 1971, *15,* 425–445.

Helson, H. *Adaptation level theory.* New York: Harper & Row, 1964.

Hewings, J., Auliciems, A., Burton, I., Schiff, M., & Taylor, C. The public use of scientific information on the quality of the environment: The case of the Ontario Air Pollution Index. In W. P. Adams & F. M. Helleiner (Eds.), *International geography.* Proceedings of 22nd International Congress, Montreal, Canada, 1972, pp. 641–643.

Hinshaw, M., & Allott, K. Environmental preferences of future housing consumers. *Journal of the American Institute of Planners,* March 1972, *38,* 102–107.

Hollingshead, A. B., & Rogler, L. H. Attitudes toward slums and public housing in Puerto Rico. In L. J. Duhl (Ed.), *The urban condition.* New York: Basic Books, 1963, p. 229–245.

Hubbert, M. U.S. energy resources: A review as of 1972. Washington, D.C.: U.S. Government Printing Office, 1974.

I.G.U. Air Pollution Study Group for the U.K. Papers on Selected Social Aspects of Air Pollution in the United Kingdom, International Geographical Union, Commission on Man and Environment, Calgary Symposium, 1972, July 23–31.

Inhaber, H. Environmental quality: Outline for a national index for Canada. *Science,* 1974, *186,* 798–805.

Ittelson, W. H., Proshansky, H. M., & Rivlin, L. G. The environmental psychology of the psychiatric ward. In H. M. Proshansky, W. H. Ittleson, & L. G. Rivlin (Eds.), *Environmental psychology: Man and his physical setting.* New York: Holt, Rinehart & Winston, 1970, pp. 419–439.

Ittelson,.W. H., Proshansky, H. M.; Rivlin, L. G., & Winkel, G. *An introduction to environmental psychology.* New York: Holt, Rinehart & Winston, 1974.

Jacoby, L. R. Perception of air, noise and water pollution in Detroit (Michigan Geographical, Publication No. 7). Ann Arbor: Department of Geography, The University of Michigan, 1972.

Jennings, B., & Murphy, J. (Eds.). *Interactions of man and his environment.* New York: Plenum Press, 1966.

Jones, G. Public testimony. *Public hearings on noise abatement and control.* Volume 7 Physiological and psychological effects (U.S. Environmental Protection Agency, Ed.), Washington, D.C.: U.S. Government Printing Office, 1971, pp. 280–292:

Jonsson, E. On the formulation of questions in medicohygienic interview investigations. *Acta Sociologica,* 1964, *7*(3), 193–202.

Jonsson, E., Arvidsson, O., Bergland, K., & Kajland, A. Methodological aspects of studies of community response to noise. In U.S. Environmental Protection Agency (1974b), pp. 611–617.

Jonsson, E., Paccagnella, B., & Sörenssen, S. Annoyance reactions to traffic noise in Italy and Sweden. *Archives of Environmental Health,* 1969, *19*(5), 692–699.

Kain, J., & Quigley, M. Evaluating the quality of the residential environment. *Environment and Planning,* 1970, *2,* 23–32.

Kaiser, E., Weiss, S., Burby, R., & Donnelly, J. Neighborhood evaluation and residential satisfaction: A survey of occupants and neighborhoods in 166 single family homes in Greensboro, N.C. Center for Urban and Regional Studies, University of North Carolina, Durham, 1970.

Kaplan, R. Predictors of environmental preference: Designers and 'clients.' In W. F. E. Preiser (Ed.), *Environmental Design Research.* Stroudsburg, Pennsylvania: Dowden, Hutchinson and Ross, 1973.

Kaplan, R. Some methods and strategies in the prediction of preference. In E. H. Zube, R. O. Brush, & J. Gy. Fabos (Eds.), *Landscape assessment: Values, perceptions and resources.* Stroudsburg, Pennsylvania: Dowden, Hutchinson and Ross, 1975.

Kaplan, S., Kaplan, R., & Wendt, J. S. Rated preference and complexity for natural and urban visual material. *Perception and Psychophysics,* 1972, *12*(4), 354–356.

Kasl, S., & Harburg, E. Perceptions of the neighborhood and the desire to move out. *Journal of the American Institute of Planners,* September 1972, *38,* 318–324.

Kasmar, J. The development of a useful lexicon of environmental descriptors. *Environment and Behavior,* 1970, *2,* 153–169.

Kates, R. W. Human perception of the environment. *International Social Science Journal,* 1970, *22,* 648–660.

Kates, R. W. National hazard in human ecological perspective: Hypotheses and models. *Economic Geography,* July 1971, *47,* 438–451.

Keller, S. *The urban neighborhood: A sociological perspective.* New York: Random House, 1968.

Kimball, T. L. Why environmental quality indices? In W. Thomas (Ed.), *Indicators of environmental quality.* New York: Plenum Press, 1972.

Kirkby, A. V. Perception of air pollution as a hazard and individual adjustments to it in three British cities. Papers on Selected Social Aspects of Air Pollution in the United Kingdom, International Geographical Union, Commission on Man and Environment, Calgary Symposium, July 23–31, 1972.

Knetsch, J., & Davis, R. Comparisons of methods for recreation evaluation. In A. Kneese & S. Smith (Eds.), *Water research.* Baltimore: Johns Hopkins University Press, 1966, pp. 125–142.

Knight, R., & Menchik, M. Residential environmental attitudes and preferences: Report of a questionnaire survey. Institute for Environmental Studies Report 24, University of Wisconsin, Madison, 1974.

Kooyoomjian, J. K., & Clesceri, N. L. Perception of water quality by select respondent groupings in inland water-based recreational environments. Rensselaer Fresh Water Institute, Rensselaer Polytechnic Institute, Troy, New York, 1973.

Kooyoomjian, K. J., & Clesceri, N. L. Perception of water quality by select respondent groupings in inland water-based recreational environments. *Water Resources Bulletin,* August 1974, *10*(4).

Kromm, D. E., & Viztak, S. Response to air pollution in Ljubljana, Yugoslavia. International Geographical Union, Commission on Man and Environment, Calgary Symposium, July 23–31, 1972.

Kryter, K. D. Scaling human reactions to the sound from aircraft. *Journal of the Acoustical Society of America,* 1959, *31,* 1415–1429.

Kryter, K. D. *The Effects of Noise on Man.* New York: Academic Press, 1970.

Ladd, F. C. Black youths view their environment: Neighborhood maps. *Environment and Behavior,* 1970, *2,* 74–99.

Ladd, F. C. Black youths view their environments: Some views of housing. *Journal of the American Institute of Planners,* March 1972, *38,* 108–116.

Lamanna, R. A. Value consensus among urban residents. *Journal of the American Institute of Planners,* November 1964, *30,* 317–323.

Lang, P. J., Rice, D. G., & Sternbach, R. A. The psychophysiology of emotion. In N. S. Greenfield & R. A. Sternbach (Eds.), *Handbook of psychophysiology.* New York: Holt, Rinehart & Winston, 1972, pp. 623–644.

Lansing, J. B. Residential location and urban mobility: The second wave of interviews. Ann Arbor: Institute for Social Research, The University of Michigan, 1966.

Lansing, J. B., & Hendricks, G. Automobile ownership and residential density. Ann Arbor: Institute for Social Research, The University of Michigan, 1967.

Lansing, J. B., & Marans, R. W. Evaluation of neighborhood quality. *Journal of the American Institute of Planners,* 1969, *35,* 195–199.

Lansing, J. B., Mueller, E., & Barth, N. Residential location and urban mobility. Ann Arbor: Institute for Social Research, The University of Michigan, 1964.

Lansing, J. B., Marans, R. W., & Zehner, R. B. Planned residential environments. Ann Arbor: Institute for Social Research, The University of Michigan, 1970.

Layton, E. *The revolt of the engineers.* Cleveland: Case Western Reserve University, 1971.

Lazarus, R. S. *Psychological stress and the coping process.* New York: McGraw-Hill, 1966.

Lee, T. Urban neighborhood as a socio-spatial scheme. *Human Relations,* 1968, *21,* 241–268.

Lefcourt, H. M. Repression-sensitization: A measure of the evaluation of emotional expression. *Journal of Consulting Psychology,* 1966, *30*(5), 444–449.

Leff, H. L., Gordon, L. R., & Ferguson, J. G. Cognitive set and environmental awareness. *Environment and Behavior,* 1974, *6,* 395–447.

Lehman, E. K. Copper-nickel mining in Minnesota—a case study in the need for responsible environmental decision-making. *Wilderness News,* Winter, 1974.

Leonard, S., & Borsky, P. N. A causal model for relating noise exposure, psychosocial variables and aircraft noise annoyance. In U.S. Environmental Protection Agency (1974b), pp. 691–705.

Leopold, A. Quantitative comparisons of some aesthetic factors among rivers. Geological Survey Circular 670, Washington, D.C., 1949.

Library of Congress Congressional Research Service. National Environmental Policy Act of 1969. Environmental Indices—Status of Development Pursuant to Sections 102(2)(B) and 204 of the Act. Washington, D.C.: U.S. Government Printing Office, 1973.

Lime, D. W. Research for determining use capacities of the boundary waters canoe area. *Naturalist,* 1970, *21*(4), 9–13.

Lime, D. W. Emerging problems of backcountry river recreation-research opportunities. North Central Forest Experiment Station, U.S. Department of Agriculture, March 1975.

Lindvall, T. On sensory evaluation of odorous air pollutant intensities: Measurements of odor intensity in the laboratory and in the field with special reference to effluents of sulfate pulp factories. Stockholm: Karolinska Institute, 1970.

Linton, D. L. The assessment of scenery as a natural resource. *Scottish Geographical Magazine,* 1968, *84,* 219–238.

Lipschutz, S. *Theory and problems of linear algebra.* New York: Schaum's Outline Series, 1968.

Litton, R. B., Jr. Aesthetic dimensions of the landscape. In J. V. Krutilla (Ed.), *Natural environments: Studies in theoretical and applied analysis.* Baltimore: Johns Hopkins University Press, 1972, pp. 262–291.

Lowenthal, D. Geography, experience and imagination: Towards a geographical episte-
mology. *Annals of the Association of American Geographers,* 1961, *51*(3), 241–
260.

Lowenthal, D. Environmental assessment: A comparative analysis of four cities. New
York: American Geographical Society, 1972. (a)

Lowenthal, D. Research in environmental perception and behavior: Perspectives on current problems. *Environment and Behavior,* 1972, *4,* 333–342. (b)

Lucas, R. C. Wilderness perception and use: The example of the boundary waters
canoe area. *Natural Resources Journal,* 1964, *3*(3), 394–411.

Lucas, R. C. The contribution of environmental research to wilderness policy decisions.
Journal of Social Issues, 1966, *22*(4), 116–126.

Lucas, R. C. User evaluation of campgrounds on two Michigan National Forests. USDA
Forest Service Research Paper NC-44. North Central Forest Experiment Station,
St. Paul, Minnesota, 1970.

Lynch, K. *The image of the city.* Cambridge: Harvard University Press, 1960.

Lynch, K., & Rivkin, M. A walk around the block. *Landscape,* 1959, *8*(3), 24–34.

Mandell, L., & Marans, R. W. *Participation in outdoor recreation: A national perspective.* Ann Arbor: Institute for Social Research, The University of Michigan, 1972.

Marans, R. W., & Mandell, L. The relative effectiveness of density-related variables.
Proceedings of the American Statistical Association Meetings, 1972, pp. 360–363.

Marans, R. W., & Rodgers, W. Toward an understanding of community satisfaction. In
A. Hawley & V. Rock (Eds.), *Metropolitan America in contemporary perspective.*
New York: Halstead Press, 1975.

Marans, R. W., Newman, S. J., Wellman, J. D., & Kruse, J. Living patterns and
attitudes of water-oriented residents. Ann Arbor: Institute for Social Research, The
University of Michigan, 1976.

Martin, P. W. *The ill-housed.* Mineola, New York: The Foundation Press, 1971.

Martin, W. S., Fruchter, B., & Mathis, W. J. An investigation of the effect of the
number of scale intervals on principal components factor analysis. *Educational and
Psychological Measurement,* Autumn, 1974, *34,* 537–545.

McEvoy, J. The American concern with environment. In W. R. Burch, Jr., N. H.
Cheek, Jr., & L. Taylor (Eds.), *Social behavior, natural resources, and the environment.* New York: Harper & Row, 1972, pp. 214–236.

McKechnie, G. E. Simulation techniques in environmental psychology. In D. Stokols
(Ed.), *Psychological perspectives on environment and behavior.* New York: Plenum
Press, 1976, in press.

McKennell, A. C. Aircraft noise annoyance around London (Heathrow) Airport. Central
Office of Information, U.K. Government Social Survey S.S. 337. London: Her
Majesty's Stationery Office, 1963.

McKennell, A. C. Methodological problems in a survey of aircraft noise annoyance.
Statistician, 1969, *19,* 1–29.

McKennell, A. C. Psycho-social factors in aircraft noise annoyance. In U.S. Environmental Protection Agency (1974b), pp. 627–644.

McKennell, A. C., & Hunt, E. A. Noise annoyance in Central London. Government
Social Survey S.S. 332 London: Her Majesty's Stationery Office, 1966.

Medalia, N. Z., & Finker, A. L. Community perception of air quality: An opinion survey in Clarkston, Washington. U.S. Department of Health, Education and Welfare PHSP No. 999-AP-10, Washington, D.C.: U.S. Government Printing Office, 1965.

Michelson, W. An empirical analysis of urban environmental preferences. *Journal of the American Institute of Planners*, 1966, *32*(6), 355–360.

Michelson, W. Analytic sampling for design information: A survey of housing experience. In H. Sanoff and S. Cohn, (Eds.), Proceedings of the 1st Annual Environmental Design Research Association Conference, 1969.

Michelson, W. *Man and his urban environment: A sociological analysis.* Reading, Massachusetts: Addison-Wesley, 1970.

Michelson, W. Environmental choice: A draft report on the social basis of family decisions on housing type and location in Greater Toronto. Ottawa: Ministry of State for Urban Affairs, 1972.

Michelson, W., & Reed, P. The time budget. In W. Michelson (Ed.), *Behavioral research methods in environmental design.* Stroudsburg, Pennsylvania: Dowden, Hutchinson and Ross, 1975.

Milbrath, L. W., & Sahr, R. C. Perceptions of environmental quality. *Social Indicators Research*, 1975, *1*, 397–438.

Miller, D. C. The allocation of priorities to urban and environmental problems by powerful leaders and organizations. In W. R. Burch, Jr., N. H. Cheek, Jr., & L. Taylor (Eds.), *Social behavior, natural resources, and the environment.* New York: Harper & Row, 1972, pp. 306–331.

Moos, R. *Evaluating treatment environments.* New York: Wiley and Sons, 1974.

Moos, R. H., & Houts, P. S. Assessment of the social atmospheres of psychiatric wards. *Journal of Abnormal Psychology*, 1968, *73*(6), 595–604.

Morris, C. *Varieties of human value.* Chicago: University of Chicago Press, 1956.

National Academy of Sciences–National Academy of Engineering. *Planning for Environmental Indices.* Washington, D.C.: Environmental Studies Board, 1975.

New Jersey Department of Transportation. *Environmental Analysis and Report for Route 18 Freeway Extension* (Vol. 1 and 2). Trenton, New Jersey: Author, 1972.

Newman, O. *Defensible space.* New York: Macmillan, 1972.

Newman, S. The residential environment and the desire to move. Ann Arbor: Institute for Social Research, The University of Michigan, 1974.

Norcross, C. Townhouses and condominiums: Residents' likes and dislikes. Washington, D.C.: Urban Land Institute, 1973.

Nunnally, J. C. *Psychometric theory.* New York: McGraw-Hill, 1967.

O'Connor, M. F. The application of multi-attribute scaling procedures to the development of indices of value. Technical Report, Engineering Psychology Laboratory, The University of Michigan, Ann Arbor, 1972.

Office of Population Censuses and Surveys. Second survey of aircraft noise annoyance around London (Heathrow) Airport. London: Her Majesty's Stationery Office, 1971.

O'Riordan, T. Public opinion and environmental quality: A reappraisal. *Environment and Behavior*, 1971, *3*, 191–214.

Orleans, P. Urban experimentation and urban sociology. Science, engineering, and the city, Washington D.C.: National Academy of Sciences, 1967.

Osgood, C., Suci, G., & Tannenbaum, P. *The measurement of meaning.* Urbana: University of Illinois Press, 1957.

Osmond, H. Function as the basis of psychiatric ward design. *Mental Hospitals,* 1957, *8,* 23–29.

Pancheri, P. Measurement of emotion: Transcultural aspects. In L. Levi (Ed.), *Emotions: Their parameters and measurement.* New York: Raven Press, 1975, pp. 439–467.

Patterson, H. P., & Connor, W. K. Community responses to aircraft noise in large and small cities in the USA. In Environmental Protection Agency (1974b), pp. 707–718.

Pearson, N. Planning a social unit. *Plan Canada,* 1962, *3*(2), 78–86.

Perin, C. Concepts and methods for studying environments in use. *Environmental design: Research and practice.* EDRA 3/AR8, Los Angeles, 1972.

Perry, C. The neighborhood unit. Regional survey for New York and its environs, Vol. VII, 1929.

Peterson, G. L. A model of preference: Qualitative analysis of the perception of the visual appearance of residential neighborhoods. *Journal of Regional Science,* 1967, *7*(1), 19–32.

Peterson, G. L. Evaluating the quality of the wilderness environment: Congruence between perception and aspiration. *Environment and Behavior,* 1974, *6*(2), 169–193. (a)

Peterson, G. L. A comparison of the sentiments and perceptions of wilderness managers and canoeists in the Boundary Waters Canoe Area. *Journal of Leisure Research,* 1974, *6*(3), 194–206. (b)

Peterson, G. L. Recreational preferences of urban teenagers: The influence of cultural and environmental attributes. Paper presented at the Symposium Fair: Children, nature, and the urban environment, Washington, D. C., May, 1975 (*Proceedings* in press).

Peterson, G. L., & Neumann, E. S. Modeling and predicting human response to the visual recreation environment. *Journal of Leisure Research,* 1969, *1,* 219–237.

Peterson, G. L., & Worrall, R. D. An analysis of individual preferences for accessibility to selected neighborhood services. Paper prepared for the 49th Annual Meeting of the Highway Research Board, Washington, D.C., 1970.

Peterson, G. L., Schofer, J. L., & Gemmel, R. S. Multidisciplinary design-interactive evaluation of large-scale projects. EDRA 5, Proceedings, Fifth Annual Conference, Environmental Design Research Association, 1974, pp. 251–272. (a)

Peterson, G. L., Schofer, J. L., & Gemmel, R. S. Assessment of environmental impacts: Multidisciplinary judgment of large-scale projects. *Ekistics,* 1974, *37*(218), 23–30. (b)

Peterson, G. L., Bishop, R. L., & Michaels, R. M. Designing play environments for children. In G. Coates (Ed.), *Alternative learning environments.* Stroudsburg, Pennsylvania: Dowden, Hutchinson and Ross, 1974, pp. 321–340. (c)

Phillips, D. K. *Abandoning method.* San Francisco: Jossey-Bass, 1973.

Poulton, E. *Environment and human efficiency.* Springfield, Illinois: Charles C Thomas, 1970.

Rabinowitz, C. B., & Coughlin, R. E. Analysis of landscape characteristics relevant to preference. RSRI Discussion Paper Series, No. 38. Regional Science Research Institute, Philadelphia, 1970.

Rabinowitz, C. B., & Coughlin, R. E. Some experiments in quantitative measurement of landscape quality. RSRI Discussion Paper Series No. 43. Regional Science Research Institute, Philadelphia, 1971.

Rainwater, L. Fear and the house as haven in the lower class. *Journal of the American Institute of Planners*, 1966, *32*, 23–31.

Rankin, R. E. Air pollution control and public apathy. *Journal of Air Pollution Control Association*, 1969 *19*(8), 565–569.

Rappaport, L., & Summers, D. A. *Human judgment and social interaction*. New York: Holt, Rinehart & Winston, 1973.

Reizenstein, J. *Why architects don't use social science*. EDRA 6 paper, 1975.

Robinson, I. M., Baer, W., Banjeree, T., & Flachsbart, P. Trade-off games. In W. Michelson (Ed.), *Behavioral research methods in environmental design*. Stroudsburg, Pennsylvania: Dowden, Hutchinson and Ross, 1975, pp. 79–118.

Rohles, F. Environmental psychology: A bucket of worms. *Psychology Today*, 1967, *1*(2), 54–63.

Rohrmann, B., Schümer, R., Shümer-Kohrs, A., Guski, A., & Finke, H. O. An interdisciplinary study of the effects of aircraft noise on man. In U.S. Environmental Protection Agency (1974b), pp. 765–776.

Rosow, I. *Social integration of the aged*. New York: The Free Press, 1964.

Rossi, P. H. *Why families move*. Glencoe, Illinois: The Free Press, 1955.

Rupp, C. W. Boundary Waters Canoe Area management. *Naturalist*, 1970, *21*(4), 2–7.

Rylander, R., Sörensen, S., & Kajland, A. Annoyance reactions from aircraft noise exposure. *Journal of Sound and Vibration*, 1972, *24*(4), 419–444.

Saarinen, T. F. *Perception of the environment*. Commission on College Geography Resource Paper No. 5. Washington, D.C.: Association of American Geographers, 1969.

Saarinen, T. F., & Cooke, R. U. Public perception of environmental quality in Tucson, Arizona. *Journal of the Arizona Academy of Science*, 1971, *6*, 250–274.

Saile, D. G., Borodah, R., & Williams, M. Families in public housing: A study of three localities in Rockford, Illinois. EDRA 3, W. Mitchell (Ed.), *Environmental design: Research and practice* Los Angeles: University of California, 1972.

Samuels, S. W. Assessment of perception of air pollution. In W. R. D. Sewell & I. Burton (Eds.), *Perceptions and attitudes in resources management*. Ottawa: Information Canada, 1971.

Sanoff, H. House form and preference. J. Archea & C. Eastman (Eds.), EDRA 2 proceedings, Pittsburgh, Pennsylvania, 1970.

Sanoff, H. Integrating user needs in environmental design. Report prepared for the National Institute of Mental Health, Washington, D.C., 1973.

Sanoff, H., & Sawhney, M. Residential livability: A socio-physical perspective. Urban Affairs and Community Service Center, North Carolina State University, Raleigh, 1971.

Santayana, G. *The sense of beauty*. New York: Charles Scribners and Sons, 1896.

Scheflen, A. E. Living space in an urban ghetto. *Family Process*, 1971, *10*(4), 429–450.

Scherer, U., & Coughin, R. E. The influence of water quality in the evaluation of stream sites. RSRI Discussion Paper Series, No. 27. Regional Science Research Institute, Philadelphia, October 1971.

Schofer, J. L., Peterson, G. L., & Gemmel, R. S. In J. E. Quon (Ed.), Impact assessment: A design-interactive strategy using a multidisciplinary panel environmental impact assessment. Midwest Universities Consortium on Environmental Education and Research, September 1974, pp. 21–47.

Schorr, A. Slums and social insecurity. U.S. Department of Health, Education and Welfare. Washington, D.C.: U.S. Government Printing Office, 1963.

Schuman, H., & Greenberg, B. Dissatisfaction with city services: Is race an important factor? In H. Hahn (Ed.), People and politics in urban society. Beverly Hills: Sage Publications, 1972, pp. 369–392.

Schusky, J. Public awareness and concern with air pollution in the St. Louis Metropolitan Area. Journal of the Air Pollution Control Association, 1966, 16(2), 72–76.

Seaton, R., & Collins, J. Validity and reliability of ratings of simulated buildings. In W. Mitchell (Ed.), Environmental design: Research and practice, volume 1. EDRA 3, 1972.

Sewell, W. R. D. Environmental perceptions and attitudes of engineers and public health officials. Environment and Behavior, 1971, 3, 23–59.

Sewell, W. R. D., & Little, B. R. Specialists, laymen and the process of environmental appraisal. Regional Studies, 1973, 7, 161.

Shafer, E. L., Jr., & Mietz, J. Aesthetic and emotional experiences rate high with Northeast wilderness hikers. Environment and Behavior, 1969, 9(2), 187–197.

Shafer, E. L., Jr., & Mietz, J. It seems possible to quantify scenic beauty in photographs. USDA Forest Service Research Paper NE-162, Northeastern Forest Experiment Station, Upper Darby, Pennsylvania, 1970.

Shafer, E. L., Jr., & Thompson, R. C. Models that describe use of Adirondack campgrounds. Forest Science, 1968, 14(4), 383–391.

Shafer, E. L., Jr., & Tooby, M. Landscape preferences: An international replication. Journal of Leisure Research, 1973, 5(3), 60–65.

Shafer, E. L., Jr., Hamilton, J. F., Jr., & Schmidt, E. A. Natural landscape preference: A predictive model. Journal of Leisure Research, 1969, 1, 1–19.

Sheldon, E. B., & Parke, R. Social indicators. Science, 1975, 188, 693–699.

Shelly, M. Analyses of satisfaction, volume 1. New York: MSS Educational Publishing Co., 1969.

Shirer, W. The rise and fall of the Third Reich. New York: Simon and Schuster, 1960.

Sierra Club, A wilderness in crisis—the Boundary Waters Canoe Area. North Star Chapter, Minneapolis, 1970.

Smith, W. S. Schueneman, J. J., & Zeidberg, L. D. Public reaction to air pollution in Nashville, Tennessee. Journal of the Air Pollution Control Association, 1964, 14(10), 418–423.

Snider, J., & Osgood, C. Semantic differential technique. Chicago: Aldine, 1969.

Sommer, R. Personal space. Englewood Cliffs, New Jersey: Prentice-Hall, 1969.

Sonnenfeld, J. Variable values in space and landscape: An inquiry into the nature of environmental necessity. Journal of Social Issues, 1966, 22(4), 71–82.

Sonnenfeld, J. Equivalence and distortion of the perceptual environment. *Environment and Behavior*, 1969, *1*(1), 83–100.

Sörensen, S. On the possibilities of changing the annoyance reaction to noise by changing the attitude to the source of annoyance. *Nordisk Hygienisk Tidskrift, Supplementum, 1*, 1970, 1–76.

Southworth, M. The sonic environment of cities. *Environment and Behavior*, 1969, *1*(1), 49–70.

Stalker, W. W., & Robinson, C. B. A method for using air pollution measurements and public opinion to establish ambient air quality standards. *Journal of the Air Pollution Control Association*, 1967 *17*(3), 142–144.

Stanky, G. A strategy for the definition and management of wilderness quality. In J. Krutilla (Ed.), *Natural environments:* Baltimore: Johns Hopkins, 1972, pp. 88–114.

Stea, D. *Environmental perception and cognition: Toward a model for residential maps.* Student publication of the School of Design, Vol. 18. North Carolina State University, Raleigh, 1969, pp. 63–76.

Stein, C. *Toward new towns for America.* New York: Reinhold Publishing, 1957.

Stevens, S. S. Measurement, psycholophysics and utility. In C. W. Churchman & P. Ratoosh (Eds.), *Measurement: Definitions and theories.* New York: Wiley and Sons, 1962, pp. 18–63.

Stotland, E. & Kolber, A. *Life and death of a mental hospital.* Seattle: University of Washington Press, 1965.

Suedfeld, P., & Ward L. M. Report on human responses to highway noise. In New Jersey Department of Transportation (1972).

Superior National Forest, U.S.D.A. Boundary Waters Canoe Area management plan and environmental statement. June 25, 1974.

Suttles, G. *The social order of the slum.* Chicago: University of Chicago Press, 1968.

Swan, J. Response to air pollution: A study of attitudes and coping strategies of high school youths. *Environment and Behavior*, 1970, *2*, 127–153.

Thomas, W. A. (Ed.). *Indicators of environmental quality.* New York: Plenum Press, 1972.

Toganacci, L., Weigel, R., Widen, M., & Vernon, D. Environmental quality: How universal is public concern? *Environment and Behavior*, 1972, *4*, 73–86.

Torgerson, W. *Theory and methods of scaling.* New York: John Wiley, 1958.

Tracor, Inc. Public reactions to sonic booms (NASA CR-1664). Washington, D.C.: National Aeronautics and Space Administration, 1970. (a)

Tracor, Inc. Community reaction to airport noise, Volume I (NASA CR-1761). Washington, D.C.: National Aeronautics and Space Administration, 1970. (b)

Troy, P. Environmental quality in four suburban areas. Canberra: Urban Research Unit, Australian National University, 1971.

Twiss, R. H. Linking the EIS to the planning process. Environmental Impact Assessment: Guidelines and Commentary. Berkeley: University Extension, University of California, 1974.

UNESCO. Programme on Man and the Biosphere (MAB): Expert Panel on Project 13: Perception of Environmental Quality. MAB Report Series No. 9. Paris: UNESCO House, 1973.

U.S. Department of Health, Education and Welfare. *Public awareness and concern with air pollution in the St. Louis metropolitan area.* Washington, D.C.: U.S. Government Printing Office, 1965.

U.S. Department of Housing and Urban Development. *Noise environment of urban and suburban areas.* Washington, D.C.: U.S. Government Printing Office, 1967. (NTIS No. N67-10225)

U.S. Environmental Protection Agency. *An assessment of noise concern in other nations* (Vol. 1) (EPA NTID300.6). Washington, D.C.: Author, 1971. (a)

U.S. Environmental Protection Agency. *Effects of noise on people* (EPA NTID300.7). Washington, D.C.: U.S. Government Printing Office, 1971. (b)

U.S. Environmental Protection Agency (Ed.). *Public hearings on noise abatement and control.* Volume 7, Physiological and psychological effects. Washington, D.C.: U.S. Government Printing Office, 1972.

U.S. Environmental Protection Agency. *Impact characterization of noise including implications of identifying and achieving levels of cumulative noise exposure* (EPA NTID 73.4). Washington, D.C.: Author, 1973.

U.S. Environmental Protection Agency. *Information on levels of environmental noise requisite to protect public health and welfare with an adequate margin for safety* (EPA 550/9-74-004). Washington, D.C.: U.S. Government Printing Office, 1974. (a)

U.S. Environmental Protection Agency. *Proceedings of the International Congress on Noise as a Public Health Problem* (EPA 550/9-73-008). Washington, D.C.: U.S. Government Printing Office, 1974. (b)

U.S. Office of Management and Budget. *Social indicators.* Washington, D.C.: U.S. Government Printing Office, 1973.

Wall, G. *Public response to air pollution in Sheffield.* Papers on Selected Social Aspects of Air Pollution in the United Kingdom. International Geographical Union, Commission on Man and Environment, Calgary Symposium, July 23–31, 1972.

Wall, G. Public response to air pollution in South Yorkshire, England. *Environment and Behavior,* 1973, *5,* 219–248.

Weiss, S., Burby, R., Kaiser, E., Donnelly, T., & Zehner, R. New Community Development: A National Study of Environmental Preferences and the Quality of Life. Research Reviews, Institute for Research in Social Science, University of North Carolina, Chapel Hill, 1973.

Wells, B. W. P. Subjective response to the lighting installation in a modern office building and their design implications. *Building Science,* January 1965, *1,* 57–68.

Werthman, C., Mandel, J. S., & Dienstfray, T. Planning and the purchase decision: Why people buy in planned communities. Institute of Regional Development, University of California, Berkeley, 1965.

Willeke, G. E. Effects of water pollution in San Francisco Bay. Report EEP-29, Program in Engineering-Economic Planning. Stanford University, Stanford, California, October, 1968.

Wilner, D. M., & Walkeley, R. P. Effects of housing on health and performance. In L. Duhl (Ed.), *The urban condition.* New York: Basic Books, 1963.

Wilner, D. M., Walkeley, R. P., Pinkerton, T. C., & Tayback, M. *The housing environment and family life.* Baltimore: Johns Hopkins University Press, 1962.

Wilson, R. L. Liveability of the city: Attitudes and urban development. In F. S. Chapin, Jr. & S. Weiss (Eds.), *Urban growth dynamics*. New York: Wiley and Sons, 1962, pp. 359–399.

Winkel, G., Malek, R., & Theil, P. The role of personality differences in judgments of roadside quality. *Environment and Behavior*, 1969, *1*, 199–223.

Wohlwill, J. F. Amount of stimulus exploration and preference as differential functions of stimulus complexity. *Perception and Psychophysics*, 1968, *4*(5), 307–312.

Wolf, E., & Lebeaux, C. Newcomers and old-timers in Lafayette Park. In *Change and renewal in an urban community*. New York: Praeger, 1969, pp. 107–137.

Yancy, W. L. Architecture, interaction, and social control: The case of a large-scale housing project. Environment and the social services: Perspectives and applications. Washington, D.C.: American Psychological Association, 1972.

York, C. M., & Baskett, G. D. A citizen panel for Atlanta area studies: Field experimentation and methodological substudies. Environmental Resources Center, Georgia Institute of Technology, Atlanta, 1971.

Zehner, R. B. Satisfaction with neighborhoods: The effects of social compatability, residential density, and site planning. Unpublished dissertation, The University of Michigan, Ann Arbor, 1972.

Zehner, R. B. Indicators of the quality of life in new communities. Unpublished report, Center for Urban and Regional Studies, University of North Carolina, Chapel Hill, 1974.

Zehner, R. B., & Chapin, F. S. *Across the city line: A white community in transition.* Lexington, Massachusetts: Lexington Books, 1974.

Zube, E. H. Cross-disciplinary and inter-mode agreement on the description and evaluation of landscape resources. *Environment and Behavior*, 1974, *6*(1), 69–89.

Zube, E. H. Perception of landscape and land use. In I. Altman & J. Wohlwill (Eds.), *Human behavior and the environment: Advances in theory and research*. New York: Plenum Press, 1976, in press.

Zube, E. H., Pitt, D. G., & Anderson, T. W. Perception and measurements of scenic resources in the southern Connecticut River valley. Amherst: Institute for Man and Environment, University of Massachusetts, 1974.

Zube, E. H., Brush, R. O., & Fabos, J. Gy. (Eds.). *Landscape assessment: Values, perceptions and resources*. Stroudsburg, Pennsylvania: Dowden, Hutchinson and Ross, 1975.

Index

307